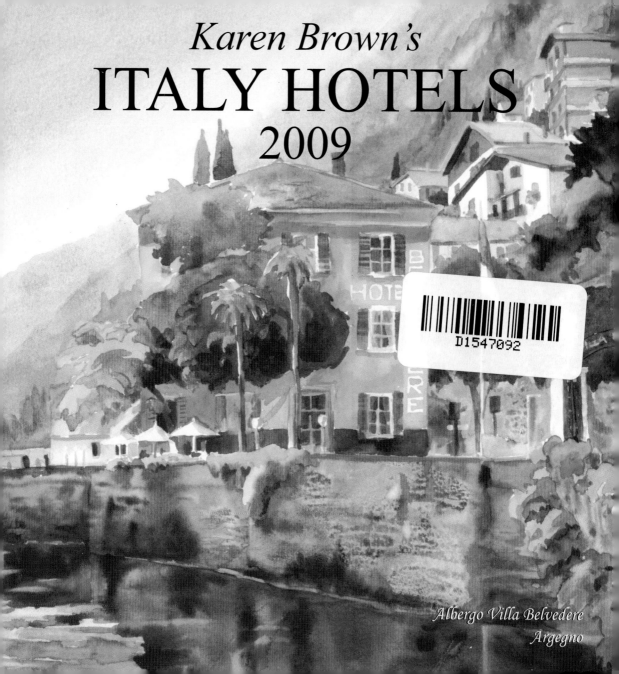

Karen Brown's
ITALY HOTELS
2009

Albergo Villa Belvedere
Argegno

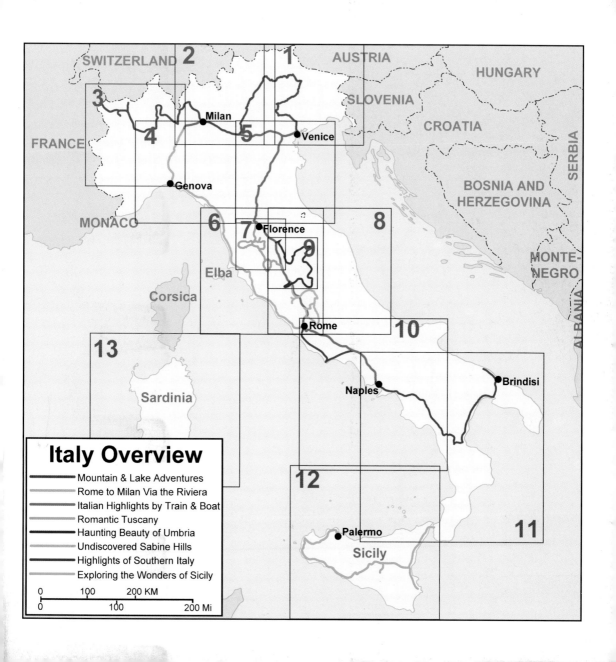

Italy Overview

- Mountain & Lake Adventures
- Rome to Milan Via the Riviera
- Italian Highlights by Train & Boat
- Romantic Tuscany
- Haunting Beauty of Umbria
- Undiscovered Sabine Hills
- Highlights of Southern Italy
- Exploring the Wonders of Sicily

0	100	200 KM
0	100	200 Mi

SWITZERLAND

FRANCE

MONACO

2

1

3

4

5

Milan

Venice

Genova

AUSTRIA

SLOVENIA

CROATIA

HUNGARY

SERBIA

BOSNIA AND HERZEGOVINA

MONTE-NEGRO

ALBANIA

6

7

Florence

9

8

Elba

Corsica

Rome

10

13

Sardinia

Naples

Brindisi

12

11

Palermo

Sicily

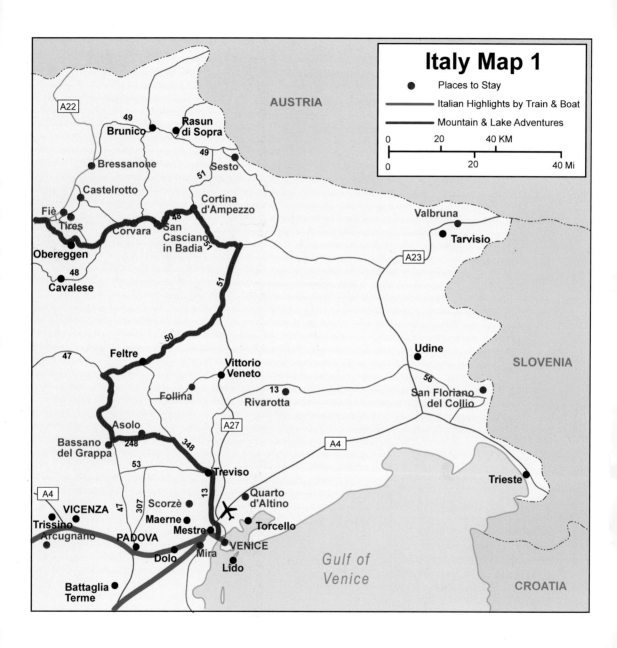

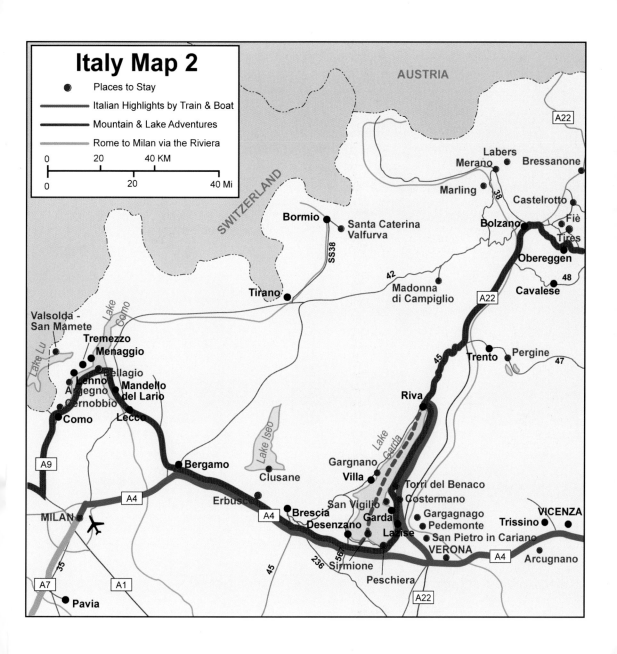

Italy Map 2

Places to Stay ●

~~~ Italian Highlights by Train & Boat

— Mountain & Lake Adventures

— Rome to Milan via the Riviera

| 0 | 20 | 40 KM |
| 0 | 20 | 40 Mi |

AUSTRIA

A22

SWITZERLAND

Labers
Merano
Bressanone
Marling
Castelrotto
38
Fiè
Bolzano
Tires
Obereggen
Bormio
Santa Caterina
Valfurva
SS38
42
48
Madonna
Cavalese
di Campiglio
Tirano
A22
45
Pergine
Lake Como
Lake Lu
Trento
47
Valsolda -
San Mamete
Tremezzo
Menaggio
Bellagio
Riva
Lenno
Mandello
Argegno
del Lario
Cernobbio
Lake Iseo
Como
Lecco
Lake Garda
A9
Gargnano
Bergamo
Villa
A4
Clusane
Torri del Benaco
MILAN
✈
Erbusco
Costermano
San Vigilio
Gargagnago
VICENZA
A4
Brescia
Garda
Pedemonte
Trissino
35
Desenzano
Lazise
San Pietro in Cariano
45
236
Sirmione
VERONA
A4
A7
A1
567
Peschiera
Arcugnano
Pavia
A22

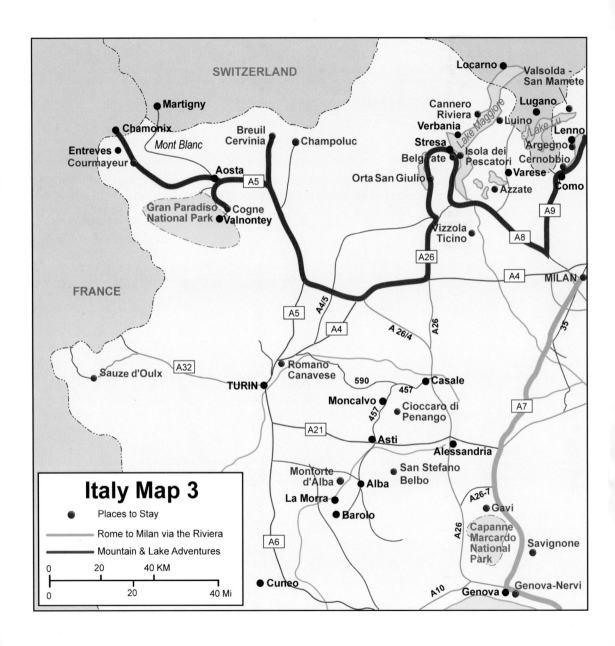

Italy Map 3

- ● Places to Stay
- — Rome to Milan via the Riviera
- — Mountain & Lake Adventures

0	20	40 KM
0	20	40 Mi

SWITZERLAND

Martigny

Chamonix

Entreves
Courmayeur

Mont Blanc

Breuil
Cervinia

Champoluc

Aosta

A5

Gran Paradiso
National Park

Cogne
Valnontey

FRANCE

Locarno

Valsolda -
San Mamete

Cannero
Riviera

Lugano

Verbania

Liuino

Lake Maggiore

Lake Lu

Lenno

Stresa

Isola dei
Pescatori

Argegno
Cernobbio

Belgirate

Varese

Orta San Giulio

Azzate

Como

A9

Vizzola
Ticino

A8

A26

A4

MILAN

A5

A4/5

A4

A 26/4

A26

35

Sauze d'Oulx

A32

Romano
Canavese

TURIN

590

Casale

457

Moncalvo

Cioccaro di
Penango

457

A7

A21

Asti

Alessandria

Monforte
d'Alba

San Stefano
Belbo

Alba

La Morra

A26-7

Barolo

Gavi

A26

Capanne
Marcardo
National
Park

Savignone

A6

Cuneo

A10

Genova

Genova-Nervi

Italy Map 4

- ● Places to Stay
- Italian Highlights by Train & Boat
- Mountain & Lake Adventures
- Rome to Milan via the Riviera

```
0        20        40 KM
0        20        40 Mi
```

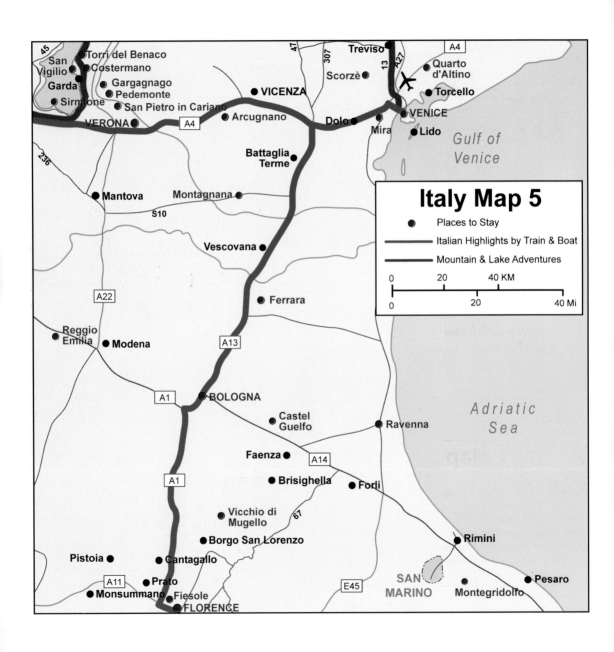

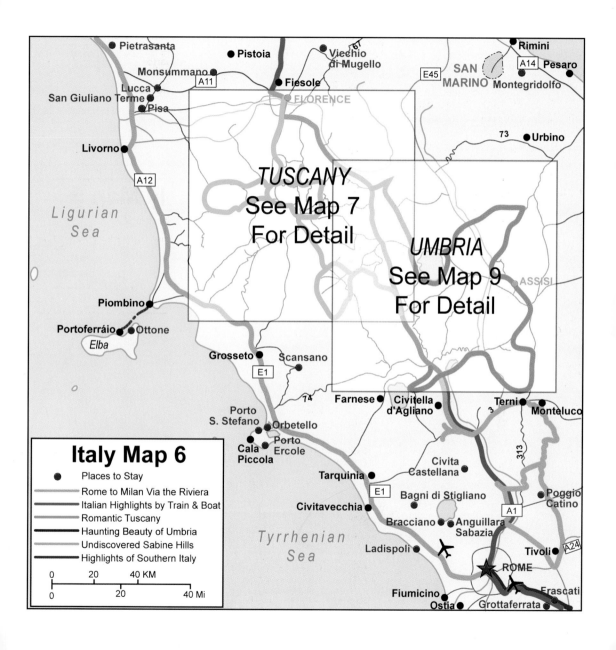

Pietrasanta

Pistoia

Vicchio
di Mugello

Monsummano

San Marino

Rimini

E45

Pesaro

A14

Lucca

A11

Fiesole

Montegridolfo

San Giuliano Terme

Pisa

FLORENCE

Livorno

73

Urbino

A12

*Ligurian
Sea*

TUSCANY
See Map 7
For Detail

UMBRIA
See Map 9
For Detail

ASSISI

Piombino

Portoferráio

Ottone

Elba

Grosseto

Scansano

E1

74

Farnese

Civitella
d'Agliano

Terni

Monteluco

Porto
S. Stefano

Orbetello

Porto
Ercole

Cala
Piccola

Civita
Castellana

313

Tarquinia

E1

Bagni di Stigliano

Poggio
Catino

Civitavecchia

A1

Bracciano

Anguillara
Sabazia

Ladispoli

Tivoli

A24

*Tyrrhenian
Sea*

ROME

Frascati

Fiumicino

Ostia

Grottaferrata

Italy Map 6

● Places to Stay

Rome to Milan Via the Riviera

Italian Highlights by Train & Boat

Romantic Tuscany

Haunting Beauty of Umbria

Undiscovered Sabine Hills

Highlights of Southern Italy

| 0 | 20 | 40 KM |

| 0 | 20 | 40 Mi |

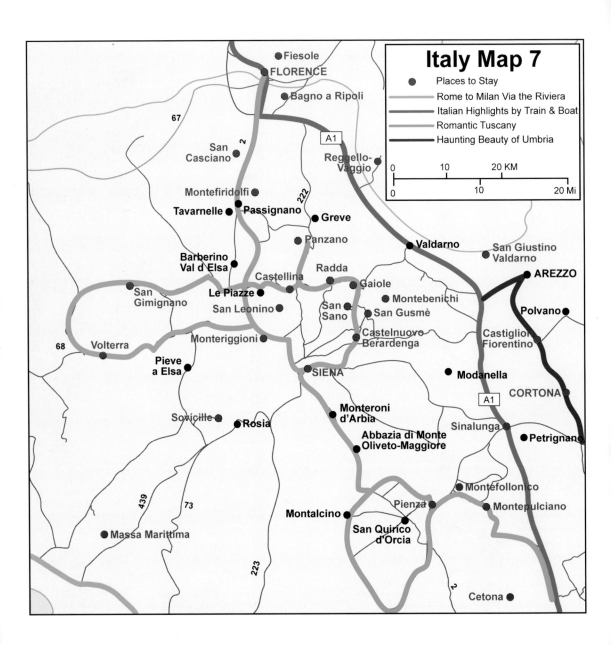

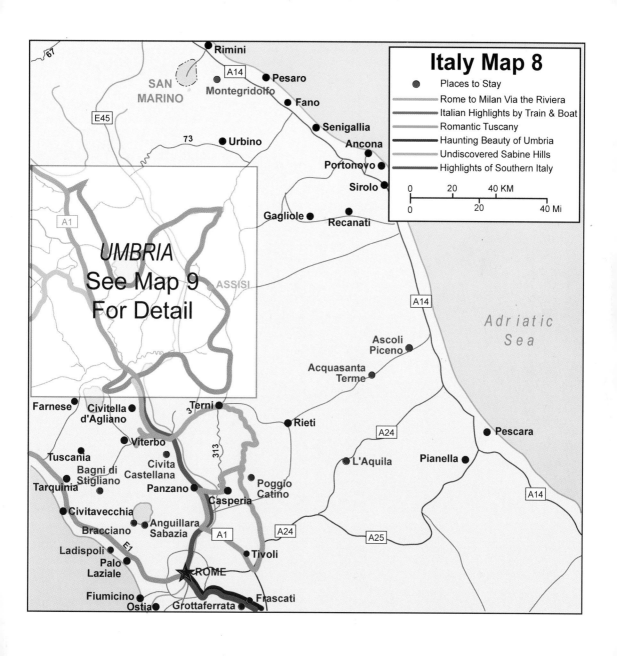

Italy Map 8

- ● Places to Stay
- Rome to Milan Via the Riviera
- Italian Highlights by Train & Boat
- Romantic Tuscany
- Haunting Beauty of Umbria
- Undiscovered Sabine Hills
- Highlights of Southern Italy

| 0 | 20 | 40 KM |
| 0 | 20 | 40 Mi |

Rimini
SAN MARINO
A14
Pesaro
Montegridolfo
Fano
E45
Senigallia
73
Urbino
Ancona
Portonovo
Sirolo
Gagliole
Recanati
A1
UMBRIA
See Map 9
For Detail
ASSISI
A14
*Adriatic
Sea*
Ascoli
Piceno
Acquasanta
Terme
Farnese
Civitella
d'Agliano
Terni
3
Rieti
Pescara
A24
Viterbo
313
Tuscania
L'Aquila
Pianella
Bagni di
Stigliano
Civita
Castellana
Tarquinia
Panzano
Casperia
Poggio
Catino
A14
Civitavecchia
Bracciano
Anguillara
Sabazia
A1
A24
A25
Ladispoli
E1
Palo
Laziale
Tivoli
Fiumicino
ROME
Ostia
Grottaferrata
Frascati
67

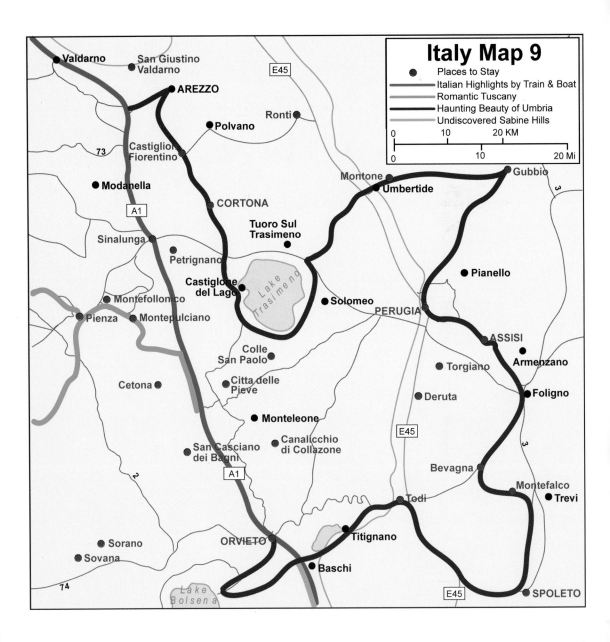

Italy Map 10

- ● Places to Stay
- ⁘ Archaeological Site
- ━━━ Highlights of Southern Italy
- ━━━ Italian Highlights by Train & Boat

0   25   50 KM

0   25   50 Mi

ROME
A1
A24
Tivoli
Frascati
Grottaferrata
148
Frosinone
A1
Latina
Anzio
Sabaudia
Formia
Gaeta
Ponza
Ventotene
Cuma
A3
NAPLES
Ischia
Castellamare
Sorrento
Capri
San Agata
Caserta
A30
Herculaneum
Pompeii
Ravello
Amalfi
Positano
Salerno
A16
A14
Foggia
A3
Potenza
Paestum
Santa Maria di
Castellabate

*Bay of
Naples*

*Bay of
Salerno*

*Tyrrhenian
Sea*

Vieste
Gargano
National Park
Monte
S. Angelo

Acquafredda
Maratea

Cittadella
del Capo

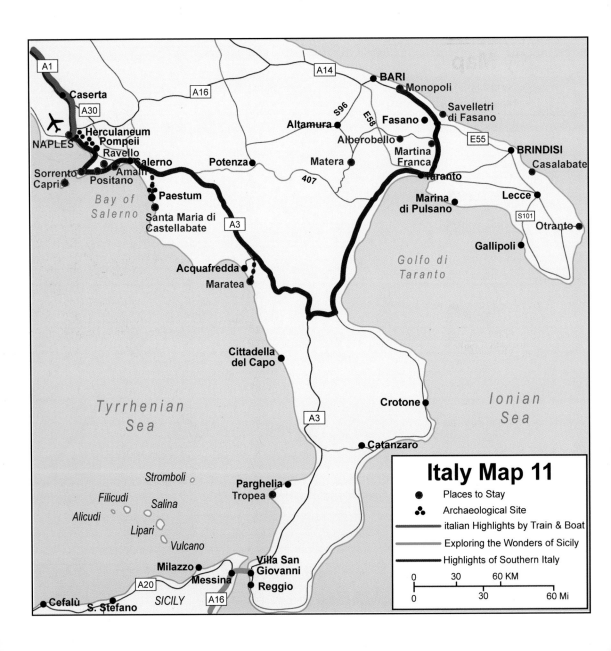

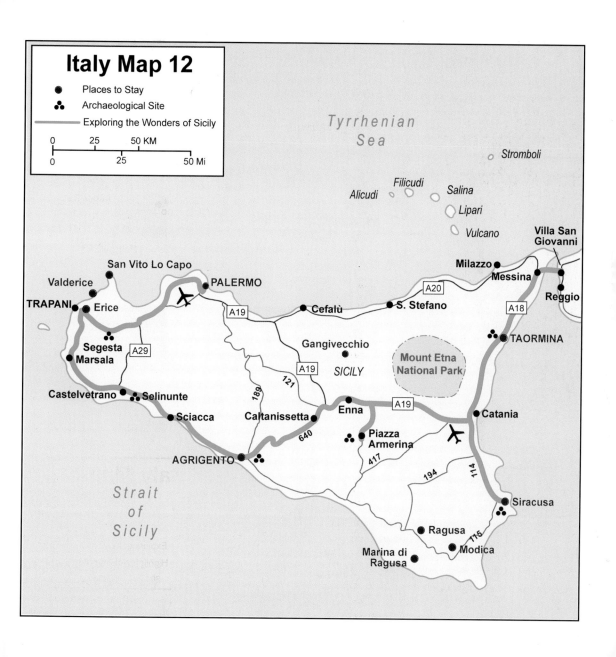

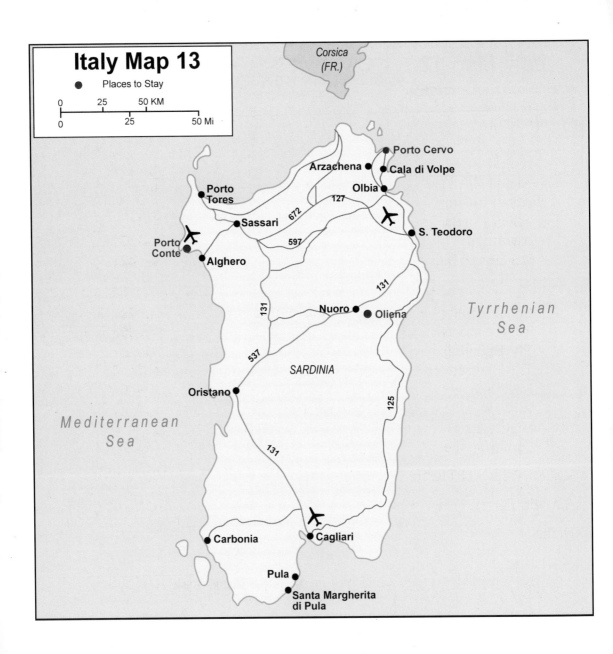

Italy Map 13

● Places to Stay

0   25   50 KM
0   25   50 Mi

Corsica
(FR.)

Porto Cervo
Arzachena   Cala di Volpe
Olbia

Porto
Tores

Sassari   672   127

597   S. Teodoro

Porto
Conte

Alghero

131

131

Nuoro   Oliena

537

SARDINIA

*Tyrrhenian
Sea*

Oristano

125

*Mediterranean
Sea*

131

Carbonia   Cagliari

Pula

Santa Margherita
di Pula

Contents

To My Best Friend, Bill,
With Whom I've Shared Over 50 Years of
Love, Laughter and Tears
plus
Many Miles of Happy Memories

2009 Cover Painting: Albergo Villa Belvedere, Argegno

Photograph front: Venice, Photograph back: Tuscany

Authors: Clare Brown and Nicole Franchini.

Editors: Clare Brown, Karen Brown, June Eveleigh Brown, Kim Brown Holmsen, William Brown, Nicole Franchini, Debbie Tokumoto, Melissa Jaworski, Terri-Jo Woellner.

Illustrations: Barbara Maclurcan Tapp and Elisabetta Franchini.

Cover painting: Jann Pollard.

Maps & Graphics: Rachael Kircher-Randolph.

Technical support: Andrew Harris.

Email: karen@karenbrown.com

Distributed by National Book Network, 15200 NBN Way, Blue Ridge Summit, PA 17214, USA.

Tel: 717-794-3800 or 1-800-462-6420, Fax: 1-800-338-4500, Email: custserv@nbnbooks.com

A catalog record for this book is available from the British Library.

ISSN 1533-4627

 # Introduction

Of all the countries in the world, there is none more magical than Italy: it is truly a tourist's paradise—a traveler's dream destination. No one could be so blasé that within Italy's narrow boot there would not be something to tantalize his fancy. For the archaeologist, there are some of the most fascinating and perfectly preserved ancient monuments existing today, just begging to be explored. For the gourmet, there is the finest food in the world. For the outdoors enthusiast, there are towering mountains to conquer and magnificent ski slopes to enjoy. For the lover of art, the museums are bursting with the genius of Italy's sons such as Michelangelo, Leonardo da Vinci, and Raphael. For the architect, Italy is a school of design—you are surrounded by the ancient buildings whose perfection still inspires the styles of today. For the history buff, Italy is a joy of wonders—her cities are veritable living museums. For the wine connoisseur, Italy produces an unbelievable selection of wine whose quality is unsurpassed. For the adventurer, Italy has intriguing medieval walled villages tucked away in every part of the country. For the beach buff, Italy's coastline and lakes hold the promise of some of the most elegant resorts in the world. For the religious pilgrim, Italy is the cradle of the Christian faith and home of some to the world's most famous saints. The miracle of Italy is that all these treasures come packaged in a gorgeous country of majestic mountains, misty lakes, idyllic islands, wonderful walled villages, and beautiful cities. In addition, the climate is ideal and the people warm and gracious. Italy is truly a perfect destination.

About This Guide

This guide is written with two main objectives: to describe the most romantic hotels throughout Italy and to tie these hotels together with itineraries that include enough details so that you can plan your own holiday. This introduction explains how to use the guide and also touches upon what to expect while traveling. After the introduction the main part of the guide is divided into three sections: itineraries, hotel descriptions, and maps. The itinerary section outlines itineraries with sightseeing suggestions along the way; the hotel description section gives a comprehensive list of recommended lodgings (appearing alphabetically by town); the map section has 13 maps to help you pinpoint each town where we suggest a place to stay. The pertinent regional map number is given at the right on the *top line* of each hotel's description.

We have personally inspected each place that we recommend and describe its ambiance and merits in our write-up, which is followed by an illustration and practical information such as address, telephone and fax numbers, rates, etc. Our choices are strictly based on hotels we think you would most enjoy. Frequently we hear, "I don't care where I stay— I'm rarely in my room except to sleep." If this is your true philosophy, then this book is *not* for you. To our way of thinking, where you stay weaves the very fabric of your trip and your choice of hotels is of absolutely prime importance. Not that the hotel needs to be expensive: a moonlit dinner on the terrace of a simple inn can be as memorable as dining at a fancy hotel—sometimes even more so because the owner is there to pamper you. The recommendations in our guide vary tremendously: some are grand hotels—fit for a king and priced accordingly; others are simple, inexpensively priced hotels tucked away in remote hamlets. We include them all if they have personality, romantic charm, and antique ambiance.

About Itineraries

In the itinerary section of this guide you'll be able to find an itinerary, or portion of an itinerary, that can be easily tailored to fit your exact time frame and suit your own particular interests. If your time is limited, you can certainly follow just a segment of an itinerary. In the itineraries we have not specified the number of nights at each destination, since to do so seemed much too confining. Some travelers like to see as much as possible in a short period of time. For others, just the thought of packing and unpacking each night makes them shudder in horror and they would never stop for less than three or four nights at any destination. A third type of tourist doesn't like to travel at all—the destination is the focus and he uses this guide to find the perfect place from which he never wanders except for daytime excursions. So, use this guide as a reference to plan your personalized trip.

Our advice is not to rush. Part of the joy of traveling is to settle in at a hotel that you like and use it as a hub from which to take side trips to explore the countryside. When you dash too quickly from place to place, you never have the opportunity to get to know the owners of the hotels and to become friends with other guests. Look at the maps in the front of this guide to find the places to stay in the areas where you want to travel. Read about each hotel in the *Hotel Descriptions* section of this book and decide which sound most suited to your taste and budget, then choose a base for each area you want to visit.

MAPS

Each itinerary is preceded by a map showing the route and each hotel listing is referenced on its top line to a map at the front of the book. All maps are an artist's renderings and are not intended to replace detailed commercial maps. We use the *Michelin Tourist and Motoring Atlas of Italy,* a book of maps with a scale of 1:300,000 (1 cm = 3 km). We also find the regional Michelin maps very useful and we state which Michelin 500-series map each hotel's town is found on in the hotel description. To outline your visit to Italy you might want to consider the one-page map of Italy, Michelin map 735. Italy hotel maps in this book can be cross-referenced with those in our companion guide, *Karen Brown's Italy: Bed & Breakfasts and Itineraries*. We sell Michelin country maps, city maps, and regional green guides (sightseeing guides) in our website store at *www.karenbrown.com*.

Another fine choice is The Touring Club Italiano map set, in an easy-to-read three-volume format divided into North, Central, and South. Even the smallest town or, better, *localita* is listed in the extensive index.

SIGHTSEEING

Ideas on what to see and do are suggested throughout the seven itineraries. However, we just touch upon some of the sightseeing highlights. There is a wealth of wonders to see in Italy, plus, of course, many local festivals and events. Before you leave, check with the tourist office for further information targeted at exactly where you plan to travel. And, once on the road, make it a habit to always make your first stop the local tourist office to pick up maps, schedules of special events, and sightseeing information. Even more important, before you drive out of your way to see a particular museum or place of interest, check when it is open. As a general guideline, most museums are closed on Mondays except for the Vatican museums, which are closed on Sundays (except for the last Sunday of the month). The most important museums now have continuous hours and either have a full- or half-day schedule but do not close for a few hours and then reopen. Smaller museums are usually open until 2 pm. Outdoor museums usually open at 9 am and close about an hour before sunset. Most monuments and museums close on national holidays—see "Holidays" on page 19. NOTE: To save waiting in line for hours to buy entrance tickets, buy tickets for most major museums well in advance on line or from travel agencies or directly from hotels.

About Hotels

BASIS FOR SELECTION

This guide does not try to appeal to everyone. It is definitely prejudiced: each hotel included is one we have seen and liked. We visit hundreds of hotels and choose only those we think are special. It might be a splendid villa elegantly positioned overlooking one of Italy's romantic lakes or a simple little chalet snuggled high in a mountain meadow. But there is a common denominator—they all have charm. Therefore, if you too prefer to travel spending your nights in romantic old villas, appealing chalets, dramatic medieval castles, ancient monasteries, converted stone cottages, and gorgeous palaces, we are kindred souls.

For some of you, cost will not be a factor if the hotel is outstanding. For others, a budget guides your choice. The appeal of a simple little inn with rustic wooden furniture beckons some, while the glamour of ornate ballrooms dressed with crystal chandeliers and gilded mirrors appeals to others. What we have tried to do is to indicate what each hotel has to offer and describe the setting, so that you can make the choice to suit your own preferences and holiday. We feel if you know what to expect, you won't be disappointed, so we have tried to be candid and honest in our appraisals.

CREDIT CARDS

Whether or not an establishment accepts credit cards is indicated in the list of icons at the bottom of each description by the symbol [CREDIT]. We have also specified in the bottom details which cards are accepted as follows: AX–American Express, MC–MasterCard, VS–Visa, or simply, all major. If the hotel does not accept any credit cards nothing will be listed. NOTE: Even if an inn does not accept credit card payment, it will perhaps request your account number as a guarantee of arrival.

GROUPS & AFFILIATIONS

A number of properties recommended in our guide books also belong to other private membership organizations. These associations impose their own criteria for selection and membership standards and have established a reputation for the particular type of property they include. The Abitare La Storia is an affiliation of accommodations in historic residences, including castles, 3, 4, and 5-star hotels and country estates. They include some of the finest places to stay in Italy. The majority of their properties are featured either in this guide or our companion guide *Karen Brown's Italy B&B: Exceptional Places to Stay & Itineraries*. Their search for quality, welcome and charm is a perfect match with our own selection criteria. Three other affiliations that are very well recognized throughout Europe are the Romantik hotel chain, the History Traveller group and Relais & Châteaux. A number of properties that we recommend are members of these prestigious organizations. If a property that we recommend is also a member of Abitare La Storia, Relais & Châteaux, or History Traveller, we note that in the bottom details of the hotel description.

ICONS

Icons allow us to provide additional information about our recommended properties. When using our website to supplement the guides, positioning the cursor over an icon will in many cases give you further details.

We have introduced the following icons in this guide to supplement each property's description. For easy reference, an icon key can also be found on the inside back cover flap. ❄ Air conditioning in rooms, ⏉ Beach nearby, ☛ Breakfast included in room rate, ⚜ Children welcome, ♨ Cooking classes offered, ▦ Credit cards accepted, ▲ Dinner served upon request, ☎ Direct-dial telephone in room, ⌖ Dogs by special request, ⛁ Elevator, ☥ Exercise room, @ Internet access available for guests, ♈ Mini-refrigerator in rooms, ⊛ Some non-smoking rooms, P Parking available (free or paid), ¶ Restaurant, ❦ Spa (treatments/massage etc.), ☈ Swimming pool, ⚘ Tennis, ▣ Television with English channels in guestrooms, ⚮ Wedding facilities, ⚷ Wheelchair friendly, W Wireless available for guests, ⚐ Golf course nearby, ⚶ Hiking trails nearby, ⚕ Horseback riding nearby, ⚶ Skiing nearby, ⚓ Water sports nearby, ♥ Wineries nearby.

RATES

In the *Hotel Descriptions* section in the back of the book each listing shows a rate range that reflects the *approximate* 2009 high-season nightly cost in euros for a room for two persons including tax, service, and continental breakfast. (Where quoted separately, breakfast prices are per person.) Breakfast included is confirmed in the list of icons at the bottom of each description by the symbol ☛. Rates do not reflect higher prices for various special holiday periods. There are a few hotels where breakfast and one other meal (either lunch or dinner) are included in the rate and, if so, this too is noted. Please use the rates given only as a general guide because each hotel has such a wide range of price possibilities that it is impossible to project with complete accuracy. Be sure to ask at the time of booking exactly what the price is and what it includes (breakfast, parking, etc.) so that you won't be in for any unpleasant surprises—sometimes rates increase after this book goes to print. When you plan your holiday, check the current exchange rate on our website, *www.karenbrown.com*, or at your bank.

HOW TO ECONOMIZE: The price for a room in Italy has soared in the last few years. However, if you study carefully the rates given in the back of this guide, you can still find a few bargains and can plan your trip using one of the less expensive hotels as your hub from which to venture out each day. We also publish *Karen Brown's Italy: Bed & Breakfasts and Itineraries*, which makes an ideal companion to this guide. The maps in both are similar, making it easy to choose a place to stay from either book. Not only can you save money by sometimes choosing a bed and breakfast for a night's accommodation, but you can also enjoy the experience of staying where you have the opportunity to know your host and fellow guests. We highly recommend choosing a combination of places to stay from both books.

For those of you who want to squeeze the most value out of each night's stay, we have several other suggestions:

1) Travel off-season—spring and fall are usually lovely in Italy and the hotels often have less expensive rates.

2) Ask for a room without a private bathroom—some hotels have very nice rooms, usually with a washbasin in the room, but with a shared bathroom down the hall.

3) Ask if there is a weekly rate—frequently hotels offer a price break for guests staying a week or more. If traveling with children, ask if there is a special family suite at a lesser price than separate rooms.

4) Ask about rates with meals included. For a stay of three days or longer, many hotels offer a special rate including meals: MAP (Modified American Plan) means two meals a day are included; AP (American Plan) means three meals a day are included.

5) Last, but not least, is the most important way to save money: stay in the countryside instead of in the cities. We cannot stress enough how much more value you receive when you avoid the cities—especially the tourist centers such as Rome, Florence, Milan, and

Venice. Of course, stay right in the heart of town if you are not watching your budget, but if you are trying to squeeze the greatest value from your euro, choose hotels in the countryside and take side trips to visit the more-pricey tourist centers.

RESERVATIONS

People frequently ask, "Do I need a hotel reservation?" The answer really depends on how flexible you want to be, how tight your time schedule is, in which season you are traveling, and how disappointed you would be if your first choice is unavailable.

It is not unusual for the major tourist cities to be completely sold out during the peak season of June through September. Be forewarned: hotel space in Rome, Florence, Milan, and Venice is really at a premium and unless you don't mind taking your chances on a last-minute cancellation or staying on the outskirts of town, make a reservation as far in advance as possible. Space in the countryside is a little easier. However, if you have your heart set on some special little hotel, you certainly should reserve as soon as your travel dates are firm. Reservations are confining. Most hotels want a deposit to hold your room and frequently you cannot get a refund if you change your plans. So it is a double bind: making reservations locks you into a solid framework, but without reservations you might be stuck with accommodations you do not like. During the height of the tourist season, some small hotels accept reservations only for a minimum of three or more nights. However, do not give up, because almost all of the hotels that have this policy will take a last-minute booking for a shorter period of time if you call along the way and there is space available. For those who like the security blanket of having each night pre-planned so that once you leave home you do not have to worry about where to rest your head, several options for making reservations are listed on the following pages.

It is important to understand that once reservations for accommodation are confirmed, whether verbally by phone or in writing, you are under contract. This means that the proprietor is obligated to provide the accommodation that was promised and that you are obligated to pay for it. If you cannot, you are liable for a portion of the accommodation charges plus your deposit. Although some proprietors do not strictly enforce a cancellation policy many, particularly the smaller properties in our book, simply cannot afford not to do so. As a courtesy to your hosts, in the case of cancellation, please advise them as soon as possible. Similarly many airline tickets cannot be changed or refunded without penalty. We recommend insurance to cover these types of additional expenses arising from cancellation due to unforeseen circumstances. A link on our website (*www.karenbrown.com*) will connect you to a variety of insurance policies that can be purchased online.

When making your reservations, be sure to identify yourself as a "Karen Brown Traveler." The hotels appreciate your visit, value their inclusion in our guide, and frequently tell us they take special care of our readers, and many offer special rates to Karen Brown members (visit our website at *www.karenbrown.com*). We hear over and over again that the people who use our guides are the most wonderful guests!

RESERVATIONS BY EMAIL: This is our preferred way of making a reservation. All properties featured on the Karen Brown website that also have email addresses have those addresses listed on their web pages (this information is constantly kept updated and correct). You can link directly to a property from its page on our website using its email hyperlink. NOTE: In any written correspondence be sure to spell out the month since Europeans reverse the American system for dates. As an example, in Italy 4/9/09 means September 4, 2009 not April 9, 2009.

FAX: If you have access to a fax machine, this is a super-efficient way to reach a hotel. The majority of hotels in Italy have fax numbers, which we have noted in the back of the book under each hotel listing. Do not forget to include your fax number for their response. Although most hotels can understand a letter written in English, on page 12 we have a form written in Italian with an English translation. Photocopy it and use it when you fax your reservation request. See comments under "Email" above, and the "Telephone" paragraph below for instructions on how to fax.

TELEPHONE: Another way to make a reservation is to telephone. You can have your answer immediately, and if space is not available, you can then decide on an alternative.

The cost is minimal if you dial direct—ask your local operator when to call for the lowest rates. Also consider what time it is in Italy when you call (even the most gracious of owners are sometimes a bit grouchy when awakened at 3 am). If you are dialing from the United States, the system is to dial 011 (the international code), then 39 (Italy code), then the city code (do *not* drop the 0 in front of the city code), and then the telephone number. Almost all of the hotels have someone who speaks English. The best chance for finding the owner or manager who speaks English is to call when it is late afternoon in Italy (Italy is six hours ahead of New York). Be aware that Italy's telephone numbers are constantly changing, so if you cannot reach a hotel, ask for operator assistance.

TRAVEL AGENT: A travel agent can be of great assistance, particularly if your own time is limited. A proficient agent can expertly handle all the details of your holiday and tie them together for you in a neat package—including hotel reservations, airline tickets, boat tickets, train reservations, ferry schedules, and theater tickets. For your airline tickets there is usually no service fee (unless you are using some kind of discount coupon), but the majority of travel agencies do charge for their other services. Talk with your agent about fees and be frank about how much you want to spend. If your travel agent is not familiar with all the small places in this guide (many are so tiny that they appear in no other major publications), you can loan him or her your book.

UNITED STATES REPRESENTATIVES: In the back of the book you'll find information on Hidden Treasures of Italy (HTI), a company that can arrange reservations for any hotel in this book. Telephone numbers are given. If you are interested, call to check on the services offered and the fees.

HOTEL RESERVATION REQUEST FORM IN ITALIAN

HOTEL NAME & ADDRESS—clearly printed or typed

Vi richiediamo la seguente prenotazione:
We would like to request the following reservation:

> Numero delle camere con bagno o doccia privata
> *Number of rooms with private bath or shower* _____

> Numero delle camere senza bagno o doccia
> *Number of rooms without private bath or shower* _____

> Data di arrivo _____   Data di partenza _____
> *Date of arrival*   *Date of departure*

Vi prego inoltre de fornirmi la seguente informazioni:
Please let me know as soon as possible the following:

> Potete riservare le camere richieste? Si / No
> *Can you reserve the space requested?   Yes / No*

> I pasti sono compresi nel prezzo? Si / No
> *Are meals included in your rate? Yes / No*

> É necessario un deposito? Si / No
> *Do you need a deposit? Yes / No*

> Prezzo alla notte
> *Price per night* _____

> Quanto é necessario come deposito?
> *How much deposit do you need?* _____

Ringraziando anticipatamente per la gentile conferma. Porgo cordiali saluti,
We thank you in advance for your confirmation. Cordial greetings,

YOUR NAME, ADDRESS, TELEPHONE & FAX NUMBERS—clearly printed or typed

RESTAURANTS

If the property has a restaurant and serves meals to non-guests, we have indicated this with the symbol ⅋ in the list of icons at the bottom of the description.

WHEELCHAIR ACCESSIBILITY

If an inn or hotel has *at least* one guestroom that is accessible by wheelchair, it is noted with the symbol ♿. This is not the same as saying it meets full disability standards. In reality, it can be anything from a basic ground-floor room to a fully equipped facility. Please discuss your requirements when you call your chosen place to stay to determine if they have accommodation that suits your needs and preference.

KAREN BROWN WEBSITE

Please visit the Karen Brown website (*www.karenbrown.com*) in conjunction with this book. It provides trip planning assistance, new discoveries, post-press updates, the opportunity to purchase goods and services that we recommend (rail tickets, car rental, travel insurance, etc.), and one-stop shopping for our guides, associated maps and prints. Most of our favorite places to stay are featured with color photos and direct website and email links. Also, we invite you to participate in the Karen Brown's Readers' Choice Awards. Be sure to visit our website and vote so your favorite properties will be honored.

About Italy

AIRFARE

Karen Brown's Guides have long recommended Auto Europe for their excellent car rental services. Their air travel division, Destination Europe, an airline broker working with major American and European carriers, offers deeply discounted coach- and business-class fares to over 200 European gateway cities. It also gives Karen Brown travelers an additional 5% discount off its already highly competitive prices (cannot be combined with any other offers or promotions). We recommend you make reservations by phone at (800) 835-1555. When phoning, be sure to use the Karen Brown ID number 99006187 to secure your discount.

BANKS

Banking hours are Monday through Friday from 8:30 am to 1:30 pm and 3 to 4 pm, with some city banks now opening on Saturday mornings. Cash machines accepting U.S. bank cash cards and credit cards are widely distributed throughout Italy. An increasingly popular and convenient way to obtain foreign currency is simply to use your bankcard at an ATM machine. You pay a fixed fee for this but, depending on the amount you withdraw, it is usually less than the percentage-based fee charged to exchange currency or travelers' checks. Be sure to check with your bank or credit card company about fees and necessary pin numbers prior to departure. *Cambio* signs outside and inside a bank indicate that it will exchange traveler's checks or give you cash from certain credit cards. Also, privately run exchange offices are available in cities with more convenient hours and comparable rates.

CURRENCY

All pricing, including room rates, is quoted in euros, using the € symbol. The euro is now the official currency of most European Union countries, including Italy, having completely replaced national currencies as of February 2002. Visit our website (*www.karenbrown.com*) for an easy-to-use online currency converter.

DRIVING

CAR RENTAL: Readers frequently ask our advice on car rental companies. We always use Auto Europe—a car rental broker that works with the major car rental companies to find the lowest possible price. They also offer motor homes and chauffeur services. Auto Europe's toll-free phone service, from every European country, connects you to their U.S.-based, 24-hour reservation center (ask for the Europe Phone Numbers Card to be mailed to you). Auto Europe offers our readers a 5% discount (cannot be combined with any other offers or promotions) and, occasionally, free upgrades. Be sure to use the Karen Brown ID number 99006187 to receive your discount and any special offers. You can make your own reservations online via our website, *www.karenbrown.com* (select *Auto Europe* from the home page), or by phone (800-223-5555).

DISTANCES: Distances are indicated in kilometers (one kilometer equals 0.621 mile). As you drive through the countryside, you will be astonished at how dramatically the scenery can change in just an hour's drive.

DRIVER'S LICENSE: A current license from your home country is valid for driving throughout Italy if you are on holiday and renting a car. However certain age limits apply. Please check on the age limit policy with the car rental company.

GASOLINE: Gas prices in Italy are the highest in Europe, and Americans often suspect a mistake when their first fill-up comes to between $120 and $150 (most of it in taxes). Most stations now accept Visa credit cards, and the ERG stations accept American Express. Besides the AGIP stations on the autostrada, which are almost always open, gas stations observe the same hours as merchants, closing in the afternoon from 12:30 pm to 4:00 pm and in the evening at 7:30 pm. Be careful not to get caught running on empty in the afternoon! Fortunately, now many stations have a self-service pump that operates on off-hours (€10 or €20 and €50 bills, and sometimes credit cards are accepted).

ROADS: The Italian roads are nothing short of spectacular, including some of the finest highways in the world. In fact, the Italians are absolute geniuses when it comes to their engineering feats (which actually is not such a surprising fact when you consider what a fantastic road system the Romans built 2,000 years ago). Nothing seems to daunt the Italian engineers: you would think the mountains are made of clay instead of solid rock, the way the roads tunnel through them. Sometimes a roadway seems endlessly suspended in mid-air as it bridges a mountain crevasse. Names of roads in Italy are as follows:

Autostrada: a large, fast (and most direct) two- or three-lane toll way, marked by green signs bearing an "A" followed by the autostrada number. (See "Toll Roads" below.)

Superstrada: a one- or two-lane freeway between secondary cities marked by blue signs and given a number. Speed limit: 110 kph.

Strada Statale: a small one-lane road marked with S.S. followed by the road number. Speed limit: 90 kph.

Raccordo or *Tangenziale*: a ring road around main cities, connecting to an autostrada and city centers.

ROAD SIGNS: Before starting on the road prepare yourself by learning the international driving signs so that you can obey all the rules. There are several basic sign shapes: triangular signs warn that there is danger ahead; circular signs indicate compulsory rules and information; square signs give information concerning telephones, parking, camping, etc. Yellow signs are for tourists and indicate a site of historical or cultural interest, hotels, and restaurants. Black-and-yellow signs indicate private companies and industries.

TOLL ROADS: Italy has a network of super expressways that makes any spot in the country an easy destination by car. Once you are on the toll roads, you can go quickly from almost any area of Italy to another, but be forewarned—these toll roads are expensive. However, every cent is well spent when you consider the alternative of creeping along within a maze of trucks and buzzing motorcycles, taking forever to go only a few kilometers. Use the toll roads for the major distances you need to cover, and then choose the small roads when you wish to meander leisurely through the countryside. Toll roads are mystifying until you learn the system—even then it is confusing because just when you think you have the operation down pat, you find it varies slightly. This is the most common routine: first follow the green expressway signs toward the toll road. Sometimes these signs begin many kilometers from the expressway, so be patient and continue the game of follow-the-sign. Each entrance to the expressway handles traffic going in both directions. As you enter into the tollgate, there is usually a red button you push and a card pops out of a slot. After going through the toll station you choose the direction you want to go. As you leave the expressway, there is a toll station where your ticket is collected and you pay according to how many kilometers you traveled. (If you lose your card, you will have to pay the equivalent amount of the distance from the beginning of the autostrada to your exit.) Tolls on Italian autostrade are quite steep, ranging from $15 to $28 for a three-hour stretch, but offering the fastest and most direct way to travel between cities. A *Viacard*, or magnetic reusable card for tolls, is available in all "toll-way" gas stations for €20–€50, or a MasterCard or Visa card can now be used in specified blue lanes (the lines for these automatic machines are always the shortest).

ELECTRICAL CURRENT

If you are taking any electrical appliances made for use in the United States, you will need a transformer plus a two-pin adapter. A voltage of 220 AC current at 50 cycles per second is almost countrywide, though in remote areas you may encounter 120V. The voltage is often displayed on the socket. Even though we recommend that you purchase appliances with dual-voltage options whenever possible, it will still be necessary to have the appropriate socket adapter. Also, be especially careful with expensive equipment such as computers—verify with the manufacturer the adapter/converter capabilities and requirements.

FOOD & DRINK

It is almost impossible to get a bad meal in Italy. Italians themselves love to eat and dining is a social occasion to be with family and friends. Restaurants are bustling not only with tourists, but also with the Italians who dawdle at the tables long after the meal is over, chatting and laughing with perhaps a glass of wine or a last cup of coffee.

You soon get in the spirit of the game of deciding which kind of restaurant to choose for your next meal. The selection is immense, all the way from the simple family trattoria where mama is cooking in the kitchen to the most elegant of gourmet restaurants with world-renowned chefs. Whichever you choose, you won't be disappointed. The Italians are artists when it comes to pasta, seen on every menu and prepared in endless, fascinating ways. Some restaurants offer a set-price tourist menu *(menu turistico)* that includes soup or pasta, a meat dish with vegetable, dessert, and mineral water or wine. A tip is usually included in the price, but it is customary to leave some small change.

Wine, of course, is offered with every meal. You rarely see an Italian family eating without their bottle of wine on the table. Unless you are a true wine connoisseur, we suggest the regional wines and if you ask your waiter to assist you with the choice, you flatter him and discover many superb wines.

Some of the most popular wines that you see on the Italian menus are: Chianti, a well-known wine produced in the Tuscany area south of Florence; Marsala, a golden sweet wine from Sicily (a favorite of Lord Nelson); Soave, a superb light white wine produced near Venice; Orvieto, a semi-sweet wine from the Umbria region near Assisi; and Est Est Est, a beautiful semi-sweet wine produced near Rome. The story that we heard about Est Est Est is lots of fun and perhaps even true. It seems that many years ago a wealthy nobleman was traveling south. Being a true gourmet both of food and drink, he sent his servant before him to pick out all the best places to eat and drink along the way. When the servant neared Rome he discovered such a divine wine that all he could relay back to his master was "Est, est, est," meaning "Yes, yes, yes." Today you will think the same about most of the wines you enjoy in Italy—the answer is still "Yes, yes, yes!"

HOLIDAYS

It is very important to know Italian holidays because most museums, shops, and offices are closed. National holidays are listed below:

New Year's Day (January 1)
Epiphany (January 6)
Easter (and the following Monday)
Liberation Day (April 25)
Labor Day (May 1)

Assumption Day (August 15)
All Saints' Day (November 1)
Christmas (December 25)
Santo Stefano (December 26)

In addition to the national holidays, each town has its own special holiday to honor its patron saint. Some of the major ones are listed below:

Bologna–St. Petronio (October 4)
Florence–St. John the Baptist (June 24)
Milan–St. Ambrose (December 7)

Palermo–Santa Rosalia (July 15)
Rome–St. Peter & St. Paul (June 29)
Venice–St. Mark (April 25)

The Vatican Museums have their own schedule and are closed on Sundays (rather than on Mondays as is the case with all other national museums), except the last Sunday of each month when admission is free of charge.

Introduction–About Italy

INFORMATION SOURCES

Italian Government Travel Offices (ENIT) can offer general information on various regions and their cultural attractions. They cannot offer specific information on restaurants and accommodations. If you have access to the Internet, visit the Italian Tourist Board's websites: *www.italiantourism.com* or *www.enit.it*. Offices are located in:

Chicago: Italian Government Travel Office, 500 N. Michigan Ave., Suite 2240, Chicago, IL 60611 USA; email: enitch@italiantourism.com, tel: (312) 644-0996, fax: (312) 644-3019.

Los Angeles: Italian Government Travel Office, 12400 Wilshire Blvd., Suite 550, Los Angeles, CA 90025, USA; email: enitla@italiantourism.com, tel: (310) 820-1898, fax: (310) 820-6357.

New York: Italian Government Travel Office, 630 5th Ave., Suite 1565, New York, NY 10111, USA; email: enitny@italiantourism.com, tel: (212) 245-4822, fax: (212) 586-9249.

Toronto: Italian Government Travel Office, 175 Bloor Street East, Suite 907, Toronto, Ontario M4W 3R8, Canada; email: enit.canada@on.aibn.com, tel: (416) 925-4882, fax: (416) 925-4799.

London: Italian State Tourist Office, 1 Princes Street, London WIB 2AY, England; email: italy@italiantourism.co.uk, tel: (020) 7408-1254, fax: (020) 7493-6695.

Sydney: Italian Government Travel Office, Level 4, 46 Market Street, Sydney NSW 2000, Australia; email: italia@italiantourism.com.au, tel: (61292) 621.666, fax: (61292) 621.677.

Rome: ENTE Nazionale Italiano per il Turismo (Italian Government Travel Office), Via Marghera, 2/6, Rome 00185, Italy; email: sedecentrale@cert.enit.it, tel: (06) 49711, fax: (06) 4463379.

PROVINCES

Italy is divided into Provinces, which appear in abbreviated form in addresses. Some of the provinces you are likely to see and their abbreviated codes are as follows:

AG	*Agrigento*	CS	*Cosenza*	MN	*Mantova*	RM	*Rome*
AL	*Alessandria*	CT	*Catania*	MO	*Modena*	RN	*Rimini*
AN	*Ancona*	CZ	*Catanzaro*	MS	*Massa*	RO	*Ravigo*
AO	*Aosta*	EN	*Enna*	MT	*Matera*	SA	*Salerno*
AP	*Ascoli Picino*	FE	*Ferrara*	NA	*Naples*	SI	*Siena*
AR	*Arezzo*	FG	*Froggia*	NO	*Novara*	SO	*Sondrio*
AT	*Asti*	FI	*Florence*	NU	*Nuoro*	SP	*La Spezia*
AV	*Avellino*	FO	*Forli*	OR	*Oristano*	SR	*Siracusa*
BA	*Bari*	GE	*Genova*	PA	*Palermo*	SV	*Savona*
BG	*Bergamo*	GO	*Gorizia*	PC	*Piacunga*	TA	*Taranto*
BL	*Belluno*	GR	*Grosseto*	PD	*Padova*	TE	*Teramo*
BN	*Benevento*	IM	*Imperia*	PE	*Pescara*	TN	*Trento*
BO	*Bologna*	IS	*Isermia*	PG	*Perugia*	TO	*Torino*
BR	*Brindisi*	LA	*Latina*	PI	*Pisa*	TR	*Terni*
BS	*Brescia*	LC	*Lecco*	PR	*Parma*	TS	*Trieste*
BZ	*Bolzano*	LE	*Lecce*	PS	*Pesaro*	TV	*Treviso*
CA	*Cagliari*	LI	*Livorno*	PT	*Pistoia*	VB	*Verbano*
CB	*Campobasso*	LT	*Latino*	PV	*Pavia*	VC	*Vercelli*
CE	*Caserta*	LU	*Lucca*	PZ	*Potenza*	VE	*Venice*
CH	*Chieti*	MC	*Macerata*	RA	*Ravenna*	VI	*Vicenza*
CO	*Como*	ME	*Messina*	RE	*Reggio Emilia*	VR	*Verona*
CR	*Cremona*	MI	*Milan*	RI	*Rieti*	VT	*Viterbo*

REGIONS

Italy is divided into 20 regions. A map and description of each region is found in the next section of this book, beginning on page 31. Below is a list of the regions and their capital cities.

REGION	*CAPITAL CITY*	REGION	*CAPITAL CITY*
Abruzzo	*L'Aquila*	Lombardy	*Milan*
Aosta Valley	*Aosta*	Marches	*Ancona*
Apulia	*Bari*	Molise	*Campobasso*
Basilicata	*Potenza*	Piedmont	*Torino*
Calabria	*Catanzaro*	Sardinia	*Cagliari*
Campania	*Naples*	Sicily	*Palermo*
Emila-Romagna	*Bologna*	Trentino-Alto Adige	*Trento & Bolzano*
Friuli-Venezia Giulia	*Trieste*	Tuscany	*Florence*
Lazio	*Rome*	Umbria	*Perugia*
Liguria	*Genova*	Veneto	*Venice*

SECURITY WHILE TRAVELING

The Italians are wonderful hosts. It seems every Italian has a brother or cousin in the United States, and so the warmth of camaraderie is further enhanced. In spite of the overall graciousness of the Italians, there are instances where cars are stolen or purses snatched, but this happens all over the world. Just be cautious. Watch your purse. Don't let your wallet stand out like a red light in your back pocket. Lock your valuables in the hotel safe. Don't leave valuables temptingly exposed in your car. Never set down luggage in train stations or airports, even for a minute. In other words, use common sense. NOTE: Whenever you travel to any country, it is wise to make a photocopy of the pages of your passport showing your picture, passport number, date, and where issued. With this photocopy in hand it is much easier to get a replacement passport.

SHOPPING

Italy is definitely a shopper's paradise. Not only are the stores brimming with tempting merchandise, but also their displays are beautiful, from the tiniest fruit market to the most chic boutique. Each region has its specialty. In Venice items made from blown glass and handmade laces are very popular. Milan is famous for its clothing and silk wear (gorgeous scarves, ties, and blouses). Florence is a paradise for leather goods (purses, shoes, wallets, gloves, suitcases) and also for gold jewelry (you can buy gold jewelry by weight). Rome is a fashion center—you can stroll the pedestrian shopping streets browsing in some of the world's most elegant, sophisticated boutiques. You can buy the very latest designer creations and, of course, religious items are available, especially near St. Peter's. Naples and the surrounding regions (Capri, Ravello, Positano) offer delightful coral jewelry and also a wonderful selection of ceramics.

For purchases over €155 an immediate cash refund of the tax amount is offered by the Italian government to non-residents of the EU. Goods must be purchased at an affiliated retail outlet with the "tax-free for tourists" sign. Ask for the store receipt **plus** the tax-free shopping receipt. At the airport go first to the customs office where they will examine the items purchased and stamp both receipts, and then to the "tax-free cash refund" point after passport control.

U.S. customs allows U.S. residents to bring in $800-worth of foreign goods duty free, after which a straight 10% of the amount above $800 is levied. Two bottles of liquor are allowed. The import of fresh cheese or meat is strictly restricted unless it is vacuum-packed.

TELEPHONES—HOW TO MAKE CALLS

The Italian phone company (TELECOM) has been an object of ridicule, a source of frustration, and a subject of heated conversation since its inception. Although more modern systems are being installed, it remains one of the most archaic and costly communication systems in the developed world. Telephone numbers can have from four to eight digits, so don't be afraid of missing numbers. Cellular phones have saved the day

(Italians wouldn't be caught dead without at least one) and are recognized by three-digit area codes beginning with 3.

IMPORTANT NOTE: All calls to Italy need to include the "0" in the area code, whether calling from abroad, within Italy, or even within the same city, whereas cell phone numbers have dropped the "0" in all cases.

Dial 113 for emergencies of all kinds—24-hour service nationwide with an English-speaking person available.
Dial 116 for Automobile Club for urgent breakdown assistance on the road.
Dial 118 for Ambulance service.

Remember that no warning is given when the time you've paid for in a public phone is about to expire (the line just goes dead), so put in plenty of change or a phone card. There are several types of phones (in various stages of modernization) in Italy.

Bright-orange pay phones, as above with attached apparatus permitting insertion of a *scheda telefonica,* reusable magnetic cards worth €5–€25, or now more rarely coins.

NOTE: Due to the ongoing modernization process of telephone lines, phone numbers are constantly being changed, making it sometimes very difficult to contact hotels (many times they are not listed under the property's name). A recording (in Italian) plays for only two months indicating the new number. If you are calling from the United States and your Italian is not up to par, we suggest you ask the overseas operator to contact the Italian operator for translation and assistance.

CALLING HOME: Calling overseas is very expensive from Italy. In addition, hotels usually add a hefty surcharge to telephone calls charged to your room. The best bet is to use one of the many available international telephone cards. With these you can make a local call within Italy and be connected with your home operator. Ask your local telephone company what access number to use. If you want to use your cell phone, ask your service provider if your phone can be set up for international calls.

TIPPING

HOTELS: Service charges are normally included in four- and five-star hotels only. It is customary to leave a token tip for staff.

RESTAURANTS: If a service charge is included, it will be indicated on the bill, otherwise 10–15% is standard tipping procedure.

TAXIS: 10%.

TRANSPORTATION

BOATS: Italy has gorgeous islands dotting her shorelines, a glorious string of lakes gracing her mountains to the north, and romantic canals in Venice. Luckily for the tourist, the country's boat system is excellent.

All of Italy's islands are linked to the mainland by a wonderful maritime network. The many outlying islands sometimes have overnight ferries that offer sleeping accommodations and facilities for cars. The closer islands usually offer a choice—the hydrofoil that zips quickly across the water or the regular ferry that is slower. Italy also offers you an enchanting selection of lakes. One of the true highlights of traveling in Italy is to explore these wondrous lakes by hopping on one of the nostalgic ferry boats that glide romantically between little villages clustered along the shorelines. Again, there is usually a choice of either the hydrofoil that darts between the hamlets, or the ferry that glides leisurely across the water and usually offers beverage and food service on board. The boat schedules are posted at each pier, or you can request a timetable from the Italian tourist office. NOTE: These little boats are punctual, to the minute. Be right at the pier with your ticket in hand so you can jump on board during the brief interlude that the boat stops at the shore. If at all possible, try to squeeze in at least one boat excursion—it is a treat you will long remember.

TRAINS: Italy has an excellent network of trains. The EUROSTAR trains between major cities are the fastest, most efficient and most frequent of all trains with a common route such as Rome-Florence taking only one hour and 40 minutes! In contrast, the local trains stop at every little town, take much longer, and are frequently delayed. Each train station is well organized. There is almost always an information desk where someone speaks English who will answer any questions and advise you as to the best schedule. There is another counter where you purchase your tickets. Still a third counter is where seat reservations are made. We strongly recommend purchasing your train tickets in advance: it is quite time-consuming to stand in two lines at each train station, only to find— particularly in summer—that the train you want is already sold out. You can purchase open tickets in the United States. However, it is almost impossible to purchase seat reservations in advance (except for major European routes). Go ahead and buy the open tickets, and then you can either purchase your seat reservations locally, or else pay the concierge at your hotel to handle this transaction for you. Seat reservations cannot be made just before getting on the train—it is best to make them as far in advance as possible.

NOTE: Your ticket must be stamped with the time and date *before* you board the train; otherwise, you will be issued a €20 fine. Tickets are stamped at small and not very obvious yellow machines near the exits to the tracks.

View of Assisi

The Eurailpass, which allows travel for varying periods of time on most trains throughout Europe, is valid in Italy. However, if you are going to travel exclusively in Italy, buy instead an Italian Rail Pass. These bargain passes which must be purchased outside of Italy include the *Tourist Pass* and the *Flexi Pass*. The *Tourist Pass* is available for unlimited travel for a period of 8, 15, 21, or 30 consecutive days. The *Flexi Pass* allows you to choose the number of days you want to travel within a month. You can buy the *Flexi Pass* for 4 days, 8 days, or 12 days of travel. All of the Italian passes can be bought for either first- or second-class travel. NOTE: In the summer when rail traffic is very heavy, unless you make dining car reservations in advance, you might not be able to have the fun of eating your meal en route. If you have not made these reservations, as soon as you board the train, stroll down to the dining car and ask to reserve a table.

If you plan to travel by train throughout Europe, you can research schedules and fares and purchase tickets and passes online. (Note that many special fares and passes are available only if purchased in the United States.) For information and the best possible fares, and to book tickets online, visit our website, *www.karenbrown.com.*

TRANSFERS INTO CITIES: Travelers from abroad normally arrive by plane in Milan, Florence, Rome, or Venice and often pick up their rental car at the airport. However, if your first destination is the city and you plan on picking up your car after your stay, approximate transfer rates are as follows:

MILAN

From Malpensa to city by taxi (70 min)	€ 80
From Malpensa to Cadorna station by train (every 30 min)	€ 12
From Malpensa several stops by bus (every 20 min)	€ 6
From Linate to city by taxi (20 min)	€ 40
From Linate to city by bus (every 20 min)	€ 6

ROME

From Da Vinci to city by train (every 30 min)	€ 12
From Da Vinci to city by taxi (45 min)	€ 50

FLORENCE

From airport to city by taxi (30 min)	€ 40

VENICE

From airport to city by waterbus (1 hour)	€ 15
From airport to city by private waterbus (40 min)	€ 100
From station to city by waterbus (15 min)	€ 15
From station to city by private waterbus	€ 110

WEATHER

Italy is blessed with lovely weather. However, unless you are a ski enthusiast following the promise of what the majestic mountains have to offer in the winter, or must travel in summer due to school holidays, we highly recommend traveling in spring or fall. Travel at either of these times has two dramatic advantages: you miss the rush of the summer tourist season when all of Italy is packed and you are more likely to have beautiful weather. In spring the meadows are painted with wildflowers. In fall the forests are a riot of color and the vineyards are mellow in shades of red and gold. Although the mountains of Italy are delightfully cool in summer, the rest of the country can be very hot, especially in the cities. NOTE: Many hotels are not air conditioned. Those that are sometimes charge extra for it.

WEBSITE

Please visit the Karen Brown website (*www.karenbrown.com*) in conjunction with this book. Our website provides trip planning assistance, new discoveries, post-press updates, feedback from you, our readers, the opportunity to purchase goods and services that we recommend (rail tickets, car rental, travel insurance, etc.), and one-stop shopping for our guides, associated maps and watercolor prints. Most of our favorite places to stay are featured with color photos and direct website and email links. Also, we invite you to participate in the Karen Brown's Readers' Choice Awards. Be sure to visit our website and vote so your favorite properties will be honored.

WHAT TO WEAR

During the day informal wear is most appropriate, including comfortable slacks for women. In the evening, if you are at a sidewalk café or a simple pizzeria, women do not need to dress up nor men to wear coats and ties. However, Italy does have some elegant restaurants where a dress and coat and tie are definitely the proper attire. A basic principle is to dress as you would in any city at home. There are perhaps a few special situations: the churches are still very conservative—shorts are definitely inappropriate, as are low-cut dresses. Some of the cathedrals still insist that women have their arms covered. It is rare that a scarf on the head is required, but to wear one is a respectful gesture. If you have an audience with the Pope, then the dress code is even more conservative. The layered effect is ideal. Italy's climate runs the gamut from usually cool in the mountains to frequently very hot in the south. The most efficient wardrobe is one where light blouses and shirts can be reinforced by layers of sweaters that can be added or peeled off as the day demands.

Florence

Regions of Italy

ABRUZZO: Although it is one of the smallest regions of Italy, rugged Abruzzo boasts the highest peaks of the Apennine range, the Gran Sasso. In fact, most of the territory is made up of majestic mountains spilling down to the coast of the Adriatic Sea. Unsuitable for agriculture, the region's economy depends on pastoral activity and specialty artisans (goldsmiths, wood and stone carvers, wrought-iron craftsmen) and  tourism. Abruzzo is the ancestral land of many Americans who return to Italy in search of their roots. The region's four major national parks and nature reserves are ideal for hiking, free climbing, and alpine, cross-country, and downhill skiing. Our favorite medieval villages to explore include Sulmona, Scanno, Penne Atri, Tagliacozzo, Saepinum and the historic capital town of L'Aquila with its Fontana delle 99 Cannelle, a fountain built in 1272 with 99 spouts. In Sulmona you find Ceramics of Castelli, a tradition since the Middle Ages. *Gastronomic specialties:* A large variety of pastas come from this region. Inland you find lamb dishes and a special variety of pecorino cheeses, while the coast offers seafood delights including stuffed squid. Highly prized wines come from Montepulciano d'Abruzzo.

AOSTA VALLEY: In the uppermost corner of northwest Italy is Valle d'Aosta, a region made up entirely of mountains, with its Alps bordering France and Switzerland. The capital city, Aosta, derives its name from Ottaviano Augusto who founded the city in 25 AD. It is one of two Italian regions that have been run as completely autonomous administrations since 1946, with its own constitution and laws. Besides  having preserved Patois, its original dialect, both French and Italian are also spoken fluently. This region has many ski resorts including: Cervinia, Courmayeur, and Mont Blanc on the French-Swiss border. You will also find 130 medieval castles in Aosta, with the Fenis and Issogne being the most famous. The Gran Paradiso National Park, with its Alpine refuges, is a haven for nature and wildlife lovers, hikers, and climbers. *Gastronomic specialties:* Fontina cheese (excellent in fondues) and many prestigious wines (including Pinot Gris) come from the Aosta Valley.

APULIA: Apulia is a delightful surprise with unique scenery barely resembling that which you see in the rest of Italy. Over the centuries it was invaded by Greeks, Arabs, Normans, Swedes, Aragonesi, Spaniards, and Saraceni, all of whom left their mark on the land. There are many castles in Apulia including: Castel del Monte, di Trani, d'Otranto, and di Copertino. Octagonal-shaped Castel del Monte is the most impressive of  the buildings commissioned by Frederick II. This region is also home to Gargano Peninsula National Park, which is heavily forested and has scenic beaches. Our favorite towns to explore are Vieste and Monte Sant'Angelo. You must also visit the whitewashed towns of Ostini, Alberobello, and Locorotondo, the touristic heart of the region and home to the trulli (whimsical-looking, cone-shaped houses). Located on the "heel" of the boot, and not to be forgotten, are the beautiful baroque cathedral cities of Lecce, San Matteo, Santa Chiara, and Santa Croce. *Gastronomic specialties:* Olive oil and wine (which are strong and full-flavored), various cheeses from sheep's milk; local ear-shaped pasta (called orecchiette), seafood dishes with mussels; fava beans and chicory are all found in the region.

BASILICATA: Basilicata, located at the "instep" of the boot, is another of Italy's smaller regions that is not often visited by tourists. It reaches the shores of the Gulf of Taranto as well as a small stretch of the Tyrrhenian Sea on the western coast. Matera is no doubt the most interesting city in this region. Its ancient neighorhood, Sassi, has been preserved as an outdoor museum with cave-like dwellings built into the  tufo rock where many citizens of this impoverished and forgotten region lived along with their livestock. While in Matera you must also visit its Romanesque cathedral and its several 9th-century churches with Byzantine frescoes. Another highlight of Basilicata is picturesque Maratea—a medieval village tucked in the hills above a beautiful coast that is enhanced by pretty beaches and hidden coves. The archaeological ruins of Eraclea and Metapontum are also part of this region.

CALABRIA: One of the most mountainous regions of Italy, Calabria, at the "toe" of the boot, is a peninsula flanked by two seas, the Ionian and the Tyrrhenian. Agriculture remains its mainstay even though the mountains are arid and the terrain subject to landslides. The rugged highlands of Aspromonte and the wooded Sila areas in the center are sparsely inhabited. Our favorite cities include: Catanzaro, Cosenza, Reggio di Calabria (ferryboats to Sicily) and Crotone. Damage from four major earthquakes and the effects of bombing in World War II have left these cities with few historic monuments. The National Museum of Magna Graecia in Reggio di Calabria (colonized by the Greeks in 750 B.C.) contains the most important art collection in southern Italy. When exploring this region, take the coastal road from Maratea going south towards Sicily which is far more scenic than the autostrada. There are gorgeous cliffs at Capo Vaticano, near Tropea, on the road from Vibo Valentia. One long beach with clear blue water runs along the Gulf coast from Reggio di Calabria all the way up to Taranto (500 km).

CAMPANIA: The Campania region, hugging the Tyrrhenian coast, is squeezed between its four neighbors: Lazio, Molise, Apulia, and Basilicata. With the country's third-major city, Naples, as its capital, Campania boasts one of the most famous coastlines in the world: the Amalfi Coast. The restored historic center of Naples (with its Piazza del Plebiscito, Palazzo Reale, Galleria Umberto, San Francesco di Paola, San Gennaro, Piazza Mercato, and Piazza Garibaldi) is definitely the highlight of this region. Nearby Naples, the archaeological sites of Pompeii, Paestum, Herculaneum, Capua, and Velia are also a must-see. Santa Maria di Castellabate and Acciaroli are two favorite towns on the Cilento coast south of the Amalfi Coast. This coastal area offers lovely, quiet, seaside resorts. Campania also boasts many gorgeous islands. After seeing the famed Capri, try lesser-known islands with more local flavor such as Ischia (specializing in thermal spas) and Procida. *Gastronomic specialties:* Campania is home of fresh Buffalo mozzarella from Paestum, pizza from Naples, and spaghetti with clams.

EMILIA-ROMAGNA: Emilia Romagna covers a large stretch of territory from the Adriatic Sea to almost the opposite side of the country. The bordering regions to the north are Veneto, Lombardy, Piedmont, and Liguria; and to the south, Tuscany and Marches. Italy's main autostrada runs right through Emilia-Romagna, dividing the flat plains to the north from the lush fertile hills to the south. There is a  wealth of precious works of art in this region from the magnificent Byzantine mosaics in Ravenna, wonderful Romanesque churches in Modena and Parma, to Renaissance art and architecture in Ferrara and Bologna. From the beaches of Rimini where international youth swarm in the summer months, dancing until dawn, to some of the most important opera and music festivals of international fame in Modena, Bologna, and Parma, this region has it all. *Gastronomic specialties:* Emilia–Romagna produces Italy's best and most famous food, starting with Parmesan cheese, Parma ham, balsamic vinegar, endless varieties of salami, tortellini and many other pastas.

FRIULI-VENEZIA GIULIA: In the far northeastern corner of Italy, is the Friuli-Venezia Giulia region. Half of its territory is made up of mountains, with the remaining area flatland bordering the Adriatic Sea. Its capital city, at the region's most easterly point, is Trieste, located on the Slovenian border and home to many shipyards. The highlighs of this region include the medieval villages of Portogruaro, Summaga, Sesto Al  Reghena, and Aquileia (the Roman colony founded in 181 B.C. whose artifacts are displayed in the Museo Archeologico). Also Cividale del Friuli, another city of ancient Roman origins (founded by none other than Caesar himself), boasts an interesting museum located in the Palladio-designed Palazzo Pretorio. If you like art, Giambattista Tiepolo, Venice's favorite 18th-century painter, is well represented in Udine, within the cathedral and Museo Diocesano. *Gastronomic specialtie*s: This region is home to some of the sweetest of prosciutto hams made in the town of San Daniele dei Friuli. Fine DOC regional wines including Pinot Bianco, Riesling, Riva Rossa, Carso Terreno, and Refosco come from this region (wine estates are concentrated around the hillsides of Gorizia).

LAZIO: It is only in the past decade or so that foreigners have begun to explore and appreciate the many historic, artistic, and natural wonders of the Lazio region, home to the nation's capital city Rome. Highlights of this region include the fascinating world of the Etruscans with more than 30 sites, a comprehensive archaeology museum in Tarquinia, and well-preserved tombs in the area of Tarquinia and Cerveteri. Lazio is  home to many famous gardens including the Tivoli and the extraordinary gardens and fountains of Villa d'Este. In addition, one of Italy's best-preserved Renaissance gardens, the Villa Lante, is also in Lazio. This region also boasts picturesque lakes. Lakes to the north of Rome include Bracciano, Bolsena, and Vico; and to the south are lakes Nemi and Albano. Rieti, backed by the Terminillo mountains and the scenic Sabine mountain area dotted with medieval villages is perfect for those seeking spots off the beaten path. Our favorite seaside attractions are the charming fishing villages on the islands of Ponza and Ventotene, plus the coast from Circeo to Gaeta. *Gastronomic specialties:* Top-rated olive oil, which rivals that of Tuscany and Puglia, is made in Riete.

LIGURIA: Liguria is best known for its Riviera tourism. The Ponente coast, including the flower capital of Italy, San Remo, is a highlight of this region. The gardens of Ventimiglia and the villages of Alassio, Albenga, Cervo, Dolceacqua, and Taggia are also worth visiting. Of course one must also visit the Levante coast which has stolen the  spotlight with such gems as Portofino, Camogli, San Fruttuoso abbey, Santa Margherita, and the very popular stretch of hill towns above the sea called Cinque Terre. We also love "Poet's Gulf," just south of the Cinque Terre where you find the charming fishing villages of Tellaro, San Terenzo, and Fiascherino. The hilly and mountainous inland areas, which give the region its verdant reputation, have yet-to-be-discovered villages (such as Uscio), and offer quiet havens from the more popular coastal destinations. A mountain excursion can be taken to Santo Stefano d'Aveto, an hour and a half's drive from the coast. *Gastronomic specialties*: Focaccia pizza using its famed olive oil, delectable pesto sauces, and many seafood specialties are common here.

LOMBARDY: The Lombardy region's capital, Milan, does not steal the  limelight from the rest of its territory, which encompasses the beloved lake regions. Still, a shopping expedition down the famed Via Monte Napoleone and a peek at Leonardo da Vinci's "Last Supper," plus the Duomo and La Scala are all a must. Regional highlights include the historic small city of Vigevano near Milan with its magnificent arcaded piazza and baroque cathedral. Our favorite Lombard cities include the beautifully austere Bergamo with its ancient stone center on the upper half of the city; Pavia with its monumental Certosa abbey and surrounding Pavese wine country; Cremona, the capital of violins and homeland of Monteverdi; and Mantova with its three interconnecting lakes. Tourists have always been highly attracted to the romantic northern lakes in Italy. Como sits at the top of the list, then Maggiore; Garda, the largest, with its fairy-tale medieval town; Sirmione; then minor lakes, Orta, Varese, Lugano, Iseo, all dotted with charming villages. The Franciacorta wine area, stretching between Brescia (Lombardy's second-biggest city), and Lake Iseo, is in this region and produces Italy's best sparkling wines.

MARCHES: The Marches, stretching along the Adriatic coast, runs  close behind Tuscany and Umbria in the way of scenic beauty, history, art, and cultural offerings. It is a prosperous region offering seaside resorts, the Sibillini mountain peaks, bucolic countryside, and Renaissance towns. Urbino, Ascoli Piceno, and Loreto are the most outstanding of the Renaissance towns in the region. Other highlights include the towns of Pesaro (on the sea and the birthplace of Rossini) and Macerata (a medieval city with summer music festivals). The scenically situated Renaissance town of Recanati is also wonderful. The Monte Conero coast south of Ancona is decidedly the most beautiful seaside area of the region, with intimate, rocky beaches and coves best reached by boat. This is a regional park with cliffs swooping down to the sea. Our favorite village here is the charming Sirolo, a walled town perched above the coast. Torre di Palma is another enchanting ancient village by the sea with delightful outdoor dining. The fascinating pink stalactite caves of Grotte di Frasassi are also worth seeing.

MOLISE: Molise, another of Italy's forgotten, mostly mountainous regions, is relatively isolated and sparsely populated. Until recently there were very few roads here, with just three main arteries cutting across the entire region. Isernia and Campobasso, the two main cities of Molise, are its highlights. Isernia has been severely damaged over the years by earthquakes and bombing and little remains of its history. It  does have, however, a museum with relics of the Paleolithic civilization recently discovered here, the most ancient finding in all of Europe to date. There are remote mountaintop villages in the area surrounding Isernia including Capracotta, Agnone, Pietrabbondante, and Scapoli, where the zampogna bagpipes, a local tradition among shepherds, are demonstrated in the yearly fair. The quaint villages of Larino, Ferrazzano, and Garanello surrounding Campobasso are lovely. The Tremiti islands of Molise and can be reached by ferryboat from Termoli or Vasto.

PIEDMONT: Piedmont is at the foothills of the Alps, which make up almost half of the region—the rest being divided between hillside and plains. Piedmont has a colorful past and today boasts one of Italy's strongest economies. Turin, the capital city of Italy until 1860 (now the home of Fiat industries) maintains an impressive historic center (Piazza San Carlo), and has the world's most important collection of Egyptian art.
The Langhe and Monferrato wine country is certainly the favorite area as far as tourism is concerned; this countryside south and east of Turin is characterized by medieval villages, ancient fortified castles, and hills lined with kilometer after kilometer of vineyards and fruit orchards. Other towns of interest include Alba, La Morra, Cherasco, Barolo, and Monforte. *Gastronomic specialties*: Risotto is common in Piedmont (the region along with Lombardy being Europe's rice capital). The region also boasts prized white truffles, and some of the country's finest wines: Barbaresco, Barbera, Barolo, and Dolcetto.

SARDINIA: Until recently, Sardinia was Italy's forgotten island, the farthest from the mainland with a rocky, arid interior covered with grazing sheep. Its Caribbean-blue waters, hidden coves, and isolated white beaches have attracted the sailing and yachting set who all converge in the summer months on the northern Emerald Coast. The rest of the year the  island is a haven for explorers discovering it's fascinating ancient history, dating back to 300 B.C. Over 7,000 ancient nuraghes (stone structures built for defense as far back as the 9th century B.C. up to the Roman period) are scattered about the entire island in various states of preservation. A vast variety of traditional festivals occur throughout the year where Sardinians, mostly dressed in traditional costumes, express their identity. These festivals are the best way to really come to understand their unique culture. The region also includes the picturesque islands of Sant'Antioco, San Pietro, La Maddalena, Caprera, and Asinara. *Gastronomic specialties:* A wide variety of good wines are made in Sardinia, especially sweet wines (Vernaccia). Recipes that are based either on lamb and wild boar or seafood specialties, including octopus, are popular.

SICILY: The culture, traditions, and history of Sicily are intensely rich. Its fertile terrain is just as varied with rugged mountains (including Europe's highest volcano, Mount Etna), flatland lined with endless citrus groves, spectacular coastlines, and 16 unique islands. The classic tour takes you to Palermo, Segesta's temple and amphitheatre, medieval  Erice, the Greek ruins at seaside Selinunte, the Valley of the Temples in Agrigento, the Roman villa and mosaics at Piazza Armerina, Siracusa, and the resort town of Taormina. Other areas worth visiting are the town of Cefalù on the northern coast, the ceramic center at Santo Stefano, Marsala and the Egadi Isles on the western coast, and the Madonie Mountains with their intact heritage. *Gastronomic specialties:* Fresh pastas made with a variety of Mediterranean vegetables; seafood combinations with sardines, tuna, and a range of local fish; rich desserts with ricotta and marzipan; and sweet wines including Moscato and Marsala, are all indicitive of this region.

TRENTINO-ALTO ADIGE: Trentino-Alto Adige combines two regions that have distinctly different flavors and traditions. Trentino is the southern tip of this far northern mountainous region, bordering Veneto's portion of the Dolomites on one side and Lombardy on the other. Whereas Trentino is Italian in tradition, the upper section of Alto Adige touching Austria is Tyrolian in flavor (more German is spoken  than Italian). The town of Trento is a highlight, featuring a 13th-century cathedral, Palazzo Pretorio, medieval tower, art museum Diocesano Tridentino, and Buonconsiglio Castle. The scenic Fassa and Fiemme valleys, a cross-country skiers' paradise where the ancient Ladin language is still in use, are also of interest. The Brenta Dolomites, where skiers gather at the Madonna di Campiglio resort, is in this region. Visit Alto Adige's capital city, Bolzano, with its Gothic cathedral and archaeological museum displaying the 5,300-year-old mummy, Otzi, discovered under the glaciers in 1991. We also love the beautiful Val Gardena valley extending to Cortina in neighboring Veneto, featuring the Siusi Alps with fairy-tale-like scenery and the centuries-old tradition of woodcarving.

TUSCANY: Tuscany has become synonymous with Italy. Travelers flock to its famous cities and well-preserved countryside not only to view the breathtaking art found here, but also to be swept away by the magic of its enchanting landscapes. Florence is a highlight with its rich display of Renaissance masterpieces all concentrated within the historical center of 3 square kilometers. One must also visit the Piazza  del Campo in Siena, one of Italy's most stunning squares, hosting the world-famous Palio horse races in July and August. The charming medieval hill towns of Montepulciano, Montalcino, and San Gimignano are home to some of the region's finest wines. The small historic cities of Lucca, Pisa, Arezzo, and Cortona, each with its own individual architectural characteristics, are also well worth visiting. Tuscany is also home to the famous Chianti area, with its endless vineyards and monumental castles. Maremma, in the southern, lesser-known reaches of the region touching the sea, is rich in Etruscan history and dotted with numerous stone villages to explore.

UMBRIA: Enchanting Umbria, bordering Tuscany, is located in the lush heart of Italy. A circular road in the center of the region touches the well-known cities of Perugia, Assisi, Spello, Spoleto, Todi, and Deruta. The two most spectacular towns outside of the loop are Gubbio and Orvieto. Highlights include the town of Perugia, a modern-day town with the stunning Palazzo Dei Priori where the majority of the finest Umbrian paintings are exhibited in the Galleria Nazionale dell'Umbria.

Assisi is another highlight with its many beautiful churches, including the mystic Basilica di San Francesco. The northern reaches of Umbria offer remote countryside and unspoiled landscapes. Umbria is home to world-famous ceramic centers, first and foremost, Deruta, and then Gubbio, producing hand-painted pieces for the past 600 years. Umbria also boasts the famous Orvieto Classico wine: varieties can be tasted at enotecas in Orvieto with its monumental cathedral and astounding façade.

VENETO: Wealthy Veneto boasts a handful of stunning artistic cities; the most beautiful slice of the Dolomites surrounding the popular resort, Cortina; the many villas of Andrea Palladio in and around Vicenza; and the eastern half of scenic Lake Garda. Venice with its 120 inlets, 100 canals, and 400 bridges is the highlight of this region. Venice's neighboring islands of Burano with its colorfully painted houses; Murano,

the glass center; and Torcello, are all of interest. Farther south you find Chioggia and its wondrous fish market; Cappella Scrovegni with Giotto's frescoed masterpiece and the 13th-century university (where Galileo taught). Verona, a magical well-preserved city, is also part of this region. Verona is famous for its still-standing 1st-century amphitheatre, its summer opera festival, the Piazza Erbe with its open market, the Renaissance square, and the Piazza dei Signori. The houses of both Romeo and Juliet in Verona are a pilgrimage point where lovers sign a book of confessions, enhancing the fairy-tale aura. Top wines from Valpolicella, Soave, and Barbarano, and grappa from Bassano del Grappa are produced in Veneto.

Coliseum, Rome

Italian Highlights
by Train & Boat–or Car

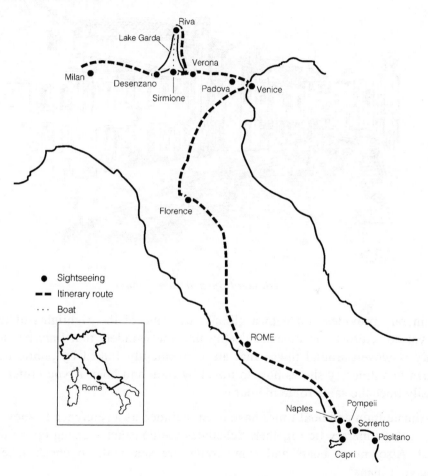

Riva

Lake Garda

Verona

Milan

Desenzano

Padova

Sirmione

Venice

Florence

● Sightseeing
▬ ▬ Itinerary route
· · · Boat

Rome

ROME

Pompeii

Naples

Sorrento

Positano

Capri

Italian Highlights by Train & Boat–or Car

Island of Burano, near Venice

This itinerary provides you with a glimpse of some of the highlights of Italy and will tempt you to return to delve more deeply into the wonders that Italy has to offer. This itinerary is woven around towns that are conveniently linked by public transportation. Although this itinerary shows how to travel by train and boat, if you prefer to drive, you can easily trace the same route in your car.

Approximate train and boat times have been included as a reference to show you how the pieces of this itinerary tie together. Schedules are constantly changing, so these must be verified. Also, many boats and some trains are seasonal, so check schedules before making your plans.

Remember to travel lightly—when burdened by heavy suitcases, the charm of public transportation quickly diminishes!

Recommended Pacing: To follow this itinerary in its entirety you need a minimum of three weeks—and this is really rushing it. We recommend two nights in Milan to see its major sights and enjoy shopping in its multitude of gorgeous boutiques, three nights in Sirmione to give you time to take boat trips on Lake Garda, two nights in Verona to wander its quaint streets and superb Roman amphitheater, three nights in Venice to enjoy its rich beauty, three nights in Florence to visit its many museums, three nights in Rome (an absolute minimum for its many sights to see and shopping), three nights in Naples to give time to visit its fabulous museums plus side trips to Pompeii and the Amalfi Drive, and three nights in Capri to just relax and play on this romantic island. If your time is limited, this itinerary lends itself well to segmentation, so if you can't include all of the suggested stops, choose just a portion of the itinerary and "finish up" on what you have missed on your next trip to Italy.

ORIGINATING CITY   MILAN

This highlight tour begins in **Milan**, a most convenient city since it is the hub of airline flights and trains. While it is a sprawling industrial city at its heart is a truly charming old section.

While in Milan you must not miss visiting the **Duomo**, the third-largest cathedral in the world. There is no denying the beauty of the interior but best of all is the exterior, so take an elevator or the stairs to the roof where you can admire the view and examine at close hand the statues that adorn this lacework fantasy.

Facing the Duomo is one of the world's most beautiful arcades, the forerunner of the modern shopping mall, but with far more style. Even if you are not a shopper, be sure to just browse and have a cup of tea in the **Galleria Vittorio Emanuele.** In this Victorian-era fantasy creation, there are two main intersecting wings, both completely domed with intricately patterned glass. Along the pedestrian-only arcades are boutiques and beautiful little restaurants with outside tables for people watching.

Duomo, Milan

After more than two decades of controversial restoration, Leonardo da Vinci's famous mural, **The Last Supper**, is once again on view in the church of **Santa Maria delle Grazie**. The mural, which covers an entire wall of the church, has been a problem for many years mainly because Leonardo experimented with painting onto drywall rather than employing the more usual fresco technique of applying paint to wet plaster. In an effort to prevent further damage, air filters, special lights, and dust-absorbing carpets have been installed, and the small groups of visitors are limited to a stay of 15 minutes. It is vital that you make an appointment in advance: from the USA 011-39 (Europe, 00-39) 0289-421146; from within Italy, (199) 19 91 00, www.cenacolovinciano.org. The unilingual Italian-speaking reservationists will make you an appointment and give you a confirmation number. Arrive at the church about 15 minutes before your appointment, confirmation number in hand, and pay cash for your ticket.

Milan's other great claim to fame is **La Scala**, one of the world's most renowned opera houses. In addition to wonderful opera, other types of performances are given here. If it is opera season, try your best to go to a performance; if not, try to get tickets for whatever is playing. It is such fun to watch the lights go down and the curtains go up in this magnificent theater with row upon row of balconies rising like layers on a wedding cake. Tickets are sold in the ticket office located around the left-hand side of the theater.

DESTINATION I   SIRMIONE

Sirmione is located on Lake Garda. The station where you need to disembark is in the town of Desenzano, which is on the main rail route between Milan and Venice. There are many trains each day between Milan and Venice, but not all stop in Desenzano. One we suggest runs as follows:

1:10 pm	depart Milan Central Station by train
2:21 pm	arrive Desenzano

When the train arrives in the ancient port of **Desenzano**, you can take a taxi to the pier where hydrofoils, steamers, and buses leave regularly for Sirmione. However, although it is more expensive, we suggest you splurge and take a taxi directly to Sirmione (about 10 kilometers away). This is definitely the most convenient means of transportation since you are taken directly to your hotel.

Sirmione is a walled medieval village fabulously located on a tiny peninsula jutting out into **Lake Garda**. This peninsula seems more like an island because it is connected to the mainland by just a thread of land. To enter the ancient town, you first cross over a moat, and then enter through massive medieval gates. Unless you are one of the lucky ones with a hotel confirmed for the night, you cannot take your automobile inside the town walls, since only pedestrians are allowed through the entrance. But if you have hotel reservations, stop near the entrance at the information office where you are given a pass to enter in taxi.

It is an easy walk to the dock in the center of town where you can study the posted schedule to decide which boat you want to take for your day's excursion. You can glide around the lake all day and have a snack on board, or get off in some small jewel of a town and enjoy lunch at a lakefront café. There is a choice of transportation: either the romantic ferry boats or the faster hydrofoils.

There are some Roman ruins on the very tip of the Sirmione peninsula which can be reached either on foot, or, if you prefer, by a miniature motorized train that shuttles back and forth between the ruins and the village.

DESTINATION II   VERONA

There are trains almost every hour that cover the half-hour journey between Desenzano and Verona. But if it is a beautiful day, it is much more romantic to incorporate sightseeing into your transportation and take a boat and bus instead of the train. If this appeals to you, the following gives an idea of how this can be done.

10:20 am   depart Sirmione by ferry
2:20 pm   arrive Riva

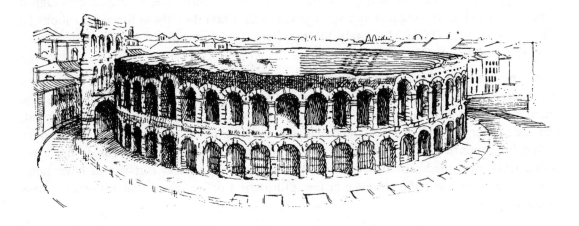

Amphitheater, Verona

You can have lunch on board the ferry or else you can wait until you reach the medieval town of **Riva**, located on the northern shore of Lake Garda. The interesting ancient core of Riva is small, so it doesn't take long to stroll through the old city.

After lunch and a walk through the old part of town, leave Riva by bus for Verona (buses run every 15 minutes in summer), tracing a scenic route along the eastern shore of the lake.

When you arrive in **Verona** you are in for a treat. This is a town that is all too frequently bypassed by the tourist, but what a prize it is. This medieval gem is the perfect city to explore on foot. Buy a detailed map and be on your way.

Definitely not to be missed is the **Roman amphitheater**, one of the largest in Italy. This dramatic arena, dating from the 1st century, has perfect acoustics and hosts operatic performances in summer. As you continue to wander through Verona's enchanting streets, you discover many delights, including the **Piazza delle Erbe** (Square of Herbs), which is the old Roman forum where chariot races used to take place. Follow your map to nearby 21 Via Cappello to find the 13th-century **Casa di Giulietta** and the balcony where Juliet rendezvoused with Romeo. Another colorful square, the **Piazza dei Signori**, features a statue of Dante in its center and 12th-and 13th-century buildings. The **Castelvecchio** (Old Castle) built by Congrande II of the Della Scala family in the 14th century, houses an art museum with paintings, sculptures, jewelry, and armaments. The 14th-century **Ponte Scaligero** (Scaliger Bridge) links the Castelvecchio with the opposite side of the river. The **Cathedral**, dating from the 12th century, is well worth a visit to see its fine red marble columns and richly adorned interior. Just across the river from the heart of the old city, visit the old **Roman theater** where performances are still held in summer.

St. Mark's Square, Venice

When you are ready to leave Verona, there is frequent train service to **Venice** so the following departure time is just a suggestion. NOTE: As you approach Venice, be sure not to get off the train at the Venice Mestre station, but instead wait for the next stop, the Santa Lucia station (about ten minutes further).

2:33 pm   depart Verona, Porto Nuova station by train
3:55 pm   arrive Venice, Santa Lucia station

As you come out of the front door of the train station, you find that the station is directly on the **Grand Canal**. It is a few short steps down to where you can board a boat to take you to your hotel. The **vaporetti** are the most popular means of transportation and are a very inexpensive means of getting about the city. They are like boat buses that constantly shuttle back and forth from the train station to St. Mark's Square. If you have a lot of luggage you might want to consider a watertaxi. The **motoscafi** (watertaxis) cost about € 50 but deliver you right to the door of your hotel, provided there is a motorboat dock (noted in the hotel description). The third choice of transportation is the **gondola**, but these are much slower and very expensive, so save your gondola ride for a romantic interlude rather than a train connection.

Venice has many hotels in every price range. In our description we give the closest boat stop to each hotel so that you know where to disembark if you come by canal from the train station. For a few of the hotels, you need to change boats at the San Marco boat stop.

Venice has so many sights—marvelous restaurants, beautiful boutiques, and fascinating little alleyways to explore—that you could happily stay for weeks.

Of course, you must savor the incomparable ambiance of **Piazza San Marco** (St. Mark's Square). Late afternoon is especially romantic as music wafts across the enormous square, courtesy of the tiny orchestras entertaining visitors as they enjoy an aperitif. A colonnaded walkway encloses the square on three sides, forming a protected path for window-shoppers at the beautiful boutiques and fancy cafés. The fourth side of the square is dominated by the **Basilica di San Marco** (St. Mark's Cathedral), richly endowed with gold and mosaics. The church dates back to the 12th century when it was built to house the remains of St. Mark. Next to the church rises the 99-meter-tall **campanile** (bell tower) where in the 15th-century priests were suspended in a cage to repent their sins. If you are in the plaza on the hour, watch the two Moors strike the hour with their huge bronze hammers as they have for 500 years. To the right of the basilica is the **Palazzo Ducale** (Doge's Palace), a sumptuous fantasy of pink and white marble— open now as a museum. The Palazzo Ducale faces on to the **Piazzetta**, a wide square opening onto the Grand Canal. The square's nickname used to be the *Piazzetta Il Broglio* (Intrigue) because in days of yore, only nobles were allowed in the square between 10 am and noon, at which time the area buzzed with plots of intrigue. Adorning the center of the square are two granite columns, one topped by the Lion of St. Mark and the other by a statue of St. Theodore.

Glass Blowing, Island of Murano

There is no better way to get into the mood of Venice than to join the crowd at St. Mark's pier as they climb aboard one of the ferries that ply the city's waterways. It is a real bargain to board the vaporetto and enjoy the many wonderful palaces bordering the Grand Canal. In addition to exploring the canals that lace Venice, you can take ferries to the outlying islands. Go either on your own or on a tour to the three islands: **Murano** (famous for its hand-blown glass), **Burano** (famous for its colorfully painted fishermen's cottages and lace making), and **Torcello** (once an important city but now just a small village with only its lovely large church to remind you of its past glories).

Another all-day outing by boat is to take the **Il Burchiello**, named for a famous 17th-century Venetian boat. From March to November, this boat departs Tuesdays, Thursdays, and Saturdays at 8:45 am from the Pontile Giardinetti pier near St. Mark's Square and travels the network of rivers and canals linking Venice and Padova. (The schedule might change, so verify dates and times.) This little boat, with an English-speaking guide on board, stops at several of the exquisite palaces en route. Lunch is served and there is time for sightseeing in **Padova** before returning to Venice by bus. Reservation office: Siamic Express, Via Trieste 42, 35121 Padova, Italy, tel: (049) 66 09 44, fax: (049) 66 28 30.

A favorite pastime in Venice is wandering—just anywhere—exploring the maze of twisting canals and crisscrossing back and forth over some of the 400 whimsical bridges. One of the most famous, the **Rialto Bridge**, arching high over the canal, is especially colorful because it is lined by shops. Also much photographed is the **Bridge of Sighs**, so named because this was the bridge prisoners passed over before their execution.

Although all of Venice is virtually an open-air museum, it also has many indoor museums. Two excellent ones are both easy to find near the Accademia boat stop. The **Galleria dell'Accademia** abounds with 14[th-] to 18[th-]century Venetian paintings. Within walking distance of the Galleria dell'Accademia is the **Peggy Guggenheim Museum**, featuring 20[th-]century art. The paintings and statues were the gift of the now-deceased wealthy American heiress, Peggy Guggenheim. The lovely museum was her canal-front home.

DESTINATION IV   FLORENCE

There are several direct trains each day from Venice to Florence: however, in summer, space is at a real premium, so be sure to reserve a seat in advance. Some of the express trains must have prior seat reservations and require a supplemental fee. NOTE: During the busy season, if you want to dine on the train, it is necessary to make advance reservations when you buy your ticket.

    11:45 am   depart Venice, Santa Lucia station (reservations obligatory)
     2:42 pm   arrive Florence

When you arrive in **Florence** take a taxi to your hotel.

Be generous with your time and do not rush Florence—there is too much to see. You must, of course, pay a visit to Michelangelo's fabulous **David** in the **Galleria dell'Accademia** located just off the **Piazza San Marco**.

Ponte Vecchio, Florence

During your explorations of Florence, you will cross many times through the **Piazza della Signoria**, located in the heart of the old city. Facing this characterful medieval square is the 13th-century **Palazzo Vecchio**, a stern stone structure topped by a crenellated gallery and dominated by a tall bell tower. It was here that the *signoria* (Florence's powerful aristocratic ruling administrators) met for two months each year while attending to government business. During this period they were forbidden to leave the palace (except for funerals) so that there could not be a hint of suspicion of intrigue or bribery. Of course, you cannot miss one of Florence's landmarks, the **Ponte Vecchio**. Spanning the Arno in the heart of Florence, this colorful bridge is lined with quaint shops just as it has been since the 14th century.

Don't miss the fantastic museums and cathedrals—the world will probably never again see a city that has produced such artistic genius. Florence's **Duomo** is one of the largest in the world. The cathedral's incredible dome (over 100 meters high) was designed by Brunelleschi. Climb the 464 steps to the top of the dome for a superb view of Florence. The **Baptistry** has beautiful mosaics and its bronze doors by Ghiberti were said by Michelangelo to be worthy of serving as the gates to paradise. The main door shows scenes from the life of John the Baptist, the north door shows the life of Jesus, and the east door shows stories from the prophets of the Old Testament. The **Uffizi Museum** (housed in a 16th-century palace) is undoubtedly one of the finest museums in the world. You can make advance reservations at the Uffizi Museum (tel: 055 23 88 651), *www.virtualuffizi.com,* or call Hidden Treasures (888) 419-6700 (U.S.). Also, do not miss the **Pitti Palace** with its fabulous art collection, including paintings by Titian and Raphael. NOTE: In addition to regular hours, museums stay open during June, July, August, and September until 11 pm. Be sure to buy a guidebook and city map at one of the many magazine stalls and study what you want to see. We just touch on the many highlights. Florence is best appreciated by wandering the historic ancient streets: poke into small boutiques; stop in churches that catch your eye—they all abound with masterpieces; sit and enjoy a cappuccino in one of the little sidewalk cafés and people watch; stroll through the

Palazzo Vecchio, Piazza della Signoria, Florence

piazzas and watch the artists at their craft—many of them incredibly clever—as they paint portraits and do sculptures for a small fee. End your day by finding the perfect small restaurant for delicious pasta made by mama in the back kitchen.

There is an excellent train service from Florence to Rome. EUROSTAR trains offer rapid, excellent service from Florence to Rome and vice versa. Trains take one hour and 38 minutes and depart several times an hour. It is probably best to take one of the midday trains—this allows you to enjoy lunch as you soak in the beauty of the Tuscany hills flowing by your window. Remember that you need both seat and dining reservations.

As the train pulls into Rome, you feel overwhelmed by its size and confusion of traffic, but once you settle into your hotel, you realize that Rome is really not as cumbersome as it looks. The ancient part of the city is manageable on foot—a fabulous city for walking with its maze of streets and captivating boutiques just begging to be explored.

"She Wolf" with Romulus and Remus

According to legend, Rome was founded in 753 B.C. by **Romulus**, who, along with his twin brother, **Remus** (whom he later conveniently "did in"), were suckled by a "she wolf." Although a far less colorful story, historians concur that it was the Etruscans who first settled here and gave the city its name. By the time Christ was born, Rome controlled the entire Italian peninsula plus many areas around the Mediterranean.

Rome is bursting with a wealth of fantastic museums, ancient monuments, spectacular cathedrals, gourmet restaurants, beautiful boutiques, colorful piazzas, whimsical fountains, inspiring statues, theater, and opera—the city itself is virtually a museum. You cannot possibly savor it all. Either before you leave home or once you arrive in Italy, purchase a comprehensive guidebook and decide what is top priority for your special interests. There are many stalls along the streets as well as bookstores throughout Rome where guidebooks are available and every hotel has brochures that tell about sightseeing tours. If there are several in your party, a private guide might be money well spent since he will custom-tailor your sightseeing—with a private guide you squeeze much more sightseeing into a short period of time.

To even begin to do justice to Rome's many wonders, this entire book would need to be devoted to its sightseeing possibilities. However, we cannot resist mentioning a few places you must see.

The first must-see is the **Vatican City** which includes in its complex **St. Peter's Basilica**, the largest church in the world. The original construction was begun in the 4th century by Emperor Constantine over the site of St. Peter's tomb. In 1447 Pope Nicolas V began plans for the new cathedral, which took over 100 years to build. It is no wonder the complex is so utterly breathtaking—all of Italy's greatest Renaissance artists were called upon to add their talents—Bramante, Michelangelo, Raphael, and Sangallo, to name just a few.

The Vatican is a miniature nation tucked within the city of Rome. It is ruled by the Pope, has its own flags, issues its own postage stamps, has its own anthem, mints its own coins, and even has its own police force—the Swiss Guard who still wear the uniform designed by Michelangelo.

Fronting the cathedral is the **Piazza San Pietro**, a breathtaking square designed by Bernini. It is so large that it can hold 400,000 people (making the square a favorite place for the Pope to address large audiences).

Vatican–Swiss Guard

St. Peter's Basilica, Rome

A double semicircle of columns encloses the square, so perfectly designed that the columns fade into each other, giving the illusion that there is a single row. In the center of the square is a towering ancient Egyptian obelisk—adorned, of course, by a Christian cross. As you stand at a distance, the **Piazza San Pietro** forms a visual frame for the cathedral.

To fully appreciate all the Vatican City has to offer, you could easily spend two days, one in St. Peter's Basilica and one day in the **Vatican museums**. The Basilica is like a museum. Not only is the structure magnificent, but the vast collection of works of art inside are almost unbelievable: imagine gazing at such masterpieces as the **Pietà** (the ethereal sculpture of Mary holding Jesus in her arms after the crucifixion, carved by Michelangelo when he was only 25) and the **Baldacchino**, the bronze canopy over the papal altar created by another master, Bernini. Also, be aware when you gaze up at the double-columned dome, that this too was designed by Michelangelo.

The **Sistine Chapel** alone is well worth a trip to Rome. Savor the breathtaking beauty of its ceiling painted by Michelangelo. In addition to St. Peter's Basilica and the Vatican museums, the gardens and the rest of the Vatican can be visited, but only on guided tours. If you are interested, inquire at the Ufficio Informazioni Pellegrini et Turisti in St. Peter's Square. NOTE: The Vatican museums are closed on Sundays, except for the last Sunday of the month when they are open free of charge.

Vatican City, as spectacular as it is, is just one small part of what Rome has to offer. You must see the gigantic **Colosseum**, the entertainment center for the citizens of ancient Rome. Here 50,000 people gathered to be entertained by flamboyant spectacles that included gladiatorial contests, races, games, and contests where Christian martyrs fought against wild beasts.

Another landmark is the **Forum**. It is difficult to make out much of this site because it is mostly in ruins, but at one time this was the heart of Rome. Once filled with elegant palaces, government buildings, and shops, it teemed with people from throughout the known world.

My favorite building in Rome is the **Pantheon**. It is difficult to imagine that this perfectly preserved jewel of a temple dates back to 27 B.C. Step beyond the heavy bronze doors which open into a relatively small, beautifully proportioned room lit only by light streaming in from an opening in the top of the dome.

No trip to Rome would be complete without a stroll down the **Via Veneto**, lined by fancy hotels and luxury boutiques. There are also many outdoor restaurants where a cup of coffee costs almost as much as a meal in a simple trattoria. However, along with your coffee, you are paying the price for the fun of people watching along one of Rome's most elite avenues.

While walking the back streets of Rome, you find many picturesque squares, usually enhanced by a fountain adorned with magnificent sculptures. Especially popular is the **Trevi Fountain** into which tourists go to throw a coin—assuring that they will return to Rome.

Rome has many festivals including the **Festa de Noantri** (Our Festival), which starts on the third Sunday in July. It takes place in **Trastevere**, which is transformed into the venue of a village fair with stalls, open-air taverns, band music, and theatrical shows throughout the entire neighborhood. The event is wrapped up with fireworks over the River Tiber.

The **Spanish Steps** is definitely a landmark of Rome. Topped by the twin spires of the Church of the Trinity of the Mountains, the wide avenue of steps leads down to the Piazza di Spagna (Spanish Square). This large square is highlighted by the Fountain of Baraccia (Fountain of the Boat), a masterpiece by Bernini. The steps are usually crowded both with tourists who come to capture the moment on film and vendors who lay out their wares to sell.

Spanish Steps, Rome

Italian Highlights by Train & Boat—or Car

Leading from the Piazza di Spagna, the Via Condotti is an avenue lined by shops and boutiques selling the finest of merchandise. Branching off the Via Condotti are the narrow lanes of Old Rome, again featuring exquisite small boutiques.

When you are ready to relax, walk to the **Villa Borghese**, a splendid large park in the center of Rome that originated in the 17th century as the private gardens of the Borghese family. Stroll through the park watching the children at play. If you are not saturated with sightseeing, there are many museums to see in the park. One of the loveliest is the **Museo di Villa Giulia**, a museum in a pretty villa that features artifacts from the Etruscan era.

DESTINATION VI NAPLES

You could spend endless weeks discovering the museum that is Rome, but if you have time to add a few more highlights, venture farther south to visit Naples, using it as a hub from which to take side trips to Pompeii, Capri, Sorrento, and the Amalfi Drive. If you want a special treat, instead of visiting romantic Capri as a day excursion, end your holiday there.

There is frequent train service from Rome to Naples. A suggestion for your departure is given below:

10:45 am   depart Rome, Termini station
12:30 pm   arrive Naples, Main station

When you arrive in Naples, take a taxi from the train station to your hotel. If you are arriving by car, be sure to buy a detailed city map in advance and mark with a highlight pen the route to your hotel. In addition, ask for exact directions when making your hotel reservation because Naples is a confusing city in which to find your way by car. However, once you get settled in your hotel, you will discover Naples an excellent city to explore on foot.

Naples, a fascinating city whose history dates back 25 centuries, reflects its rich heritage in its architecture and culture. It seems everyone at one time claimed Naples as "theirs," including the Greeks, the Romans, the French, and the Spanish. Until the unification of Italy, Naples was an important European capital, and is still today a vibrant, exciting city with a stunning setting on the edge of the sea. For many years Naples had the reputation of being a dirty city that was plagued by petty crime. Most tourists came to see its fabulous Museo Archeologico Nazionale and then move quickly on. However, recently a great effort has been made to freshen up the entire city plus deal with the crime issue. Today a great transformation has taken place and Naples is indeed well worth a visit. It is a wonderful city filled with intriguing small squares, an unbelievable assortment of churches, a colorful waterfront, palaces, fortresses and world-class museums. Plus Naples makes an excellent base from which to take side trips.

Below are some suggestions on what to see and do in and around Naples:

SIGHTSEEING IN NAPLES

If you enjoy walking, you can visit almost all of the sights listed on foot. Or, at least walk one way and return to your hotel by taxi.

Museo Archeologico Nazionale: The Museo Archeologico Nazionale is considered one of the finest museums in the world, and rightly so. It has an incredible collection of jewels of antiquity, including unbelievably well-preserved statues, intricate mosaics, and delicate frescoes. There are endless marvels to see. You are bound to be awestruck as you stroll through the corridors lined with the dazzling Farnese collection of ancient sculptures. You could spend endless hours gazing in wonder at the huge statues and deftly carved marble busts that line the well-lit hallways. If you include a visit to Pompeii (which you *must*) you will find that the originals of the most outstanding mosaics and sculptures have been transferred to the Museo Archeologico Nazionale for safekeeping. The mosaics alone are worth a trip to Naples.

Within the museum there is an "off limits" section that is called the *secret cabinet* which is a series of rooms that display a collection of quite risqué paintings, sculptures and mosaics discovered under the ash at Pompeii (only a limited number of people are allowed in at a time and you need a special ticket that can be bought when you arrive at the museum).

Arrive at the Museo Archeologico Nazionale when it opens in the morning in order to be among the first visitors. As the day progresses, busloads of tourists descend. After looking at your map, if you decide walking round trip is too strenuous, we suggest taking a taxi to the museum then strolling back to your hotel since the return will be downhill. NOTE: Museum closed on Tuesdays.

Capodimonte Hill: Perched on Capodimonte Hill, which rises above the city, is a splendid park with over 4,000 varieties of centuries-old trees. Within these grounds is the Palazzo Capodimonte, built in 1738 as a hunting lodge for the King Charles III. Housed within the palace is the Museo e Gallerie Nazionale di Capodimonte featuring a breathtaking art collection of the wealthy Bourbon kings, including works by such masters as Bellini, Michelangelo, Titian, and Botticelli.

You can walk to Capodimonte from the Museo Archeologico, but it is a steep, uphill climb so you might well want to take a taxi, or save the excursion for a separate day. NOTE: Museum closed on Mondays.

Italian Highlights by Train & Boat—or Car

Spaccanapoli District: For savoring the delights and charm of Naples, our favorite tour is in the Spaccanapoli District. Here, on the site of the old Greek-Roman city, you find tiny plazas, little boutiques, outdoor restaurants, coffee shops, markets, and a seemingly endless number of churches. Make your way to the pretty **Piazza Gesù Nuovo**, where you will find the tourist office facing the square. Pop in here and ask for their map that outlines a walk exploring the Spaccanapoli District. If for any reason, the office is closed, the route is easy to find on your own. Basically what you do is follow streets in a rectangular pattern, returning where you began in Piazza Gesù Nuovo. Leaving the square, head east on Via Benedetto Croce that soon changes its name to Via San Biagio dei Librai. Continue on until you come to Via Duomo where you turn left and go a couple of streets to until you see on your right the **Cathedral (Duomo di San Gennaro)**. Next, retrace your steps on Via Duomo for a half a block and turn right, heading west on Via Tribunali. When the road dead-ends at Via San Sebastiano, turn left, go one block, turn right and you are back where you began. You will see many churches along your way, including two that are on the Piazza Gesù Nuovo (The **Church of Guesù Nuovo** and the **Cloister of Santa Chiara**). Most of the churches are open only during services, but the fun of this walk is not so much sightseeing as savoring the flavor of this colorful, ancient part of the city. Make this a leisurely stroll, looking into the little shops, sitting in the small square, maybe a cappuccino at a small café or a pizza, which originated in Naples.

The Piazza Plebiscito and Places to Visit Nearby: The Piazza Plebiscito is a large, bustling square located just at the lower part of one of Naples's principal boulevards, Via Toledo. This is a major square, so it is not surprising there are many monuments and museums nearby. Listed below are some of the recommended places to visit.

Palazzo Reale: Dominating the east side of the Piazza Plebiscito is the large, impressive Palazzo Reale, an outstanding palace that was built for the Spanish Viceroys in 1600, in honor of King Philip II's arrival in Naples. Accenting the façade are niches with statues of the kings of Naples. This is a massive complex, and it might take a while to find your way to the ticket office. Once you have your tickets, you climb an imposing double

Palazzo Real, Naples

staircase that sweeps to the floor above where the royal quarters have been opened as a museum. You might want to rent a cassette which gives commentary on what you will be seeing. It is fun to wander through the endless rooms in this noble residence, including the queen's private chapel, the throne room, a quaint 18th-century theater, and an assortment of sumptuously adorned apartments. NOTE: Closed on Wednesdays.

Theatre San Carlo: Just around the corner from the Piazza Plebiscito, in a wing of the Palazzo Reale that faces the Piazza Trieste e Trento, you find the dazzling Theatre San Carlos. Commissioned by Charles of Bourbon in 1737, this jewel is reminiscent of La Scala Theatre in Milan. It looks like an ornate wedding cake with 186 private, gilt adorned boxes that rise in six tiers that face an imposing stage. Sometimes there are tours of the theater so you might want to drop by to check the schedule before visiting the museum in the Palazzo Reale.

The Umberto Gallery: Just to the north of Piazza Plebiscito, facing a second small square, the Piazza Trieste e Trento, is the belle-époque-style Umberto Gallery, a shopping arcade dating to 1887 which is made of four wings radiating like a cross from its core (if you have been to Milan, the Umberto Gallery is similar to the Galleria there). Wander in to admire the handsome mosaic floor and the ornate, glass-domed ceiling which soars over 50 meters.

Castel Nuovo: Just to the east of the Palazzo Reale, the Castel Nuovo rises on a bluff above the Porto Beverello, the dock from which the ferries leave for Capri and Sorrento. The Castel Nuovo (New Castle) certainly isn't very new—it dates back to the 13th century. The building is definitely dramatic, a rectangular stone building punctuated by huge round stone towers. In the 15th century a splendid white marble Triumphal Arch was added, a true masterpiece whose beauty contrasts pleasantly with the stern, fortress like castle. A deep moat, originally filled with sea water, embraces the fortress. Within the museum you can visit the Museo Civico that contains 14th-century frescoes. It is also possible to visit the Palatine Chapel and the Baron's Hall.

Castel Nuovo, Naples

Castel dell'Ovo: Leaving the Piazza Plebiscito, head down to the waterfront and turn right, following the Via Nazario Sauro as it traces the waterfront. As it rounds a bend, the name of the boulevard changes to Via Partenope, which is fronted by deluxe hotels that face onto Santa Lucia Harbor. Built on a rocky peninsula, that juts into the sea and forms one side of the harbor, is the Castel dell'Ovo built by the Norman King William I in the

12th century. The name means Castle of the Egg, which supposedly originated from a legend that a magic egg was buried in the castle, and if ever broken, bad luck would descend upon Naples.

SIDE EXCURSIONS FROM NAPLES

Naples makes a convenient hub from which to make side trips to some of Italy's jewels, including Sorrento, the Amalfi Drive, Capri and the archaeological sites of Herculaneum and Pompeii, all accessible by either organized tour or "do it yourself" by public transportation.

Pompeii & Herculaneum: Near Naples are two exciting archaeological wonders: Herculaneum and Pompeii. Both are fascinating, but if you don't have time to visit both, don't miss Pompeii. You can choose between joining a guided tour or taking a train to the site. A company called **Circumvesuviana** has narrow-gauge trains leaving Naples' Central Station about every half hour, arriving at the Pompeii Villa dei Misteri station (located across from the entrance to the site) about 40 minutes later. At the entrance to Pompeii, we suggest either buying a map explaining what to see or hiring a certified guide.

An aura of mystery lingers in the air as you wander the streets of Pompeii. All visitors are touched by this ancient city of an estimated 25,000 inhabitants, which in one day became frozen for all time. Probably there is nowhere else in the world where you can so vividly step back in time. Much of what you see today has been reproduced, but the reality is pure. Plaster was poured into molds formed by the lava that demolished the buildings and buried so many families that fateful day. Thus it became possible for latter-day archaeologists to reconstruct houses and make reproductions of people and pets. Walk through the town along the sunken streets crossed by high stepping stones, strategically placed so that pedestrians did not get their feet wet on rainy days. Be sure not to miss some of the reconstructed villas that allow you a glimpse into the daily life of long ago. The **Casa del Fauno**, a fine example of how the wealthy lived, has two inner courtyards and several dining rooms. The **Casa del Poeta Tragico**, a more modest home, has a sign in mosaic saying "Cave Canem" (beware of the dog). At the **Villa di Giulia Felice** you see the example of an entrepreneur—in addition to using it as a private villa, the owner rented out rooms, had shops on the ground floor, and operated an adjacent bathhouse. If traveling with children, you might want to go alone into the **Lupanare** (Pompeii's brothel) where there are erotic paintings on the walls. At the **Terme Stabiane** you see a sophisticated underground water-heating system.

There are many more places to visit than those listed above. As you explore Pompeii, there is no need to watch the time. There is a narrow-gauge train departing from the Pompeii Villa dei Misteri station about every 20 minutes for the half-hour scenic journey to Sorrento.

Sorrento: Sorrento is a charming city that sits on the top of a bluff overlooking the sea. Below is a colorful harbor with ferries constantly gliding in and out, en route to such picturesque destinations as Capri, Positano and Amalfi. The historic center is charming, richly reflecting its ancient Greek and Roman legacy. Pretty boutiques and outdoor cafes beckon as you stroll the narrow streets and explore intimate plazas. The same Circumvesuviana trains that depart Naples's Central Station for Pompeii, continue on to Sorrento. The total time is a little over an hour. Another option for visiting Sorrento, is to take one of the hydrofoils that ply between the two towns.

Amalfi Coast: The strip of coast that runs south from Sorrento to Salerno is world famous for its beauty. A two lane road hugs the steep, winding coastline, capturing breathtaking views as the bluffs fold around the brilliant blue Mediterranean. Enchanting villages dot the coast, further enhancing its idyllic beauty. One of the most accessible of these villages is **Positano**, a postcard-perfect fishing hamlet snuggled in a cove that is wrapped by an exceedingly steep hill. Colorfully painted houses, trendy boutiques, cute restaurants, and cascades of brilliant bougainvillea add to the appeal of this jewel. From Naples you can take a ferry to Sorrento and then on to Positano, or take the train to Sorrento and a bus from there (the buses leave from the train station).

Capri: Several shipping companies have ferries that leave frequently from Naples to the romantic island of Capri, leaving from Molo Beverello, the dock below Castel Nuovo. By choosing an early morning departure, it is easy to visit Capri and return in time for dinner in Naples. However, if time permits, we would suggest spending a few days in this beautiful small island. For sightseeing in Capri, see the following destination.

DESTINATION VII   CAPRI

There is frequent boat service between Naples and Capri. Boats leave from either the Mergellina Pier (Boat Companies: Alilauro and S.N.A.V.) or the Molo Beverello Pier (Boat Companies: Caremar and N.L.G.). You can take a ferry (traghetto), which takes one hour and fifteen minutes or a hydorfoil (aliscafo), which takes forty-five minutes.

Your boat arrives at the **Marina Grande**, a small harbor filled with colorful boats and edged by brightly painted shops. When the boat docks, you find hotel porters on the pier along with carrier services that go to all of the hotels. They relieve you of your luggage and take it directly to the hotel of your choice, freeing you to take either a minibus or the funicular to the main town of Capri, which is located on a flat saddle of land high above the sea. There are many charming places to stay on Capri.

Capri has many wonders. The most famous is its submerged cave, the **Blue Grotto**, which can be accessed by boat when the seas are calm. Large boats begin leaving the harbor every day at 9 am for the short ride to the entrance to the grotto, where you are transferred into tiny rowboats. The earlier you go the better since the seas are calmer in the morning. The excursion is an adventure in itself. As you approach the tiny cave opening, it seems impossible that there is adequate room for a boat to enter, but suddenly the sea surges forward and in you squeeze. Like magic, you see it—the mysterious, stunning blue light reflecting from some hidden source that illuminates the grotto. The cost isn't great, but be aware of the system: You pay for a ticket for the motorboat that takes you to the cave, and then you pay again, on site, to the oarsman who skillfully maneuvers his little rowboat through the hole and into the grotto. It is appropriate to tip

Marina Grande, Capri

your boatman—he will do his best to make your short ride memorable and quite probably serenade you within the cave.

Capri is a superb island for walking. As you stroll the trails, all your senses are treated by the fragrant flowers, the gorgeous vistas of the brilliant blue waters, and the sound of birds luring you ever onward. There are many spectacular walks. Follow the trail winding down the cliffs to the small harbor **Marina Piccola**, located on the opposite side of the island from the ferry dock. At the Marina Piccola there are lovely views of the shimmering aqua waters as you make your way to the small beach where you can enjoy a swim before your return. Instead of walking back up the hill, take the little bus that delivers you quickly back to the main square.

Another absolutely spectacular walk—although a long one of at least 45 minutes each way—is to Emperor Tiberius's Palace, **Villa Jovis**, perched high among the trees on the cliffs on the western tip of the island. This is the grandest of the palaces left by Tiberius. Although it is mostly in ruins, you can easily appreciate its former magnificence as you climb about exploring the ruins of the terraced rooms. From the palace there are stunning panoramic vistas: you have an overview of the whole island and can watch the ferries shuttling back and forth to the mainland. A much shorter walk, but one equally beautiful, is to the **Cannone Belvedere**. This path guides you near delightful private villas hidden behind high walls (you get glimpses through the gates) and on to a promontory overlooking the sea.

Another excursion is to **Anacapri**, the only other town on the island, to visit the **Villa San Michel**, a lovely villa overlooking the sea that was the home of the Swedish scientist Axel Munthe. His residence is now open as a museum. Anacapri is a bit too far to walk easily but buses leave regularly from the main square in town.

During the day, Capri is swarming with tourists on package tours that descend like a swarm of locusts from the constant stream of hydrofoils and ferries. You might surmise that in the evening the activity subsides, but it isn't so. The tour groups leave at dusk but then a new group of people emerges from the secreted villas and fancy hotels. Guests in chic clothes and fancy jewelry stroll the streets—both to see and be seen.

When the real world calls and you must leave Capri, there is frequent ferry or hydrofoil service back to Naples. From Naples, you can take a train to Rome or a plane to your next destination.

Capri

Romantic Tuscany

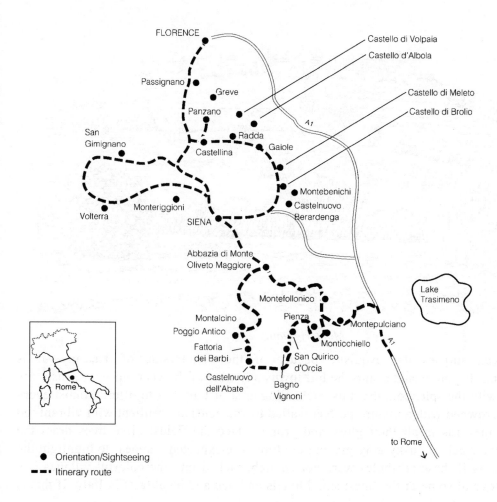

FLORENCE

Castello di Volpaia
Castello d'Albola

Passignano

Greve

Panzano

Castello di Meleto
Castello di Brolio

San Gimignano

Radda

Castellina

Gaiole

A_1

Montebenichi
Castelnuovo Berardenga

Volterra

Monteriggioni

SIENA

Abbazia di Monte Oliveto Maggiore

Lake Trasimeno

Montefollonico

Montepulciano

Montalcino
Poggio Antico

Pienza

A_1

Fattoria dei Barbi

Monticchiello

San Quirico d'Orcia

Castelnuovo dell'Abate

Bagno Vignoni

Rome

to Rome
↓

● Orientation/Sightseeing
▪▪▪ Itinerary route

73

Romantic Tuscany

Monteriggioni

Nothing can surpass the exquisite beauty of the countryside of Tuscany—it is breathtaking. If you meander into the hill towns any time of the year, all your senses are rewarded with the splendors that this enchanting area of Italy has to offer. Almost every hillock is crowned with a picture-perfect walled town; fields are brilliant with vibrant red poppies; vineyards in all their glory and promise lace the fields; olive trees dress the hillsides in a frock of dusky gray-green; pine forests unexpectedly appear to highlight the landscape. As if these attributes were not enough, tucked into the colorful villages is a treasure-trove of some of the finest small hotels and bed and breakfasts in Italy. If this is still not sufficient to tempt you away from the normal tourist route, remember that the food and wines are unsurpassed.

If you are planning to include Florence on your trip to Italy, slip away into the countryside and treat yourself to Tuscany. You will be well rewarded with a wealth of memories that will linger long after you return home. The following itinerary suggests two stops—one in Chianti Classico wine region and the other in Southern Tuscany.

A convenient place to begin your journey is in **Florence**, Tuscany's jewel. Magnificent art is not confined to the city limits of Florence and you will see impressive cathedrals and museums hosting spellbinding works of art throughout Tuscany. See the *Italian Highlights by Train & Boat—or Car* itinerary for sightseeing suggestions for Florence.

Pacing: To explore the hill towns of Tuscany you need at least a week (in addition to the time you allocate to Florence). We recommend a minimum of four nights in the heart of Tuscany's Classico Wine Region, which stretches from Florence south to Siena. This will give the minimum time needed to enjoy the tranquil beauty of the hill towns and to sample the delicious Chianti wines. The second suggested stop is southern Tuscany where we suggest three nights to explore the stunning small towns that dot the hillsides, visit breathtaking monasteries, and taste more of Italy's superb wines: Vino Nobile, grown near Montepulciano, and Brunello, grown near Montacino.

Tuscany is laced with narrow roads that twist through the picturesque countryside. Take a detailed map so that if you get lost, you can find your way home, but part of the joy of Tuscany is to be unstructured. Enjoy the freedom to discover your own perfect village, your own charming restaurant, and your own favorite wine. Although in your wanderings you are sure to find some very special places that we have missed, we share below some of the towns we find irresistible and vineyards that are especially fun to visit.

CHIANTI CLASSICO WINE REGION

This idyllic area lives up to every dream of Tuscany—hills crowned by picture-perfect villages, medieval walled towns, straight rows of towering cypresses, romantic villas, ancient stone farmhouses, vast fields of brilliant poppies, forests of pine trees, vineyards stretching to the horizon. Instead of moving about, packing and unpacking, choose a place to stay anywhere within the area and use it us your hub for exploring this utterly beguiling region of Italy. Below we give suggestions for towns to visit and some of our favorite wineries.

SUGGESTED SIGHTSEEING: TOWNS TO VISIT

Monteriggioni: If you are looking for a town that is truly storybook-perfect, none can surpass the tiny, magical hamlet of Monteriggioni. It is such a gem that it is hard to believe it is real and not a creation by Disney! You can spot it from afar, nestled on the top of a small hill, with 14 towers punctuating the perfectly preserved enclosing walls.

Monteriggioni

No cars are allowed here, so you have to park in the designated area below the walls before walking up to the town, which is composed almost entirely of a main square with small streets radiating from it. On the square you find a Romanesque church, restaurants, boutiques, and shops selling olive oil, cheeses, and wine. It takes only a few minutes to stroll from one end of the town to the other but I assure you, you will be enchanted. As a bonus, Monteriggioni produces its own fine wine, Castello di Monteriggioni.

Passignano in Chianti: Passignano in Chianti is rarely on a tourist route, but we can't help mentioning this tiny hamlet that exudes such a tranquil beauty. For sightseeing, there really isn't much to see except the **Badia a Passignano Abbey**, founded by Benedictine monks in the 11th century. The abbey is set in a pocket of lush landscape and dominates the village, which is no more than a cluster of houses and a restaurant. However, as you drive into the valley, approaching from the west, the abbey with its towering ring of cypresses has such an idyllic setting that it is one of our favorites—a photographer's delight. The abbey can be visited on Sundays at 3 pm; tours leave from the church (please check to verify the abbey is open the Sunday you want to visit). Fine wines, produced by the abbey's vineyards, can be purchased at the Osteria, tel: (055) 80 71 278.

Radda: Located in the very heart of the Chianti wine region, Radda makes a good base of operations. However, not only is the town very conveniently located for sightseeing, it is also extremely quaint and some of its walls are still intact. It was in Radda in 1924 that 33 producers gathered to create a consortium to protect a very special blend of wine that was known as **Chianti Classico**. Only vintners who maintain the standards of the consortium are allowed to proudly display its symbol of the black rooster.

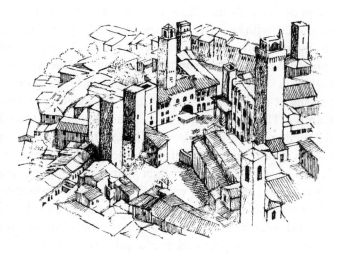

San Gimignano: During your exploration of Tuscany, one town you must not miss is San Gimignano. What is so dramatic about San Gimignano is that at one time the walls of the town were punctuated by 72 towers. During the Middle Ages it was a status symbol for noble families to build their own personal towers for their protection—the higher the tower,

San Gimignano

the greater the image of wealth and importance. It is amazing that 14 of the original towers are still standing. They make a striking silhouette, soaring like skyscrapers, and on a clear day you can see them on the horizon from far away. San Gimignano is truly a jewel—plan to spend at least a day here. There are many shops and marvelous restaurants tucked along the maze of streets. On Fridays there are walking tours with English-speaking guides that leave from the Porta San Giovanni at 11 am (best check with the tourist office to be sure the time and day haven't changed). One of our favorite restaurants in San Gimignano is the delightful **Ristorante Dorando,** which has great food served in cozy rooms with coved ceilings that create the ambiance of an old wine cellar. Located on Vicolo del Oro 2, a small side street just off Piazza Duomo, tel: (0577) 94 18 62. Another favorite, **Ristorante Il Pino**, offers mouthwatering homemade pastas—some of the best we have ever eaten. Located on Via Collolese, 8–10, just down the street from L'Antico Pozzo, tel: (0577) 94 04 15.

Siena: This is an entrancing walled hill town that deserves many hours to savor its rich delights—you should allow yourself at least one full day here. The ramparts are perfectly preserved with a series of massive gates guarding a meticulously maintained medieval stronghold. Drive as close as you can to the main square, park your car, and set out to explore on foot. You cannot drive into the center of the city, but there are designated parking areas (marked by "P") near each of the gates. One of the most convenient is the parking at the Porta Romana. Once you leave your car, strike off for the giant **Piazza del Campo**. This central piazza is immense and, instead of being square, is fan-shaped and slopes downward like a bowl. Eleven streets surrounding the square converge into it like spokes of a massive wheel. Like the Spanish Steps in Rome, the Piazza del Campo is a favorite for tourists who linger here just enjoying the medieval ambiance. It is in this gigantic piazza that the colorful **Palio delle Contrade** (dating back to the 11th century) takes place twice a year, on July 2 and August 16. The horse race is only a part of a colorful spectacle of medieval costumes, impressive banners, and parades, and the festivities extend beyond the actual date of the races. Monopolizing one side of the Piazza del Campo is the 13th-century Gothic **Palazzo Pubblico** (Town Hall) whose graceful arches are embellished with Siena's coat of arms. The Palazzo Pubblico is open as a museum where you can stroll through the governor's living quarters.

Although Siena looks like a large city, it is easily negotiable on foot and most of the museums are in one small area. After visiting the Piazza del Campo, most of the other major places of interest are just a few minutes' walk away, clustered about the Piazza del Duomo. There are excellent tourist signs that will guide you along the maze of narrow streets to all the museums.

You absolutely must not miss Siena's 12th-century **Duomo**, facing the Piazza del Duomo. This is one of Italy's most astounding cathedrals. Not only is its exterior breathtaking, but once you enter, you will be overwhelmed by its dramatic black-and-white, zebra-striped marble columns. Don't miss the intricately carved, 13th-century panels depicting the life of Christ on the octagonal pulpit. Also, be sure to see the **Piccolomini Library**. You need to buy a ticket to enter, but it is well worth it. This relatively small room is totally frescoed with gorgeous murals in still-vibrant colors portraying the life of Pope Pius II. The cathedral also has 59 fabulous inlaid-marble mosaic panels on the floor depicting religious scenes. However, some of the most precious of these are covered to protect them and are on display only from the end of August to the first of October.

After visiting the Duomo, the following museums are just steps away. One of our favorites is the **Ospedale di Santa Maria della Scala**, located across from the entrance to the Duomo. At first glance, it is difficult to truly appreciate its wealth of things to see. The museum goes on and on—it is enormous. Just when you think you have finished, a discreet sign will lead you ever downwards to a lower level and a stunning array of artifacts. The building, dating back to the 800s, was originally constructed as a hospital. Be sure not to miss the former infirmary with its lushly colored frescoes by the master Domenico di Bartolo depicting scenes of patients being treated by their doctors. Another nearby museum is the **Baptistry**, a small museum that, as its name implies, houses the baptismal font for the Duomo. In addition to its beautifully frescoed walls and vaulted ceiling, of prime interest is the 15th-century baptismal font, which is adorned by religious scenes cast in bronze by some of Italy's most famous Renaissance masters, including one panel by Donatello. The **Museo dell'Opera Metropolitana** is worth a visit if for no other reason than to see the sublime *Maestá* by Duccio, painted in 1311. The central scene of the Virgin Mary is truly awesome. For art lovers, the **Museo Civico** must not be missed. Here you will see stunning masterpieces by Ambrogio Lorenzetti, Spinello

Aretino, and Simone Martini. It is overwhelming to ponder how Italy could have produced so many geniuses.

NOTE: There is a comprehensive ticket valid for three days that allows you entrance into many of Siena's prime sightseeing attractions—this is a bargain compared to buying individual tickets. When you buy your ticket for the first museum ask about it and which museums it includes.

Volterra: Just a short drive from San Gimignano, Volterra is a delightful, non-touristy town enclosed by still-intact, 12th-century walls. Like so many of the cities founded by the Etruscans, Volterra is built upon the flat top of a steep hill. As you drive toward the city, the landscape becomes increasingly barren, since the soil is not conducive to growing grapes or olive trees. Instead, alabaster is king here and objects made of alabaster are sold in all of the shops. Not to be missed is the alabaster museum called **Museo Etrusco Guaracci**, which has a fabulous collection of works of art, including sculptures and beautiful vases, displayed with great taste in a series of interlinking rooms that show the art to perfection. There is an adjacent shop selling many alabaster items. The whole town is a jewel whose charm is best experienced by strolling through the narrow cobbled streets. Its main square, **Piazza dei Priori**, the heart of the town, is surrounded by fine examples of beautifully preserved medieval buildings and with its towers, splendid town hall (the oldest in Tuscany), and Romanesque church, it is considered by some to be one of the finest squares in Tuscany. Stroll to visit one of the main gates, the **Porta all'Arco**, the origins of which date back to the 7th century B.C. During World War II, the loyal citizens of Volterra buried the stones of the gate to keep the Nazis from blowing it up.

SUGGESTED SIGHTSEEING WINERIES:

The production of wine plays an enormous role throughout Tuscany, and between Florence and Siena (where **Chianti Classico** is produced) you are constantly reminded of this as you pass through vast rolling hills splendidly adorned with neatly tended vineyards. The Chianti Classico area covers over 172,000 acres, with Siena and Florence being the two "capitals" of the region. Included in the area are the towns of Castellina, Gaiole, Greve, Radda, and some of Barberino Val d'Elsa, Castelnuovo Berardenga, Poggibonsi, San Casciano Val di Pesa, and Tavarnelle Val di Pesa. Even if you are not a wine connoisseur, it would be a pity not to make at least one winery stop both for the fun of observing the production process and for an understanding of the industry that is so central to the soul and character of Tuscany. Many of the wineries also have gift shops and sell marvelous olive oils and cheeses in addition to wine.

As you meander through the countryside you see signs with Chianti Classico's black rooster symbol and you can buy directly from the producer where you see *Vendita Diretta*. In some cases there are also tours of the winery (these are sometimes free, but sometimes there is a charge). A *Cantina* sign means that the winery has a shop where wine is sold and can usually be sampled. One of the delights of touring the back roads of Tuscany is just to stop on whim. When you spot a *Vendita Diretta*, drive in, introduce yourself, and sample some wines. You might well discover one that will become one of your favorites.

Some of our favorite wineries to visit are listed below:

Castello di Brolio: If you visit only one winery, Castello di Brolio should be it since this is not only one of the oldest wineries the world, but also where Chianti wine was "born." Although the production of wine in Tuscany dates back to Etruscan times, the enormously wealthy Ricasoli family, owners of the Castello di Brolio since 1167, are responsible for the special blending of grapes we now consider "Chianti Classico." At one time the extremely powerful Ricasoli family owned most of the land and castles lying between Florence and Siena. The remote family castle, Castello di Brolio, had largely been abandoned when Bettino Ricasoli decided to move into it (so the story goes) after becoming jealous at a winter ball in Florence when his young bride danced a bit too closely to one of her young admirers. Thinking it best to take his wife away from temptation, he rebuilt the huge, remote, crenellated castle, replanted the vineyards, and experimented with the blending of grapes, coming up with the original formula that forms the basis of what is known today as Chianti Classico. The fortified castle tops a high, forested hill. You leave your car in the designated parking area and climb for about 20 minutes up a path or on the road through a parklike forest to the castle gates. Open daily from 9 am to noon and 3 pm to sunset. The castle is located about 10 kilometers south of Gaiole. Tel: (0577) 73 02 20, *www.ricasoli.it.*

Castello d'Albola, winetasting

Castello d'Albola: The Castello d'Albola, a spectacular property just a short drive north of Radda on a gentle hill laced with grapes, is owned by the Zonin family, who have restored the entire medieval complex beautifully. This is an intimate, extremely pretty place to taste wines and take a tour. What we particularly like about the Castello d'Albola is that it is in such a beautiful setting and offers delightfully informal, friendly, free tours. Drive up the hill to the castle, leave your car in the parking area, and walk into an inner castle courtyard, off which you find the winetasting room and cantina. Before or after winetasting, your hostess leads you on a short, professional tour showing you how fine wines are produced. The owner has other enormous estates as well as the Castello d'Albola and is one of the largest producers of wine in the world. Tours start at noon, 2 pm, and 5 pm daily. The cantina is open for complimentary wine tasting daily, April to

October from 10 am to 6:30 pm (9 am to 5 pm November to March). Tel: (0577) 73 80 19, *www.albola.it.*

Castello di Volpaia: The 12th-century Castello di Volpaia, located on a narrow lane about 7 kilometers north of Radda, is one of our favorite places for winetasting. Plan to spend a day on this outing, with ample time to meander through the countryside en route, tour the winery, taste the superb wines, and enjoy a wonderful lunch at the winery's excellent restaurant, La Bottega. Although the winery is called *Castello* it really isn't located inside a castle at all, but rather in various medieval stone houses in a picture-perfect village wrapped by vineyards where you find a small church, a cluster of houses, La Bottega Ristorante, and the winetasting room. You need to preplan this wine tour and also make reservations for lunch since both are very popular and usually booked far in advance. There is a fee for the tour based on the number of people in the group. Tel: (0577) 73 80 66, *www.volpaia.com.*

Castello di Meleto: Another favorite destination for wine-tasting is the beautiful Castello di Meleto, which has an idyllic setting in the gentle hills near the town of Gaiole. Just across from the dramatic castle you find a pretty winetasting room and gift shop where fine wines and olive oils produced on the estate can be purchased. On request, tastings of olive oil and aromatic vinegars can be arranged. What makes this a very special experience is that there is an added bonus: not only can you sample wines, but you can

Castello di Meleto

also visit the beautiful interior of the castle. In addition to splendidly frescoed rooms, the castle has one exceptionally intriguing feature—a whimsical private theater complete with its original stage settings. Call ahead, tel: (0577) 73 80 66, to find out the time and cost of the guided tours of the cellars and castle. The Castello di Meleto also offers bed & breakfast accommodation.

SOUTHERN TUSCANY

The area of Tuscany that lies south/southeast of Siena is famous for its superb wines. A great bonus is that these vineyards are in one of Italy's most picturesque regions, filled with quaint villages and amazing abbeys, thus making your adventures even more enchanting. Whereas Chianti Classico wine is renowned in the area between Florence and Siena, the vineyards farther south also produce some of the mostly highly regarded wines in the world, the most famous of these being **Vino Nobile**, grown near Montepulciano, and **Brunello**, grown near Montacino. There are many wineries open to the public where wine can be tasted and purchased. Many winetastings are free, although some wineries charge a minimal fee. As you drive through the countryside look for signs reading *Cantina* (wine shop) or *Vendita Diretta* (direct sales).

LOOP VISITING WINERIES, ABBEYS, AND QUAINT VILLAGES

We suggest a loop that covers some of our favorite wineries, medieval towns, and picturesque abbeys. It would be impossible to squeeze everything in this itinerary into one day unless you rush madly from place to place. Therefore, if your time is limited, don't stop at each place suggested but just choose a few of the sightseeing suggestions below that most appeal to you. But better yet, take several days and follow the itinerary in its entirety, covering a small section each day at a leisurely pace.

This loop begins in **Montepulciano**, a rare jewel of a walled hill town that not only oozes charm in its narrow, cobbled streets but is also center stage for the delicious Vino Nobile di Montepulciano. This wealthy town was home to many aristocrats who built magnificent palaces here. The heart of the city is the **Piazza Grande** where you find the dramatic 13th-century **Palazzo Comunale** accented by a stone tower. Also facing the square is the picturesque **Palazzo Contucci**, fronted by a charming Renaissance well decorated with the Medici coat of arms and highlighted by two stone lions. Leading off the Pizza Grande are small streets that crisscross the town, connected by staircases.

A masterpiece you absolutely must not miss when visiting Montepulciano is the **Temple of San Biagio**, a stunning church located on the west edge of town. You can walk from town, but it is a long way down the hill and then back up again, so you might want to drive, especially in hot weather. Made of creamy travertine, the church's façade is extremely picturesque and its elegant interior is equally lovely—nothing cluttered or dark but rather light and airy, with fine marble pastel-colored walls.

Within Montepulciano there are many boutiques, restaurants, and cantinas selling wine. Our favorite wine shop here is an extremely special one, the very old **Cantina del Redi**, located just down the street from the Piazza Grande with its entrance next to the Palazzo Ricco. Once you enter, an ancient staircase leads ever deeper into the hillside, passing rooms filled with huge wooden casks of wine. When you finally reach the lowest level, you wind your way through more casks until you arrive at the cantina where you can sample and purchase wine. When finished, you discover that you have descended quite a way down the hillside and the main entrance to the winery faces onto a lower terrace.

Another of our favorite wineries, **Dei**, is just a few kilometers outside Montepulciano's city walls. What is especially fun about this winery is that it is family-owned and managed by the lovely daughter, Maria Caterina Dei, who still lives in the beautiful family villa on the property. Maria Caterina is passionate about wine and with great professionalism can explain about the production of the Dei wines, which have won many awards. Before taking over the family's vineyards, the multi-talented Maria Caterina trained in music and the theater, and sometimes she entertains the guests during wine tours. There is a fee for tours, depending upon what is requested. Lunches and winetasting can be prearranged. Call in advance for tours: Dei, Villa Martiena, Montepulciano, tel: (0578) 71 68 78, *www.cantinedei.com.*

Leaving Montepulciano, take the S146 west toward Pienza. After driving about 3 kilometers, take a small road on the left marked to **Monticchiello**. You soon arrive at a sweet, tiny, charming walled town whose allure is its unpretentious, non-touristy ambiance. Park your car in the designated area outside the main gate. As you enter through the gate, you will see on your left La Porta, a charming restaurant with an outside terrace sitting on the town walls—a great place to stop for lunch. As you stroll through Monticchiello (it won't take you long), take a look inside the 13th-century church where you will see a beautiful altarpiece by Pietro Lorenzetti.

Il Chostro di Pienza, Pienza

From Monticchiello, continue on the back road to **Pienza**. This is one of our favorite walled hill towns in Tuscany, a real gem that mustn't be missed. The town is perched on the top of a hill and is pedestrian-only so you need to park your car outside the walls. It is no wonder that the town is so perfect even though so tiny: it was here in the 15th century that Pope Pius II hired a famous architect, Bernardo Rossellino, to totally redesign the town where he was born, making it into a masterpiece. You will find many restaurants if you are inclined to dine.

Leaving Pienza, take S146 west to **San Quirico d'Orcia**, a very attractive small medieval town with a lovely Romanesque church. If you stop to see the town, you must not miss its lovely garden, called **Horti Leonini**. An entrance about a block from the main square leads into a tranquil Renaissance garden, originally designed as a beautiful resting place for the pilgrims who stopped here on the road to Rome. This cool oasis with clipped box hedges and shade trees makes an interesting stop. If you are hungry, the **Osteria del Leone** makes a good choice for lunch.

From San Quirico d'Orcia, head south on S2 for about 6 kilometers and watch for a small road to the right leading to **Bagno Vignoni**. This is a most unusual, very small town, known for the curative value of its hot sulphur springs. In the center of town, you find what would have been the town square made into a huge sulphur bath built by the Medicis. The pool is surrounded by picturesque medieval buildings that complete the interesting scene.

Leaving Bagno Vignoni, don't continue on the S2, but take S323 directly south for 12 kilometers and then turn right following signs to Montalcino. In a few minutes you come to **Castelnuovo dell'Abate** where, just a few minutes outside town, you will find the superb Romanesque **Abbey Sant'Antimo**, whose origins date back to the 9th century when it was founded as a Benedictine monastery. The abbey—a simple, pastel-pinkish stone church serenely set amongst fields of olive trees—makes a beautiful picture. Try to arrive at 11 am or 2:45 pm when the Benedictine monks, clad in long, pure-white robes, gather at the altar to chant their prayers in Latin. This is a haunting, beautiful experience.

The singing lasts only a short time, and the times might vary from the ones we mention above, so to confirm the schedule call, tel: (0577) 83 56 59.

Leaving Castelnuovo dell'Abate, drive north on the road for Montalcino. In a few minutes you will see a sign to the **Fattoria dei Barbi**. Turn right and follow a small road up the hill to the Barbi winery, an excellent winery to visit. It is extremely pretty with many gardens and a charming cantina where you can sample the vineyard's fine wines and purchase wine and other gift items. Its restaurant serves wonderful meals made with only the freshest products, accompanied, of course, by their own wines. Free tours of the winery are given hourly from 10 am to noon and 3 pm to 5 pm, tel: (0577) 84 82 77, *www.fattoriadeibarbi.it.*

After your visit to the Fattoria dei Barbi, continue north for 5 kilometers to **Montalcino**, which is world famous, along with Montepulciano, for its superb wine, Brunello di Montalcino. There are many places in town where wine can be tasted and purchased. In addition to wine, the town is famous for its fine honey, which can be purchased in many of the shops. Montalcino is fun for wandering—it is not large and you can in no time at all cover the area within the walls by foot. On the east edge of town is an imposing 14th century fortress.

From Montalcino, head south on the road to Grosetto for a little over 3 kilometers to another of our favorite wineries, **Poggio Antico**. Excellent tours are offered and, of course, you can also sample the superb wines. These tours are very popular so you should reserve in advance at tel: (0577) 84 80 44, *www.poggioantico.com.* For dining, the winery's **Ristorante Poggio Antico** serves outstanding Tuscany cuisine. Reservations for the restaurant are also highly recommended—tel: (0577) 84 92 00, email: rist.poggio.antico@libero.it.

After visiting Poggio Antico, retrace your way north to Montalcino and continue on for 9 kilometers to where the road intersects with the S2. Turn left here, going north toward Siena. In 10 kilometers, turn right on S451 and continue for another 10 kilometers to the **Abbazia di Monte Oliveto Maggiore**. Founded in the early 14th century by wealthy merchants from Siena as a Benedictine retreat, this fascinating abbey is well worth a detour. Be prepared to walk since you must park your car and follow a long path through the forest to the abbey's entrance, which is through a gatehouse crowned by a beautiful della Robbia terracotta. Once through the gate, you continue through the woodlands to the huge brick complex. After visiting the church, it seems you could wander forever through the various hallways. Before you get too distracted, however, ask directions to the cloister because you don't want to miss this marvel. Here you find 36 frescoes depicting scenes of the life of St. Benedict, some painted by Luca Signorelli, others by Antonio Bazzi.

In the region around the abbey you will come across an entirely different type of landscape, called the *crete*. Here, tucked among the green rolling hills, you unexpectedly come across bleak, canyon-like craters, caused by erosion. These are especially out of character as the surrounding scenery is so soft and gentle.

From Abbazia di Monte Oliveto Maggiore, weave your way through the small back roads to Montepulciano. Follow signs to San Giovanni d'Asso, then Montisi, then Madongino, then **Montefollonico**. Take time to stop in Montefollonico because this is another "sleeper"—a quaint, small, medieval walled town that is fun to explore. For the gourmet, there is a superb restaurant on the edge of town called **La Chiusa.**

From Montefollonico, go south on S327. When you come to the S146, turn left to complete your loop back to Montepulciano.

Duomo, Orvieto

The Haunting Beauty of Umbria

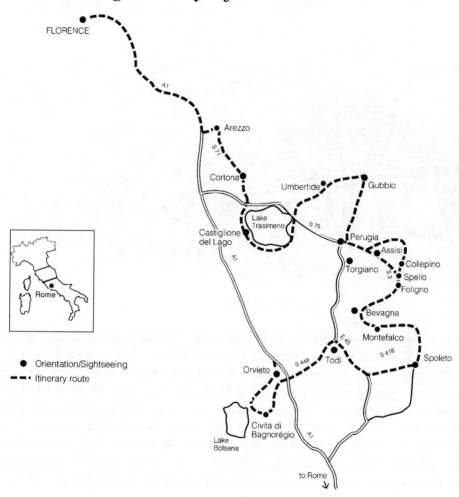

The Haunting Beauty of Umbria

Assisi

Tuscany is so popular that travelers frequently forget to visit Umbria, snuggled just "next door." Although similar in many ways to Tuscany, Umbria has its own haunting beauty and the advantage of fewer tourists. This is a region seeped in history and imbued with romantic charm. Here you find a beguiling landscape—a blend of rolling hills, craggy forests, rushing rivers, lush valleys, chestnut groves, and hillsides laced with vineyards. Adding further to Umbria's magic is that its hills and valleys radiate a soft mellow light, gleaming gently in the sun. It is not just the landscape that makes Umbria so delightful. It also has stunning medieval castles, incredible cathedrals, ancient monasteries, art treasures, fine wines, beautiful ceramics, and captivating towns perched on hilltops.

Pacing: You can conveniently follow this itinerary either before or after a tour of Tuscany. If you already have visited Tuscany on a previous trip to Italy, this itinerary stands alone. After the finishing the itinerary, you can loop back to Florence by heading north on the A1, or head south on the A1 to Rome. Whichever way you choose, in order to capture its beauty and many sightseeing possibilities, you need at least five nights in the Umbria region: We suggest three nights in the eastern part of Umbria. Choose a place to stay and in use it as a hub from which to journey out each day to explore a different sightseeing target. Next, loop south and choose a place to stay for two nights in the western part of Umbria, somewhere near Orvieto.

EASTERN UMBRIA

NOTE: This itinerary of Eastern Umbria is much too long for one day. Use it only as a framework for how the most interesting towns can be looped together. Once you choose which town you are going to use as the hub for your explorations, tailor the itinerary to visit the places mentioned in the itinerary that most appeal to you.

As you depart from Florence you are bound to run into a lot of traffic, but there are many signs to the expressway. Follow signs that lead to the A1 and take it south toward Rome.

Arezzo: About 65 kilometers after leaving Florence you come to a turnoff to **Arezzo,** located about 10 kilometers east of the highway. Arezzo is still in Tuscany, but since it is so close to Umbria and "on the way," now is the time for a visit. Arezzo has a rich history dating back to the Etruscan era, but is not as quaint as some of its smaller neighbors. It is well known as one of the largest gold centers in Europe and has many shops selling gold jewelry. Arezzo is also famous for its **Antique Fair** that is held in the Piazza Grande on the first Saturday and Sunday of every month. Here you find many unusual items such as antique coins, jewelry, furniture, stained glass remnants, paintings, light fixtures, handmade linens, pottery, trunks, etc. The fair is considered one of the most important ones in Italy and so popular that people come from far and near to browse the rich collection of antiques. Arezzo was the birthplace of Guido Monaco who around the year 1000 A.D. devised musical notes and scales. One of Arrezo's famous inhabitants was the powerful 14th-century poet Pietro Aretino who took great glee in writing scandalous poetry about the rich and famous. Aretino's greatest skill was gentle blackmail, extorting great sums from princes and popes who paid him not to expose their indiscretions in poetry.

Cortona: From Arezzo follow S71 south to Cortona, a gem of a walled town terraced up a steep hillside covered with olive trees and vineyards. Like Arezzo, Cortona is still in Tuscany, but fits more conveniently into the itinerary for Umbria since it is on the route. Stop to enjoy the atmosphere of this medieval town: its narrow, twisting, cobbled streets, jumble of small squares, lovely boutiques, excellent restaurants, and colorful buildings are delightful. The heart of the town is the **Piazza della Repubblica**, the main square, which has many narrow streets feeding into it. If you are up for walking, climb the twisting streets to the old fortress standing guard over the town.

Lake Trasimeno: Leaving Cortona, continue driving south on S71 toward Lake Trasimeno. In about 11 kilometers you come to a four-lane expressway. Do not get on the highway, but instead continue south on S71, which traces the west shore of Lake Trasimeno, Italy's fourth largest lake, which is fed by underground channels linked to the Tiber river basin. Fascinatingly, the early Romans built these underground waterways many centuries ago. Follow the road south for 9 kilometers to **Castiglione del Lago**, the most interesting town on the lake. Built on a high rocky promontory that juts out into the water, the old walled city with its battlements and towers has lots of character. Artifacts and tombs nearby indicate it was originally an Etruscan settlement, but what you see today dates from the Middle Ages. In the 1500s it was the dukedom of the Corgna. In the church of Santa Maria Maddalena you can see a 16th-century panel with paintings of the Madonna and Child by Eusebio da San Giorgio. Also visit the Palazzo del Capitano del Popolo, the Palazzo della Cornna, and the Leone fortress.

Umbertide: Continue the loop around the lake then take the road toward Magione, which is just before the junction with the expressway heading to Perugia. In a few minutes, you see the four-lane expressway, but do not get on it. Instead, continue over the highway and follow the back roads through the countryside to Umbertide. Stop for a short visit to this small, 10th-century town that hugs the banks of the Tevere River. In addition to the castle, you might want to visit the Church of Santa Maria della Reggia, which is an intriguing octagonal, three-tired building topped by a cupola. Another church, the Holy Cross, is famous for its lovely painting by Signorelli, called *Deposition from the Cross*.

Gubbio: Leaving Umbertide, take the road that passes over the highway E45 and continue on to Gubbio. This splendidly preserved, medieval walled town is perched high on the slopes of Monte Ingino. The setting is superb and the view from the plaza that sits like a shelf overlooking the countryside is breathtaking. The narrow, cobbled streets and walkways lacing the hillside are delightful to explore. The town is filled with architectural masterpieces, one of these, the Basilica, dominates the town. There is much to see including the Cathedral, the Consuls Palace, the Piazza Pensile, the Pretorio Palace, and the Santa Maria Nuova church where you can see Ottaviano Nelli's *Madonna del Belvedere*. Outside the city walls, nestled below the town, there are the remains of a Roman theater—another reminder of how important the city was in its prime.

Perugia: From Gubbio head south on S298 in the direction of Perugia. There is a turnoff to Perugia, which is surrounded by many modern commercial buildings. If time is short, bypass Perugia (which is not as pristine as many of Umbria's other jewels) and continue on to the junction of S75 and continue east following signs to Assisi. However, if you want to "see it all," Perugia is rich in history and has many delights. Perugia is a large medieval city surrounded by ramparts. An important Umbrian city since Etruscan days, the old town has at its heart the **Piazza IV Novembre**, a beautiful square with an appealing fountain, the **Fontana Maggiore**, built in the late 13th century.

Assisi: Coming from either Perugia or Gubbio, take S75 east following signs for Assisi, one of our favorite targets in Umbria. Built up the steep slopes of Mount Subasio, this magical city is a tribute to St. Francis. Although he was born into a family of wealth, after several visions in which Christ appeared to him, St. Francis left his privileged life. He was obviously a person with a deeply poetic soul and his tender teachings of reverence for the beauties of nature and kindness to all animals and birds still appeal to

St. Francis of Assisi

us today. To remember your visit, you might want to buy a statue of St. Francis to bring home. You will find statues in all sizes and price ranges in the many shops.

Even if it were not for the lingering memory of the gentle St. Francis, Assisi would be a "must see" for it is one of the most spectacular hill towns in Umbria. Perhaps there are a few too many souvenir shops, but this is a small price to pay for the privilege of experiencing such a very special place. The town walls begin on the valley floor and completely enclose the city as it climbs the steep hillside to the enormous castle at its summit. Assisi with its maze of tiny streets is a marvelous town for walking (you must wear sturdy shoes) and it is great fun as you come across intriguing little lanes opening into small squares. When you stop to rest, there are breathtaking vistas of the lovely Umbrian fields stretching out below. Along with many other historic buildings, Assisi's most famous monument, **St. Francis' Basilica,** was severely damaged by an earthquake in September 1997. However, all of the repairs have now been completed and the town looks remarkably "back to normal." The basilica, which also houses a monastery, faces onto a large square bound by columns forming vaulted covered walkways. In addition to the monastery, there are two basilicas—upper and lower. Both are adorned with excellent frescoes that were unfortunately damaged by the earthquake. Also while in Assisi, visit **Santa Chiara** (St. Clara's Church). Clara, a close friend of St. Francis, founded the Order of St. Clares. Go into the church to view the lovely frescoes of Santa Clara and her sisters. Part of the enjoyment of Assisi is just to stroll through its narrow, cobbled streets—the whole town is like a living museum. If you have time, hike up to the **Rocca Medioevale**, an enormous 14th-century fortress perched on the hillside overlooking the city. From here you have a magnificent bird's-eye view of Assisi and beyond to the enchanting Umbrian countryside sweeping out to the distant hills.

Collepino: From Assisi you can continue on the S75 in the direction of Foligno. However, if you feel adventuresome and enjoy getting off the beaten path, there is a narrow, twisting, very scenic back road that leads through the hills making a loop from Assisi that ends up back on the S75 in Spello, about 5 kilometers before Foligno. The driving is difficult, but you can enjoy the beauty of the rugged forested mountains, an area of Umbria seldom seen by tourists. The road begins at the upper part of Assisi. Follow signs in the direction of Gualdo Tadino, but before you get there, take the road marked to Armenzano where you continue on following signs to Spello. After going through Armenzano, the road passes the adorable secluded hamlet of Collepino, which oozes charm with its winding cobbled streets and stone houses. It is so tiny that you quickly see it all. After Collepino, it is 7 kilometers on to Spello, where the road joins the S75, which you take going south.

Bevagna: Five kilometers south of Spello you come to **Foligno** where we suggest leaving the S75 and taking instead the back roads that to enjoy the lovely villages and scenery. From Foligno S316 toward Bevagna, which you reach after about 8 kilometers. Bevagna is an enticing, intimate, charming walled village, founded by the Romans. In addition to just enjoying the allure of the town, there is much to see including a stunning 19th-century opera house, the beautiful San Michele church, well-preserved mosaics in the old Roman baths, and a paper press making paper just as it has been for centuries. If it is mealtime, there is a wonderful place for lunch, L'Orto degli Angeli.

Montefalco: From Bevagna, take the road marked to Montefalco (located 7 kilometers from Bevagna). Montefalco is a walled town that crowns a hill with sweeping views of the Umbrian countryside. The town is a maze of small, narrow streets. For sightseeing, the main attraction is **San Francisco**, a church now converted into a museum that displays some of the finest work of Benozzo Gozzoli, including the fresco *Life of St. Francis*. Also, a delicious wine, *Sagrantino*, is produced here.

Spoleto: From Montefalco, loop back to the main road, S75, and continue south following signs to Spoleto. Not only is medieval Spoleto dramatically perched atop a hill, but it also has an almost unbelievable bridge dating from Roman times. This **Ponte delle Torri**, spanning the deep ravine between Spoleto and the adjoining mountain, was built over an aqueduct existing in the 14th century. This incredible engineering wonder is 230 meters long and soars 81 meters high. It is supported by a series of ten Gothic arches and has a fort at the far end as well as a balcony in the center. The 12th-century **Cathedral** in Spoleto is also so lovely that it alone would make a stop in this charming town worth a detour. The exterior of this very old cathedral, with its beautiful rose window and intricate mosaics, is truly charming. Although a great sightseeing destination at any time of the year, Spoleto is very popular in late June and early July when it hosts the world-famous Spoleto Festival, featuring great music, dance, and theater. During the festival season rooms are usually more expensive and almost impossible to secure so should be booked far in advance.

Torgiano: Torgiano, in the center of a rich wine region, has a lovely small wine museum. You would never dream that such a tiny town could boast such a gem, but it is not a coincidence: the Lungarotti family owns the vineyards for many kilometers in every direction. Signor Lungarotti furnished the museum with artifacts pertaining to every aspect of wine production from the earliest days, creating an interesting and beautifully displayed collection worthy of a detour by anyone interested in wines. In the center of town, the Lungarotti family owns, **Le Tre Vaselle**, a charming choice for lunch.

WESTERN UMBRIA

From Spoleto, a scenic route connecting the eastern part of Umbria to the western part of Umbria is to take the S418, which twists west from Spoleto for 25 kilometers through beautiful hills to the E45. Turn north on E45 for about 21 kilometers and turn west on S448, following signs to the A1 and Orvieto.

Todi: The picture-perfect village of Todi makes a great midway stop between Spoleto and Orvieto. It is located near the junction of E45 and S448 and is well signposted. This adorable small town crowning a hilltop like icing on a cake is one of our favorites. No, there isn't much to see—it is the town itself that is so picturesque. It is just fun to wander the twisting cobblestone streets, enjoy the medieval ambiance, and stop to enjoy a cappuccino in one of the sidewalk cafés. As you stroll through the small village, watch for the Cathedral, the People's Square, the intimate San Ilario Church, and the Roman/Etruscan Museum.

When you come to the A1, don't get onto the freeway, but instead follow signs to Orvieto. NOTE: When deciding on a town in the area to use as a hub for sightseeing don't limit your choice to those in Umbria. You will also find a rich selection of places to stay very nearby in Tuscany and Lazio.

Orvieto: Originally founded by the Etruscans, Orvieto later became a prosperous Roman city, famous for its production of ceramics. Orvieto is spread across the top of a hill that drops down on every side in steep volcanic cliffs to the Umbrian plain 200 meters below—you wonder how the town could ever have been built! Drive as far as you can up to the town, park your car, and proceed on foot. Have a good map handy because you pass so many churches and squares that it is difficult to orient yourself—Orvieto is a maze of tiny piazzas and narrow twisting streets. Continue on to Orvieto's center where a glorious **Duomo** dominates the immense piazza. You may think you have seen sufficient stunning cathedrals to last a lifetime, but just wait—Orvieto's is truly special, one of the finest examples of Romanesque-Gothic architecture in Italy. It is brilliantly embellished with intricate mosaic designs and accented by lacy slender spires stretching gracefully into the sky. Within the Duomo, you absolutely must not miss the **Chapel of San Brizio;** here you find frescos by Fra Angelico and Luca Signorelli. Also of interest in Orvieto is **St. Patrick's Well**, hewn out of solid volcanic rock. Pope Clement VII took refuge in Orvieto in 1527 and to ensure the town's water supply in case of siege, he ordered the digging of this 62-meter-deep well. It is unique for the 70 windows that illuminate it and the two spiral staircases that wind up and down without meeting. Other sights to see include the Papal Palace, the Town Hall, and the archaeological museum.

Civita di Bagnorégio: Although **Civita di Bagnorégio** is not in Umbria, it's located just southwest of Orvieto, so it conveniently ties in with this itinerary. If you are a photographer and love picturesque walled villages, few can surpass the setting of this small town. Take the N71, which twists west from Orvieto toward **Lake Bolsena**. Stay on N71 for about 20 kilometers and then turn left heading to Bagnorégio. Go into town and follow signs to Civita, which crowns the top of a steep, circular-shaped, rocky outcrop. There is no road into the village—the only access is by walking over a long, narrow suspension bridge that joins the two sides of a deep ravine. Once you arrive, you will find a few shops, some Etruscan artifacts, a church, and a restaurant. However, the main focus is the town itself with its narrow arcaded alleyways and a dramatic 180-degree view of the desolate, rocky canyons that stretch out around the town with a haunting beauty.

The Undiscovered Sabine Hills

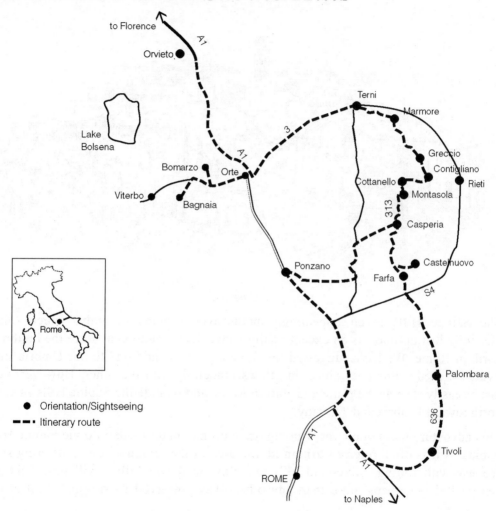

The Undiscovered Sabine Hills

Casperia

The Sabine Hills is an appealingly undiscovered niche of Italy, which—although blissfully lost in time—is an exceptionally convenient area to visit since the region is just north of Rome. We have suggested this itinerary as an "add on" to our Umbria itinerary (which precedes this one) since one flows gracefully into the other. However, you can just as easily reverse the route and start in Rome and include the Sabine Hills as you head north toward Umbria and Tuscany.

This adventure takes you over winding, tranquil mountain roads into the Sabine Hills (or Sabina as it is often referred to), an idyllic area in the region of Lazio offering splendid scenery with rolling, olive-clad hills and tiny, medieval hilltop villages. This part of central Italy—perhaps more than any other—has preserved its original rural character, and, not withstanding its proximity to Rome, is one of the least populated parts of the country. A wonderful time to visit is spring when the countryside explodes in color with yellow broom and fields of sunflowers, accented by the silver green of the olive trees which produce some of Italy's finest extra virgin olive oils.

Pacing: We suggest spending a minimum of two nights in this region of northern Lazio to savor the authentic charm of the long-forgotten villages in the Sabine Hills. Since the area is small, choose one town as your base of operation and go out from there each day for sightseeing.

As you study the map at the beginning of this itinerary, it is obvious that you could begin your drive to the Sabine Hills from numerous places in Umbria or Tuscany. However, since we ended the Umbria itinerary near Orvieto, we have chosen it as a suggested starting point. If your time is limited, the quickest way to get to Sabina from Orvieto is to take the A1 south and exit at Ponzano/Soratte, but we suggest in our itinerary a more leisurely approach through the less discovered corners of northern Lazio.

Parco dei Mostri and Villa Lante: Leaving Orvieto, drive south toward Rome on the A1. Because they are convenient to your route, we suggest stopping to visit two extraordinary gardens: the Parco dei Mostri and the Villa Lante. For these excursions, exit the A1 at Orte, and then take the superstrada 204 west toward Viterbo. About 27 kilometers after leaving the A1, take the exit marked to **Bomarzo** where the sacred garden of **Parco dei Mostri** is located. Dating back to 1552, the park was designed by Pirro Ligorio, who also created the incredible gardens of Villa d'Este in Tivoli. He is also responsible for the completion of Saint Peter's Cathedral, a commission he took over after the death of Michelangelo. A 30-minute walk through the wooded park with gigantic hidden statues of animals and mythological characters makes this a great destination for children. After visiting Parco dei Mostri, it is just a short drive on to the enchanting gardens of **Villa Lante.**

To reach Villa Lante from Parco dei Mostri, follow a small, ancient road flanked by olive and hazelnut groves in the direction of Viterbo. Before reaching Viterbo, follow signs for

Bagnaia, where you find the classic Italian renaissance gardens of **Villa Lante**, which date back to 1568. The lavish life style of those in the aristocracy of the Catholic Church is clearly evident; an opulent villa surrounded by sensational gardens seems to have been a perk of being a Cardinal. Villa Lante was built by Cardinal Gianfrancesco Gambara and later was occupied by a succession of Popes until the Lante family bought the property in 1657. The Duchess of Lante was born in France and when she moved to her new home in Italy, she brought with her a French agronomist who added a French flavor to the Villa Lante gardens. Open 9 am to 4:30 pm in winter, 9 am to 7:30 pm in summer.

Terni: After visiting both gardens, return east toward Orte. When you reach the A1, do not get on the freeway but continue east to Terni, which is on the border of Umbria and Lazio. Because it was rebuilt after extensive damage in World War II, Terni is a city of modern architecture. Although it does not have an old world ambiance, it is worth a stop for those who love fashionable couture—it seems every Italian designer is represented here. Our suggestion is to drive through Terni and get onto the smaller roads that lead to Marmore.

Marmore: From the center of Terni take route 79 to Marmore, a tiny village where **Cascata delle Marmore** is located. If you are a nature lover, you will not want to miss this side trip to the highest waterfall in Europe, which was created in 290 B.C. when the Romans changed the course of the River Velino. To admire the falls, leave your car and enter the parkland. The viewpoint is open year round for two hours a day: 1pm to 2pm and 4pm to 5pm. The times vary each month but you can check them on Google (Marmore waterfalls opening). The waterfall can be admired from below or above. You view the falls from above on the way to Greccio.

Greccio: As you leave Marmore the road divides. At this point, leave Route 79 that goes on to Rieti and take instead a very small road that parallels the river Velino. After 12 kilometers you will reach Greccio, a peaceful monastery in a spectacular position on the slopes of Mount Lacerone with views stretching across the green plain below to the peaks of Mount Terminillo. It was here in December, 1223, that Saint Francis of Assisi, along with the local noblemen, enacted the first live nativity scene. The tradition has continued ever since the 12th century and each year at Christmas people flock from all over Italy to see this traditional event in which a cast of a hundred people participate dressed in splendid costumes: the convent is open 9:30am to 1pm and 3pm to 6pm. After visiting the Greccio sanctuary, drive back down the steep winding road and continue south toward Sabina, following signposts for Contigliano. Before entering the town, make a sharp right. You find yourself on a mountain road with no traffic at all.

Cottanello: The first hilltop village you come to is Cottanello, a tiny, remote, picturesque hill town surrounded by mountains instead of olive groves. The inhabitants are mostly shepherds and you might need to stop along the way to let a shepherd with his flock of sheep cross the road. The typical regional products of the area are pecorino and ricotta cheese made with sheep's milk. Just outside this sleepy town is the tiny medieval cliff-side **Hermitage of Saint Cataldo**, carved out of rock hanging over the road. It is possible to have a guide open the hermitage for you if you have an appointment and arrive before lunchtime. Also of interest is the nearby archaeological remains of a Roman farmhouse, which belonged to Lucius Cotta, the brother in law of Julius Caesar, and features a lovely mosaic floor. The site is hard to find and rarely visited, so a reservation is essential. For both of these stops, call the Comune of Cottanello (0746) 66 122 or Sig. Stefano Petrucci, a guide, whose cell phone is (3287) 42 50 58. If you pass by in the afternoon and are planning to stay at one of the hotels or bed and breakfasts in the Sabine Hills, your hosts can call for you and make an appointment for the next morning.

Jewels of the Sabine Hills: Passing Cottanello, turn left at the bottom of the hill toward Poggio Mirteto and Casperia. As the road descends, the panorama widens to include the rolling plains of Lazio and the Tiber valley. You are now in the heart of Sabina which hasn't changed much in the last 1,000 years. Here you will discover authentic, off the beaten path, hilltop villages such as Casperia, Montasola, Roccantica, Poggio Catino, Farfa, and Stroncone and a romantic landscape of olive farms, abbeys and castles. To add to the enchantment, there is a total lack of souvenir shops and tour buses—a treat for those who enjoy experiencing the life of the local people. What fun it is to not rush about. Relax in one of hill towns where time seems to have stood still; enjoy a cappuccino or sip a glass of wine in the piazza and peer over the medieval walls at the inspiring landscape of the Tiber Valley. Happily, the area offers a rich selection of places to stay. Choose one of these as your hub for a few nights stay and venture out to explore the area, visiting the towns and sites featured in the following part of this itinerary. You will soon discover why the Roman emperor, Hadrian, chose Sabina as one of his favorite getaways from Rome. Some of the jewels of the Sabine hills are featured below.

Montasola: This tiny, intact medieval hilltop village, typical of the region, has no more than 80 inhabitants. The entrance gate, dominated by a medieval tower, leads into the village. There are no famous monuments here, but stop to take some photos and enjoy the splendid panoramas (the town is at an altitude of 600 meters).

Montasola

Casperia: Perched on a rocky outcrop and bound by the remains of its original stone walls and watchtowers, Casperia is one of the most picturesque medieval villages in the Sabine Hills. While enjoying the local food and wine, you can often listen to a live jazz pianist as you watch the sun set over Mount Soratte. In this completely pedestrian town every turning along the narrow cobble stoned alleyways offers a photo opportunity. A local craftsman, Gianni, has been making a wonderful model of the village for the last 10 years as a setting for the Christmas nativity crib. Every year he adds more. The model is located in the church of San Giovanni Battista, which is usually open in the afternoons around 5pm. A favorite place on a summer's evening is the panoramic café in the piazza of Casperia.

In 1852 the famous German historian, Gregorovius, described Casperia in his book *Wandering in Italy* "In all my travels I have never beheld a panorama of such heroic beauty as that offered to me from the top of the hill in the territory of Aspra (the old name for Casperia). It is truly a paradise on earth! A majestic solitude dominates both the nearby mountains where timeless castles stood, and the villages of the Sabines where ancient families still dwell, solidly preserving the customs and the ways of life of the past...the ideal place to dream." Little has changed since Gregorovius fell in love with Casperia and the Sabine Hills.

Abbey of Farfa

Farfa: Not to be missed is the **Abbey of Farfa**, one of the most famous European religious buildings of the Middle Ages, found in the town of the same name. Charlemagne was its protector, and at the height of his empire, a vast part of central Italy was owned by the abbey. A visit is not complete without including the magnificent, recently refurbished, library that contains more than 60,000 volumes and original manuscripts, including one of the first books ever printed. The staff in the herb store will arrange your visit. Do not miss a well preserved Roman sarcophagus that was found on the premises, attesting to the fact that the 6th-century abbey was built on the site of a Roman villa: tel: (0765) 27 73 15 (not much English spoken).

Castelnuovo di Farfa: A small winding road leads to the nearby village of Castelnuovo di Farfa where a contemporary museum of olive oil is located, the first of its kind in Italy. It has an unusual exhibit that interprets the history of the olive, which has always dominated the landscape of Sabina. International artists have participated in creating the exhibit, which also features a rare collection of oil presses. The museum is open weekends and on request for small groups, tel: (0765) 36 370.

Castel San Pietro: This small picturesque hilltop village built around a large 17th-century palace makes a fun place to stop for lunch after having visited Farfa. There is a great restaurant here, Re Burlone, located in the cellars of the palazzo.

Fara Sabina: The highest village in the Sabine hills is Fara Sabina. Once a Lombard stronghold the village offers the most spectacular view of the rolling plains of Lazio—the land of the Latins and birthplace of our western civilization. You can see across the Tiber valley as far as Rome, and, on a clear day, the dome of Saint Peter's is visible.

Tivoli, Villa d'Este, and Villa Adriana: While based in Sabina, enjoy a daytrip to one or more of Italy's famous renaissance gardens and the archeological site of Villa Adriana. To reach Tivoli, drive south from Fara Sabina, crossing the Via Salaria S4 and continuing on the small backroad 636 to Palombara Sabina. Then continue on to Tivoli. In Tivoli you find the Villa d'Este with its 16th-century fountains—a must see for Renaissance garden lovers. Nearby you find Villa Adriana, an incredible archaeological site with 300 acres of grounds.

After visiting Villa d'Este and Villa Adriana, take the link road to A1, direction Florence (the entrance is just a few kilometers from Tivoli). Exit at Ponzano/Soratte and head east, making your way back to your base in the Sabine hills. NOTE: Villa D'Este and Villa Adriana can also be visited en route to Rome, if this is your next destination.

Mountain & Lake Adventures

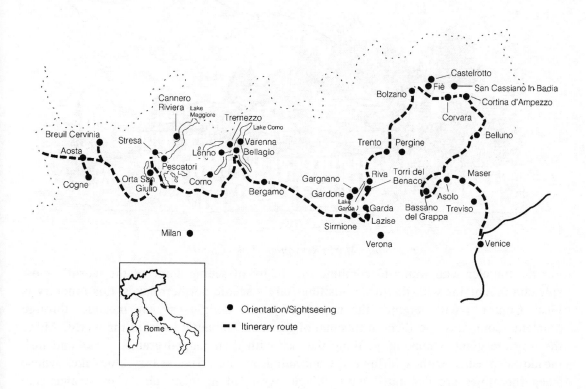

Castelrotto
Fiè
San Cassiano In Badia
Bolzano
Cortina d'Ampezzo
Corvara
Cannero
Riviera
Lake Maggiore
Tremezzo
Belluno
Lake Como
Trento
Pergine
Breuil Cervinia
Stresa
Varenna
Bellagio
Aosta
Lenno
Pescatori
Gargnano
Riva
Torri del Benaco
Maser
Cogne
Orta San Giulio
Como
Bergamo
Gardone
Gardone
Asolo
Lake Garda
Bassano del Grappa
Treviso
Garda
Sirmione
Lazise
Milan
Verona
Venice

Rome

● Orientation/Sightseeing
- - - Itinerary route

Mountain & Lake Adventures

Santa Maria Rezzónico, Lake Como

For the traveler who wants to combine the magic of seeing some of the world's most splendid mountains with the joy of visiting Italy's scenic northern lakes, this itinerary is ideal. Contrasts will heighten the impact of visual delights as you meander through dramatic mountains and then on to some of the most romantic lakes in the world. Along the way are giant mountains piercing the sky with their jagged granite peaks and lush meadows splashed with wildflowers. Continuing on you arrive at lazy blue lakes whose steep shorelines are decorated with villages wrapped in misty cloaks of siennas and ochres. This itinerary can stand alone. However, it is also perfect for the traveler arriving in or departing from neighboring countries. All too often the tourist thinks he has finished Italy when his tour ends in Venice, and he rushes north into Austria or Switzerland. What a waste—a very picturesque region still remains. Please linger to enjoy the mountains and lakes that truly are some of Italy's greatest natural treasures.

Recommended Pacing: To do this itinerary "well" you need three weeks. This may seem to be dawdling a bit, but less time than indicated would not allow you to enjoy your destinations. Remember that three nights really means only two full days with travel in between. Allow at least three nights in Venice—more would be preferable, especially if you want to explore some of the small islands such as Murano (famous for its hand-blown glass) and Burano (well-known for its colorful cottages and hand-made lace). Your next stop, Asolo, needs two nights. Not only is the town delightful, but also you will want to visit some of the Palladian mansions in the area. Your next suggested stop, the Dolomites, needs another three nights. The scenery is spectacular and you will want time to explore some of the exquisite mountain back roads and take hikes. From the Dolomites your next destination is spectacular Lake Garda. Again, you need three nights. You must have time to take advantage of the romantic boat trips around the lake and also a side trip to nearby Verona. Your next stop is another exquisite highlight, Lake Como. Here you need three nights to enjoy the boat excursions around the lake. From Lake Como, it is on to Lake Maggiore, another lovely destination. Here you need three nights to enjoy both boat trips around the lake and visits to the romantic islands in the lake. After Lake Maggiore it is on to Lake Orta, a much smaller lake with great personality. Because it is not so large, two nights should suffice here. From Lake Orta you leave the Lake District and are in the splendid Aosta Valley in the Alps, which trace the border with France and Switzerland. Here you need another two nights in order to have sufficient time to take walks and enjoy the awesome parks. You might not have the luxury of time to spend three weeks on this "*Mountain & Lake Adventures*." If not, tailor this itinerary for your own schedule. Perhaps visit just one of the lakes instead of all four, or save the lakes for another trip and leisurely enjoy just Venice and the Dolomites. Whatever your choice, you are in for a special treat in this incredibly beautiful region of Italy.

VENICE: This itinerary begins in **Venice**, one of the most romantic cities in the world. Venice's many narrow waterways are crisscrossed by storybook bridges and shadowed by majestic palaces whose soft hues reflect warmly in the shimmering water. Black gondolas quietly glide through the narrow canals as the gondolier in his red-and-white-striped shirt softly serenades his passengers with an operatic selection.

Venice is not a traditional city with streets and automobile traffic, but rather an archipelago of 117 islands glued together by 400 bridges.

There is a wealth of things to do and see in Venice. See our itinerary *Italian Highlights by Train & Boat–or Car* for sightseeing suggestions.

When it is time to leave Venice for Asolo, you need to take a boat to your car since all the "streets" in Venice are canals. If you are renting a car, take the boat to **Piazzale Roma** where most of the car rental companies are located. Also in the Piazzale Roma there are overnight car parks for storing your car if you drive into Venice. The choice of conveyance to the Piazzale Roma, Venice's hub of transportation, will depend upon your budget and your inclination. The **vaporetti** are the most reasonable: similar to river buses. They leave regularly from St. Mark's Square, stopping along the way to pick up passengers. It is approximately a half-hour ride to the Piazzale Roma. The **motoscafi** are motorboats that duck through the back canals and usually take about 15 minutes to the Piazzale Roma. The motoscafi are like private cabs and are much more expensive than the "bus," but can be very convenient, especially if your hotel has a private motorboat landing. The most romantic mode of transportation is by private **gondola**: however, these are very expensive and usually take about an hour to reach the Piazzale Roma.

Once you have retrieved your car from the parking garage, head north from Venice toward **Treviso**, about an hour's drive. If time allows, stop here. Stroll through this picturesque city spider-webbed with canals and surrounded by 15th-century ramparts— perhaps have a cup of coffee or a bite of lunch. Treviso is famous for its arcaded streets, churches lavishly decorated with frescoes, and painted houses. You might want to climb the ramparts for a view of the Alps beckoning you on.

ASOLO: From Treviso it is approximately another hour north to Asolo. However, just a few kilometers before you reach Asolo you see signs for the town of **Maser** where the **Villa di Maser** (sometimes called by the name of **Villa Bararo**) is located. This is a splendid villa designed by **Andrea Palladio** and fabulously decorated with frescoes by Paolo Veronese. It also has a very interesting museum of old carriages and antique cars. This elegant villa has erratic days and hours when it is open to the public—usually in late afternoons on Tuesdays, Saturdays, and Sundays. However, it is only about 1½ kilometers out of your way, so it is well worth a detour to investigate.

Your prize tonight is **Asolo**, a gem of a medieval village snuggled on the side of a hill with exquisite views of the countryside. The town is so romantic that it is no wonder Robert Browning was captivated by it and chose Asolo as his home. As you drive toward Asolo, the terrain does not seem to hold much promise—just modern towns and industry. Then a side road winds up a lovely hillside and into the intimate little town. Although definitely a tourist destination, Asolo maintains the atmosphere of a *real* town with colorful fruit stands, candy shops, and the neighborhood grocer for those lucky few who live here. In addition, there are boutiques with exquisite merchandise for the tourist. Of course, a castle adorns the hill above the village—mostly in ruins but setting the proper stage. Naturally, there is a wonderful cathedral dominating the square, just as it should. You will find all this plus vineyards and olive trees on the hillsides and the scent of roses in the air.

There are a couple of towns that are worth seeing while you are in the Asolo area. If brandy holds a special interest for you, visit **Bassano del Grappa**, an old town famous for its production of grappa (or brandy). The town is also a pottery center. However, Bassano del Grappa is rather large and, in our estimation, much less interesting than **Marostica**, a tiny town just a few kilometers farther on. If you are in this area in September, check your calendar and consider a stop in Marostica. Here, during the first part of September (in alternate years) the central square is transformed into a giant chessboard and local citizens become the human chess pieces. Even if it isn't the year of the chess game, you will enjoy this picturesque little medieval town encircled by ramparts, its pretty central square enclosed by colorful buildings and castle walls. There is also a second castle guarding the town from the top of the hill.

THE DOLOMITES: From Asolo, you head north to one of the most stunning regions of Italy, the **Dolomites**—breathtaking mountains. It is important to have a very detailed map of the region because this is a confusing area for driving. Adding to the confusion of finding your way is the fact that most of the towns have two names: one Italian and one German. Before World War I this section of Italy belonged to the Austrian Empire, and most of the towns have retained their original names along with their new ones. The food is a mixture of Italian and German—strudel is the favorite dessert and ravioli stuffed with meat, vegetables, and cream cheese is called either ravioletti or schulpfkrapfeln.

There are various routes for driving north into the Dolomites. The major highway heads north through **Feltre** and **Belluno** and then goes on to Cortina d'Ampezzo. However, if the day is nice and your spirit of adventure high, there is really nothing more fun than taking the back roads through the mountains. Journey through tiny hamlets and gorgeous mountain valleys far from the normal tourist path—always keeping a map accessible so that you don't wind up hopelessly lost.

Mountain & Lake Adventures

You might want to travel casually and stop in a village that captures your heart as you drive through the picturesque Dolomite valleys. A good base for exploring the region is **Corvara**, a small village ringed by breathtaking mountains. Another excellent choice is **Cortina d'Ampezzo**, a tourist center that is larger due to its excellent skiing facilities. Its location is truly breathtaking—the town spreads across a sunny meadow ringed by gigantic granite peaks. Although the true allure of Cortina is its beauty, there are a few other attractions—the lovely frescoes in the Romanesque **Church of SS Filippo e Giacomo**; the **stadium** where the 1956 Olympic ice-skating competition was held; and the **Museo Ciasa de Ra Regoles** with its geological display and contemporary art exhibition.

This is a mountain lover's area where the roads are slow and winding. The scenery is beautiful, with green valleys dominated by the stark mountain walls, but the driving is hard, with lots of hairpin bends. Many routes are spectacular. The 48 and 241 from Cortina to Bolzano form the stupendous **Great Dolomite Road** (*Grande Strada delle Dolomiti*). Another lovely route runs through the **Alpe di Siusi,** high Alpine meadowlands beneath towering mountains. (From the Verona-Brennero autostrada exit at Bolzano Nord and follow a route through Völs [Fiè allo Sciliar], Siusi, and Castelrotto.) It continues on into the **Val Gardena** (Grödner Tal) to **Ortisei** (Sankt Ulrich) and up to the **Sella Pass**. We enjoyed a sensational 50-kilometer drive over four mountain passes that ring the **Gruppo Sella** mountain group—from Corvara we took the Gardena Pass, the Sella Pass, the Podoi Pass, and the Campolongo Pass, which returned us to Corvara.

The only relaxing (albeit strenuous) way to truly appreciate the Dolomites is to get out of your car and walk the well-marked trails that feather out into the hills. Cable cars and ski lifts run in summer and are excellent ways to assist the walker to higher altitudes. At gift shops or tourist offices you can purchase detailed hiking maps that show every little path.

LAKE GARDA: Your next stop is Lake Garda. From the mountains, drive to Bolzano where you join the expressway (E7), heading south toward Trento (Trent). **Trent** is best known as the town where the Catholic Council met in the 16th century to establish important articles of faith that emphasized the authority of the Catholic Church.

Leave the freeway at Trent and head west on 45 toward the small, but lovely, green **Lake Toblino**, which is enhanced by a superb castle on its north shore where you can stop for lunch. From Toblino head south on the pretty country road, lined with fruit trees and vineyards, heading directly south toward Lake Garda, Italy's largest lake. When you come to Arco, the road splits. Take the road to the left and continue south to Lake Garda and then follow the 249 as it curves along the eastern shore of the lake.

Lake Garda abounds with romance. Don't rush. Take time to explore the lake by boat. Get off at colorful small hamlets that capture your fancy; it is hard to choose since each seems impossibly tempting. Have lunch, then hop back on a later boat to continue along your way. The boat schedules are posted at each dock, and if you ask the attendant, he can usually give you a printed timetable.

There are many alluring villages you should not miss, each a gem. One of the most charming towns is **Sirmione**, accessible by a picturesque drawbridge. This walled medieval village at the south end of Lake Garda is positioned on a miniature peninsula that juts into the lake. During the summer Sirmione is absolutely bursting with tourists, but you can easily understand why: this is another one of Italy's "stage-set" villages, almost too perfect to be real.

At the north end of the lake is the larger town of **Riva.** Although much of the town is of new construction, it has at its medieval core the **Piazza III Novembre** and 13th-century **Tower of Apponale**. A good place to eat lunch is on the terrace of the **Hotel Sole**, located directly across from the boat dock.

Along the western shore of the lake our favorite villages are **Gargnano** and its tiny adjacent neighbor, **Villa di Gargnano**. Both are medieval jewels hugging the waterfront with colorful fishing boats tucked into little harbors—truly adorable towns.

Also on the western shore of Lake Garda is **Gardone Riviera**. From here it is just a short drive to a **Vittoriale**, once the home of Gabriele d'Annunzio, the celebrated Italian poet. (For those who are fascinated by stories of romance, **Gabriele d'Annunzio** is also famous for his love affair with Eleanora Duse.)

The east side of Lake Garda also abounds with unbelievably quaint towns, each so perfect that you want to get out your camera or sketchbook to capture the beauty. Our favorites are the medieval walled towns of **Garda**, **Lazise**, and **Torri del Benaco**—each a gem. You mustn't miss them. Of the three, Torri del Benaco is our favorite.

It will be easier to leave the Lake Garda knowing that beautiful Lake Como awaits your arrival.

On your way from Lake Garda to Lake Como, stop at **Bergamo**, about an hour's drive west on the A4. As you approach Bergamo, the congested city doesn't appear to be worth a stop—but it is. The shell of the city is deceiving because it hides a lovely kernel, the **Cita Alta**, or high city. The lower part of Bergamo is modern and a bit dreary, but the old medieval city snuggled on the top of the hill holds such treasures as the **Piazza Vecchia**, the **Colleoni**

Chapel, and the **Church of St. Mary Major**. Should you want to time your stop in Bergamo with lunch, there are several excellent restaurants. One suggestion would be the **Agnello d'Oro**, a cozy, charming, 17th-century inn in the Cita Alta. From Bergamo it is a short drive on to **Lake Como**.

LAKE COMO: Lake Como is spectacular. The lower half of the lake is divided into two legs, the western branch called Lake Como and the eastern branch called **Lake Lecco**, enclosed by soaring cliffs that give a fjord-like beauty to the area. On the tip of land where the two lower sections of the lake join, is one of the lake's most delightful towns, **Bellagio**, a medieval jewel that exudes great charm. The town traces the shore of the lake and has a medieval walled entrance into the picture-perfect central square from which narrow lanes lined with colorful boutiques and restaurants lead up hill. Views of mountains, painted medieval buildings, flowers everywhere, promenades around the lake, and paths into the hills enhance your stay here. A particularly appealing walk follows a path that climbs up the wooded hill behind Bellagio and drops down into a tiny village, Pescallo, that nestles in a small cove on the other side of the peninsula.

Bellagio, Lake Como

In addition to Bellagio there is a rich selection of gems on the lake—picturesque, softly hued little hamlets, tucked into intimate coves around the shore. Most of these villages are accessible by boat. You can settle onto a steamer equipped with bar and restaurant and from your armchair lazily enjoy the constantly changing but always intriguing shoreline as the boat maneuvers in and out of the colorful little harbors, past elegant private villas, by enchanting villages. It is great fun to hop aboard one of the ferries and get off at one of the towns for lunch. There are also some swift hydrofoils that will whisk you about the lake and car ferries that transverse the lake, making it convenient to travel from one side to the other without going all around the lake.

Another bonus of Lake Como (besides the quaint towns to explore) is that it has exceptional villas to visit, many accessible by ferry. One of these on the western shore near **Tremezzo** is the **Villa Carlotta**, a fairy-tale-like 18th-century palace—worthy of the Prussian Princess Carlotta for whom it was named. Built by the Marquis Clerici, the villa with its surrounding formal gardens filled with rare plants and trees is outstanding. From the terrace you have an enchanting view over the lake to Bellagio. You reach the villa by a short drive from the ferry landing at Tremezzo along the beautiful tree-lined Via del Paradiso, *www.villacarlotta.it*. The interior of the villa with its prominent art collection and statues is open every day from 9 am to 6 pm from April to September. It is also open in March and October from 9 am to 11:30 am in the morning and in the afternoon from 2 pm to 4:30 pm.

Our favorite villa to visit because of its extraordinary beauty and romantic setting is **Villa del Balbianello** at **Lenno**, located on the west side of Lake Como. Built in 1700 by Cardinal Durini, this picture-postcard perfect villa is so beautiful it looks like a painting (and many artists have captured it on canvas). It is perched on the tip of a tiny peninsula with terraced gardens down to the lake. Have your camera ready and charged because as the ferry approaches the town of Lenno you will see the villa to your left and won't be able to stop taking photos. When your ferry arrives into Lenno, ask for directions to Sala Comacina, where you take a special motorboat to the landing where a flight of steps leads up to the gardens that are open to the public from the beginning of April until the end of

October on Tuesday, Thursday, Friday, Saturday, and Sunday from 10 am to 12:30 pm and again in the afternoon from 3:30 pm to 6 pm.

Como, located at the southern tip of Lake Como, is one of the larger towns on the lake. It is a pretty walled town with excellent shopping—including a colorful market every Saturday. Como is easily accessible from Milan and has many ferry departures from its dock.

Varenna is another small lakeside town accessible by ferry that is exceptionally attractive. Located about midway up the east side of the lake, it nestles on a promontory with great views. The heart of the town has a quaint, tiny square lined by medieval buildings. From Varenna about a half-an-hour hike takes you up to **Castello di Vezio,** a 13th-century castle with beautiful views of Lake Como. Varenna is a main hub for ferries, including car ferries that shuttle back and forth from Varenna to Bellagio and **Menaggio**, enabling you to quickly cross the lake without having to drive around it.

Cannero Riviera–Lake Maggiore

LAKE MAGGIORE: From Lake Como, the next stop is Lake Maggiore. Take advantage of the expressways to make your drive as easy as possible because there is usually heavy traffic in this part of Italy. It is best to head directly south in the direction of Milan to pick up the freeway.

Keep on the bypass that skirts the north side of Milan and take the freeway northwest to Lake Maggiore. Like Lake Garda and Lake Como, Maggiore offers ferries to many of its quaint towns and adds a special treat, the **Borromean Islands**, a small archipelago of three small islands, **Isola Bella**, **Isola Madre**, and **Isola dei Pescatori**. These enchanting islands can be reached by ferry from Stresa, Baveno, or Pallanza, but the most convenient of these departure points is **Stresa.** There are private taxi-boats available, but the most reasonable transportation is by public ferry.

Our two favorites of the Borromean Islands are Isola Bella and Isola dei Pescatori. You can easily visit them both in one day. If you enjoy gardens, be sure not to miss Isola Bella (Beautiful Island). Allow enough time to see its sumptuous palace, which is bound by formal gardens that terrace down to the lake. Fountains and sculptures make the gardens even more alluring. Afterwards, head to Isola dei Pescatori (Fisherman's Island) for lunch. Isola dei Pescatori is an enchanting island with twisting, narrow, alley-like streets and colorful fishermen's cottages. As the name implies, this is still an active fishing village. During the tourist season the island teems with people and the streets are lined with souvenir shops, but it is hard to dull the charm of this quaint town.

Another sightseeing excursion on Lake Maggiore is to the park at **Villa Taranto**. Its gardens, created in the 20th century by a Scottish captain, Neil McEacharn, are splendid with over 2000 species of plants, including huge water lilies, giant rhododendrons, and colorful azaleas. Adding to the botanical masterpiece, are fountains, waterfalls, beautiful trees and sculptures.

Isola Bella, Lake Maggiore

LAKE ORTA: Lake Orta, situated just west of Lake Maggiore, is one of our favorite lakes. Because it is so close to Lake Maggiore, it can be visited as a day trip from there. However, because it so appealing, we feel it deserves a stopover on its own. One doesn't hear much about Lake Orta, although it abounds with a charm and is filled with of Romanesque and Baroque treasures. It is probably less known because it is so small and doesn't have many quaint towns tucked along its shoreline. However, it does have one outstanding village, **Orta San Giulio**. It is picture perfect with a tiny square facing the water, narrow cobbled streets, noble mansions, a wonderful, very old, town hall, many boutiques, fragrant gardens, painted houses, and picturesque churches.

Adding to the perfection, just across from the town, you see **Isola San Giulio** shimmering in the water. You can take a boat out to this tiny island where you can walk the narrow street that circles the island and visit the Romanesque style church with 15th- and 16th-century frescoes.

THE ALPS: After visiting Lake Orta, drive south to the main freeway and head west on A4 toward Turin heading for the Italian Alps. Before Turin, when the freeway branches, take A5 heading northwest toward Aosta and beyond to the French border. As you head into the mountains, many small roads lead off to narrow valleys accented by gorgeous meadows, blanketed in summer with wildflowers. Most of these roads dead end when they are stopped by impregnable mountain ranges. In the winter, this is a paradise for downhill or cross-country skiing. One of the most famous ski areas is **Breuil-Cervinia**, almost at the Swiss border, just over the mountain from the Swiss resort, Zermatt. In summer the mountains beckon one to explore the beautiful paths that lead off in every direction.

Cogne-Valnontey

Our favorite place for walking or hiking is in the **Grand Paradis National Park**, just south of **Cogne**. To reach the park, from the A5, take the road south to Cogne. From here you can walk through a glorious meadow that stretches to the foot of the Grand Paradis, a majestic mountain that soars over 4,000 meters into the sky. If you drive a few kilometers beyond Cogne to where the road ends, you find Valnontey, a stunning hamlet of rustic, centuries-old, stone houses enhanced by pots of geraniums. As you stroll through the tiny village, it seems you have stepped back many centuries—it is so perfect, so untouched.

When it is time to continue your journey, the A5 continues on through the Mont Blanc tunnel and into France.

The Dolomites

Mountain & Lake Adventures

Rome to Milan via the Italian Riviera

MILAN

Pavia Carthusian Monastery

SAVIGNONE

Genova   A12

Camogli

Portofino

Sestri Levante

Levanto

Colonnata

Monterosso al Mare

Carrara

Cinque Terre

La Spezia

Lucca

Portovenere

Pisa

Livorno

FLORENCE

Rome

Elba

Orbetello Peninsula

Orbetello

Porto San Stefano

Porto Ercole

Tarquinia

Civitavecchia

ROME

● Orientation/Sightseeing

▬ ▬ Itinerary route

Rome to Milan via the Italian Riviera

Vernazza, Cinque Terre

This itinerary traces the western coast of Italy as far as Genova before heading north for the final stretch to Milan. To break the journey, the first stop is Tarquinia for sightseeing, then Orbetello, a picturesque peninsula-like island joined to the coast by three spits of land. The next destination is Cinque Terre—a string of five tiny fishing villages along the coast that have not yet fallen prey to a great influx of tourists. As you follow the highway up the coast, it becomes a masterpiece of engineering—bridging deep ravines and tunneling in and out of the cliffs, which rise steeply from the sea. Along the way you pass picturesque small towns snuggled into small coves. Then it's on to Portofino—one of Italy's most treasured jewels—before the final destination of Milan.

Recommended Pacing: This itinerary can be run quickly if it is being used as simply as a means of transportation between Rome and Milan (or visa versa), but it is much more fun to savor the small towns along the way. You need a minimum of three nights in Rome—you could spend a week and still only touch on what this fabulous "living museum" has to offer. Once on your way between Rome and Milan, there are outstanding places to stay and things to see along the coast. However, if your time is strictly limited, choose just one of the three stopovers we recommend (Porto Ercole, Cinque Terre or Portofino) and plan to stay for three nights. Ideally, if you have the luxury to meander along the way, then plan to spend at least two nights in all three. Every suggested stopover is lovely in its own way and will give you a glimpse of the beauty of Italy's small, delightful, coastal towns.

This itinerary begins in **Rome**, a perfect introduction to Italy. The joy of Rome is that every place you walk you are immersed in history. The whole of the city is a virtual museum—buildings over 2,000 years old, ancient fountains designed by the world's greatest masters, the Vatican, Renaissance paintings that have never been surpassed in beauty. Buy a guidebook at one of the many bookstores or magazine stands to plan what you most want to see and do. Also buy a detailed city map and mark each day's excursion. Most places are within walking distance—if not, consider taking the subway, which stretches to most of the major points of interest.

For sightseeing suggestions in Rome, see the *Italian Highlights by Train & Boat—or Car* itinerary.

From Rome follow the well-marked signs for the expressway heading west toward the Leonardo da Vinci airport. About 5 kilometers before you arrive at the airport, head north on A12 in the direction of **Civitavecchia**.

About 13 kilometers beyond the Civitavecchia Nord exit, turn right (east) on S1 BIS in the direction of Viterbo. Continue a bit more than 3 kilometers and turn left toward **Tarquinia**, an Etruscan city that historians date back to the 12th century B.C. Even if it is not quite that old, archaeologists have established that people were living here as early as

600 years before Christ. Before you reach Tarquinia, you will see on your right an open-air museum—an open field dotted with **Etruscan tombs**. The site is not well-marked, but your clue will be tour buses lining the road. Park your car, buy a ticket at the gate, and explore the fascinating tombs. There are over a thousand tombs stretching over 5 kilometers, but only a small, select group is open to the public. You can wander at leisure. Each tomb has a sign describing what drawings are found within. You will find a rich treasure trove of paintings depicting the life of the ancient Etruscans, including scenes of hunting, dining, fishing, drinking, and frolicking. All of the burial sites are underground. To access a tomb, you have to climb down a narrow flight of steps and when you reach the bottom, everything is semidarkness. However, when you push a button, the tomb is magically illuminated behind a glass window. Each tomb is individually decorated with paintings that offer a poignant glimpse of life over a thousand years ago. There is no way you can visit all the burial chambers, but one of the most popular is the **Tomb of the Leopards** where there is a well-preserved banquet scene.

After viewing the tombs, ask the attendant at the gate for directions to the **Museo Nazionale Tarquiniese** which is located in the center of town in the 15th-century **Vitelleschi Palace**. Even if you do not have time to savor all of the beautiful Etruscan vases and handsome carved stone sarcophagi, you must make at least a brief stop to view the astonishing winged horses dramatically displayed in a large room on an upper floor. You will be spellbound by these superb horses on an ornate relief that adorned the altar of the Queen's temple.

After your brush with Etruscan civilization, continue north for approximately 50 kilometers to Scalo/Orbetello where you turn west. The road crosses 6 kilometers of lagoons on a narrow spit of land (going through the town of Orbetello) before reaching the large, bulbous peninsula dominated by Mount Argentario. Turn left when you reach the peninsula to reach the fishing village of **Porto Ercole** or right for the larger port town of **Porto Santo Stefano** where ferryboats depart for the islands of Giglio, Gianutri and Corsica. Beyond the town is a spectacular coastal cliff drive overlooking the sea.

Return to S1 and head north on the highway as it follows the coast. About 35 kilometers before you come to the large city of Livorno (which you want to avoid at all costs), the road divides. One split goes to Livorno and the other becomes the A12, which heads inland and bypasses the city. The next large town after Livorno is **Pisa.** Take the Pisa Nord exit which takes you directly to the city walls and the historic part of the old town. Your target is the **Piazza del Duomo**, a huge square studded by fabulous buildings, including Pisa's landmark, its **Leaning Tower.** However, it is not only the Leaning Tower that makes the Piazza del Duomo such a winner, it is studded with many other magnificent buildings, all of which are outstanding architectural jewels and happily are open to the public as museums. You can buy one ticket allowing entrance to all. Climb to the top of the Leaning Tower (which is once again open for visitors after being strengthened by massive cables). Also, don't miss the breathtaking **Duomo** or the **Baptistery**. Since we first visited Pisa many years ago, an awesome transformation has taken place. The buildings have been scrubbed cleaned and returned to their original splendor, making Pisa a joy to visit.

Leaning Tower of Pisa

About 25 kilometers northeast of Pisa is the extremely picturesque city of **Lucca.** Lucca too is an ancient, perfectly preserved city. Completely surrounding the town is an enormous wall—a wall so wide that it even supports pretty, small parks and a path that runs along the top that is a favorite for joggers. Lucca is truly a jewel. Take time to wander through her maze of narrow streets, admiring imposing mansions and colorful squares.

Leaving Lucca, return to the expressway A12 and head north to Genova. Along the way you see what appears to be a glacier shimmering white in the mountains that rise in the distance to the right of the highway. This is not snow at all, but rather your introduction to the renowned white Italian marble. Detour to visit some of the marble quarries. Exit the highway at Carrara and take the winding drive up into the hills to the ancient village of **Colonnata**—famous through the ages for its marvelous white marble. As you wander this tiny town you're following the footsteps of Michelangelo, who used to come to here to choose huge blocks of marble from which to carve his masterpieces.

Take the small road from Carrara west to join the A12 and continue north for an entirely different kind of experience—exploring the lovely, remote coast called **Cinque Terre**.

This area is quickly becoming linked with civilization, so do not tarry if you love the thrill of discovering old fishing villages hardly touched by time. En route you come to an exit to **La Spezia**, a large seaport and navy town. If you want to take a detour, go to La Spezia and from there take the short drive to the tip of the peninsula south of town to visit the old fishing village of **Portovenere** which clings to the steep rocks rising from the sea. This was one of Lord Byron's haunts when he lived across the bay at **San Terenzo**. After Portovenere, return to the A12 and continue north.

Along the Cinque Terre there used to be five completely isolated fishing villages dotted along the coast between La Spezia to the south and Levanto to the north. First, only a footpath connected these hamlets, then a train was installed, and now civilization is encroaching, with a road under construction, which will open them up to greater commercialism. Three of these little villages, (**Riomaggiore, Monterosso and Manarola**) are already accessible by road. Still completely cut off from car traffic are the colorful fishing hamlets of **Vernazza** and **Corniglia**.

If you want to spend the night in one of the villages along the Cinque Terre, **Monterosso al Mare** offers the best selection of accommodations. To reach the town of Monterosso al Mare, exit the A12 at Carrodano and follow signs to Levanto. From Levanto take the road up the hill at the south end of town, signposted Monterosso al Mare. A massive rock formation jutting into the sea divides Monterosso al Mare into two distinct sections that are connected by a train tunnel. You can walk between the two parts of town, but you cannot drive. So if you leave your car in the public parking area, which is located in the "north" village, you will need to take a taxi to hotels located in the "south" village.

You do not need a car to enjoy the Cinque Terre: this is a region that lures those who love to hike and be out of doors. You can explore the villages by train,

Cinque Terre

boat, or walking: the most fun is to combine all three. If you have the time, plan to spend several days here. If the weather is pleasant, hike the trail that traces the rocky coast and links the villages, stopping for lunch along the way (one of our favorite restaurants is the Pensione Cecio in Corniglia). After lunch, hop aboard one of the frequent trains (each of the towns has a train station and the schedules are clearly posted) or take one of the ferries (which only operate in the summer season) to return "home." Let your mood and the weather dictate your explorations. Although this is a remote coast, be prepared that you will not be alone: the path along the Cinque Terre is popular and always busy—filled with the vacationers who have come to enjoy the natural beauty.

If you have time to see only one of the scenic towns, **Vernazza**, which clings perilously to a rocky headland above a tiny harbor, is the most picturesque. This colorful jewel has brightly painted fishermen's houses, quaint restaurants, a harbor with small boats bobbing in the clear, turquoise water, and a maze of twisting narrow steps that lead up to the promontory overlooking the village.

Leaving Cinque Terre, continue north beside the coast. Stop in **Sestri Levante**, one of the most picturesque coastal villages en route. Continue along the small coastal road that goes through Chiàvari and on to San Margherita where you take the small road south for the short drive to the picture-book village of **Portofino**. This last section of the road, especially in summer, is jammed with traffic, but the prize at the end is worth the trials endured to reach it. Portofino is by no means undiscovered, but is well deserving of its accolades—it is one of the most picturesque tiny harbors in the world.

Portofino is a national treasure—it truly is a jewel. Its tiny harbor is filled with glamorous yachts, small ferries, and colorful fishing boats. Enveloping the harbor are narrow fishermen's cottages, poetically painted in warm tones of sienna, ochre, and pink and all sporting green shutters. Bright flower boxes accent the windows and the laundry flaps gaily in the breeze.

Vivid reflections of these quaint little houses shimmer in the emerald water. In the center of town is a small square, lined with restaurants, which faces the harbor. Forming a backdrop to the town are steep, heavily forested hills, which complete this idyllic scene.

Portofino

When it is time to leave Portofino, return to the A12 highway and continue west for about 30 kilometers to Genova. As you go through the city, watch for the A7 going north to Milan. An interesting detour on the last leg of your journey is the **Pavia Carthusian Monastery** (*Certosa di Pavia*). Probably the simplest way to find it is to watch for the turnoff to Pavia (96 kilometers north of Genova): take the road east to Pavia and from there go north about 10 kilometers to the monastery. Lavishly built in the 15th century, this splendid monastery is claimed by some to be one of the finest buildings in Italy. (Check carefully the days and hours open—the monastery is usually closed on Mondays and for several hours midday.) The outside of the building is lavishly designed with colorful marble and intricate designs. Inside, the small cloisters are especially charming with 122 arches framed by beautiful terracotta moldings. It also has a baroque fountain and several small gardens. Next to the monastery you find the **Palace of the Dukes of Milan**, which is now a museum. After your tour of the monastery it is approximately 26 kilometers farther north to **Milan**.

The outskirts of Milan are not very inviting—you find frustrating traffic and modern commercial buildings. However, the heart of Milan has much to offer. Take time to see Leonardo da Vinci's famous mural, **The Last Supper**, in the church of **Santa Maria delle Grazie**. It is vital that you make an appointment in advance: from the USA call 011-39 (Europe, 00-39) 0289-421146; from within Italy, (199) 19 91 00. The unilingual Italian-speaking reservationists will make you an appointment and give you a confirmation number. Arrive at the church about 15 minutes before your appointment, confirmation number in hand, and pay cash for your ticket.

If you enjoy shopping (and Milan has some of the finest shops in Italy), pay a visit to the splendid **Galleria Vittorio Emanuele**, one of the prettiest shopping arcades in the world. Even if you are not a shopper, you should take time to browse. Located between Milan's other two sightseeing stars, the Duomo and La Scala, the Galleria Vittorio Emanuele is the forerunner of the modern shopping mall, but with much more pizzazz. In this Victorian-era fantasy there are two main, intersecting wings, both completely domed with intricately patterned glass. Along the pedestrian-only arcades you find many boutiques and colorful restaurants with outside tables.

After a stroll through the arcade, you emerge into an imposing square dominated by the truly spectacular **Duomo**, the third-largest cathedral in the world. Not only is the size impressive, but this sensational cathedral has a multicolored marble façade enhanced by over 100 slender spires piercing the sky. This spectacular cathedral faces onto an enormous square lined with cafés, office buildings, and shops. Stop to have a snack at one of the outdoor restaurants—you could sit for hours just watching the people go by.

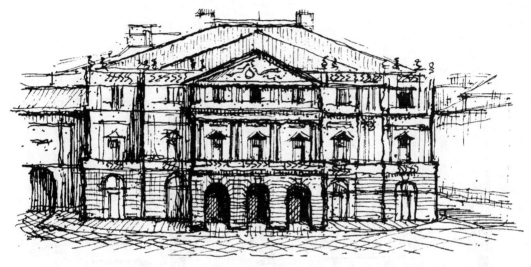

La Scala, Milan

Another site not to be missed is Milan's opera house. Every opera buff knows about **La Scala**. Even if you have not been an opera enthusiast in the past, if you are going to be in Milan during the opera season (which usually runs from December to May), write ahead and try to get tickets. The theater is stunning and an experience not to be missed. When it is not opera season, there is usually some other performance or concert featured. If you haven't purchased seats in advance, you can try to buy them on the day of the performance (the ticket office is located down a flight of stairs to the left of the opera house).

Highlights of Southern Italy

ROME

Abbey of
Monte Cassino

Anzio
Nettuno

Trani

Polignano
a Mare

Castel del Monte

Monopoli

to Corfu-Greece

Naples   Pompeii
Sorrento   Salerno
Capri

Matera

Alberobello

Brindisi

Positano
Amalfi
Ravello

Paestum

Taranto

Maratea

Sibari

● Orientation/Sightseeing
■ ■ ■ Itinerary route
· · · · · Suggested sidetrips

Messina

PALERMO

Erice
Trapani
Marsala

Villa San Giovanni

Taormina

Selinunte

Enna

Catania

Agrigento

Piazza
Armerina

Siracusa

Rome

137

Highlights of Southern Italy

Amalfi Coast

Memories of childhood history lessons vaguely call forth such names as Pompeii, Herculaneum, and Paestum, yet, all too frequently, the urge to visit these jewels is lost in the misconception that southern Italy is a rather lackluster destination. What a mistake! Southern Italy has fascinating archaeological sites, appealing medieval towns, white sand beaches and the dazzling Amalfi Coast with its picture-perfect villages. Travelers who venture south from Rome are thrilled when they wander through the fabulous Greek site of Paestum with its splendidly preserved temples rivaling those found in Greece or discover the mysterious town of Alberobello with its twisting streets lined by cute, whitewashed, beehive-like Trulli houses.

Recommended Pacing: Spend a minimum of three nights in Rome. Then, choose one town along the Amalfi Coast and stay for a minimum of five nights so that you will have time to make an excursion to Capri. Your next stop, Maratea, does not have much sightseeing but is a perfect place to relax for a couple of nights. The final destination is near the "heel" of Italy. Choose one place to use as your home base in Apulia and plan to spend at least three nights so that you will have time to explore this remote, beautiful part of Italy.

This itinerary makes a circle of the south in order to suit the travel needs of a wide selection of tourists. Follow the entire route or select the portion best for you since this itinerary is particularly suitable for the traveler who wants to take only a segment. For instance, the journey from Rome to Brindisi is a favorite one for the lucky tourists on their way to Greece, while the west coast is a popular drive for the tourist who wants to visit Sicily and then return to Rome by air or ferry. Most popular of all is the segment from Rome to the Amalfi Drive. This itinerary allows you to custom tailor your journey and gives you tantalizing sightseeing along the way.

Rome is a most convenient starting point to begin a tour of southern Italy, since its airport is the destination of planes from all over the world. In Rome you can immerse yourself in a wealth of history, art, architecture, museums, and monuments—and build a foundation for the sights that will be encountered on your journey southward. For sightseeing suggestions in Rome, refer to the chapter *Italian Highlights by Train & Boat—or Car*.

If you arrive into Rome by plane, do not reserve your rental car until the day of your departure. Just take a taxi to your hotel or board the train from the airport that whisks you to the center of the city. When it is time to leave Rome bear in mind that the city has a monumental traffic problem. To guide you, look for strategically placed signs indicating that there is an expressway ahead. It might be quite a distance, but be patient as these signs lead you to the outskirts of Rome to the highway that makes a ring around the city with various spokes going off to different destinations. Follow the ring and take the exit for the A2, the expressway heading south toward Naples. Continue south for approximately 128 kilometers to the exit for **Cassino** where you leave the expressway. Actually, you can spot your destination from several kilometers away—the **Abbey of Monte Cassino** crowns the top of a large mountain to the left of the highway as you drive south. The road that winds up to the summit of the mountain to the Abbey is clearly marked about midway through Cassino. This abbey, founded by St. Benedict in 529 A.D., is extremely interesting both religiously and historically. For war historians it brings back many battle memories—this is where the Germans staunchly held out against the Allied forces for almost a year in World War II. When the mountain was finally conquered in May 1944, it opened the way for the Allies to move into Rome. As you read your history books, it seems strange that one fort could hold out for so long, but when you see the abbey you understand: it is an enormous building on the crest of a precipitous mountain. In the siege the abbey was almost destroyed, but it has been rebuilt according to the original plans.

NOTE: For those of you who for sentimental or for historical reasons are especially interested in World War II, there is another destination you might well want to visit in this day's journey. **Anzio** is a town on the coast about 56 kilometers south of Rome and could easily be included as a stop before Cassino. It was at Anzio that the British and Americans forces landed in January 1944. The emotional reminder of this terrible battle is a few kilometers south at **Nettuno** where 8,000 white crosses and stars of David range—row after row across the green lawn. There is a circular drive around the beautifully manicured, parklike grounds where you also find a memorial chapel and small war museum. For those who lost family or friends during the invasion, there is an information office to the right as you drive in, where you can stop to find out exactly where your loved ones are buried—you will need help because the park is huge.

From Cassino return to the expressway and continue south for about 60 kilometers until you see the sign for **Pompeii**. Unless you have absolutely NO interest in archaeology, you must see the city of your childhood history books. This is where time was frozen in 79 A.D. for the 25,000 people who were smothered by lava from the eruption of **Mount Vesuvius**. If you are a dedicated student of archaeology, you must also visit the **Museo**

Archeologico Nazionale (National Archaeological Museum) in Naples, which houses many of the artifacts from Pompeii.

Time slips back 2,000 years and you feel the pulse of how people lived in ancient times as you wander the streets of Pompeii and visit the temples, lovely homes, wine shops, bakeries, and public baths. Many of the private homes have been reconstructed so you can marvel at the pretty inner courtyards, sumptuous dining rooms in Pompeii-red with intricate paintings on the walls, fountains, servants' quarters, bathrooms, and gardens. At the entrance to Pompeii there are souvenir stands where you can purchase a guidebook to the city, or, if you prefer, you can hire a private guide at the entrance. There is a nice terrace restaurant by the entrance and also a café inside.

Much of what you see today has been reproduced, but the reality is pure. Plaster was poured into molds formed by the lava that demolished the buildings and buried so many families that fateful day. Thus it became possible for latter-day archaeologists to reconstruct houses and make reproductions of people and pets. Walk through the town along the sunken streets crossed by high stepping stones, strategically placed so that pedestrians did not get their feet wet on rainy days. Be sure not to miss some of the reconstructed villas that allow you a glimpse into the daily life of long ago. The **Casa del Fauno**, a fine example of how the wealthy lived, has two inner courtyards and several dining rooms. The **Casa del Poeta Tragico**, a more modest home, has a sign in mosaic saying *Cave Canem* (beware of the dog). At the **Villa di Giulia Felice** you see the example of an entrepreneur—in addition to using it as a private villa, the owner rented out rooms, had shops on the ground floor, and operated an adjacent bathhouse. If traveling with children, you might want to go alone into the **Lupanare** (Pompeii's brothel) where there are erotic paintings on the walls. At the **Terme Stabiane** you see a sophisticated underground water-heating system.

If you have time, visit the nearby ruins of **Herculaneum** which was also buried in the lava of Vesuvius.

Leaving Pompeii, head to the coast in the direction of Sorrento where the **Amalfi Drive** begins, tracing one of the most beautiful stretches of shoreline in the world. Be sure to make the journey in daylight because you want to savor every magnificent vista as well as safely negotiate this extremely twisty and precipitous road.

It is hard to recommend our favorite town along the Amalfi Drive since each has its own personality: **Sorrento**, is an old fishing town perched on a rocky bluff overlooking the sea. It makes an especially convenient place to stay if you want to make a side trip to Capri by ferry or hydrofoil. **Ravello** is a tiny village tucked high in the hills above the coast with absolutely dazzling views down to the sea. **Positano** is an especially romantic coastal town with a picturesque medley of whitewashed houses terracing down an ever-so-steep embankment to a pebble beach dotted with brightly painted fishing boats. **Amalfi** is a small harbor town nestled in a narrow ravine.

From whatever hub you choose as your hotel base, venture out to do some exploring. The traffic during the tourist season is staggering, with buses, trucks, and cars all jockeying for position on the narrow twisting roads. Prepare for much shouting, waving of hands, honking, and general bedlam as long buses inch around the hairpin curves. The best advice is to relax and consider the colorful scene part of the sightseeing. Also, begin your excursions as early in the day as possible to try to avoid the major traffic.

If you are not overnighting in **Ravello**, you must plan to take the narrow winding road up to this romantic clifftop town. When you arrive, leave your car in one of the designated parking areas, pick up a map at the tourist office, then walk along the well-marked path to the **Villa Rufolo** and the **Villa Cimbrone**—both have beautiful gardens that are open to the public and enchanting views of the Bay of Salerno.

If you are not overnighting in **Positano**, by all means make this a day's excursion. The town is a photographer's dream—houses painted a dazzling white step down the impossibly steep hillside to a pebble beach lapped by brilliant blue water. To reach the small plaza dominated by a church topped by a colorful mosaic-tiled dome you have to climb one of the town's many staircases. Today Positano attracts artists and tourists from

Positano

around the world, but in the 16th and 17th centuries it was an important seaport with tall-masted ships bringing in wares from around the world. When steamships came into vogue in the 19th century, Positano's prosperity declined and three-quarters of its population immigrated to the United States.

If you have not been able to include an interlude on **Capri** during your Italian holiday, it is easy to arrange an excursion to this enchanted island as a side trip from the Amalfi Coast. Steamers and hydrofoils depart regularly from Sorrento, Amalfi, and Positano. Ask at the tourist bureau or your hotel for the schedule.

We also highly recommend spending a day in **Naples**, which, although not on the Amalfi Coast, is conveniently close. Since it is quite difficult to drive into Naples without getting lost, we suggest the following options: Train from Sorrento, boat from Sorrento, or boat from Positano. Naples, the third largest city in Italy, is well worth a side trip; it has many places of interest plus one of the world's finest archaeological museums, the **Museo Archeologico Nazionale,** where most of the original artifacts from Pompeii are displayed. For more in depth suggestions for what to see and do in Naples, read the itinerary *Italian Highlights by Train & Boat—or Car.*

While exploring the Amalfi Coast, be sure to include the **Emerald Grotto**, located between the towns of Amalfi and Positano. After parking, buy a ticket and descend by elevator down the steep cliff to a small rocky terrace. Upon entering the water-filled cave, you're rowed about the grotto in a small boat. Your guide explains how the effect of shimmering green water is created by a secret tunnel allowing sunlight to filter from deep below the surface. The cave is filled with colorful stalactites and stalagmites which further enhance the mysterious mood. There is also a nativity scene below the water which mysteriously appears and then drifts again from view.

When it is time to leave the Amalfi area, take the coastal road south as it twists and turns along the dramatic cliffs toward Salerno. At Salerno, join the expressway A3 for about 19 kilometers until the turnoff for **Paestum** which is located on a side road about a half-hour drive from the freeway. Magically, when you enter the gates of the ancient city, you enter a peaceful environment of a lovely country meadow dotted with some of the world's best-preserved Greek temples. As you walk along the remains of streets crisscrossing the city, your senses are thrilled by the sound of birds singing and the scent of roses.

From Paestum return to the A3 and continue south until you come to the Lagonegro Nord-Maratea exit. Do not be tempted by some of the short cuts you see on the map that lead to the coast, but stay on the main road 585. In about 25 kilometers the road comes to the sea where you turn north at Castrocucco, following signs to **Maratea**. Plan on spending several days in the Maratea area.

Not well known to foreigners, this lovely section of coast, known as the **Gulf of Policastro**, is a popular resort area for Italians. The loveliest section of the road is between Maratea and Sapri where the road traces the sea along a high corniche, providing lovely vistas of small coves and rocky promontories. This is not an area for intensive sightseeing, but provides a quiet interlude for several days of relaxation.

Maratea, Gulf of Policastro

From the Gulf of Policastro, take road 585 back to the A3 and continue south for about 75 kilometers, turning east at Frascineto-Castrovillari toward the instep of Italy's boot. After about 25 kilometers you near the coast. Here you turn left on 106 to **Taranto**. Stop to see this ancient port, which is connected by a bridge to the modern city. Even if you are not interested in ancient history, it is fun to see the Italian naval ships—giant gray monsters—sitting in the protected harbor.

From Taranto take 172 north and continue on for about 45 kilometers following signs to **Alberobello**. You are now in the province of **Apulia**, not a well-known destination, but all the more fun to visit because it is off the beaten path. Choose a hotel in the area as your hub, venture out to explore the fascinating sights that follow:

Trulli District: Trulli houses (whose origins date back to at least the 13th century) are some of the strangest structures in Italy—circular stone buildings, usually in small clusters, standing crisply white with conical slate roofs and whimsical, twisted chimneys. Outside ladders frequently lead to upper stories. Often several of these houses are joined together to form a larger complex. What a strange and fascinating sight—these beehive-like little houses intertwined with cobbled streets form a jumble of a small village that looks as though it should be inhabited by elves instead of *real* people. The heart of the Trulli region is **Alberobello** where there are so many Trulli houses (more than 1,000 along the narrow streets) that the Trulli district of town has been declared a national monument.

Trulli Houses, Alberobello

Trulli houses are not confined just to the town of Alberobello though this is where you find them composing an entire village. In fact, the Trulli houses you see outside Alberobello are sometimes more interesting than those in the town itself. As you drive along the small roads, you spot gorgeous villas cleverly converted from Trulli houses, now obviously the homes of wealthy Italians. Others are now farmhouses with goats munching their lunch in the front yard. Occasionally you spot a charming old Trulli home nestled cozily in the center of a vineyard. But most fun of all are the Trulli homes of the free spirits: their homes, instead of displaying the typical white exteriors, have been painted a brilliant yellow, pink, or bright green with contrasting shutters.

Grotte di Castellana: As you are exploring the countryside near Alberobello, take the short drive north to see the Castellana Caves—the largest in Italy. In a two-hour tour you see many rooms of richly colored stalagmites and stalactites.

Coastal Villages: Be sure to include in your sightseeing some of the characterful towns along the coast. They look entirely different from the colorful fishing villages in the north of Italy. These are Moorish-looking, with stark-white houses lining narrow, alley-like streets. The Adriatic looks an even deeper blue as it laps against the white buildings, many of which rise from the sea with small windows perched over the water. Besides **Monopoli** other coastal towns to see are **Polignano a Mare** and **Trani**.

Castel del Monte: On the same day that you explore the coastal villages, include a visit to the 13th-century Castel del Monte. Built by Emperor Frederick II of Swab, it is somewhat of a mystery, having none of the fortifications usually associated with a medieval castle. Nevertheless, it is dramatic—a huge stone structure crowning the top of a hill with eight circular towers, which stretch 24 meters into the sky. There are stunning views in every direction.

Matera: Plan one full day to visit Matera, an intriguing town of stark beauty (so extraordinary UNESCO has listed it as a World Heritage site). As you approach Matera, you can't help but wonder what is so special—it looks like quite an ordinary, modern city. But, continue on, following signs for "Sassi." Upon arrival, park your car and go to the central plaza in the heart of the old city. From the plaza, steps lead down to a secreted town beneath, hugging the walls of a steep canyon laced by narrow alley-like lanes and ancient houses. These dwellings, called **Sassi**, have facades fronting cave-like homes. The scene is haunting with a jumble of monotone houses and churches clinging to, and blending with, the hillside. There is not a hint of color to liven the scene. Some scholars think that this site, which began thousands of years ago as cave homes, might well be the oldest inhabited place in Italy. The city had been almost totally abandoned by the mid-1900s, but it is being rediscovered and, as a result, art galleries, restaurants, shops, and a few places to spend the night are reappearing. Mel Gibson is responsible for some of the most recent interest in the town, since he filmed here for his movie, *The Passion of the Christ*. The only way to explore this ancient part of Matera is on foot (the tourist office provides maps with various suggested routes).

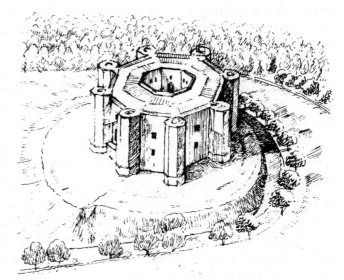

Castel del Monte

When it is time to leave Apulia, you can breeze back to Rome by an expressway. Or, if your next destination is Greece, it is just a short drive to **Brindisi** where you can board the ferry for Corfu, Igoumenitsa, or Patras. Best of all, if you can extend your holiday in Sicily (see *Exploring the Wonders of Sicily* itinerary).

Exploring the Wonders of Sicily

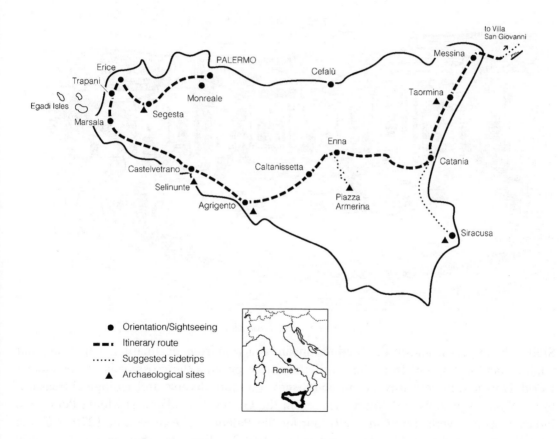

- ● Orientation/Sightseeing
- ■ ■ ■ Itinerary route
- ⋯⋯ Suggested sidetrips
- ▲ Archaeological sites

Exploring the Wonders of Sicily

Greek Theater, Taormina

Sicily, the largest island in the Mediterranean, is a wondrous destination. This triangular hunk of land jutting out from the tip of Italy's toe became the crossroads of the ancient world. Nowhere in your travels can you discover a more diverse archaeological treasure-trove. Stone-Age tools and figures carved in the Grotta di Addaura at Monte Pellegrino indicate people were living in Sicily during the Paleolithic Age. About 1270 B.C. the island was invaded by a Mediterranean tribe called Siculians, but they were not the only settlers: excavations show the arrival of tribes from Asia. Beginning in the 10th century B.C., pioneering Phoenicians took a fancy to this fertile land, followed later by their descendants, the Carthaginians. However, the true dawn of Sicily's reign of glory began with the colonization by the Greeks whose enormous influence permeates Sicily today. However, the rich fabric of Sicily's heritage does not end with the Greek influence: later the Romans invaded, then the Normans, then the Spanish, and on and on. This resulting melting pot of cultures makes Sicily an absolute MUST for those who delight in the romance of archaeology. The true magic of Sicily is that most of the ruins are so natural in their setting. Frequently you discover you are alone—the only tourist walking through a field of wildflowers to gaze in awe at an exquisite temple.

Recommended Pacing: We recommend a minimum of a week to follow this itinerary. If you are passionate about archaeology, you could stay in Sicily for a month or more to delve in depth with its many glorious sites. Plan to spend two nights in Taormina (one of Sicily's most attractive cities) two nights in Agrigento to see the incredible temples in the *Valle dei Templi*, and then three nights in northwest Sicily (Palermo or another hub) to visit Palermo, Segesta, Monreale, and Erice.

The greatest age of glory for Sicily began when the Greeks founded their first colony here about 770 B.C. Apparently these early Greeks left their native country for economic and political reasons, but many were also undoubtedly motivated by pure curiosity—the desire to discover what awaited across the sea. Like the immigrants who came to America, the early settlers wanted a fresh start in a new land and an opportunity to establish a better life for themselves. And they did. Prospering enormously from the richness of the fertile soil, the early Greeks became extremely wealthy. As the *nouveaux riches* tend to do, they flaunted their success, building great cities, elaborate houses, theaters, spas, and stadiums—all bigger and better than those they left at home. Siracusa, the mightiest city in Sicily, eventually became more powerful than Athens. The temples they built surpassed in size and splendor those left in their native land. Not losing their passion for sports, every four years the new colonialists sent their finest athletes back to Greece where they dominated the Olympic games.

Twice an hour ferries cross the narrow channel from **Villa San Giovanni** to **Messina**, Sicily. After buying your ticket, go to the indicated lane and wait with all the trucks, campers, and other cars for the signal to drive onto the boat. When on board, you may leave your car and go upstairs to the lounge area where you can buy snacks while traversing the short channel. In 35 minutes the large ferry draws up to the pier in Messina and you drive off to begin your adventures.

If you prefer to fly to Sicily, just reverse this itinerary. Start in Palermo and finish in Taormina. Alternatively, you can take a ferry from Naples to Palermo (a ten-hour journey).

Picture-perfect **Taormina** with the dramatic peak of **Mont Etna** as a backdrop, hugs the crest of a small peninsula that juts out to the sea. Steep cliffs drop to the unbelievably blue sea. Quaint streets wind through the colorful town where you can browse in the many smart boutiques, sip a cappuccino at a small café, or simply enjoy the incredible view. The scent of oranges is in the air and brilliantly colored bougainvilleas lace the medieval buildings.

However, it is not just the natural beauty of its spectacular setting that makes Taormina so popular. As in all of Sicily, your leisure pleasure is enhanced with fabulous sights to see. The prime archaeological target for your sightseeing is the **Greek Theater**. From the center of town an easy walk up Via Teatro Greco takes you to a magnificent theater dug into the sloping hillside above the town. Built by the Greeks in the 3rd century B.C., the open-air amphitheater has only a token few of its original columns remaining, making the effect even more romantic. As you gaze beyond the rows of seats to the stage below and out to the vivid blue sea beyond, you will think there is no prettier picture in all of Italy.

After visiting the Greek Theater, most of the remainder of your sightseeing can be done informally while strolling through town. First pick up a map and general information at the tourist office in the **Palazzo Corvaia**, a 15th-century palace located on the Piazza Vittorio Emanuele. From the Palazzo Corvaia, continue through town and stop at the 17th-century **St. Giuseppe Church** in Piazza Nove Aprile. As you walk on, be sure to step inside the 13th-century **Cathedral** in the Piazza del Duomo to enjoy the paintings. Farther on you come to the 12th-century **Torre dell'Orologio**, the portal that leads into the oldest and most colorful part of Taormina, **Borgo Medieval**.

Leaving Taormina, follow the A18 south toward Catania. When you reach Catania, take the A19 west in the direction of Palermo, then when the highway splits (not long after passing Enna), instead of continuing north to Palermo, head southwest in the direction of Caltanissetta and Agrigento. After Caltanissetta, the expressway ends and you are on a two-lane road for the final leg of your journey to Agrigento.

Along the route from Taormina to Agrigento, we recommend two excursions. It would make your day too long to include them both, but if you get an early start, you will have enough time to squeeze in one of them.

Suggested Excursion I: If you are a Greek history buff, take this 128-kilometer detour to see one of the wealthiest, most powerful cities of the ancient Greek Empire (rivaling only Athens in importance). When you reach Catania, don't turn west toward Palermo, but continue south, following signs to **Siracusa**, founded in 734 B.C. by the Corinthians. In the **Archaeological Park** at the edge of town are two theaters—a 6th-century B.C. **Greek Theater** (one of the most magnificly preserved in the world) and the ruins of a 2nd-century A.D. **Roman Amphitheater** (one of the largest arenas the Romans ever built). From the Archaeological Park, skip the sprawling modern city and cross the Ponte Nuovo that spans Siracusa's harbor to **Ortygia**, the island where the Greeks first founded Siracusa. Visit the two main squares, the beautiful **Piazza del Duomo** where the cathedral (built upon the ancient temple of Minerva) is located and the **Piazza Archimede** enhanced by a baroque fountain. After sightseeing in Siracusa, return to Catania and take A19 west in the direction of Palermo.

Suggested Excursion II: If you are a Roman history buff, take this 74-kilometer round-trip excursion to visit the Villa of Casale. En route from Taormina to Agrigento on the A19, turn south at Enna to **Piazza Armerina**. Continue southwest beyond Piazza Armerina for 5 kilometers to your sightseeing target, the **Villa of Casale**, rivaling in splendor the home built by Tiberius on the island of Capri. The foundations of this sumptuous Roman villa were hidden under a blanket of mud for 700 years—not discovered by archaeologists until 1950. The fact that this ostentatious villa was built when the Roman Empire was on the verge of financial ruin is all the more fascinating. You cannot help wondering if the obviously vast expense of its construction was indicative of the flamboyant spending style that led to the collapse of the Roman Empire.

Built in the 3rd century A.D., this mansion surely must have belonged to someone of enormous importance—perhaps Emperor Maximilian. The ruins are beautifully displayed in a covered museum with walkways guiding you from one opulent room to the next, each overlooking courtyards. But don't start until you have studied a mockup as you

enter showing an artist's rendering of what the huge villa looked like in its prime—a look at this will increase your appreciation of the incredible grandeur of what you will be seeing. In all, the home covers an area almost three times the size of a football field. The outstanding feature is the 3,500 square meters of mosaics that decorated the floors of this splendid villa. Following the home's foundations are 40 amazing mosaic floors of extraordinary quality. These beautifully preserved ancient Roman mosaics are considered the finest in the world. Slip back almost 1,700 years and imagine what life must have been like: the scenes show hunting expeditions, wild animals, mythical sea creatures, chariot races, cupids fishing, slaves working, girls cavorting. Once you have visited this Roman showplace, return north to Enna, then turn west following the route to Agrigento.

Exploring the Wonders of Sicily

Agrigento is a congested, not very pretty city. We recommend you stay instead outside the heart of the city near the archeological zone. Follow the signs for the **Valle dei Templi**. The name is misleading: the archeological site is actually on a plateau to the west of town—not in a valley at all.

Plan to spend two nights in Agrigento so that you can spend one entire day leisurely seeing the ruins. A wide pedestrian road connects the temples—start at one end and savor the haunting beauty of each. Most of these Doric temples are in ruins, with only enough columns remaining to give you an idea of what they used to be in their glory. The best preserved is the **Temple of Concord** which dates back to 440 B.C. See them all: the **Temple of Juno**, the **Temple of Hercules**, the **Temple of Dioscuri**, the **Temple of Jupiter**, and the **Temple of Castor and Pollux**. The setting is beautiful with the sea in the distance and colorful wildflowers in the surrounding fields. It is a thrill to stroll from one temple to the other, marveling at their grandeur and trying to envision what these incredible structures dedicated to Greek gods looked like 2,000 years ago.

To complement your sightseeing at the temples, take a walk to the **Archaeological Museum**. The museum has a mock-up of the Temple of Jupiter, plus many vases and artifacts from the site.

From Agrigento, continue west on 115 toward Castelvetrano. About 10 kilometers before you arrive in Castelvetrano, turn left onto the 115 dir toward the coast, signposted to Selinunte. For such major ruins, there is little commercialism. You might well miss the main east entrance on the 115 dir—as you drive toward the coast, look for a parking area to the right of the road (if you go under the railroad tracks, you have gone too far).

Park your car in the designated area, buy your ticket, and walk through the tunnel into the enormous field where the remains of the temples of Selinunte lie scattered amongst the wildflowers. In its prime, **Selinunte** was one of the finest cities in Sicily. It met disaster in 407 B.C. when the Carthaginians (it is thought under the command of Hannibal) razed the city, slaughtered 16,000 people, and took thousands into slavery. The giant temples, however, were probably destroyed by earthquake, not by the sword. Here, spread along a huge plateau overlooking the ocean, are the impressive remains of some of the most gigantic temples built by the Greeks. It is staggering to imagine how more than 2,500 years ago they had the skill and technology to lift and piece together these huge blocks of stone weighing over 100 tons each (slaves undoubtedly helped). Of the original seven temples, only one has been reconstructed, but the massive columns lying on the ground indicate the scope and grandeur of what used to be.

From Selinunte, return to the 115, taking the coastal route to Erice. En route, stop for lunch at one of the restaurants along the seafront promenade in **Mazara del Vallo**, an ancient city that was at one time a colony of Selinunte. Browse through the historic center of town to see the beautiful **Piazza della Repubblica** and the **Cathedral**.

The next large town after Mazara del Vallo is **Marsala**, a city well known throughout the world for its excellent wine. Ironically, it was not an Italian, but an Englishman, named John Woodhouse, who experimented by lacing the native wine with an extra bit of alcohol. Based on Woodhouse's formula, Marsala quickly became one of the staples of the British Navy and a special favorite of Lord Nelson. Along the road between Selinunte and Marsala are various wineries that are open to the public. One of the most popular is the **Florio Winery**—one of the three original companies to produce Marsala.

Exploring the Wonders of Sicily

Erice, Sicily

From Marsala, the road heads north to Trapani. Bypass Trapani and head northeast to **Erice**. Positioned over 750 meters above the coast (about 10 kilometers from Trapani), Erice is a delightful medieval walled town, cooled by breezes from the sea. Park your car and walk through the **Porta Trapani** and up the cobbled street. Erice is best discovered by exploring on foot. Narrow cobblestone streets and steep stairways form a maze throughout the town, which is so small that you cannot get lost for long. Just wander, discovering tiny old churches, picturesque squares, characterful stone houses, arcaded passageways, and shops selling the locally produced handmade carpets with colorful geometric designs. Walk to the Castello Normanno, built upon the ruins of the Temple of Venus. From the tower you have a splendid view looking over the town of Trapani and out to the sea.

If you like to get off the beaten path, from Erice drive down to Trapani and take a hydrofoil to the **Egadi Isles,** all less than an hour away. Just a short distance off shore, **Favignana**, the largest of the three islands, was once a great center for tuna. The major cannery was owned by Ignazio Florio (the same Florio who founded the Florio Winery). **Levanzo**, the smallest of the islands, has a very small population due to its lack of fresh water. The island farthest from Trapani, **Maréttimo**, is basically a fishermen's island.

Wind down the hill from Erice and turn left on the A29 going east in the direction of Palermo. Thirty kilometers after getting on the freeway, take the Segesta exit and follow signs for the **Segesta** archaeological site, located close the highway. Although you have seen many ruins by this stage of your holiday in Sicily, don't miss this one—it is special. First drive to the designated parking area and walk up the hillside to visit what most experts believe to be the world's finest example of a **Doric temple**. The temple with 36 columns looks much as it must have in 400 B.C. There is no roof—there never was because this isolated temple to some unknown god was never completed. One of the most superb aspects of this temple is its setting—there is nothing to jar the senses. The temple stands alone in a field of wildflowers with great natural beauty all around. Enjoy the romance of this gem at your leisure, then drive down the hill and park your car by the information center where there is a nice restaurant. Eat lunch here and then walk the marked path to see the Greek Theater. It is about a kilometer away, but a lovely walk through untouched fields. There are so few signs, you'll wonder if you are going the right way and be tempted to verify your destination with a fellow tourist you pass en route. Again, the location is what makes this theater so special. What an eye the Greeks had for beauty: the stage is set in such a way that the spectators look out across the mountains to the sea. The theater is mostly in ruins, but sit on one of the ancient benches, enjoy the beautiful surroundings, and imagine dramas that took place over 2,000 years ago.

Continue to **Palermo**. Palermo is a commercial, traffic-congested city, but there are some very interesting places to see both within the city and on its outskirts.

The most dramatic sightseeing excursion (just 8 kilometers south of Palermo) is to visit **Monreale**, an awesome cathedral built by William II in 1174. It seems that William II was visited in a dream by an angel who told him of a secret treasure, and with his new-found wealth he built Monreale, one of the world's greatest medieval monuments. From the outside, the cathedral doesn't look special, but just wait: the interior is stunning. When you step inside you find 130 panels of shimmering mosaic, illustrating stories from both the Old and the New Testaments. The bronze doors of the cathedral are spectacular, designed by Bonanno Pisano in the 12th century. This is a cathedral not to be missed.

Another sight near Palermo is **Monte Pellegrino**, a 600-meter mountain rising on the west edge of the city. There are several caves in the mountain. The **Grotta di Addaura** is a three-chamber cave with carvings dating to the Paleolithic Age. Another cave has been transformed into a chapel, the **Sanctuary of Santa Rosalia**, commemorating Santa Rosalia, the niece of King William II, who became a hermit—living and dying in this cave. You need to obtain permission from the National Archaeological Museum in Palermo if you want to visit these caves.

Another recommended side trip from Palermo is to visit the ancient fishing village of **Cefalù** built on a rocky peninsula about an hour's drive east from Palermo. Not only is this a very colorful fishing village, complete with brightly-hued boats and twisting narrow streets, but there is also a splendid Norman **Cathedral** built by King Roger II in the 12th century in fulfillment of a promise he made to God for sparing his life during a storm at sea.

From Palermo you can take one of the many flights to Rome, board a ferry to Naples, or complete your circle of Sicily by driving to Messina for the short ferry ride back to the mainland.

Taormina, Greek Theater

Hotel Descriptions

The Castel di Luco is an imposing medieval fortress whose history goes back to at least 1052. This incredibly well-preserved castle, crowning the top of a small hill in the countryside near Aquasanta Terme, has passed down for five centuries in the same family. The Amici family continues to live in the fortress, but part has been converted into a stunning restaurant where guests dine in medieval vaulted halls enriched by original frescoes. Diners climb an ancient stairway carved into the rock to enjoy romantic meals by candlelight featuring regional cuisine prepared by Sra Amici and her daughter, Laura. This is totally a family operation and Laura and her gracious brother Francesco have poured their hearts and souls into expanding the family business by converting two stone houses in the small hamlet at the base of the castle into a tiny hotel. The four suites all have brick floors, stone walls, beamed ceilings, a small sitting room, a separate bedroom, and a very modern bathroom. The decor is simple as befits the rustic nature of the stone buildings, but they are all very tastefully furnished, have every modern comfort, and feature pretty antique beds in all the bedrooms. My favorite, Elena, has a wonderful large terrace with a beautiful view up onto the hills. The Castel di Luco is a great base for sightseeing and for exploring the beautiful adjacent National Park of the Gran Sasso. *Directions:* Ask for detailed instructions.

CASTEL DI LUCO
Owners: Laura & Francesco Amici
Località Castel di Luco
Acquasanta Terme, (AP) 63041, Italy
Tel & Fax: (0736) 80 23 19
4 Suites: €155
Restaurant closed Sun & Mon
Open: all year, Credit cards: all major
4 km SE of Acquasanta, 157 km NW of Rome
Region: Marches, Michelin Map: 563

We were delighted when one of our favorite hotels in Agrigento, the Foresteria Baglio della Luna, opened a second property, the Hotel Domus Aurea, located just 350 meters away. Most places to stay in Agrigento are in the city center and quite bland. The prime location for accommodation is to be as close as possible to the archaeological park. Although not within walking distance, the new Hotel Domus Aurea is actually within the territory of the land site, and has been transformed from a private noble residence dating from 1781. The stately yellow villa with a front-side fountain is surrounded by Mediterranean gardens and has a distant view of the Valley of the Temples. The décor within maintains the ambiance of an elegant private home with all modern amenities. A variety of superior, deluxe, and junior suites are appointed in classic style with marble floors and impeccable bathrooms. Bedrooms are divided between two floors with the last two located up on the rooftop surrounded by a large terrace. Common rooms with period paintings and antiques include a comfortable English-style lounge, a breakfast room, and an outdoor terrace. Dinner is served at the nearby "Il Dehor" restaurant located in their sister hotel, Baglio della Luna. *Directions:* Take the S.S. 115 from Menfi to Agrigento. At Porto Emedocle, bear left at the fork towards Siracusa. After 3.5 km, exit after the underpass and turn right. The hotel is on the right-hand side of the road.

※ ■ ✄ 💳 ☎ 🏠 ♨ @ 🍸 P 🚭 🖼 ♿ ⚓

HOTEL DOMUS AUREA
Manager: Ignazio Altieri
C. da Maddalusa S.S. 640, Km 4
150, Valle dei Templi
Agrigento, (AG) 92100, Italy
Tel: (0922) 51 15 00, Fax: (0922) 51 24 06
20 Rooms, Double: €180–€300
Open: all year, Credit cards: MC, VS
127 km SE of Palermo, 212 km SW of Taormina
Region: Sicily, Michelin Map: 565

The Foresteria Baglio della Luna is a charming hotel within a few minutes' drive of Agrigento's jewel—the Valley of the Temples. The oldest part of the complex is a 13th-century square tower. Later, more buildings were added, and in the 18th century the property became a private countryside estate, which today has been cleverly converted into an appealing inn. You enter from a quiet lane through high walls into an attractive inner courtyard with an ancient well in the center. At the far end of the courtyard a doorway through the stone wall leads down to beautiful terraced gardens. The spacious, deluxe suites (all with Jacuzzi tubs) are located in the tower, but even the standard guestrooms are very comfortable and prettily furnished with antique headboards, tiled floors, handmade rugs, and attractive, color-coordinated fabrics on the drapes and bedspreads. Along one side of the courtyard are the public rooms: a cozy bar, a pretty lounge with lots of paintings on the walls and comfortable leather sofas, and the restaurant, which specializes in regional Sicilian and Italian dishes. The attractive, formal restaurant is one of the best in Sicily, managed by chef Damian Ferraro. The restaurant opens onto one of the most outstanding features of this intimate hotel—a delightful indoor-outdoor dining room with walls of glass that fold back completely so that the room is totally open to the cool breezes.

❄ ☕ ⚗ ☕ CREDIT 🐕 @ 🍷 P 🍴 🚭 ⊙ 🛋 ♿ ⚓ 🦯 🍇

FORESTERIA BAGLIO DELLA LUNA
Manager: Ignazio Altieri
Contrada Maddalusa-Valle dei Templi
Agrigento, Sicily, (AG) 92100, Italy
Tel: (0922) 51 10 61, Fax: (0922) 59 88 02
24 Rooms, Double: €200–€400
Open: all year, Credit cards: all major
128 km SE of Palermo, 212 km SW of Taormina
Region: Sicily, Michelin Map: 565

There is a fascinating area in southeastern Italy with a collection of strange round white buildings with gray-stone conical-shaped roofs. These ancient houses, which seem to be left over from some Moorish tribe that must have inhabited this part of Italy long ago, are called Trulli and are usually seen in groups of two or three throughout the countryside. In the town of Alberobello you will discover a whole village of these whimsical little houses whose jumble of domed roofs, whitewashed walls, and crooked little chimneys creates a most unusual sight. Be sure to stroll through the pedestrian zone of Alberobello, which oozes charm. Fortunately there is a good hotel in the area that is located within walking distance of the center of the Trulli village. Not only is its location excellent, but the hotel captures the mood of the area since it is constructed within some of the Trulli houses. Small bungalows are scattered around a large park-like area connected by winding pathways under the pine trees. Each bungalow is a suite with a living room with fireplace, one or more bedrooms, and a private patio. The suites are spacious and have attractively tiled bathrooms. The dining rooms and the reception area each occupy their own Trulli. Within the grounds are a pool and children's play yard. If you are on your way to Greece, you will find the Hotel dei Trulli a convenient choice: very close to Brindisi and Bari, the two major ferry ports.

HOTEL DEI TRULLI
Manager: Luigi Farace
Via Cadore, 32
Alberobello, (BA) 70011, Italy
Tel: (080) 43 23 555, Fax: (080) 43 23 560
32 Rooms, Double: €200–€220*
*Includes breakfast & dinner
Open: all year, Credit cards: all major
68 km NW of Brindisi, 55 km SW of Bari
Region: Apulia, Michelin Map: 564

In Amalfi, we highly recommend the luxurious Hotel Santa Caterina. However, if you are looking for a more modestly priced place to stay, the Hotel Marina Riviera is an excellent, alternate choice. Although a simpler hotel, it also offers exceptional warmth of hospitality and a high level of comfort. This is not surprising when you know that Giusi Gargano is also part owner (along with her sister) of the Hotel Santa Caterina. The Hotel Marina Riviera, an old noble villa that has been in the Gargano family for many years, has been tastefully renovated and walls opened to create spacious, bright, and airy rooms. An elevator, or a staircase, leads up one floor from the street to the lounge that opens onto a terrace with a splendid view of the harbor and the colorful town of Amalfi, an easy walk from the hotel. The bedrooms are all pleasantly decorated in color-coordinated fabrics and have modern bathrooms, some with Jacuzzi tubs. All of the bedrooms look out to the harbor; the more expensive ones are larger and have the best views. A bountiful buffet breakfast is served each morning. There is no restaurant, but this is not a problem since on the street level just below the hotel, there is an excellent place to dine, the Ristorante Eolo, owned by the Garganos' talented daughter. The hotel has a unique rooftop sun deck for guests to enjoy. The hotel has an arrangement with a garage in town. *Directions:* Located on the main road, on the south end of town.

✳ ☕ 🍽 💳 ☎ 👥 🍸 P 🚭 👨‍👩‍👧 🐾 ♿ ⚓

HOTEL MARINA RIVIERA
Owners: Giusi & Antonio Gargano
Via Pantaleone Comite, 19
Amalfi, (SA) 84011, Italy
Tel: (089) 87 11 04, Fax: (089) 87 10 24
32 Rooms, Double: €210–€550
Open: Easter to Nov, Credit cards: all major
69 km S of Naples, 24 km N of Salerno
Region: Campania, Michelin Map: 564

The choice place to stay in Amalfi is the deluxe Hotel Santa Caterina. It is not in the town center, but since Amalfi has the main highway separating it from the sea, the hotel has a far superior setting—just to the north of town on a cliff rising above the blue Mediterranean. Although larger than most hotels in our guide, the Santa Caterina has the intimacy and warmth of a small hotel. Since 1880 the property has belonged to the Gambardella family who has imbued in their excellent staff the art of making each guest feel special and with over 100 staff members for 62 rooms, you can understand how everyone is properly pampered. The hotel terraces down the hill from the highway to the sea where you find a large saltwater swimming pool. Guestrooms, all individual in decor, are charming, with whitewashed walls, antique furniture accents, and colorful, local, handmade tiles on the floors and in the bathrooms. Many rooms have a balcony with a view to the sea. The main dining room is cheerful, with coved ceiling and sunlight streaming in through walls of glass. However, most guests choose to dine outside on the bougainvillea-bedecked terrace. On a terrace above the pool is a second outdoor restaurant where lunch is served. Almost all of the fruits and vegetables used in the restaurant are freshly gathered from the hotel's own gardens. If you want to splurge, there are several cottages tucked in amongst the lemon orchards.

HOTEL SANTA CATERINA
Owner: Gambardella family
S.S. Amalfitana, 9
Amalfi, (SA) 84011, Italy
Tel: (089) 87 10 12, Fax: (089) 87 13 51
62 Rooms, Double: €430–€1450
Open: all year, Credit cards: all major
69 km S of Naples, 24 km N of Salerno
Region: Campania, Michelin Map: 564

Named for its position between the two Roman lakes of Bracciano and Martignano, I Due Laghi was born 13 years ago with all the characteristics of an agritourism farm—and has remained the only one around Lake Bracciano. It has developed over time into more of a country hotel with all the service and upgraded amenities of a four-star establishment, yet conserves the informal, rustic flavor of a ranch. On 375 acres of cultivated fields and woods, horses and cattle graze and sports activities take center stage, from riding (even drag hunts) and biking to swimming in the pool. In addition, you can enjoy two nearby golf courses, tennis courts, and lake sailing. Its close proximity to Rome and surrounding Etruscan towns makes it a relaxing and peaceful haven for travelers. The equestrian theme prevails in the bar and lounge area and there is a large restaurant, La Posta de Cavalieri, which has received a Veronelli rating. Matteo and his staff are very attentive to guests' needs and are thorough believers in the beauty that the area offers the more adventurous guest. Bedrooms, rather standard in decor, are all off one wing of the main house with suites that have separate garden entrances. The hotel is an easy 40-minute train ride from Rome. *Directions:* From Rome leave the GRA ring road at exit 5-Cassia Bis and follow it to the Bracciano-Anguillara exit left. Turn left again at the lake and follow signs to I Due Laghi. 49 km from the airport.

COUNTRY RELAIS I DUE LAGHI
Owner: Alba Cella
Via della Marmotta
Anguillara Sabazia, (RM) 00061, Italy
Tel: (06) 99 60 70 59, Fax: (06) 99 60 70 68
24 Rooms, Double: €170
7 Suites: €290
Open: all year, Credit cards: all major
39 km NW of Rome
Region: Lazio, Michelin Map: 563

For those yearning to take a closer look at the architectural marvels of 14th-century master Andrea Palladio, among other treasures of the Veneto region, the Villa Michelangelo could not be a more idyllic base. Scenically positioned in the Berici Hills surrounding historic Vicenza, this very appealing countryside retreat allows easy access to the 23 Palladian palazzos within the city plus 16 country villas scattered about the province. Formerly an 18th-century private residence, the extensive L-shaped main building includes a dining room with outdoor porticos serving excellent regional specialties. The very comfortable bedrooms and suites, with many amenities, are classically appointed in soft-peach or celestial-blue hues. Some have beamed ceilings and others have delightfully soothing views over an expansive manicured lawn bordered by a stone wall and balustrade up to the wooded hillsides. A cleverly designed indoor/outdoor pool, tucked below the lawn level, looks out over this same stunning panorama. Impeccably kept grounds add much to the overall peaceful and romantic ambiance. Attractions abound, including golf, concerts and local festivals, wine estates, jewelry and silversmith artisans, and medieval villages to explore. *Directions:* Exit the A4 at Vicenza Ovest and at the rotunda turn right. At the stop sign head for Arcugnano and continue up through the town. Turn right at the hotel sign onto a narrow road.

VILLA MICHELANGELO
Owner: Alessandra Dalla Fontana
Via Sacco, 35
Arcugnano, (VI) 36057, Italy
Tel: (0444) 55 03 00, Fax: (0444) 55 04 90
52 Rooms, Double: €200–€250
Open: all year, Credit cards: all major
4 km S of Vicenza, 60 km W of Venice
Region: Veneto, Michelin Map: 562

If you've ever dreamed of waking up in an Italian villa and throwing open your shutters to a breathtaking view, the Albergo Villa Belvedere will surely capture your heart. This enticing 18th-century villa with mustard-yellow façade, crisp-white trim, and dove-gray shutters has a superb setting. Only a private terrace separates it from Lake Como. This intimate inn is an incredible value—but do not expect a luxury hotel: the furnishings are simple. (Since we first visited the Villa Belvedere many years ago it has been constantly upgraded.) What you get is much more: an incomparable setting, great warmth of welcome, and old-fashioned comfort enhanced by faultless housekeeping. What makes Villa Belvedere so outstanding is the Cappelletti family's genuine hospitality. Jane Cappelletti (born in Scotland) met and fell in love with her husband, Giorgio when visiting Italy. Sadly, Giorgio passed away in 2004. He is greatly missed by all who knew him and loved his warmth and happy disposition. Jane continues to run the small hotel, ably assisted by her charming, efficient daughter, Michela. The Villa Belvedere is steps from the dock, where you can board a ferry to explore beautiful Lake Como with its clusters of romantic villages. Splurge on a lakefront room (such as 7 or 15)—these are quieter with spectacular vistas. *Directions:* Take A9 north from Milan and exit at Como Nord. Take N340 north toward Menággio—after about 15 km you come to Argegno.

ALBERGO VILLA BELVEDERE   ***Cover painting***
Owner: Jane Cappelletti
Via Milano, 8
Argegno, Lake Como, (CO) 22010, Italy
Tel: (031) 82 11 16, Fax: (031) 82 15 71
16 Rooms, Double: €230*
*Includes breakfast & dinner
Open: mid-Mar to mid-Nov, Credit cards: MC, VS
65 km N of Milan, 20 km N of Como
Region: Lombardy, Michelin Map: 561

The ancient city of Ascoli Piceno, with an idyllic setting between hillside and sea, comes as a pleasant surprise to the traveler in exploration of Italy's lesser known treasures. The city center still preserves examples of Romanic, Gothic, Renaissance and Baroque periods, sometimes mixed together in layers of history. The Palazzo Giuderocchi is an excellent choice from which to tour the lower half the Marches and parts of Abruzzo. Twenty-three well-furnished rooms with original antiques are spread about the upper two floors of the historic palace, while the remaining nine are situated in another residence of aristocratic origins around the corner and on the main square of the city. Bedrooms vary in size and décor with fabrics in celestial blues, yellow or peach tones, many enhanced by lovely views over the picturesque rooftops of the nearby historic palazzos. The authentic original atmosphere is generated from the brick and wood beamed ceilings, terra cotta floors, and magnificent frescoed ceilings in main rooms. The hotel has its own restaurant, the Rua dei Notari, which is light and airy with vaulted ceilings and opens to an inner courtyard. A very pleasant surprise for location, service, comfort, and rate. *Directions:* From Rome on the A24, exit at Teramo, follow signs for Teramo Centro and reach Piazza Garibaldi; turn right in Viale Bovio S.S.81. After 40 km follow signs for A14, turn towards Roma. Exit at Ascoli Porta Cartara. Turn left and follow to city center.

PALAZZO GUIDEROCCHI
Manager: Danilo Di Pasquale
Via Cesare Battisti 3
Ascoli Piceno, (AP) 63100, Italy
Tel: (0736) 24 40 11, Fax: (0736) 24 34 41
32 Rooms, Double: €99–€399
Open: all year, Credit cards: all major
Historic Center of city
Region: Marches, Michelin Map: 563

Asolo, a jewel of a village tucked into hills northwest of Venice, is one of Italy's best-kept secrets. While once again exploring this magical town, we looked up from the main square and saw the pretty mustard-yellow Albergo al Sole nestled on the hill above us. Albergo al Sole has a wonderful location in this very special town, with its famous Palladian villas and world reputation for the production of wonderful wines. With excellent quality and pretty furnishings throughout, the Albergo al Sole is a terrific value. The guestrooms are spacious and decorated appealingly. The bathrooms too are exceptionally large and prettily tiled. All the rooms have satellite LCD TV and mini-bar. If you are on a budget, even the least expensive rooms are very lovely, although they do not have the same village view as the more expensive rooms. If you are looking for a truly special room, you need not splurge on a suite, but rather ask for a deluxe double. Our favorite, the Eleonora Duse, is a very pretty corner room decorated with antiques and with large windows overlooking Asolo. The entire hotel follows a basic color scheme that combines the cheerful colors of pretty pinks and yellows. The hotel has a wonderful informal terrace restaurant "La Terrazza" with a panoramic view overlooking the town of Asolo. Ask about the gourmet dinners in the exclusive 16th century "Cave of Bacco." The hotel also offers cooking classes, a fitness center, and massages.

❄ ☕ ✂ ☕ 💳 🏠 🛗 🏋 @ W Ⓨ P 🍴 🚭 🌸 🖼 ♿ 🎿 🏃 🏇 🍇

ALBERGO AL SOLE
Manager: Silvia De Checchi
Via Collegio, 33
Asolo, (TV) 31011, Italy
Tel: (0423) 95 13 32, Fax: (0423) 95 10 07
22 Rooms, Double: €145–€285
1 Suite: €240–€280
Open: all year, Credit cards: all major
65 km NW of Venice, 14 km E of Bassano
Region: Veneto, Michelin Map: 562

Asolo is a beautiful medieval town in the low-lying hills northwest of Venice, dominated by castle ruins on the hillside above and filled with charming streets, Gothic arcades, and frescoed façades. Here in this magical town one of our favorite hotels in Italy, the Villa Cipriani, is secreted in a garden just a short stroll from the center of the village. However, since the price tag at the Cipriani does not fit everyone's budget, for those who do not want to splurge on accommodations, a good alternative choice is the Hotel Duse. Its location is superb—right in the very heart of Asolo, surrounded by quaint streets lined with elegant shops. There is a tiny reception lobby leading up to freshly renovated guestrooms. Although small, each room is attractively decorated with a cozy provincial charm. The decor is similar throughout, with nicely framed prints over the beds, a pretty ribbon tied in a bow accenting the frame. The fabric matches the shades on the reading lamps. The cozy mood prevails in each room—only the color scheme varies. Although the rooms are very reasonably priced, they all offer air conditioning, satellite television, direct-dial phone, Internet connection, mini-bar, and a spotlessly clean bathroom. The hotel has changed hands since our last visit.

❄ ✎ 💳 ☎ 🛗 @ ⅄ P 🍴 🚭 🖼 🚶 🏃 🐎 🎿 ⛷ 🍇

HOTEL DUSE
Manager: Alessandro Zavattiero
Via Browning, 190
Asolo, (TV) 31011, Italy
Tel: (0423) 55 24 1, Fax: (0423) 98 04 04
*14 Rooms, Double: €100–€130**
**Breakfast not included: €8*
Open: all year, Credit cards: all major
65 km NW of Venice, 14 km E of Bassano
Region: Veneto, Michelin Map: 562

The Villa Cipriani is just as I had envisioned in every dream of Italy: an old villa snuggled on a hill, her softly faded exterior emphasized by dark-green shutters, masses of roses creeping over trellises, columns adorned with vines, lazy views over rolling green hills, faded ochre-colored walls half-hidden by tall cypress trees dotting nearby hilltops, birds singing in the garden, the sentimental rhythmical peal of church bells, a pianist on the terrace playing old love songs, the fragrance of flowers drifting through the air like the finest perfume—perfection. My impression of a romantic paradise must not have been a unique experience for in the garden was a wedding party. A beautiful bride, a handsome groom, they had fallen in love at the Cipriani and had returned with family and friends from the United States for their marriage. The Villa Cipriani is located in Asolo, a charming, small, medieval walled hilltown less than two hours northwest of Venice which has an atmosphere so delightful that Robert Browning chose it as a residence. And the home he chose? The Cipriani. Luckily, his home is now a hotel and you, too, can live for a while in Asolo. Although the Villa Cipriani is a sophisticated, polished hotel, the warmth of reception is as gracious as in a small, family-run inn: all the guests are properly pampered.

VILLA CIPRIANI
Manager: Mr. Silver Carpanese
Via Canova, 298
Asolo, (TV) 31011, Italy
Tel: (0423) 52 34 11, Fax: (0423) 95 20 95
31 Rooms, Double: €307–€470
Open: all year, Credit cards: all major
65 km NW of Venice, 14 km E of Bassano
Region: Veneto, Michelin Map: 562

A reader highly recommended La Fortezza, saying that it was a wonderful bargain and that he enjoyed the best meal of his entire trip there. We too were immediately captivated by this simple, charming place to stay in the center of Assisi. The restaurant seems to be the star attraction, with Guglielmo Chiocchetti in the kitchen cooking while his wife, Tina, takes care of the many dinner guests. Their two wonderful sons, Luca and Lorenzo, are also totally involved in this family operation, helping out wherever needed, assisted by Luca's pretty wife who was serving the day we stopped by. Without a doubt, it is the gentle, caring Chiocchetti family with their exceptional warmth that makes La Fortezza so special. Their restaurant's superior food features many Umbrian dishes, served in a cozy dining room with vaulted stone ceiling and wooden chairs painted a cheerful red. The guestrooms, which are an outstanding value, are located on two floors above the restaurant. Although not large, each is spotlessly clean and very tastefully decorated in a simple, country style. The choice bedroom even has its own little terrace. The hotel is hidden up a lane of stone steps at the northeast corner of the Piazza del Comune. There are lots of steps getting to the hotel, but then this is true throughout Assisi, which seems pasted to the side of the hillside. Just remember, bring a small suitcase. Closest parking: Piazza Matteotti.

LA FORTEZZA
Owner: Chiocchetti family
Above NE corner of Piazza del Comune
Assisi, (PG) 06081, Italy
Tel: (075) 81 24 18, Fax: (075) 81 98 035
7 Rooms, Double: €65
Restaurant closed Thursdays
Closed: Feb, Credit cards: all major
117 km N of Rome, 26 km E of Perugia
Region: Umbria, Michelin Map: 563

Il Palazzo, a three-star hotel in the heart of Assisi, offers surprisingly attractive accommodations for a modest price. Built in the 1500s as a palace for the prosperous Bindangoli-Bartocci family, its foundations date back even further. Amazingly, the hotel is still owned by Bartocci descendants. Indications of the palace's rich heritage can still be seen in the many important oil paintings and 18th-century tempera mythical scenes. As you enter off the street there is a simple reception area. Beyond is a large, beamed-ceilinged living room with comfortable sitting areas. The right wing of the palace has been turned into a restaurant serving local dishes. A buffet breakfast is served on the main level. To reach the bedrooms, you walk out into a central courtyard and then up an exterior steel staircase. I assure you the climb is worthwhile because once you throw open the shutters of your bedroom, you are treated to a stunning panorama of the Umbrian countryside. Definitely splurge—request one of the superior bedrooms, all very spacious and attractively furnished with appealing antiques. One of my favorites, 204, has twin beds with pretty, painted iron headboards. Room 203, a corner room, is also a real winner with a canopy bed—it would be my first choice except that the bathroom is not very large. As with all the hotels in Assisi, take just a small overnight suitcase. Closest parking: Piazza San Francesco.

IL PALAZZO
Manager: Arianna Bartocci Fontana
Via San Francesco, 8
Assisi, (PG) 06081, Italy
Tel: (075) 81 68 41, Fax: (075) 81 23 70
11 Rooms, Double: €100–€140*
1 Suite: €120–€160*
*Dinner by prior request
Closed: mid-Jan to mid-Mar, Credit cards: all major
177 km N of Rome, 26 km E of Perugia
Region: Umbria, Michelin Map: 563

Assisi is one of our favorite places to stay and our guide can never recommend enough hotels here, so we were delighted to find the Residenza d'Epoca San Crispino, a fabulous, enchanting new hotel. Dating back to the 14th century when it was a religious site for the order of San Crispino, the hotel has been tenderly restored to maintain its rich heritage while adding every comfort for the 21st century. Almost all of the furnishings are beautiful antiques previously used in a nunnery. Throughout this tiny inn you find simple, uncluttered, tasteful decor with white walls, stone floors, crisp white embroidered curtains, bouquets of fresh flowers, and handsome antiques. The mood is set as you enter through very old double doors into a courtyard, bound on one side by the small, 5th-century church of San Biagio. From the courtyard, steps lead up to the foyer where the reception desk is an antique confessional. Accommodations are all suites, varying in size from a studio to a two-bedroom, two-bath apartment. Every room has an armoire, which conceals a small refrigerator, minibar, espresso machine, hot plate, dishes, and utensils for preparing light snacks. Laundry service is available upon request. Each room is a dream, but my very favorite is The Moon and The Stars, which not only has a lovely view, but also its own huge private garden. This small hotel is really special and a marvelous value.

RESIDENZA D'EPOCA SAN CRISPINO
Manager: Ilaria Cocco
Via San Agnese, 11
Assisi, (PG) 06081, Italy
Tel & Fax: (075) 81 55 124
7 Rooms, Double: €140–€310
Open: all year, Credit cards: all major
177 km N of Rome, 26 km E of Perugia
Region: Umbria, Michelin Map: 563

For a moderately priced place to stay in the heart of Assisi, the Hotel Umbra is an unbeatable choice. The hotel is located just a few steps down a narrow little alley that leads off the Piazza del Comune, one of the central plazas in town. The entrance is through wrought-iron gates that open to a tiny patio where you are treated to an idyllic oasis with tables set under a trellis covered by vines creating a lacy pattern of shadows. There is a lovely view from this intimate terrace. After passing through the patio, you enter into a lounge/reception area with doors opening into the dining room where very good meals are served. The public rooms have accents of antiques, but have a homey rather than grand ambiance. Steps lead to the simple bedrooms, which are individually decorated and very pleasant. Splurge and ask for a room (such as 34) with a panoramic vista of the Umbrian valley. However, do not be disappointed if one is not available—the rooms (such as 35) overlooking the jumble of tiled roofs are also very nice. If you like small, family-run hotels that are not decorator-perfect in every detail, but offer great heart and hospitality, the Hotel Umbra is an excellent choice. The delightful Alberto Laudenzi family oversees every detail of this small inn and makes guests feel at home. The staff too is extremely gracious and accommodating. The location is absolutely perfect.

❄ ☕ ✂ ♨▭ ☎ @ W ￥ ⑪ 🏃 👫 🍇

HOTEL UMBRA
Owner: Alberto Laudenzi family
Via Degli Archi, 6-Piazza del Comune
Assisi, (PG) 06081, Italy
Tel: (075) 81 22 40, Fax: (075) 81 36 53
24 Rooms, Double: €100–€125
Restaurant closed Sundays
Closed: mid-Jan to mid-Mar, Credit cards: all major
26 km E of Perugia, 177 N of Rome
Region: Umbria, Michelin Map: 563

As the road twists and turns ever further into the wooded hills above Assisi, one can't help wondering what treasure awaits at the trail's end, or if anyone could possibly have found this romantic hideaway before you. What a surprise then to finally turn off the graveled road and discover the parking lot filled with luxury cars. In this glorious hillside setting with its sweeping panorama of wooded hills, worldly cares quickly melt away. Although the hotel is built into a cluster of 10th-century stone houses, all the modern-day luxuries are present including a beautiful swimming pool on the right as you enter and, on a lower terrace, tennis courts. Behind the main building is a separate stone house where you find a most appealing lounge with deep-green sofas and chairs grouped around a giant fireplace. Doors from the lounge lead into an intimate little bar and beyond to a dining room with honey-colored stone walls, beamed ceiling, and terracotta floors with tables dressed in the finest of linens. Marvelous meals are served, prepared almost totally from ingredients from the hotel's own farm, which is part of the property. The individually decorated bedrooms sport a rustic, yet elegant, ambiance. The hotel is located 10 km outside of Assisi in the charming village of Armenzano. *Directions:* From Assisi follow signs toward Gualdo-Tadino and as you leave the town walls of Assisi take the road to the right signposted Armenzano. From Armenzano, the hotel is well marked.

ROMANTIK HOTEL LE SILVE DI ARMENZANO
Owner: Marco Sirignani family
Assisi–Armenzano, (PG) 06081, Italy
Tel: (075) 80 19 000, Fax: (075) 80 19 005
21 Rooms, Double: €180–€220
13 Apartments: €600 weekly
Open: Mar to mid-Nov, Credit cards: all major
Romantik Hotels
10 km E of Assisi
Region: Umbria, Michelin Map: 563

If you are flying into or out of Milan, the Locanda dei Mai Intees, a charming, family-run hotel with wonderful, traditional Italian cooking, about half an hour's drive north of Malpensa Airport, makes a delightful choice for a place to spend the night. This small inn is managed by your charming host, Paolo Crosta, whose gracious mother, Carla, oversees the kitchen. Azzate, a town near Lake Varese, seems characterless from the outskirts, but at its historic heart you find a cluster of medieval buildings, including the Locanda dei Mai Intees. The hotel used to be several separate buildings and what was once the village square is now the hotel's courtyard where meals are served in warm weather. On chilly evenings, dinner is served in one of several cozy dining rooms warmed by a roaring fire, where tables are beautifully set with fine linens. The original stone staircase leads up to guestrooms decorated with personal photographs, paintings, and antique furnishings. My favorite, Carla, a larger corner room, has windows on two sides, while Juliet has a cute carved wooden balcony. No matter what room you choose, you will be charmed by the warmth of the Crosta family, who welcome guests as friends. *Directions:* From Malpensa Airport, head north on A8 toward Varese. Exit at Azzate. Do not turn at the Azzate sign, but continue for 3 km and go left at the roundabout. Go 300 meters, turn left at the roundabout, and continue for 200 meters to the hotel.

❄ ☕ ✄ CREDIT ☎ Y ¶ 🕴

HOTEL LOCANDA DEI MAI INTEES
Manager: Paolo Crosta
Via Monte Grappa, 22
Azzate, (VA) 21022, Italy
Tel: (0332) 45 72 23, Fax: (0332) 45 93 39
13 Rooms, Double: €185–€250
Restaurant closed Mondays
Open: all year, Credit cards: all major
Abitare La Storia
54 km NW of Milan, 30 km W of Como
Region: Lombardy, Michelin Map: 561

The Grand Hotel Terme di Stigliano, which opened in 2006 just north of Rome, has the unique feature of having its own ancient thermal waters running right through the 60-acre property. Abundant evidence of having been an important Roman bath center has been found, including an underground natural vapor cave, one of nine sources of the therapeutic waters. The Gargallo family had the large ex-hotel completely refurbished and have re-created a haven for weary travelers. Immersed in a wooded, hilly park complete with two small babbling rivers, the hotel offers a wellness center offering a complete line of treatments. There is also an outdoor swimming pool, sauna, and a hydro jet pool with thermal waters. Some of the 50 similarly appointed bedrooms in the main house have a terrace, and all enjoy pure, unspoiled landscapes—thanks to the surrounding Park Reserves. French Jouy bedspreads and curtains in yellow or blue accent otherwise plain rooms. The rooms on the top floor have wood beamed mansard ceilings. All the paintings, lighting decorations, and trompe d'oeil work on door frames have been done by the owner and her daughter. The Ninfeo restaurant serves traditional Italian fare. *Directions:* From Rome take the CASSIA S2 towards Viterbo and exit Bracciano. Pass through Lake Bracciano, Manziana and proceed to Canale Monterano. Before town turn left for Bagni di Stigliano.

GRAND HOTEL TERME DI STIGLIANO
Owner: Marchesi Gargallo family
Via Bagni di Stigliano
Casale Monterano
Bagni di Stigliano, (RM) 00060, Italy
Tel: (06) 99 67 49 10, Fax: (06) 99 63 428
52 Rooms, Double: €280–€350
Open: all year, Credit cards: all major
53 km NW of Rome
Region: Lazio, Michelin Map: 563

The recently-restored Villa Olmi, located on the outskirts of Florence, offers three types of luxury accommodations: suites within an historic villa, standard rooms in the former farmhouse, or two fully-equipped spacious apartments. Set on a flat 15-acre property facing distant hills, the 700-year-old villa, farmhouses, barns and surrounding land once belonged to a prosperous Florentine family. The more commercial "Fattoria" building holds 38 new bedrooms with marble bathrooms, reception and lounge areas, a breakfast veranda overlooking the orchards to the pool, and the restaurant, "Il Cavaliere", where the chef creates fine Tuscan cuisine. A vaulted brick wine cellar offers wine-tasting from an extensive list. The 18th century villa however steals the spotlight—flaunting 12 luxuriously appointed suites all joined by a grand salon adorned with enormous Murano chandeliers. A laborious restoration project, under the regulations of the National Art Preservation Ministry, brought to light the splendid pastel-colored frescoes on walls and ceilings, which compliment selective antiques, canopy beds and sumptuous fabrics in the exclusive suites. Many personalized services are arranged by the courteous staff. The advantageous location of the complex allows easy touring of the Chianti area as well as Florence (complimentary shuttle service provided to and from the city center). *Directions:* Exit Firenze Sud from the A1 and follow signs for Bagno di Ripoli and the hotel.

VILLA OLMI
Manager: Enzo Cadirni
Via degli Olmi 4/8, Bagno a Ripoli, (FI) 50012, Italy
Tel: (055) 63 77 10, Fax: (055) 63 77 16 00
50 Rooms, Double: €330–€1300*
3 Suites: €1600–€2100*
2 Apartments: €1600 daily*, €8000 weekly*
*Breakfast not included: €30
Open: all year, Credit cards: all major
8 km from city center
Region: Tuscany, Michelin Map: 563

The Villa Ca'Sette is a refreshingly stylish accommodation with a friendly staff, set in a typical 18th-century Veneto villa, once a private summer home to nobility. Well known since the '50s for its excellent Michelin-star restaurant, it was completely refurbished as a hotel in 2001. Cleverly combining modern design with antique touches, guestrooms are divided among the main villa and the adjacent "barchessa." Upstairs in the more classic villa with frescoes and antiques is the sitting area off which is two double bedrooms and a grand suite, and can be rented as a separate apartment. Besides a convenient two-level family suite, there are another 14 clean and contemporary-style beamed bedrooms, which harmonize well with natural materials such as wood and stone. The sleek bathrooms with rain showers are created in varying shades of marble and travertine. The light and airy, elegant restaurant on the ground floor, with large windows looking over the garden, serves produce of the season and local meats and fish, each dish presented as a work of art. At the foot of the Dolomites, the charming ancient town of Bassano is an hour from Venice, and near Asolo, Marostica, Padova, Vicenza, and Verona. *Directions:* From Padova, drive north to Bassano and at Rosà exit for the encircling highway around Bassano. Leave at the second Romano d'Ezzelino exit towards Bassano city. The hotel is on the left side 1 km before town.

❄ ☕ 🏃 ☕ 💳 ☎ 🏠 🚻 @ W Ⓨ P 🍴 🚭 🖼 🔔 ♿ ⚓ 🚶 👫 🏇 ⛷ 🍇

HOTEL VILLA CA'SETTE
Owner: Renzo Zonta
Via Cunizza da Romano, 4
Bassano del Grappa, (VI) 36061, Italy
Tel: (0424) 38 33 50, Fax: (0424) 39 32 87
19 Rooms, Double: €180–€230
2 Suites: €300–€500
Open: all year, Credit cards: all major
1 km N of Bassano del Grappa, 76 km N of Venice
Region: Veneto, Michelin Map: 562

If you want to feel like a guest of royalty, shamelessly pampered and enveloped in the lap of luxury, make a reservation at the Villa Dal Pozzo d'Annone. Nestled on a hillside across the road from Lake Maggiore, this splendid mansion offers incredible, sweeping lake and mountain views. Here you will be warmly welcomed as a guest, for this is the private home of the Marchesi Dal Pozzo d'Annone, a member of one of Italy's oldest, most prestigious families, and while many gorgeous properties have been made into deluxe hotels, here you will find that nothing feels contrived. Everything is absolutely authentic, with exquisite antique furniture (some dating back to the 15th century) placed as it has been for generations, museum-quality portraits adorning the walls, and family treasures displayed on desks and tables. There are six large, elegantly furnished guestrooms in the villa, each with satellite TV, mini-bar, luxurious bathroom, and direct-dial telephones. Everything is of the finest quality, including the linens, the towels, and the thick bathrobes. The 12-acre estate is like a splendid natural park with woodlands, ponds, gardens, waterfalls, streams, Roman statues, rare trees, and a swimming pool. Since our last visit, 12 new lake-view suites in a charming house in the garden have been added. There is also a restaurant, Bistrot Stendhal, for guests, a private gym, and sauna with Turkish bath. *Directions:* Drive south from Stresa 3 km and the villa is on the right.

❋ ☕ 🚴 💳 ☎ 👫 🍸 @ W ⅞ P 🍴 🐾 ≋ 🎿 🖼 ⚓ ✈ 🎋 🚶 🐎 ⛵

VILLA DAL POZZO D'ANNONE
Owner: Marchesi Dal Pozzo d'Annone
S. Strada del Sempione, 5
Belgirate, (VB) 28832, Italy
Tel: (0322) 72 55, Fax: (0322) 77 20 21
18 Rooms, Double: €250–€620
Open: Apr to Oct, Credit cards: all major
Abitare La Storia
74 km NW of Milan, 3 km S of Stresa
Region: Piedmont, Michelin Map: 561

The Hotel Florence offers moderately priced accommodations in the charming ancient port of Bellagio. The location is prime—facing the lake in the heart of the old part of town. Across the road from the hotel, next to the lake, is a romantic, wisteria-covered terrace where meals are served when the weather is balmy. If you are lucky enough to snare a front room with a balcony, you can step out through your French doors and be treated to a splendid view of Lake Como. The lounge, which is just off the reception area, is the oldest part of the building, dating back to the 18th century. Here you find a beamed ceiling and a large fireplace. A staircase leads to the upper floor where the guest dining room is located—it has no view of the lake, but does have a fireplace to warm the room on chilly days. There is also a gourmet restaurant open to the public and a spa with massage services. All of the individually decorated guestrooms have antique furnishings, satellite TVs, safety boxes, and hairdryers. Splurge and ask for the corner room with French doors opening onto a large terrace with lounge chairs invitingly set for viewing the lake. The hotel is owned by the Ketzlar family, who are real pros—the inn has been in their family for over 150 years. It is now managed by Freidl Ketzlar, her daughter Roberta, and her nephews Christian, Timothy and Aaron. The family tradition lives on.

HOTEL FLORENCE
Owner: Ketzlar family
Piazza Mazzini, 46
Bellagio, (CO) 22021, Italy
Tel: (031) 95 03 42, Fax: (031) 95 17 22
27 Rooms, Double: €140–€200
3 Suites: €230–€260
Open: Apr to Oct, Credit cards: all major
Lakefront, 80 km N of Milan, 31 km NE of Como
Region: Lombardy, Michelin Map: 561

The Grand Hotel Villa Serbelloni is certainly appropriately named—it is definitely "grand." Indeed, the public rooms will take your breath away with their intricately frescoed ceilings, gold mirrors, ornate columns, Oriental carpets, gilded chairs, massive chandeliers, and a sweeping marble staircase. The bedrooms too are lovely and the quality throughout is superb: fine percale sheets, soft down pillows, and large towels. The service excels, with a friendly staff eager to please. The park-like grounds, enhanced by colorful beds of well-tended flowers, stretch to the very edge of the lake where a large swimming pool holds center stage. There are two more indoor pools (one for adults and one for children) opening to the garden. In addition, there are two tennis courts, a fitness/beauty center, and a squash court. The hotel has two restaurants, one terrace restaurant and the gourmet Mistral. For sightseeing and shopping, the quaint port of Bellagio is adjacent to the hotel. If you want to explore some of the other charming lakeside villages, the ferry is just steps away, or the concierge can arrange a private boat to pick you up at the hotel's pier. For opulent surroundings and palatial splendor, the Grand Hotel Villa Serbelloni can't be beat. The hotel also has 13 apartments with cooking facilities available, one-week minimum. *Directions:* In the center of Bellagio.

GRAND HOTEL VILLA SERBELLONI
Manager: Giuseppe Spinelli
Bellagio, (CO) 22021, Italy
Tel: (031) 95 02 16, Fax: (031) 95 15 29
96 Rooms, Double: €380–€1000
4 Suites: €1000–€1050
Open: Mar 27 to Nov 17, Credit cards: all major
80 km N of Milan, 31 km NE of Como
Region: Lombardy, Michelin Map: 561

La Pergola is an attractive, moderately-priced small hotel nestled in a quaint hamlet just a short walk over the hill from Bellagio. Although it officially rates only one star, in my estimation it deserves far more. Originally a 15th-century convent, it came into Marilena Mazzoni's family in 1732 and has been passed down from generation to generation ever since. The pretty, creamy-yellow building with dark-green shutters snuggles right by the lake and features an enchanting terrace-restaurant at the edge of the water. The charm of the hotel continues within where a fresh, uncluttered, old-world ambiance is displayed throughout. The dining room is most attractive, with fresh white walls accented by copper pots, wooden chairs and tables, and a vaulted ceiling. The guestrooms vary in size but each is tastefully decorated using some antique furnishings; all have modern tiled bathrooms. I was captivated by La Pergola, but when I first met Signora Mazzoni, she was reluctant to have her property in our guide for fear that it would attract the wrong kind of guests—those looking for more amenities than her simple hotel provides. I assured her our readers are different, valuing charm and comfort rather than luxurious amenities. *Directions:* Take the road from Como to Bellagio. Just before Bellagio, turn right toward Lecco, then left toward Pescallo. The hotel is in the town plaza.

LA PERGOLA
Owners: Livio & Lara Gatti, Marilena Mazzoni
Piazza Del Porto, 4
Bellagio-Pescallo, (CO) 22021, Italy
Tel: (031) 95 02 63, Fax: (031) 95 02 53
9 Rooms, Double: €110–€130
Restaurant closed Tuedays
Open: Mar to Dec, Credit cards: none
80 km N of Milan, 31 km NE of Como
Region: Lombardy, Michelin Map: 561

L'Orto degli Angeli is a rare jewel. Located in the historic center of Bevagna (a small, picture-perfect walled village of Roman origin), this intimate inn exudes the genuine warmth of a private home, yet offers the comfort and sophistication of a fine hotel. The handsome stone house has been in the family of your gracious host, Francesco Antonini, since 1788. He and his sweet wife, Tiziana, welcome guests with such a gentle kindness that you will be immediately captivated by their charm. An impressive staircase leads up to the guest lounge, which has a stunning frescoed ceiling and comfortable sofa and chairs grouped around an immense stone fireplace. Main meals are served in the Redibis restaurant set in a well-preserved part of the ambulatory of the ancient Roman theater built in the 1st century A.D. All of the individually decorated guestrooms have pretty, tiled bathrooms, some antique furnishings, fireplaces, and color-coordinating fabrics on the bedspreads and curtains. Many of the rooms overlook a central garden, built upon the old Roman theatre. Bevagna is rich in historical importance—don't miss the stunning little 19th-century opera house, the well-preserved mosaics in the Roman baths, and the picturesque churches. *Directions:* From Perugia take 75 to Assisi-Foligno. Exit to the 316 to Bevagna and look for L'Orto degli Angeli signs.

L'ORTO DEGLI ANGELI
Owners: Tiziana & Francesco Antonini
Via Dante Alighieri, 1
Bevagna, (PG) 06031, Italy
Tel: (0742) 36 01 30, Fax: (0742) 36 17 56
5 Rooms, Double: €200–€220, 9 Suites: €280–€350
Restaurant closed Tuesdays
Closed: Jan to Feb, Credit cards: all major
History Traveller
25 km S of Assisi
Region: Umbria, Michelin Map: 563

Although surrounded by a sprawling, uninteresting concrete metropolis, the center of Bologna shelters a fascinating maze of ancient twisting streets, arcaded passageways, a vast selection of cultural activities, marvelous shopping under porticoed walkways, and some of the best food in all of Italy. The revamped Corona d'Oro, the best in town in the heart of the medieval quarter, is a small, well-managed hotel whose elegantly designed construction conserves architectural elements of various periods, predominately the art nouveau. In the atrium courtyard entrance with original marble floors and fresh white sofas, you can admire a portico that dates back to the 14th century. The main hall and stairwell, exquisitely done in the Liberty style of the early 1900s, lead up to the bedrooms, which are individually decorated, mostly with modern furnishings, but with a touch of the traditional in the sedate color schemes and prints nicely displayed on the walls. Some of the rooms have recessed block-panel ceilings with paintings of coats of arms and landscapes dating back to the 15th and 16th centuries. A few rooms also have small balconies or terraces. Service and tourist assistance outstanding. For a more zen-like experience there is also the owner's Novecento Hotel nearby. *Directions:* Located on a small side street just a few blocks from the large, central plaza. The best bet is to arrive by train and take a cab. If driving, ask the hotel for detailed directions.

❄ ☕ ✗ CREDIT ☎ 🐕 🚻 @ W ⟨ P ♨ ♿

HOTEL CORONA D'ORO
Manager: Mauro Orsi
Via Oberdan, 12
Bologna, (BO) 40126, Italy
Tel: (051) 74 57 611, Fax: (051) 74 57 622
40 Rooms, Double: €209–€357
3 Suites: €305–€510
Closed: Aug, Credit cards: all major
In the heart of Bologna
Region: Emilia-Romagna, Michelin Map: 562

The Villa Clementina is a gem of a small hotel, romantically secreted behind high walls. It is not until the green gates swing slowly open that the stunning gardens and charming inn come magically into view. This gorgeous property was once the home of a famous artist, Lorenzo Vespignani, and your enchanting young host, Dimitri Bonetti, is also a well-known painter and studied under Vespignani. Today Dimitri uses the same light-filled studio that was once his mentor's. However, one of his greatest masterpieces isn't on canvas—it is the Villa Clementina. The property is truly a work of art: each room has hand-painted frescoed walls, lamps and beds made by Dimitri, furniture placed in perfect positions, handsome fabrics, and quality in every detail. My favorite guestroom, Romana, is a particularly spacious room with a fireplace and replicas of ancient Roman frescoes enhancing the walls. The inn is built within several houses nestled on terraces that step down a gentle hill. The grounds are like a beautiful park, with many exotic trees and perfectly manicured gardens filled with the fragrance of jasmine and the sweet song of birds. On one of the terraces there is a charming restaurant, on another a large swimming pool, and on the lowest level, a clay tennis court. The Villa Clementina's location is superb: it is within an easy drive of the Rome airport and about a half-hour train ride into the heart of Rome.

HOTEL VILLA CLEMENTINA
Owner: Dimitri Bonetti
Via Traversa Quarto del Lago, 12
Bracciano, (RM) 00062, Italy
Tel: (06) 99 86 268, Fax: (06) 99 80 94 28
7 Rooms, Double: €135–€185, 2 Suites: €225–€290
Dinner by request
Open: Apr to Nov (or by request)
Credit cards: all major
30 km NW of Rome
Region: Lazio, Michelin Map: 563

In 1550, King John of Portugal decided to give a "little" gift to the Emperor Ferdinand of Austria, so he purchased an elephant in India, shipped it to Genoa, then planned to walk it to Austria. This giant beast grew weary about the time it reached Bressanone and was stabled for two weeks at the Am Hohen Feld Inn. Young and old came from far and wide to see this impromptu circus. The proprietor of the Am Hohen Feld was obviously a master at marketing: to maintain the fame of his establishment, he promptly renamed his hotel—you guessed it—the Elephant. A picture of our friend the elephant was painted on the front of the building to commemorate the sensational event. But even without an elephant story this hotel is a winner with its old-fashioned charm. The sitting room, hallways, and dining rooms (three cozy rooms) incorporate antiques, museum-quality paintings, and magnificent paneling. The Elephant is also well known for its good food—fresh fruits come from the adjacent walled garden where you also find the swimming pool and an old home that has been converted into very nice bedrooms. I particularly liked our room 12 for its spaciousness, room 11 for its corner location, and room 29 for its comfortable decor and balcony. *Directions:* Leave the autostrada at Bressanone and follow the main road through town. The hotel is well signposted in the quiet pedestrian zone.

🍵 🥂 💳 🕿 🏠 🏨 🏋 @ W Y P 🍴 ✿ ≋ 🏃 🖼 🐾 ⛷ 🚶 🏇 ⛷ 🍇 🎿

HOTEL ELEPHANT
Manager: Elisabeth Heiss
Via Rio Bianco, 4
Bressanone, (BZ) 39042, Italy
Tel: (0472) 83 27 50, Fax: (0472) 83 65 79
44 Rooms, Double: €160–€243
Restaurant closed Thursdays
Open: Mar to Nov & Christmas, Credit cards: MC, VS
History Traveller
40 km NE of Bolzano, near Brenner Pass
Region: Trentino-Alto Adige, Michelin Map: 562

Hotel Hermitage is our recommendation for the best accommodations in Breuil Cervinia, well known throughout the world for its fine skiing. Its mighty mountains back right up to the Matterhorn and skiers can ski into Switzerland and have lunch in Zermatt. Summer is also a glorious time of year here, with fabulous hiking trails. Most of the hotels in town are high-rise buildings without much style or charm but happily this is not the case with the Hermitage. The setting is excellent: the hotel is snuggled on the side of the mountain, looking over the village below to incredible mountain peaks across the narrow valley. Although not an old building, it is constructed in the traditional chalet style seen throughout the region. The sturdy stone-and-wood façade, enhanced in summer with balconies laden with colorful geraniums, presents an appealing first impression. Inside, the decor is filled with old-world charm. The walls are paneled with blond wood that came from a 17th-century mountain chalet. There are many antiques and bouquets of fresh flowers throughout to further enhance the cozy mountain ambiance. The guestrooms, too, are charming and each has a balcony capturing a view of the mountains. The final touch of perfection for the Hotel Hermitage is that it is owned and managed by the gracious Neyroz family. *Directions:* From the A5, exit at Chatillon and follow signs to Breuil Cervinia. The hotel is signposted in the village.

HOTEL HERMITAGE
Owner: Corrado Neyroz
Breuil Cervinia, (AO) 11021, Italy
Tel: (0166) 94 89 98, Fax: (0166) 94 90 32
30 Rooms, Double: €300–€600
7 Suites: €600–€1200
Closed: May–Jun & Sep–Oct, Credit cards: all major
Relais & Châteaux
55 km NE of Aosta, 187 km NW of Milan
Region: Aosta Valley, Michelin Map: 561

The Cenobio dei Dogi was formerly the summer home of the Genovese doges, so it is no wonder that it has such an idyllic location nestled on a small hill that forms one end of Camogli's miniature half-moon bay. From the hotel terrace there is an enchanting view of the tiny cove lined with marvelous narrow old fishermen's cottages painted in all shades of ochres and siennas. The hotel has a very nice swimming pool, as well as a private (though pebbly) beach. Many of the bedrooms have balconies boasting romantic views of this storybook scene. There is a tennis court for tennis buffs, although I cannot imagine anyone wanting to play tennis with all the beautiful walking trails, which make enticing spider-web designs on the peninsula. The Cenobio dei Dogi is a larger hotel than most that appear in this guide, but the hotel possesses a solid, comfortable, no-nonsense kind of charm. Both public and guestrooms have been completely renovated, and they have done a beautiful job. It is not chic in the jet-set style of hotels frequently found on the Riviera, but has a lovely, fresh appeal. If you are enticed by pretty flower gardens and exceptional views, you will certainly like the Cenobio dei Dogi. *Directions:* To reach the hotel, exit the A12 at Recco and follow signs to Camogli. The hotel is located at the east end of town.

HOTEL CENOBIO DEI DOGI
Manager: Mauro Siri
Via Nicolo Cuneo, 34
Camogli, (GE) 16032, Italy
Tel: (0185) 72 41, Fax: (0185) 77 27 96
105 Rooms, Double: €155–€375
5 Suites: €380–€480
Open: all year, Credit cards: all major
Abitare La Storia
Near Portofino-Italian Riviera, 20 km SE of Genoa
Region: Liguria, Michelin Map: 561

Relais Il Canalicchio is snuggled within a medieval village on a hilltop overlooking a breathtaking vista of vineyards, olive groves, tiny villages, and forested hills that melt into the horizon. Because the hotel occupies almost the entire romantic village, it has secret little terraces and enchanting nooks to explore. The castle dates back to the 13th century and in its excellent restoration great care was taken to preserve its original architectural features such as terracotta floor tiles, beamed ceilings, thick stone walls, massive fireplaces, and arched brick doorways. The ancient Roman fortified walls of the village are incorporated into one side of the hotel and allow for a romantic lush garden that stretches to the edge of the wall and, on a lower terrace, a splendid swimming pool and a panoramic restaurant. Giant terracotta pots filled with brilliant red geraniums add color to the immaculately tended grounds. Inside, everything is decorator-perfect with a homelike, comfortable ambiance created by the use of fine antiques and lovely fabrics. The spacious bedrooms have the feel of an English country manor, with pretty floral fabrics, coordinating wallpapers, and accents of antiques. A footbridge takes you to an adjacent building with 16 new country suites, all with private entrances. *Directions:* From Perugia go south on E45 in the direction of Roma/Terni, exit at Ripabianca-Foligno, and follow signs to the hotel.

RELAIS IL CANALICCHIO
Manager: Federico Pittaluga
Via della Piazza, 4
Canalicchio di Collazzone, (PG) 06050, Italy
Tel: (075) 87 07 325, Fax: (075) 87 07 296
47 Rooms, Double: €155–€260
Open: Mar–Nov & New Years, Credit cards: all major
39 km SW of Assisi, 20 km N of Todi
Region: Umbria, Michelin Map: 563

Since 1902, the Gallinotto family has presided over the Cannero Lakeside Hotel just south of the Swiss border. With Maria Carla Gallinotto's presence, and her five children (Felice, Samuele, Annalisa, Alfredo, and Giuliana) working alongside her, you can be certain that you will meet caring family members during your stay. This little lakeside resort is composed of two main historical buildings, one a former monastery and the other a house of the "Baron di Sant'Agabio." Ferries that visit all the delightful resorts and islands of Lake Maggiore leave from the dock in front of the hotel. However, do not confine your explorations to the lake, for the valleys and mountains to the west offer spectacular scenery. On the other hand, the hotel is so delightful that you may wish to limit your excursions to the pool and strolls along the lakeside pedestrian promenade. Suites are decorated in the Lombardy style with breathtaking views. Lake-facing bedrooms are found on four floors—all are charming. Additional guestrooms look out to the swimming pool, as do ten self-catering apartments that can accommodate from two to four persons. Dinner is served in the lovely lakefront restaurant. *Directions:* Arriving at the lake, drive north along the pedestrian promenade to the hotel. If space is not available next to the hotel, you will be directed to the hotel's parking lot in the village.

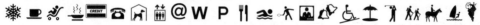

CANNERO LAKESIDE HOTEL
Owner: Gallinotto family
Cannero Riviera, Lake Maggiore, (VB) 28821, Italy
Tel: (0323) 78 80 46, Fax: (0323) 78 80 48
45 Rooms, Double: €116–€156
10 Suites: €176–€220
Open: Mar 10 to Nov 3, Credit cards: all major
12 km N of Verbania, 20 km S of Locarno
Region: Piedmont, Michelin Map: 561

The brochure of this stunning luxury hotel proudly proclaims "the most breathtaking view in the whole world" and indeed they may be right. With its seemingly precarious clifftop position one thousand feet above the turquoise sea, your vision captures the entire Bay of Naples including the tip of Sorrento, Mount Vesuvius, Ischia island and the rest of Capri below. You are off to a great start as you take in these views from the panoramic terrace bordering the spacious and luminous sitting rooms and bar of the main hall, from all bedrooms, or from the spectacular bi-level swimming pool. The Signorini family have personally overseen the complete renovation of the hotel including all the refined decorating details adding family antiques and artwork. The 56 rooms with balconies or front gardens are dispersed about several floors of the main residence and a smaller guesthouse above the pool. Many suites and jr suites are available all with head-spinning views like the one with the whirlpool tub looking directly out to Sorrento. After a day of touring the island, drinks await you poolside, served while watching another sunset sink into the sea. Dining on Mediterranean seafood at the Terrazzo di Lucollo facing the pool and lush garden is another divine experience not to be missed. *Directions:* From Naples, take the jetfoil from the ports of Mergellino or Beverello. A car pickup at Capri port can be arranged to Anacapri.

❄ ☕ 💳 ☎ ♿ @ ♈ P 🍴 🚭 ≈ 🖼 ⛷ ⚓ 🏄

HOTEL CAESAR AUGUSTUS   **New**
Manager: Giovanni Padula
Via G. Orlandi 4
Capri, (NA) 80071, Italy
Tel: (081) 83 73 395, Fax: (081) 83 71 444
52 Rooms, Double: €430–€680
4 Suites: €840–€1450
Open: all year, Credit cards: all major
Relais & Châteaux
Island of Capri, ferry from Sorrento or Naples
Region: Campania, Michelin Map: 564

The Hotel Luna savors one of the most beautiful, tranquil locations on the island of Capri. It is just a short walk from the village yet, in atmosphere, it seems a world away from the bustle and noise. The overall mood at the hotel is set by its delightful approach, a covered trellis pathway which in summer is completely shaded by brilliant bougainvillea and grapevines and bordered by flowers: a wonderful introduction to the Hotel Luna and to a restful interlude by the sea. To the left of the path as you approach the hotel, you see the Luna's large swimming pool surrounded by flowers and a view to the sea. The hotel is perched on the cliffs overlooking a spectacular coastline of green hills dropping straight into the sea, from which emerge giant rock formations. On two sides of the hotel there is a terrace with comfortable chairs where guests may enjoy this spectacular view. Just below the terrace is an open-air bar set on a balcony that hangs out over the cliffs with an unsurpassed panorama of the sea. The reception area and the lounges are attractively decorated using a pleasing, fresh color scheme of white, blue, and yellow. The bar is especially appealing with slipcovered chairs that pick up the rich colors in the tiled floors. There are a few antiques around to add charm. The guestrooms are also attractive. If you want to splurge, ask for one of the guestrooms facing the sea—the vista is memorable.

@ W

HOTEL LUNA
Owner: Luisa Vuotto
Viale Giacomo Matteotti, 3
Capri, (NA) 80073, Italy
Tel: (081) 83 70 433, Fax: (081) 83 77 459
50 Rooms, Double: €285–€460
Open: Apr to Oct, Credit cards: all major
Island of Capri, ferry from Sorrento or Naples
Region: Campania, Michelin Map: 564

The Villa Brunella is a tiny jewel located on the picturesque Via Tragara, only a ten-minute walk to the center of town. This romantic hotel, overlooking the Marina Piccola, squeezes the greatest advantage from its narrow, deep lot. It is built on terraces starting at street level where its superb restaurant with a view balcony is located, and steps down the steep hillside to the blue swimming pool. The hotel is run more like a private home than a commercial hotel. The charming owner, Vincenzo Ruggiero (whose father was a fisherman) was born on Capri. He built the villa and named it after his lovely wife Brunella. This is a family operation: Vincenzo and Brunella are now ably assisted by their three handsome sons (Massimo, Salvatore, and Luigi) and charming daughter (Antonella). The whole family seems to take genuine pleasure making guests feel welcome. The 20 bedrooms are tastefully decorated with pretty bedspreads and coordinating curtains. The cool ceramic-tiled floors, creamy-white walls, and potted plants add greatly to the charm. Splurge and ask for one of the deluxe-category rooms located above the swimming pool such as number 60 (54 and 55 are also very special). These offer dramatic views of the sea and islands from their own private terraces. Simply heavenly. The hillside setting is spectacular.

VILLA BRUNELLA
Owners: Brunella & Vincenzo Ruggiero
Via Tragara, 24
Capri, (NA) 80073, Italy
Tel: (081) 83 70 122, Fax: (081) 83 70 430
7 Rooms, Double: €280–€370
13 Suites: €360–€460
Open: Mar 29 to Nov 6, Credit cards: all major
Island of Capri, ferry from Sorrento or Naples
Region: Campania, Michelin Map: 564

Snuggled in the secluded, wooded hills of Anacapri, the stunning 19th-century Villa Le Scale is on a small lane leading to the museum, Villa San Michele, once the residence of the Swedish writer/philosopher/physician, Axel Munthe. For 20 years, Villa Le Scale was the private home of your charming hostess, Anna Maria Coronato, who has converted it into a sumptuous small hotel. It is no wonder that the finished project is so outstanding, since Anna Maria is a well-known antique and art dealer who has traveled the world collecting treasures for her clients. You enter into a beautiful park that abounds with mature shade trees. Manicured gardens, sculptures, and a very attractive swimming pool enhance the appealing scene. A broad stairway shaded by a trellis and bordered by white columns leads to a fairy-tale white villa that nestles on a gentle hill. Once inside, it is instantly obvious that this is a very special, luxurious hotel. The sun-filled rooms are spacious, and tastefully display museum quality antiques and art. Each of the eight guestrooms is individually decorated around a theme with every piece lovingly selected. One of my favorites, the Venetian Room, has a spectacular Venetian bookcase framing the entrance to the bathroom featuring a handsomely tiled, very large, Turkish shower. The bedroom opens onto a spacious private terrace, where you enjoy breakfast to the serenade of birds. *Directions:* Located on the lane to Villa San Michele.

VILLA LE SCALE
Owner: Anna Maria Coronato
Via Capodimonte 64, Anacapri
Capri, Anacapri, (NA) 80071, Italy
Tel: (081) 83 82 190, Fax: (081) 83 82 796
8 Rooms, Double: €300–€1100
Entire villa can be rented by the week
Open: Apr to Nov, Credit cards: all major
History Traveller
Island of Capri, ferry from Sorrento or Naples
Region: Campania, Michelin Map: 564

The Salento area in the province of Lecce stretches down to the southern most tip of the heel and, as a peninsula, is surrounded on all sides by the sea. Scenic countryside within these parameters is characterized by endless kilometers of enormous, gnarled olive trees divided in sections with stone walls as property lines. The most treasured aspects of this regions are all represented at the Monacelli inn, a 15th century masseria and mill minutes away from the turquoise sea, surrounded by olive groves, plus warm Pugliese hospitality, and divine local food. The twelve bedrooms and suites are found among two fortress stone farmhouses complete with inner courtyard and watch tower and have been tastefully appointed with antique furnishings, canopy beds and modern bathrooms and many amenities. The Piccini family's challenge was to restore the estate with guest's comfort in mind and provide activities for all interests. The restaurant, Rifugio del Re, decorated naturally by the sand-colored stone walls enhanced by red tablecloths, uses all the farm's own organic products. Even soaps and cosmetics are produced using the precious oil. A light lunch can be served at the edge of an expansive infinity pool set among the olive trees. A busy place and a good glimpse of life in Puglia. *Directions:* Exit highway A14 at Bari Nord and follow for Brindisi. Take the expressway and exit at Squinzano, Casalabate, Cerrate. Follow signs for Casalabate and then for the Tenuta Monacelli.

❄ ☕ ♨ 💳 📷 🐕 🍴 @ ♈ P 🍽 🚭 🏊 🖼 🐾 ⛷ ⚓ 🚶 🏇 🍇

TENUTA MONACELLI   **New**
Owners: Annalisa & Giuseppe Fedele Piccini
Località: Cerrate
Casalabate, (LE) 73100, Italy
Tel: (0832) 38 20 37, Fax: (0832) 38 20 27
10 Rooms, Double: €180–€220
2 Suites: €220–€300
Open: all year, Credit cards: all major
10 km NE of Lecce
Region: Apulia, Michelin Map: 564

The Solarola, a sunny yellow villa, as its name implies, in the flat countryside around Bologna is, in a word, "perfect." This gorgeous turn-of-the-last-century was once a private home and was transformed into a guesthouse with five double rooms, a restaurant, living room, billiard room, outdoor gazebo, and beautiful swimming pool by the previous owners Antonella and Valentino. Additional rooms with air conditioning and all amenities were opened after that in the former barn directly in front with downstairs living room and library. Antonella decorated the guest villas to be romantic and refined, yet warm and inviting. Each room is named after a flower and everything—wallpaper, botanical prints, fluffy comforters, motifs on lampshades and bed frames, bouquets, and even room fragrance—conforms to the floral theme. Victoriana abounds in details such as antique cabinets filled with china, lace curtains and doilies, dried-flower bouquets, old family photos, and Tiffany lamps. Ghearado Casini and his wife purchased the hotel from Antonella and Valentino and continue with the same traditions and service. The real treat at Solarola is the inventive cuisine created by the skilled chef Roy Caceres who has been awarded one Michelin star. *Directions:* Exit from autostrada A14 at Castel S. Pietro and turn right towards Medicina for 5 km. Turn right at Via S. Paolo, follow the road to the end then turn right on Via S. Croce to the Solarola.

LOCANDA SOLAROLA
Owners: Gherardo Casini & Francesca Tugnoli
Via San Croce, 5
Castel Guelfo, (BO) 40023, Italy
Tel: (0542) 67 01 02, Fax: (0542) 67 02 22
14 Rooms, Double: €120–€180
2 Suites: €180–€207
Restaurant closed Mon & Tue for lunch
Open: all year, Credit cards: all major
28 km E of Bologna
Region: Emilia-Romagna, Michelin Map: 562

If your dream is to discover a small luxury hotel in Tuscany that is truly "off the beaten path" look no further—the romantic Locanda Le Piazze is about as remote as you will find. Tucked in the heart of Tuscany's richest wine-growing region, the hotel crowns a gentle hill. In every direction there is nothing but a breathtaking patchwork of vineyards sweeping like the open sea across undulating hills, dotted with enchanting old farmhouses. After three years in which the buildings were totally renovated and a beautiful pool added, the hotel opened to guests in the summer of 1995. It is no wonder the design and decor are in absolutely faultless taste: the owner, Maureen Bonini, has for over 40 years been a design consultant in Florence. All of the hotel's rooms exude sophisticated country elegance. Huge bouquets of fresh flowers highlight white walls, terracotta floors, and beamed ceilings. Each of the guestrooms has its own personality, but all exude a similar comfortable, homelike ambiance. The fabrics used throughout are all from Maureen's good friend, Ralph Lauren. The stunning swimming pool, tucked in the vineyards, is reached by a path through fragrant beds of lavender. *Directions:* From Castellina in Chianti take the road to Poggibonsi, S.S. 429. As you leave Castellina, turn left at the first road, SP130 Castagnoli, marked to Gagliole, Castellare, and Castagnoli and follow signs to the hotel—a 10-minute drive (ask for directions).

LOCANDA LE PIAZZE
Owner: Maureen Bonini
Localita: Le Piazze
Castellina in Chianti, (SI) 53011, Italy
Tel: (0577) 74 31 90, Fax: (0577) 74 31 91
20 Rooms, Double: €120–€160
Dinner by reservation: €35, light lunches, closed Wed
Open: Apr to Oct, Credit cards: all major
Midway between Castellina & Poggibonsi
Region: Tuscany, Michelin Map: 563

The Tenuta di Ricavo is unique—not a hotel at all in the usual connotation, but rather a tiny, very old, Tuscan hamlet with peasants' cottages that have been transformed into delightful guestrooms. The stables are now the dining room and the barn is now the office. Unlike many of the over-renovated hotels in Tuscany where most of what you see is actually new construction, Ricavo is all real. The guestrooms have been lovingly restored to enhance their original rustic charm and are attractively furnished with country antiques. You enter the large property following a lane through a vast pine forest that leads to the cluster of weathered stone cottages, romantically embellished by climbing roses. Flowers are everywhere and in one of the gardens are two swimming pools. Before it became a hotel, the village was the summer-holiday retreat of a Swiss family who, after World War II, transformed their home into a unique, village-style hotel. However, the Tenuta di Ricavo is not for everyone. It is quiet. But it is a haven for the traveler for whom a good book, a walk through the forest, and a delicious dinner are fulfillment. Excellent English is spoken—especially by the gracious owner, Christina Lobrano, whose charming husband, Alessandro, is the talented chef. NOTE: There is a three-night minimum during high season. *Directions:* From Castellina, take the road to San Donato. A long way out of town, the hotel is on your right.

TENUTA DI RICAVO
Owners: Christina & Alessandro Lobrano
Castellina in Chianti, (SI) 53011, Italy
Tel: (0577) 74 02 21, Fax: (0577) 74 10 14
18 Rooms, Double: €170–€250
5 Suites: €260–€420
Minimum Stay Required: 3 nights in high season
Restaurant closed Sundays, reservations required
Open: Apr to Nov, Credit cards: MC, VS
Region: Tuscany, Michelin Map: 563

At Le Fontanelle it seems that wherever your eye wanders it is rewarded; from the impeccably decorated interiors, lush gardens and inviting terraced lawns looking on to picture-perfect Tuscan views. Spacious guestrooms of varying dimensions are dispersed about the large stone main building with front courtyard and annexes, all similarly appointed using crisp white linens, classic English and French fabrics, and traditional Tuscan furnishings. Most have either a private garden or terrace from which to absorb the beauty and stillness of this timeless landscape. Simple elegance characteristic of true Tuscan style prevails throughout the many common spaces and a sense of luxury is derived from the many thoughtful details, complimentary amenities, and attentive staff. Refined Tuscan cuisine is presented in the pristine dining room whose large panoramic windows replace the need for paintings and whose name, La Colonna, comes from the stone pillar conserved in the center of the room. Alternatives areas for meals are up at the swimming pool grill or the corner terrace outside the restaurant, appropriately name Belvedere for the magnificent vistas. To top it all off, a heated indoor pool, hydro-jet pool, sauna, steam room and spa treatments are all available for extra pampering. *Directions:* From the Siena-Sinalunga highway, take the 408 road. Fontanelle is 1 km after the turnoff for Pianella.

HOTEL LE FONTANELLE
Manager: Marion Winski
Strada Provinciale 408
Castelnuovo Berardenga, Pianella, (SI) 53019, Italy
Tel: (0577) 35 751, Fax: (0577) 35 75 55
17 Rooms, Double: €350–€800
7 Suites: €800–€1450
Open: Mar to Nov, Credit cards: all major
Region: Tuscany, Michelin Map: 563

The Hotel Relais Borgo San Felice, located in the heart of Tuscany, is built within a feudal hamlet consisting of a cluster of stone, ivy-laced buildings linked by quaint cobbled lanes. The various buildings, including a small chapel, have been cleverly converted into reception area, guestrooms, dining rooms, lounges, conference room, and bar. The tiny village is not entirely consecrated to the hotel: local farmers still live in some of the buildings and olive oil and wine are produced. The San Felice wines, produced from grapes grown on the 2,400 surrounding acres, are some of Italy's finest. Although the hotel is secluded deep in the countryside, there is no need for guests to sacrifice any creature comforts. The Borgo San Felice, a member of the prestigious Relais & Châteaux group, is a sophisticated property offering all the amenities and services of a deluxe hotel. Although the façade is rustic, the interior exudes a gracious charm and the guestrooms, which are decorated with soft, pleasing colors, floral fabrics, and many antiques, offer every amenity. When not exploring the wealth of fascinating towns and historic sites round about, guests can relax by a large swimming pool with a view terrace, enjoy a game of tennis, or be pampered at the beauty center. *Directions:* From Florence take S2 south, until the road ends. Follow signs toward Arezzo-Monteaperti to San Felice, which is between the towns of Pianella and Villa a Sesta.

HOTEL RELAIS BORGO SAN FELICE
Manager: Cinzia Fanciulli
Localita San Felice
Castelnuovo Berardenga, (SI) 53019, Italy
Tel: (0577) 39 64, Fax: (0577) 35 90 89
43 Rooms, Double: €300–€670
Open: May to Nov (or by request)
Credit cards: all major
Relais & Châteaux
19 km E Siena
Region: Tuscany, Michelin Map: 563

Castelrotto is the loveliest of medieval towns in the western Dolomites. Surrounded by high mountain meadows dotted with chalets and backed by towering mountains, it's a sight to behold. Snuggled in the heart of town, the 14th-century Cavallino d'Oro has a deep-mustard-color façade highlighted by dark-green shutters and flower boxes overflowing with geraniums. There is an old-world atmosphere throughout this small inn. The guestrooms are individual in decor, and delightfully furnished in a typical Tyrolean style—three rooms with light-pine, four-poster beds are especially pretty. The rooms face the medieval market square or have a balcony with a view of the Dolomites. From its beginning the Cavallino has offered accommodations, originally being a coaching station providing food and rooms for weary travelers and facilities for the horses. This hospitality is certainly ongoing—Susanne and Stefan (both of whom speak excellent English) have now taken over as the third generation of the Urthaler family to run the hotel. Not only do they exude boundless enthusiasm and gracious warmth of welcome, they are also constantly improving their small hotel by incorporating more antiques into the decor and continuously renovating and upgrading. The restaurant has an excellent reputation, specializing in regional dishes. *Directions:* Exit at Bolzano Nord from the Verona-Brennero autostrada and follow signs for Alpe Di Siusi and Castelrotto.

HOTEL CAVALLINO D'ORO
Owners: Susanne & Stefan Urthaler
Castelrotto, (BZ) 39040, Italy
Tel: (0471) 70 63 37, Fax: (0471) 70 71 72
18 Rooms, Double: €80–€125
40 Suites: €90–€150
Open: all year, Credit cards: all major
140 km S of Innsbruck, 24 km NE of Bolzano
Region: Trentino-Alto Adige, Michelin Map: 562

The family-run Relais San Pietro is an absolute dream. It offers the finest quality throughout, gorgeous views, excellent location, spectacular swimming pool, and outstanding cuisine, all at remarkably reasonable prices. This gem of a little hotel has the added benefit of superb hospitality: Luigi Protti, your host, radiates a gentle, old-fashioned, welcoming kindness. Upon retirement he and his wife, Antonietta, decided to move back to Tuscany and open a hotel. They bought a long-neglected farmhouse only a few kilometers from the town where Signora Protti had been born and a small, intimate hotel. The Protti family recently renovated the 300 year old "Canonica" (priests' house) adding four elegant and spacious suites. The interior of the hotel has a refreshing light, uncluttered appeal. All of the original architectural features such as beamed ceilings and beautiful brick archways have been meticulously preserved. Bedrooms feature beautiful wrought-iron headboards, white bedspreads, excellent lighting, doors painted with regional designs, and superb bathrooms. The romantic dining rooms occupy what were formerly the stables. Signora Protti and her daughter-in-law preside over the kitchen and the food is fabulous. *Directions:* From Cortona, go north on 71 toward Arezzo. At Castiglion Fiorentino, turn right toward Città di Castello. After 6 km, turn left at a sign to Polvano. Go up the hill. Relais San Pietro is on the left.

❄ ☕ ✄ 💳 ☎ @ W P ⁉ 🚭 ≈ 🏃 🖼 ⚓ 🚶 🏇 🚣 ❦

RELAIS SAN PIETRO
Owner: Protti Family
Polvano, Castiglion Fiorentino, (AR) 52043, Italy
Tel: (0575) 65 01 00, Fax: (0575) 65 02 55
5 Rooms, Double: €180–€230
5 Suites: €240–€300
Meals for hotel guests
Closed: Nov to Apr, Credit cards: all major
14 km N of Cortona
Region: Tuscany, Michelin Map: 563

A book on the most charming hotels in Italy would not be complete without including one of the world's premier hotels, the Villa d'Este. Originally the hotel was a private villa built in 1568 by Cardinal Tolomeo Gallio. He obviously had elegant taste, for the Villa d'Este is truly a fantasy come true. From the moment you step into the vast lobby with its sweeping staircase, huge Venetian-glass chandeliers, marble columns, statues, and soaring ceiling, you will feel you are entering a dream. The bedrooms are all elegantly furnished—no two are alike, but all are beautiful with color-coordinated carpets, wall-coverings, and bedspreads. Some of the bedrooms have prime locations with enchanting views out over the lake. Although the interior is outstanding, it is the outside where the fun really begins. The hotel opens onto a large terrace where guests relax with refreshing drinks. Just a short distance beyond the terrace is the lake where there is a dock for boats and a very large swimming pool that extends out over the water, plus an indoor pool and a very popular state-of-the-art spa. Tucked away in the park there are eight tennis courts, and in the area, seven golf courses. However, the most stunning feature of the Villa d'Este is the park: it surrounds the hotel with lovely pathways winding between the trees, statues, and even a formal garden with dramatic mosaic colonnade. *Directions:* Well-signposted in the center of Cernobbio.

VILLA D'ESTE
Manager: Danilo Zucchetti
Via Regina, 40
Lake Como
Cernobbio, (CO) 22012, Italy
Tel: (031) 34 81, Fax: (031) 34 88 44
78 Rooms, Double: €510–€1300
7 Suites: €850–€1900
Open: Mar to mid-Nov, Credit cards: all major
53 km N of Milan, 5 km N of Como (town)
Region: Lombardy, Michelin Map: 561

La Frateria di Padre Eligio, a very special, enchanting hotel, makes an outstanding base for exploring the beauties of Tuscany and Umbria. The guestrooms of this 13th-century convent (founded by St. Francis) are the original guest quarters where the friars lodged passing pilgrims. They are simply, yet tastefully, furnished with antiques. There is nothing to interrupt the enchantment—bathrooms and telephones are the only concessions to the modern era. The silence is sweetened by the song of birds and the air by the fragrance of flowers. A centuries-old forest surrounds the hotel with beckoning paths where you can stroll in perfect stillness. The restoration of this masterpiece of history is superb, but the miracle is how it was accomplished. La Frateria di Padre Eligio, in addition to housing a deluxe hotel, is home to a commune of once-troubled young people who toiled for 12 years to restore the Convento San Francesco to its former beauty. Today these remarkable young men and women awaken at dawn to begin long days of labor. They meticulously groom the gardens, tend the vegetable garden, run the hotel, bake the fresh breads, prepare the meals (exclusively using produce from the farm), and serve in the restaurant. *Directions:* Exit the A1 at Chiusi Chianciano and follow signs to Cetona. Go through town towards Sarteano. Just after leaving Cetona, turn left at a sign "Mondo X—La Frateria di P. Eligio." Go 700 meters to the hotel.

❄ ☕ ✁ 💳 ☎ @ W ⅄ P ‖ ⚲ 🎱 🚶 🐎 ♨ 🍇

LA FRATERIA DI PADRE ELIGIO
Manager: Maria Grazia Daolio
Convento San Francesco
Cetona, (SI) 53040, Italy
Tel: (0578) 23 82 61, Fax: (0578) 23 92 20
5 Rooms, Double: €240
2 Suites: €300
Open: all year, Credit cards: MC, VS
89 km SE of Siena, 62 km NW of Orvieto
Region: Tuscany, Michelin Map: 563

The Villa Anna Maria is located in Champoluc, a small town at the end of the beautiful Ayas Valley, which stretches north into the Alps almost to the Swiss border. The glaciers of the Monte Rosa (one of the 4,000-meter peaks of the Alps) provide a glorious backdrop as you drive up the valley. Champoluc is a well-known ski center in winter as well as a favorite mountain summer resort. The Villa Anna Maria is not a luxury hotel, but rather a simple, charming mountain chalet with great warmth of welcome from Miki Origone and his gracious son, Jean Noël. Together they run the villa with meticulous care for every comfort of their guests. Inside there is a delightful dining room that exudes a romantic coziness with its wooden Alpine-style country chairs, wooden tables, and gay red-checked curtains—just the place to return to for a good lunch or dinner after walking in the mountains (organized walks can be arranged). Upstairs, the bedrooms are spotlessly clean and very comfortable, with wooden paneling on the walls and a rustic ambiance. The atmosphere is homey—wonderful for those seeking a friendly, family-oriented country inn in a mountain village. *Directions:* Exit the A5 at Verres and follow the valley up to Champoluc. Drive through Champoluc and you see a small sign for the hotel on the right side of the road just before you leave town. Turn right on this little lane, which winds up the hill, and the Anna Maria is on your right.

VILLA ANNA MARIA
Owners: Miki & Jean Noël Origone
Via Croues, 5
Champoluc, (AO) 11020, Italy
Tel: (0125) 30 71 28, Fax: (0125) 30 79 84
20 Rooms, Double: €146–€160*
*Includes breakfast & dinner
Open: all year, Credit cards: MC, VS
64 km NE of Aosta, 175 km NW of Milan
Region: Aosta Valley, Michelin Map: 561

The Ca'Peo, a well-known restaurant serving some of the finest food in Italy, is located high in the coastal hills south of Genoa. You might think you will never arrive as the road winds ever upward from the coast through groves of olive and chestnut trees, but the way is well signposted, and just about the time you might be ready to despair, you will find a wonderful old farmhouse, owned by the charming Franco Solari, who is host and in charge of the wines, and his talented wife, Melly, who is the chef. Their enchanting daughter, Nicoletta, who will immediately win your heart, helps out wherever needed. The intimate dining room, which has only nine tables, is enclosed on three sides by large arched windows to take advantage of a sweeping view to the sea. Dining is definitely the main feature, and if you appreciate fine food and wines it is superb; however, in a modern annex there are five rooms (most are suites) available for guests who want to spend the night. The decor here is simple, but after lingering over a wonderful meal accompanied by delicious wines, how nice to walk just a few steps to your bed. The Ca'Peo is only about half-an-hour's drive from the popular resort of Portofino, so you might want to stay here instead or treat yourself to a memorable meal—but reservations are necessary. *Directions:* Exit the A12 at Chiavari. Follow signs to Leivi, then pick up and follow signs to Ca'Peo.

CA'PEO
Owners: Melly & Franco Solari
Via dei Caduti, 80
Chiavari a Leivi, (GE) 16040, Italy
Tel: (0185) 31 96 96, Fax: (0185) 31 96 71
5 Rooms, Double: €104–€129
Restaurant closed Mondays
Closed: Nov, Credit cards: all major
44 km SE of Genoa, 22 km NE of Portofino
Region: Liguria, Michelin Map: 561

The 16th-century Locanda del Sant'Uffizio, originally a Dominican monastery and then a farm, has been converted over the years into a delightful resort offering 40 guestrooms and an exquisite restaurant serving the finest of Piedmontese cuisine. The red brick hotel is surrounded by gently rolling hills dotted by woodlands and laced by vineyards which have been producing fine wines for many centuries (some of the wines served at the locanda are from their own estate). All furnishings are antique and every detail of the decor has been rigorously overseen, with the result being a very tasteful, elegant, yet relaxed hotel. It is surrounded by beautifully manicured gardens and has its own swimming pool and tennis courts cozily nestled amongst vineyards. Our favorite bedrooms are the cloister rooms looking towards the swimming pool with either terrace or balcony. An ambiance of warmth and hospitality radiates throughout the hotel. Guests come from far and near to dine here—the food is outstanding, as would be expected in a one-Michelin-star restaurant. A complimentary aperitif is offered every evening from 7:30 pm to all hotel guests who have reserved a table in the restaurant. *Directions:* Exit the A21 at Asti Est, turn right, then next right on the 457 towards Casale Monferrato. After passing through Calliano go 1 km and turn right for Cioccaro then follow signs to the Locanda.

❄ 🍴 🥂 ☕ 💳 ☎ 🐕 🏹 @ W ⛱ P 🍴 ≈ 🚶 🏞 🐾 ♿ 🏌 🏃 🐎 🍇 ❦

LOCANDA DEL SANT'UFFIZIO
Manager: Vito Andresini
Cioccaro di Penango, (AT) 14030, Italy
Tel: (0141) 91 62 92, Fax: (0141) 91 60 68
40 Rooms, Double: €180–€240
17 Suites: €240–€480
Open: all year, Credit cards: all major
5 km SE of Moncalvo, 60 km E of Turin
Region: Piedmont, Michelin Map: 561

Just on the border between Umbria and Tuscany and conveniently close to the walled town of Citta della Pieve, the Relais dei Magi is an excellent choice for accommodations in this enchanting part of Italy. A quiet, tree-lined lane leads up to the handsome 18th-century yellow villa with symmetrical windows accented by green shutters and roof adorned by rustic tile. The setting is utterly tranquil, with idyllic views in every direction—over 160 acres of woodlands, olive groves, and meadows stretch out as far as the eye can see. To the right of the villa, perfectly positioned to capture the view, is a stunning swimming pool romantically nestled on a grassy terrace amongst beds of flowers and towering cypresses. In the villa there are five deluxe suites, two with stunning view terraces and all with fireplaces and Jacuzzi tubs. Also in the villa are comfortable lounges and a beautiful dining room where a set-menu dinner is offered. A homelike ambiance prevails, with comfortable yet decorator-perfect furnishings throughout. Additional suites are found in a wing of rooms near the pool, while for longer stays or for families/friends there are apartments for two to six persons with kitchens complete with dishwashers and every modern amenity. Spa facilities include a fitness center, sauna, Turkish bath, and small heated pool. *Directions:* From Citta della Pieve take N220 toward Perugia. The hotel is on the left side of the road.

RELAIS DEI MAGI
Owner: Paolo De Marchis
Localita Le Selve Nuove, 45
Citta della Pieve, (PG) 06062, Italy
Tel: (0578) 29 81 33, Fax: (0578) 29 88 58
8 Rooms, Double: €170–€195
5 Suites: €300–€350
Closed: Jan & Feb, Credit cards: all major
43 km N of Orvieto, 79 km S of Arezzo
Region: Umbria, Michelin Map: 563

The Relais Falisco is a recently restored property situated in the Lazio region between Lake Bracciano and Etruscan Viterbo. Easily reached from the autostrada, the hotel is found within the historic center of the town of Civita Castellana with its Etruscan museum and ceramic center, and offers really the only base at this level from which to explore this interesting area. The 17th-century home, originally a private residence now offers 43 bedrooms on the two upper floors, with several suites taking over the top tower and lending superb views from private terraces over rooftops and distant countryside. Original architectural features were carefully preserved, thankfully, and are the highlights in contrast to the rather standard hotel furnishings including reproduction paintings, furniture and oriental carpets throughout the hotel. Most bedrooms have high ceilings with stenciled beamed ceilings. The breakfast room is reached through a series of sitting areas lined with black leather armchairs, small living room with red sofas and fireplace. The advantages here are the excellent rates and very helpful staff. *Directions:* Exit from the A1 autostrada at Magliano Sabina and follow signs for Civita Castellana (15 km). Both the Cassia S.S.2 and the Flaminia S.S.3 lead to Civita from Rome. Follow for city center and signs lead to Via Don Minzoni. Parking available in hotel's inner courtyard.

RELAIS FALISCO
Manager: Nicole Berruet
Via Don Minzoni 19
Civita Castellana, (VT) 01033, Italy
Tel: (0761) 54 98, Fax: (0761) 59 84 32
43 Rooms, Double: €140–€210
Open: all year, Credit cards: all major
35 km SE of Viterbo, 48 km NE of Rome
Region: Lazio, Michelin Map: 563

Romantik Hotel Relais Mirabella is a delightful hotel nestled on a hillside with lovely views overlooking Lake Iseo, a small, charming lake just west of Lake Garda. The vast property has been in the Anessi family for many generations and what makes this hotel especially delightful is that the family is personally involved in its management, supervising every detail of its operation and seeing that all guests are warmly welcomed and well taken care of. In addition to the hotel's own elegant restaurant, Conte di Carmagnola, which has a delightful outdoor dining terrace 300 meters up the hill, the family also owns and operates another restaurant, La Catilina, which exudes rustic charm. The heart of the hotel is within two farmhouses that have been meticulously renovated to the highest of modern standards. A collection of old paintings adorns the walls of the public rooms and a few of the guestrooms, which are decorated with antiques. In addition, there is a new wing of rooms that blends in well with the original buildings. The guestrooms in this new wing do not have antiques but are large, decorated with excellent taste, and have the advantage of individual terraces. All of the rooms have a view of the lake. There is also a marvelous swimming pool, nestled on the hillside, surrounded by well-tended gardens and with gorgeous views. *Directions:* Just west of Clusane, the hotel is marked on the main lake road.

ROMANTIK HOTEL RELAIS MIRABELLA
Owner: Anessi family
Via Mirabella, 34
Clusane, Lake Iseo, (BS) 25049, Italy
Tel: (0309) 89 80 51, Fax: (0309) 89 80 52
28 Rooms, Double: €110–€160,* 1 Suite: €150–€170*
*Breakfast not included: €12
Closed: Jan to Apr, Credit cards: all major
Romantik Hotels
5 km W of Iseo, 75 km NE of Milan
Region: Lombardy, Michelin Map: 561

The setting of the Hotel Bellevue is stunning—it's nestled on a gorgeous meadow enclosed by Italy's highest mountains. Paths from the hotel lead across the lush meadow to the Grand Paradis National Park, a heavenly place to enjoy nature. From the outside, this hotel looks like many others that you encounter in mountain resorts—an attractive, well-maintained building with balconies and window boxes. However, from the moment you step inside, it becomes instantly apparent that this is a very, very special inn. It absolutely oozes charm and although the façade is not old, the interior certainly is. Parts of centuries-old farmhouses and regional artifacts have been cleverly incorporated into the enchanting interior, including mellow paneling, intricate beamed ceilings, carved doors, lovely fireplaces, planked-wood floors, antique light fixtures, and wrought-iron ornaments. All of the furnishings are either family heirlooms or 15th- to 17th-century antiques that came from farmhouses in the Valle d'Aosta. Every room is absolutely picture perfect. Every tiny detail throughout shows love, and the quality is superb. Boundless amenities include 3 restaurants, an indoor pool, saunas, and Turkish baths. The Jeantet-Roullet family's genuine warmth and tender care of guests adds the final touch of perfection. *Directions:* Exit the A5 at Aosta west and follow signs to Cogne. The hotel is on the main road on your right as you leave town.

HOTEL BELLEVUE
Owner: Jeantet-Roullet family
Rue Grand Paradis, 22
Cogne, (AO) 11012, Italy
Tel: (0165) 74 825, Fax: (0165) 74 91 92
38 Rooms, Double: €180–€340
7 suites: €350-€430: 3 chalets
Closed: early Oct to early Dec, Credit cards: all major
History Traveller, Relais & Châteaux
27 km S of Aosta, 110 km N of Turin
Region: Aosta Valley, Michelin Map: 561

Leaving behind the road from Perugia with its developing industries, a country gravel road takes you up to the splendid 17th-century Villa di Montesolare overlooking in all directions its hilly estate of olive groves and vineyards. A wide, gray-stone staircase leads up to an elegant salon with marble fireplace and crystal chandelier off which are eight lovely guestrooms and two suites on two floors. They are individually appointed with authentic period antiques, which harmonize perfectly with the original features of the villa left intact. Seven newer suites and nine bedrooms are located within two 350-year-old farmhouses just down the road, offering magnificent views and utter tranquility. A separate breakfast room is inside one of these two houses. Back at the main house, guests enjoy a drink at the bar before dinner served in one of the two intimate, frescoed dining rooms where varied Umbrian cuisine is presented along with a selection of 350 Umbrian wines. Summer concerts are held in a chapel in the formal Italian garden. Enjoy activities such as swimming in one of two hillside pools, tennis, theme menus, and the on site spa and beauty farm. Gracious and warm hosts Filippo and Rosemarie do an absolutely superb job of making guests feel totally pampered at their romantic retreat. *Directions:* From Perugia take S.S. 220 toward Citta di Pieve. After Fontignano (3 km), turn right at Colle Sao Paolo to the villa (4 km).

✻ ☕ 🏂 ♨ 💳 ☎ 🏠 @ W Y P 🍴 ❀ ≈ 🚶 🖼 🏃 👣 🏇 🍲

HOTEL VILLA DI MONTESOLARE
Owners: Rosemarie & Filippo Strunk Iannarone
Panicale
Colle San Paolo, (PG) 06064, Italy
Tel: (075) 83 23 76, Fax: (075) 83 55 462
15 Rooms, Double: €200–€280
10 Suites: €300–€450
Open: all year, Credit cards: all major
25 km SW of Perugia
Region: Umbria, Michelin Map: 563

The Hotel Menardi, over 200 years old, was originally a centrally located farmhouse, but as Cortina's popularity as a fabulous ski center has spread, so has growth and new construction, and the farm is located just on the outskirts of town. The Menardi farm naturally evolved into a hotel as at first it gave shelter to the men carting loads over the Cimabanche Pass who needed a place to sleep. Today the inn is a simple but wonderful small hotel whose special ingredient is the old-fashioned warmth and hospitality of the gracious Menardi family—Franca Menardi assisted by her three sons Antonio, Alberto, and Andrea. The hotel maintains a country flavor with old prints on the walls, antique clocks, giant dowry chests, Oriental carpets, and beautiful hanging cupboards all set off by the warmth and gaiety of flowers everywhere. The dining room is most appealing and an excellent hearty dinner is served—be sure to request the half-pension rate. The individually decorated bedrooms are all attractive, several have balconies and all have double-glazing to guard against road noise. Several delightful rooms are located across the garden, with three lovely rooms sacrificing a mountain view for a private terrace. *Directions:* Arriving in Cortina, follow the one-way system around town and signposts for Dobbiaco. You find the hotel on your right on the outskirts of town.

🛏 🏃 💳 ☎ @ W P ⍾ ❀ 🖼 🔔 🏃 🏇 ⛷

HOTEL MENARDI
Owner: Menardi family
112 Via Majon
Cortina d'Ampezzo, (BL) 32043, Italy
Tel: (0436) 24 00, Fax: (0436) 86 21 83
49 Rooms, Double: €90–€230
Open: Jun 1 to Sep 2 & Dec 7 to Apr 12
Credit cards: all major
133 km E of Bolzano, 71 km N of Belluno
Region: Veneto, Michelin Map: 562

As Cortina has grown from a mountain outpost to a chic resort, so the Hotel de la Poste has grown from a simple mail coach stop to one of the top accommodations, the last big expansion being made to accommodate visitors during the 1956 Olympics. The Manaigo family has been at the helm for the last century. Currently Marisa, her nephew Gottardo, and her daughter Michela continues to keep the hotel's long-standing reputation afloat, while offering guests the warmest of welcomes. Bedrooms vary from a sumptuous suite in the oldest, thick-walled building to a snug single room with small shower room in the new wing. You can choose from mountain views to town views and decor that varies from traditional to modern. Breakfast is taken in the corner breakfast room or outside on the patio in sunny weather, a great spot for people-watching on the main street of town. Dinner is enjoyed in the grand dining room with its soaring ceiling and ornate plasterwork. Other scattered sitting rooms have a definite old-fashioned charm. In winter skiing is de rigueur, while in summer hiking on a wide variety of trails, shopping in the sophisticated stores, and simply just enjoying stunning views of the Dolomites are the order of the day. *Directions:* When you arrive in Cortina keep on the one-way system round town until you come to the Hotel de la Poste garage. Park here to unload. You can leave your car here (€16 per day) or at a free car park 150 meters from the hotel.

HOTEL DE LA POSTE
Owner: Manaigo family
Cortina d'Ampezzo, (BL) 32043, Italy
Tel: (0436) 42 71, Fax: (0436) 86 84 35
51 Rooms, Double: €200–€374
4 Suites: €280–€494
Closed: Apr to Jun & Oct to Dec 23
Credit cards: all major
133 km E of Bolzano, 71 km N of Belluno
Region: Veneto, Michelin Map: 562

Hotel Descriptions   219

If you want to find the perfect little hotel to use as a base to explore the wonders of Tuscany and Umbria, look no farther than Il Falconiere—a jewel snuggled in the countryside just a few kilometers outside Cortona. From this convenient location you can venture out each day to such beauties as Siena, Florence, Assisi, San Gimignano, Orvieto, and Pienza, all easily accessible by car. The joy is that you can return each evening to relax by the gorgeous swimming pool, enjoy some of the best food in Italy, then sleep peacefully in the hushed tranquility of the countryside. And what a value! You can stay here for much less than you would pay for a deluxe room in Florence or Rome. Il Falconiere is owned by Silvia and Riccardo Baracchi, a charming, talented young couple who have achieved amazing results from their labor of love and long years of hard work. Riccardo inherited the property from his grandmother. His wife, Silvia, is the incredibly talented chef whose superb meals have earned their restaurant a Michelin star. The guestrooms are individually decorated with great flair. Many antiques are used throughout, creating a comfortable, quietly sophisticated elegance. Il Falconiere is truly a very special place offering superb quality, charm, and genuine hospitality. Another bonus: the hotel has a wonderful wellness center and has recently restored the beautiful Baracchi estate winery just east of Cortona. *Directions:* Just north of Cortona, signposted off the road to Arezzo.

IL FALCONIERE RELAIS E RISTORANTE
Owners: Silvia & Riccardo Baracchi
Localita: San Martino
Cortona, (AR) 52044, Italy
Tel: (0575) 61 26 79, Fax: (0575) 61 29 27
19 Rooms, Double: €270–€570
Open: all year, Credit cards: all major
Relais & Châteaux
3 km N of Cortona
Region: Tuscany, Michelin Map: 563

The Villa di Piazzano is an enchanting inn with all the ingredients to make it very special: an historic villa, a lovely landscape, a convenient location, beautiful decor, pretty antiques, and, best of all, the heart-felt hospitality of the Wimpole family who pamper guests and welcome them like friends. As their surname suggests, your hosts are not all Italian-born. Damien Wimpole, an Australian, met his Italian wife, Adriana, in Rome. After their marriage, they traveled extensively throughout the world and, as a result, their charming daughter, Alessandra, is fluent in several languages. When searching for a perfect property to convert to a small hotel, they discovered the stunning but long-neglected Villa di Piazzano, one of the oldest villas in Umbria. The task to bring the property back to its original splendor was awesome, but well worth the effort. Today the delightful villa, set amidst romantic gardens, is a jewel—the interior decorator-perfect with handsome fabrics and many antiques. Everything has been thought of to make a stay here special, including a large swimming pool and wireless Internet access. There is a lovely restaurant specializing in fine Tuscan cuisine. The villa is officially in Umbria, but part of the property is in Tuscany, making it a great choice for those who want a base for exploring both areas. The hotel is located 5 km outside of Cortona. *Directions:* Ask for detailed driving instructions.

VILLA DI PIAZZANO
Owner: Wimpole family
Località: Piazzano
Cortona, Tuoro Sul Trasimeno, (AR) 06069, Italy
Tel: (075) 82 62 26, Fax: (075) 82 63 36
18 Rooms, Double: €160–€340
Closed: Dec to Mar, Credit cards: all major
5 km SE of Cortona
Region: Tuscany, Michelin Map: 563

Cortona, a picturesque walled city in Tuscany, is a favorite with tourists. On the main road that wraps around the east side of the city, the Villa Marsili has the advantages of parking facilities and of being easy to find, and is within walking distance of the center of town. A gated entrance leads into the front courtyard of this handsome yellow villa accented by dark-green shutters and beds of colorful flowers. Inside, the villa has been totally remodeled into a deluxe hotel with every modern amenity. The staff is exceptionally cordial, so even though there is a commercial air, the welcome by the well-trained staff is warm and gracious. The management is happy to help you plan your excursions and they even offer cooking classes. The bedrooms are all tastefully decorated and have all the comforts and appointments of a first-class hotel. Throughout the hotel a quiet, refined ambiance prevails, with soft colors enhanced by antique furniture and ceilings adorned by frescoes. Breakfast is a wonderful buffet of Tuscan specialties. There is no restaurant, but guests can enjoy a complimentary aperitif on the garden terrace with a view of the Val di Chiana valley and Lake Trasimeno before walking to a rich selection of restaurants. *Directions:* Located on the east side of Cortona on the road to Arezzo.

❄ ☕ ⚕ ♨ 💳 ☎ 🐕 ⛪ @ W Ⓨ P 🖼 ♿ ⚓ 🚶 👫 🏇 🍷 ❦

VILLA MARSILI
Manager: Stefano Meacci
Viale C. Battisti, 13
Cortona, (AR) 52044, Italy
Tel: (0575) 60 52 52, Fax: (0575) 60 56 18
26 Rooms, Double: €135–€230
3 Suites: €270–€340
Closed: Feb, Credit cards: all major
Abitare La Storia
51 km NW of Perugia
Region: Tuscany, Michelin Map: 563

The Relais alla Corte del Sole has a superb location—conveniently close to Cortona and Montepulciano, yet snuggled in the tranquil countryside. This gem of a small hotel is owned by the gracious Spiganti family whose famed Tonino Restaurant in Cortona prepares such exceptional cuisine that the late Pope invited the chef to prepare his Christmas dinner. To complement their restaurant, the Spiganti family restored five 16th-century brick farmhouses into an elegantly rustic hotel that is run by their charming daughter, Ilaria, one of the most endearing, gracious hostesses you will ever meet. No two bedrooms are alike and each has been individually decorated with fine brocade fabrics and antiques that enhance the country simplicity of beams and brick floors. The bathrooms have been personalized by a local artist whose whimsical designs reflect the various room names. The restaurant, La Corte del Sole, has a wonderful outside terrace with view. A passion for flowers is evident in the surrounding garden, which leads to a large swimming pool. Bordering Umbria and Tuscany, the Relais alla Corte del Sole is the perfect spot from which to easily explore both regions. *Directions:* Exit the A1 at Val di Chiana and follow signs for Perugia. Take the second Cortona exit towards Montepulciano and drive 7 km to the turnoff for Petrignano-Pozzolo. The hotel is after Petrignano.

RELAIS ALLA CORTE DEL SOLE
Owner: Ilaria Spiganti
Localita: I Giorgi
Cortona–Petrignano del Lago, (PG) 06061, Italy
Tel: (075) 96 89 008, Fax: (075) 96 89 070
18 Rooms, Double: €166–€450
2 Suites: €213–€450
Open: all year, Credit cards: MC, VS
16 km S of Cortona
Region: Umbria, Michelin Map: 563

Corvara is a lovely Alpine village sitting high in the Dolomites and ringed by towering peaks. Fortunately, it's one of those places that combines an exquisite setting with a superb upscale hotel run by the most welcoming of families, the Costas. From the exterior the hotel looks like another typical Alpine hotel but once inside you realize that this is very different—all seven intimate paneled dining rooms and enoteca have been rebuilt from antique local homes. The conservatory breakfast room offers the largest breakfast selection I have ever seen, from fresh-squeezed juices to eggs cooked any way you want them. The indoor swimming pool with its whirlpool features is a swimming adventure, though if you prefer swimming outdoors, there is also a large garden pool. Bedrooms are absolutely delightful, ranging from romantic rooms with balconies offering stunning mountain views to two exquisite junior suites decked out in white pine accented by blue-and-white fabric. In winter this is a paradise for skiers and in summer for hikers and an ideal base for exploring the magnificent Dolomites. The hotel also offers guests a wine therapy spa with treatments using natural grape products. *Directions:* Corvara is 50 km west of Cortina d'Ampezzo. Arriving in the town, you find the hotel on the hill next to the old church.

HOTEL LA PERLA
Owner: Costa family
Corvara, (BZ) 39033, Italy
Tel: (0471) 83 10 00, Fax: (0471) 83 65 68
21 Rooms, Double: €140–€260*
30 Suites: €195–€280*
*Includes breakfast & dinner, restaurant closed Mon
Open: Jun to Sep & Dec to Easter
Credit cards: all major
65 km E of Bolzano, 47 km W of Cortina
Region: Trentino-Alto Adige, Michelin Map: 562

For many years the Locanda San Vigilio, tucked on a small peninsula on Lake Garda, has been featured in our guides. In 2002 the owners opened the Locanda San Verolo, a romantic small inn—once a farmhouse—nestled in the rolling hills of the tranquil countryside about a 15-minute drive away. Beyond the outer stone wall you find a courtyard where tables are set for open-air dining in balmy weather. The restaurant, reception area, and some of the guestrooms are in the largest of the ochre-colored houses facing the courtyard, while the other guestrooms are in three other buildings. My favorite accommodations are on the top floor of the main house because of the beautiful views. All the spacious, individually furnished guestrooms are decorated perfectly and are exceptionally appealing, with a simple elegance appropriate for a farmhouse. Gorgeous fabrics, fine antiques, original art, rich colors, hand-painted wooden headboards, fine linens, and splendid large bathrooms are featured in all. Obviously no expense was spared to make this a luxurious yet rustic hideaway. A path leads up a gentle slope to a large swimming pool terraced on the hillside with a beautiful view of the countryside and to the bell tower of a tiny church peeking out of the trees just below the hotel. *Directions:* From Garda take the road to Caprino. At Costermano, turn left toward Castion and Zeno. In a few minutes you will see a sign on the right for the hotel.

※ ⚞ CREDIT ☎ 🐕 @ W Y P ¶ ≈ ⚓ 🏃 👫 🏇 ⚓ 🍇

LOCANDA SAN VEROLO
Owners: Agostino & Guarienti di Brenzone
Localita San Verolo
Costermano, (VR) 37010, Italy
Tel: (045) 72 00 930, Fax: (045) 62 01 166
13 Rooms, Double: €250–€380*
*Breakfast not included: €15
Open: all year, Credit cards: all major
History Traveller
78 km S of Trento, 68 km E of Brescia
Region: Veneto, Michelin Map: 562

Most hotels in the stunning mountain resort of Courmayeur are located in the chic center of town. However, if you prefer to stay in a more tranquil setting that also offers astounding scenery, the Maison Lo Campagnar makes a perfect choice. This small hotel is located just 800 meters away from Courmayeur in Dolonne, a quaint hamlet consisting of a cluster of old farmhouses topped by the typical stone roofs of the region. This inn is newly built in traditional style and blends in beautifully with its much older neighbors. A meadow, where sheep graze in summer, stretches out in front of the hotel to the base of the mountain, making it possible in winter to ski home at the end of the day. Inside, the hotel is exceptionally pretty, and exudes an appealing, rustic country charm. A talented local artisan built the hotel and is responsible for its beautiful hand-made, alpine-style furniture and intricately carved woodwork. The guestrooms are very pretty and exude a rustic country ambiance. In addition to its appealing décor and top notch quality throughout, the hotel has another huge advantage—an unobstructed, superb view of one of the world's most beautiful mountains, Mont Blanc. *Directions:* Exit the A 4 at the Courmayeur. At the plaza, turn left, go under the bridge, following signs to Dolonne. After a small supermarket "Economica" on your right, turn right. At the end of the road turn left, then right at the first street to the hotel.

❄ ☕ 🎿 CREDIT ☎ P 🍴 👫 🎿

MAISON LO CAMPAGNAR
Owner: Fabio Ferrari
Rue des Granges
14, Fraz. Dolonne
Courmayeur, (AO) 11013, Italy
Tel: (0165) 84 68 40, Fax: (0165) 84 65 34
12 Rooms, Double: €180–€210
Closed: Oct, Nov & May, Credit cards: all major
35 km W of Aosta, 24 km S of Chamonix
Region: Aosta Valley, Michelin Map: 561

Romantik Hotel Villa Novecento, located in the alluring village of Courmayeur, opened its doors to guests in 2002 after several years of meticulous renovation. This gem is on a quiet street, just steps from chic boutiques and enticing restaurants. The four-story, cream-colored mansion with windows framed by brown shutters is very attractive. However, the hotel's true charm comes to life when you step inside. The rooms have gorgeous antiques, soft lighting, sumptuous fabrics, polished hardwood floors, magnificent paintings, mellow wood paneling, oriental carpets, and bouquets of fresh flowers. To add perfection, the hotel's restaurant is exceptional. The hotel is owned by the gracious Cavaliere family, experienced hoteliers and masters in hospitality, who also own the elegant Romantik Hotel Villa Pagoda near Genova. Mrs. Cavaliere is a talented decorator and an avid collector of antiques. Her treasures are artistically displayed throughout the hotel. You will also be amazed by the warmth of welcome. It seems as if you are a guest in a lavish home. The guestrooms are all lovely, with superb linens and top notch quality in every detail. The suites are much larger than the standard rooms, and if you really want to splurge, "1951" is especially charming—a spacious room with a raftered ceiling, a fireplace, and a king-sized bed highlighted by a romantic painted headboard. *Directions:* Drive to the town plaza, follow signs to the hotel.

ROMANTIK HOTEL VILLA NOVECENTO
Owner: Francesco Cavaliere
Viale Monte Bianco, 64
Courmayeur, (AO) 11013, Italy
Tel: (0165) 84 30 00, Fax: (0165) 84 40 30
24 Rooms, Double: €110–€300
2 Suites: €210–€620
Closed: Oct & May, Credit cards: all major
Romantik Hotels
Region: Aosta Valley, Michelin Map: 561

L'Antico Forziere in the capable hands of Daniela and her industrious family, formerly the manager of another hotel in the guide, is a pleasant and strategic place from which to tour the highlights of Umbria. The ancient stone fortress building on the Tiber river, is located just off the main road which leads to Deruta, one of Italy's most famous ceramic centers. The views from the house and swimming pool over the valley are quite lovely. Attention has been given to the preservation of the centuries-old building, with exposed stone walls, handmade brickwork, wood beamed ceilings. Accommodation within 3 suites with independent garden entrance or 6 double rooms are appointed in typical Umbrian style with iron wrought beds, hand-woven local fabrics and simple country furniture and many amenities. High emphasis has been given to the restaurant where sons, Stefano and Andrea continue to work wonders, serving excellent local fare including fish and meat specialties within the vaulted brick and stone dining room where many come for a specially-prepared regional meal. Daniela's husband and third son, Samuele, take care of the general property and serve in the restaurant. Perugia, Assisi, Todi, Orvieto and Spoleto are all within 30 minutes of this base. Excellent value and hospitality. *Directions:* From Perugia, exit at Casalina just after Deruta and follow signs to the hotel for 1 km.

L' ANTICO FORZIERE
Owners: Daniela Taddia & Alessandro Rodella family
Via Rocca, 2 – Località Casalina
Deruta, (PG) 06051, Italy
Tel: (075) 97 24 314, Fax: (075) 97 29 392
6 Rooms, Double: €85–€100
3 Suites: €125–€150
Restaurant closed Mondays
Open: all year, Credit cards: all major
12 km S of Perugia, 3 km S of Deruta
Region: Umbria, Michelin Map: 563

To the west of famous Lake Garda lies the smaller, lesser known Lake Iseo. Here, tucked into the gentle Franciacorta hills, you find L'Albereta, a deluxe property with intimacy and tranquility at its heart. The owner, Carmen Moretti de Rosa, has collaborated with Henri Chenot and his wife, Dominique, to create the hotel's spa, Espace Vitalité, offering several well-being programs. You feel a happy ambiance as soon as you enter the sunny reception area with light streaming in through walls of glass. To the right is a charming, intimate sitting area with comfortable chairs set off by checkerboard-pattern walls. The foyer steps lead down to a swimming pool with windows that slide open to the pretty garden. Carmen decorated the bedrooms and each has its own personality with subdued elegance and excellent taste throughout. The walls in the bedrooms and hallways are whimsically painted with individual designs that tie in with the color and decor. The most dramatic rooms are the suites in the tower, one of which was occupied by the actress Sophia Loren. The hotel's fine restaurant features the famous cuisine of Gualtiero Marchesi and the dining room is serenely furnished in muted tones of green with a wall of windows that look out over the wooded hills, capturing a splendid view of Lake Iseo in the distance. *Directions:* From the A4, take the Rovato exit and follow signs to Sarnico. After 3 km, turn right at the sign for the hotel

L'ALBERETA
Owner: Carmen Moretti de Rosa
Via Vittorio Emanuele, 23
Erbusco, Lake Iseo, (BS) 25030, Italy
Tel: (03077) 60 550, Fax: (03077) 60 573
57 Rooms, Double: €240–€940, Breakfast not included
Restaurant closed mid-Jan to Mar
Open: all year, Credit cards: all major
Relais & Châteaux
60 km W of Verona, 65 km E of Milan
Region: Lombardy, Michelin Map: 561

Hugging the crest of a rocky coastal mountain rising 750 meters above Trapani, Erice's authentic testimony to yesteryear is broken only by several tall communication towers just outside the ancient walls. This appealing town of twisting cobbled streets makes a convenient overnight stop when visiting the Greek temple and theater at Segesta. As you wind up the hill toward Erice, watch for the parking area near Porta Trapani: leave your car here and walk through the arched stone entrance and up the Via Vittorio Emanuele to the Hotel Moderno. The intimate reception area has a definite old-fashioned feeling. A hallway leads to a lounge accented by chairs grouped around small round tables where guests can just relax or enjoy a cold drink from the adjacent bar. A stone staircase leads up to the modest guestrooms in the main building, all of which are immaculately clean and fresh with whitewashed walls and white-tiled floors. Some bedrooms are decorated with light knotty-pine furniture; others have an antique motif. One of my favorites, room 35, has a handsome king-sized iron headboard with brass trim and an antique armoire. About half of the guestrooms are located in an annex just across the street in another very old building that has been renovated. These guestrooms are a bit more spacious and equally pleasant. Of the total 40 bedrooms, six have a balcony.

HOTEL MODERNO
Owner: Giuseppe Catalano
Via Vittorio Emanuele, 63
Erice, Sicily, (TP) 91016, Italy
Tel: (0923) 86 93 00, Fax: (0923) 86 91 39
40 Rooms, Double: €100–€130
Restaurant closed Mondays
Open: all year, Credit cards: all major
15 km NE of Trapani, 96 km SW of Palermo
Region: Sicily, Michelin Map: 565

Located in the historic heart of Ferrara, the five-star Duchessa Isabella Hotel is absolute perfection. You are totally immersed in breathtaking opulence from the moment you step into the stunning reception hall with its soaring, ornately decorated ceiling and handsome marble staircase sweeping up to a second foyer enhanced by Greek columns, Persian carpets, two huge gilt candelabra, fine paintings, soft lighting, and ornate antique furniture. Sometimes such spectacular palaces reflect a faded elegance, but not this one: it is so well maintained that it looks as beautiful as when the palace was built in the 16th century. This world of refinement is orchestrated by Evelina Bonzagni, an attractive, hard-working woman who reflects the image of the gracious hostess, warmly greeting returning clients as friends and watching every detail of the management with a keen eye. All the guestrooms are splendidly decorated with antiques, as are the dining rooms. Dinner at the Duchessa Isabella is an exquisite affair. Not only is the food superb, but also the dining rooms are absolutely gorgeous. There is not one large restaurant, but rather a series of lovely, intimate dining rooms, with beautiful painted wooden ceilings bordered in gold, authentic doors dating back to the 16th century, chairs richly upholstered in fine fabrics, and incredible frescoes. *Directions:* The Via Palestro is a main street that runs into the piazza where the cathedral is.

HOTEL DUCHESSA ISABELLA
Owner: Evelina Bonzagni
Via Palestro, 70
Ferrara, (FE) 44100, Italy
Tel: (0532) 20 21 21, Fax: (0532) 20 26 38
28 Rooms, Double: €299–€850
Restaurant closed Sundays & Monday dinners
Closed: Aug, Credit cards: all major
Relais & Châteaux
51 km NE of Bologna, 110 km SW of Venice
Region: Emilia-Romagna, Michelin Map: 562

Opened for guests in 2000, the Locanda della Duchessina is the latest of Evelina Bonzagni's artistic creations. Each of her hotels in Ferrara has its own personality and is outstanding in its own way. The Locanda della Duchessina is the most intimate, giving guests the feeling of staying in a private home. Painted a soft pastel pink with windows enhanced by shutters and boxes of geraniums, the building is instantly appealing. Evelina Bonzagni's decor in her other two hotels ranges from opulent splendor to sedate grandeur, whereas the Locanda della Duchessina's rooms are decorated in gentle pastel colors with walls enhanced by lovely papers. It is not surprising that the charmingly decorated bedrooms have a feminine flair since each of the five bedrooms is named for the daughter of one of Ferrara's wealthy noble families. Wallpapers in pink check, pastel plaids, miniature florals, or pretty blue designs set the decor in each with coordinating bedspreads and draperies, lacy white curtains, and pillows with matching fabrics. The guestrooms are not large, but each is perfect and has a beautiful bathroom where the tiles pick up the room's decor. In the rear of the hotel is a romantic little garden, gently shaded by trees and enhanced by flowers. The Locanda offers incredible value with beautifully decorated rooms and superb quality. *Directions:* Located on a tiny street off Via Palestro, just steps from the Hotel Duchessa Isabella.

❋ ⚕ CREDIT ☎ 🏠 @ Ⴘ P 🚭 ♿ 🕴

LOCANDA DELLA DUCHESSINA
Owner: Evelina Bonzagni
Vicolo del Voltino, 11
Ferrara, (FE) 44100, Italy
Tel: (0532) 20 69 81, Fax: (0532) 20 26 38
5 Rooms, Double: €150–€175*
*Breakfast not included: €13
Closed: Aug, Credit cards: all major
51 km NE of Bologna, 110 km SW of Venice
Region: Emilia-Romagna, Michelin Map: 562

If you don't need the ultimate in luxury provided by Ferrara's opulent Duchessa Isabella Hotel, her "sister" hotel just around the corner, the Principessa Leonora, which is also owned by Evelina Bonzagni, is equally outstanding in its own way. The mood here is one of subdued, quiet elegance. Here Evelina Bonzagni again shows her impeccable taste, but the style is more sedate—less gilt and fewer ornate antiques. This 16th-century residence was once the home of Leonardo Mascheraio, whose fame for making masks was so great that the street was named for him, and the hotel's beautiful suites are named in honor of the many illustrious guests who visited the mansion. The standard bedrooms are designated by their past use, such as the stable, the wine cellar, the oil press, olive store, etc. Guestrooms offer every latest modern amenity such as Internet access with modem, satellite TV, safety deposit box, and mini-bar. Behind the hotel is a charming garden where guests can relax after a day of sightseeing and, for the more active, there is also a fitness room. The hotel is exceptionally attractive with terracotta floors, marble columns, many fireplaces, beamed ceilings, centuries-old arched doorways, thick walls, Oriental carpets on polished floors, walls enhanced with a fabulous collection of French tapestries, and fine antiques throughout. *Directions:* Via Mascheraio runs from the Via Palestro where the Duchessa Isabella Hotel is located.

❅ ☕ ✂ CREDIT ☎ ♿ 🍴 @ ♂ P ⊘ 🖼 ♿ 🚶 🏇 ⛵

HOTEL PRINCIPESSA LEONORA
Owner: Evelina Bonzagni
Via Mascheraio, 39
Ferrara, (FE) 44100, Italy
Tel: (0532) 20 60 20, Fax: (0532) 24 27 07
21 Rooms, Double: €190
1 Suite: €299
Open: all year, Credit cards: all major
51 km NE of Bologna, 110 km SW of Venice
Region: Emilia-Romagna, Michelin Map: 562

Sitting high above the valley, the delightful village of Völs nestles beneath the Schlern Mountain—hence you see local signposts for Völs am Schlern. At the heart of the village the Romantik Hotel Turm dates back to the 13th century when it functioned as a castle. Today it is certainly not a castle of drafty corridors and sparse rooms but a delightful hotel that displays its castle origins in its barrel-vaulted rooms and thick stone walls. Instead of a gloomy dungeon you have an indoor whirlpool-jacuzzi (as well as an outdoor one set on a grassy garden terrace). The art collection, started by Karl Pramstrahler, lines every available inch of wall space and includes everything from old oil paintings to contemporary art. Stefan Pramstrahler is responsible for the delicious food and runs the hotel. Bedrooms come in all shapes and sizes, from lovely rooms set beneath the eaves to a turret suite with a four-poster bed and a little house (Wagenhaus) with a sitting room and child's bedroom downstairs, and a master bedroom upstairs. Amenities include a full spa with swimming pool, whirlpool, sauna, wine bath, solarium, and massage services. *Directions:* Exit at Bolzano Nord from the Verona-Brennero autostrada. Follow signs for Siusi and Fiè (also called Völs), at the main intersection in the village turn left, following the road to the hotel, next to the church

ROMANTIK HOTEL TURM
Owner: Stefan Pramstrahler
Kirchplatz, 9, (Völs), Fiè, (BZ) 39050, Italy
Tel: (0471) 72 50 14, Fax: (0471) 72 54 74
30 Rooms, Double: €200–€355, 6 Suites: €320–€410
Restaurant closed Thursdays
Closed: Nov 13 to Dec 20, Jan 8 to Jan 26
Credit cards: MC, VS
Romantik Hotels
16 km E of Bolzano, 7 km S of Siusi (Seis)
Region: Trentino-Alto Adige, Michelin Map: 562

The Punta Est is a delightful villa perched on a hilltop overlooking the sea. When the home was converted to a hotel, an annex was added to provide more bedrooms, but it still radiates the friendly ambiance of a private home. This warmth of reception and attention to detail are the result of the management of the gracious Podestà family who own and personally manage the inn. They seem dedicated to making your stay as enjoyable as possible. This small hotel is constantly being maintained with loving care. Every time we visit the property has been upgraded, the latest addition being a wellness area in the nature cave. There are little terraces with lovely views snuggled at various levels among the trees and on one of these terraces is a swimming pool. There is also access to the public beach, which can easily be reached by walking down the path to the main highway and following the tunnel beneath the highway to the beach. The rooms in the main villa are smaller and more old fashioned than those in the newer annex, which are more reminiscent of an American motel. Meals are served daily in the hotel's restaurant, which also has outdoor seating in front of the sea. The hotel is located east of Finale Ligure, just before the tunnel.

❄ ☕ 🥗 CREDIT ☎ 🐕 ♨ @ W Υ P ⁇ ❀ ≈ 👤 ⛱ ⚓ 🏃 🥾 🐎 🍇

HOTEL PUNTA EST
Owner: Podestà family
Via Aurelia N.1
Finale Ligure, (SV) 17024, Italy
Tel & Fax: (019) 60 06 11
31 Rooms, Double: €180–€270
6 Suites: €270–€450
Open: May to Oct, Credit cards: all major
72 km SW of Genoa
Region: Liguria, Michelin Map: 561

Hotel Albergotto, situated on a corner of the elegant Via de Tornabuoni with its austere Renaissance palazzos and designer boutiques, could not be more central. It existed for the past century as a small hotel once hosting illustrious musical and literary artists like Verdi, Elliot, and Donizetti, but had been virtually forgotten in recent decades. A complete renovation has brought it back to life and it is an excellent choice in the middle price range. From the street entrance you take a red-carpeted flight of stairs to reach the elevator up to the rooms on the top three floors. Beyond the reception desk are two breakfast rooms and a comfortable living room decorated in royal-blue tones with large windows looking out to Tornabuoni. Light-wood floors throughout the hotel give the place a fresh and newer look. Very pleasant, cheerful bedrooms in mustard hues with matching floral bedspreads have amenities such as air conditioning, satellite TV, and mini-bar. The double-paned windows keep out any traffic noise from the main street. Most delightful is the large mansard suite with wood-beamed ceilings and views over the city's rooftops and bell towers. The friendly staff will help you to enjoy your stay. *Directions:* Via de Tornabuoni is three blocks north of the River Arno and two blocks west of Piazza della Repubblica.

HOTEL ALBERGOTTO
Owner: Carlo Martelli
Via de Tornabuoni 13
Florence, (FI) 50123, Italy
Tel: (055) 23 96 464, Fax: (055) 23 98 108
22 Rooms, Double: €132–€285
Open: all year, Credit cards: all major
In the heart of Florence
Region: Tuscany, Michelin Map: 563

In the new category of accommodation in historic residences, the Antica Torre is at the top of the list. The top floors of this ancient fortified palazzo, in the very center of Florence, has been converted into a luxurious and stunning hotel. An elevator takes guests up to the top-floor sitting/bar area and breakfast room where large windows allow heart-stopping full 360-degree views over Florence's terracotta tiled roofs, major monuments, Arno river, and distant hillside backdrop. Take a closer look by stepping out on the large rooftop terrace complete with turrets to have an eye-level peek at Brunelleschi's grand cupola. On the two floors below you find 12 upscale and extra-spacious bedrooms with many amenities, each featuring more unique views or private terraces. The classically styled rooms have been well appointed in soft hues of gold or celestial blue, many with large open windows, perfect for drinking in the marvelous cityscape, virtually identical to that of the Renaissance period. Attentive and energetic young staff definitely keep guests' every comfort in mind, and can arrange anything from special events on the terrace, to taking over the whole accommodation for family reunions or other gatherings. Magical does not even come close to describing the sensation at sunset from this special perch. *Directions:* The Antica Torre entrance is located half a block north of the Arno river on Via Tornabuoni.

❄ ☕ 🛵 CREDIT ☎ ⛹ @ W Y 🍴 🖼

ANTICA TORRE DI VIA TORNABUONI
Manager: Paola Bini
Via Tornabuoni, 1
Florence, (FI) 50123, Italy
Tel: (055) 26 58 161, Fax: (055) 21 88 41
12 Rooms, Double: €180–€290
3 Apartments: €360–€450 daily, €1200–€1600 weekly
Open: all year, Credit cards: all major
In the heart of Florence
Region: Tuscany, Michelin Map: 563

Moderately priced accommodations are rare in Florence, so we were happy to discover the Hotel Il Guelfo Bianco, which combines reasonable rates with a choice location in the heart of Florence. Most importantly, this small hotel has an owner, Alessandro Bargiacchi, whose presence is seen and felt. He speaks only a little English, but his smile and genuine warmth of welcome make guests feel right at home. Everyone who assists him is exceptionally friendly and all converse in several languages, including the gracious manager, Antonella Rocchini. Federico is also very charming. The inviting lobby sets the tone of the hotel with a bright reception area with exposed brick walls and contrasting abstract paintings and modern light fixtures. There is a lounge bar where guests can relax and enjoy a drink and a reading room with Internet access. Breakfast is served in a pretty room with a delightful courtyard that is very popular with guests in pleasant weather. The bedrooms vary in size and shape, as one would expect in an historical 16th-century building. All are decorated with individual antiques and some even have celestial frescos on the ceilings. On a busy street, the more quiet rooms look over a back garden. The Hotel Il Guelfo Bianco is not a deluxe hotel, nor does it pretend to be, but it makes an excellent choice for a friendly, pleasant place to stay in the heart of Florence.

HOTEL IL GUELFO BIANCO
Owner: Alessandro Bargiacchi
Via Cavour, 29
Florence, (FI) 50129, Italy
Tel: (055) 28 83 30, Fax: (055) 29 52 03
40 Rooms, Double: €150–€250
7 Suites: €160–€225
Open: all year, Credit cards: all major
In the heart of Florence
Region: Tuscany, Michelin Map: 563

In our estimation, the Hotel Helvetia and Bristol is one of the finest luxury hotels in the center of Florence. Nothing has been spared to make this showplace a true beauty—the decor is outstanding. The lounges, exquisitely decorated with an elegant, yet extremely comfortable, homelike ambiance, exude quality without flamboyance. Each of the guestrooms is also superbly decorated, and, as in a private home, no two are alike. Abundant use of exquisite padded-fabric wall coverings, with color-coordinated draperies, upholstered chairs, and bedspreads along with lovely antiques make each one special. I fell in love with all of the rooms, but my very favorites were the mini-suites: room 257 in gorgeous shades of muted green and room 363 in lovely golds, creams, and dusty pinks, with a sumptuous marble bathroom with Jacuzzi tub, heated towel racks, plus the added bonus of a tiny terrace. The "Hostaria Bibendum" restaurant and bar is a marvelous retreat—light and airy with its alfresco terrace. The restaurant serves lunch, dinner and afternoon tea and the menu features Tuscan specialties made from the freshest local ingredients. The Helvetia and Bristol is expensive, but no more so than the other luxury hotels in Florence, and for those who appreciate quality and refinement, it is unsurpassed.

HOTEL HELVETIA AND BRISTOL
Manager: Stefano Venturi
Via dei Pescioni, 2
Florence, (FI) 50123, Italy
Tel: (055) 26 651, Fax: (055) 23 99 897
67 Rooms, Double: €350–€650*
30 Suites: €450–€1900*
*Breakfast not included: €28
Open: all year, Credit cards: all major
In the heart of Florence
Region: Tuscany, Michelin Map: 563

The Hotel Lungarno, one of our favorite hotels, is superbly located directly on the River Arno, a few minutes' walk from the Ponte Vecchio. Of more recent construction, the architect has cleverly incorporated into the hotel an ancient stone tower, which houses several romantic suites. The decor is superb, with fine-quality furnishings and gorgeous fabrics accented by an appealing color scheme of blues and creamy whites. The hotel has been totally refurbished with all the latest modern conveniences in smartly styled rooms that have a great appeal. In addition to classic guestrooms are six splendid two-bedroom, two-bath apartments, which are an exceptional value if you are traveling with friends or family. Throughout the hotel a gracious ambiance of understated elegance prevails, enhanced by the admirable management and warm reception. Bountiful bouquets of fresh flowers and an outstanding collection of original 20th century paintings (over 450 works) add the final touch of perfection. If you plan far in advance, you might even be lucky enough to snare a room with a large terrace overlooking the river—these are very special and well worth the extra cost. What a treat to sit on your own terrace in the evening and watch the Arno fade into gold in the setting sun. The alternative is a drink at the Lungarno's sophisticated bar or chic Borgo San Jacopo restaurant, with incomparable river views accompanied by precious Picasso, Cocteau and Rosai paintings. Top-class.

HOTEL LUNGARNO
Manager: Mr. Sandro Alfano
Borgo San Jacopo, 14
Florence, (FI) 50125, Italy
Tel: (055) 27 26 40 00, Fax: (055) 26 84 37
60 Rooms, Double: €310–€630
13 Suites: €670–€1500
Restaurant closed Tuesdays
Open: all year, Credit cards: all major
On the Arno near Ponte Vecchio
Region: Tuscany, Michelin Map: 563

The hills immediately surrounding Florence, dotted with stately villas and country homes dating back to the Renaissance, offered Florentine aristocrats cool respite in summer from the higher temperatures in the city below. The gracious Bulleri family chose this alternative to the city some 30 years ago, and after a successful career in the fashion industry, Claudio and Paola transformed their splendid wooded property into a top-notch inn for discerning guests. Nine very comfortable, immaculate rooms, personally decorated by Paola, have been created in a house across from the family's villa. This includes an elegant main living and dining room with fireplace and large windows looking out over the garden. Classic-style bedrooms have parquet floors, matching fabrics for beds and drapes, and spacious sparkling-white bathrooms. Amenities include satellite TV, wireless Internet, mini-bar, safe, air conditioning, and a selection from the wine cellar. A full country breakfast is served out in the gazebo (in winter sliding glass doors keep the gazebo warm). The swimming pool has gorgeous hillside views over olive groves. The Bulleris share their personal lifestyle: charming son Lorenzo assists guests with local itineraries, guides and museum or concert ticketing, and Paola conducts cooking lessons, while Claudio accompanies guests to his nearby golf club.

MARIGNOLLE RELAIS & CHARME
Owner: Claudio Bulleri family
Via di San Quirichino, 16
Florence, (FI) 50124, Italy
Tel: (055) 22 86 910, Fax: (055) 20 47 396
7 Rooms, Double: €140–€245
2 Suites: €235–€375
Lunch & dinner on request
Open: all year, Credit cards: all major
3.5 km from heart of Florence
Region: Tuscany, Michelin Map: 563

The Montartino-Villa Le Piazzole is located on the outskirts of Florence with the advantage of being easy to find with convenient parking. Bus and taxi service to Florence are readily available. Villa Le Piazzole was built in the 16th century as a watchtower to ensure safe transit for goods coming into Florence. As you enter the gates and wind up to the enchanting small villa crowning the hilltop, you can quickly see why this site was chosen for protection since the Ema Valley stretches below as far as the eye can see. You feel like a guest in a secluded country estate, yet Florence is only 3 kilometers away. The house has been lovingly restored, with great care taken to retain its original architectural features. Terracotta floors, whitewashed walls, beamed ceilings, handsome wooden furniture, and many beautiful antiques create the ambiance of a noble home. The guestrooms are spacious and the decor luxurious. All rooms and apartments have air conditioning, satellite TV, safe, mini-bar, direct-dial phone, and computer line and wireless connection. Added bonuses: a chapel for weddings, pool, Jacuzzi, and steam bath. In the cellar, tastings of their private-label wines and olive oil can be arranged with their English-speaking sommelier. *Directions:* From A1 take the Florence Certosa exit. At the second light turn right on Via Gherardo Silvani for 1.3 km. When the road splits, keep to the right. The hotel is on the left, behind a gated entrance.

❄ ☕ 🍴 ♨ 💳 ☎ @ W Y P ≈ 🖼 ⛷ ♿ 🕺 🐎 🍇

MONTARTINO-VILLA LE PIAZZOLE
Manager: Benedetta Listri
Via Gherardo Silvani, 147-149
Via Suor Maria Celeste 28, Florence, (FI) 50125, Italy
Tel: (055) 22 35 20, Fax: (055) 22 34 95
4 Rooms, Double: €200–€275
2 Suites: €250–€350
Breakfast included, other meals by prior arrangement
Open: Jan 1 to Nov 2, Credit cards: all major
3 km S of Ponte Vecchio
Region: Tuscany, Michelin Map: 563

The stunning Palazzo Magnani Feroni, an ancient private residence of the Giannotti family, dating back to the 1500s, is on the "left bank" of the River Arno four blocks away from the Ponte Vecchio. The sensation of being in a true palace is captured immediately upon entering the grand foyer with vaulted ceilings, marble busts, statues, and precious period paintings, many from the owners' world travels. This is a unique all-suite upscale accommodation in that they have purposefully avoided adding any obvious signs of its being a hotel (a small reception room sits off the main entrance) in order to retain the aura of living in an elegant historical residence. Sumptuous bedrooms with soaring ceilings, mostly enormous suites, have retained their original architectural features and have been appointed with antique and reproduction pieces, gilded framed mirrors, Oriental carpets, brocaded gold fabrics on sofas, and tapestries. Suites on the ground floor look out onto an inner courtyard and one has two walls entirely covered with a fresco depicting a bucolic countryside scene. Breakfast is served in the suites or in the long upstairs dining room with its showcase displaying antique silk fabrics left over from the days when the palazzo was also an antique gallery. Another highlight includes a rooftop terrace with superb views over the city, where in summer the Palace Bar opens every evening. The hotel also offers complimentary in-suite dinner for late arrivals.

❄ ☕ ✗ ☕ ▦ ☎ ⇕ 🛎 @ W ⌕ P 🔔 ⚘ ⅄ ⅄⅄ ⅄ 🍇

PALAZZO MAGNANI FERONI
Owners: Dr. & Sra. Alberto Giannotti
Borgo San Frediano, 5
Florence, (FI) 50124, Italy
Tel: (055) 23 99 544, Fax: (055) 26 08 908
12 Suites: €230–€850
Open: all year, Credit cards: all major
History Traveller
Center of Florence
Region: Tuscany, Michelin Map: 563

Palazzo Niccolini is one of the few hotels in Florence within a new category called Historic Residences. Dating from the 16th century, this fascinating palazzo has a prime location directly facing the Duomo Cathedral. The Niccolini family, descendants of the original owners, reside in part of the palazzo and have very meticulously restored the building, offering ten elegant, spacious bedrooms and suites for guests. Entered from the street level, the reception area is up one flight of stairs (or elevator) near the grand living room with period paintings, antiques, grand chandeliers. Breakfast is served in the elegant living room, making one feel like a private house guest. Each bedroom is elegantly decorated with antiques and all have sparkling, marble bathrooms; some with frescoed walls or ceilings. However, the "pieće de resistance" is the priceless suite upstairs that will leave guests in awe. Open the door, climb up ten steps into the glassed-in living room, and gaze right into the side of Brunelleschi's Cupola. You will never get a better view of the detailed, marble façade and roof tiles. In addition, behind the white sofa (which is located directly in front of the enormous windows) is a two-person hydro jet tub hidden among the plants. The bedroom and bathroom are accessed off to the side. *Directions:* The palazzo is on the corner of the Duomo square and Via dei Servi.

❄ ☕ ⚡ CREDIT ☎ 🐕 ♿ @ W Ⴤ P ⑪ ⊘ 🏛 ⚘ ♿ 🍇

PALAZZO NICCOLINI AL DUOMO
Manager: Marchesi Filippo
Via dei Servi, 2
Florence, (FI) 50122, Italy
Tel: (055) 28 24 12, Fax: (055) 29 09 79
5 Rooms, Double: €200–€340
5 Suites: €300–€500
Open: all year, Credit cards: all major
Next to the Duomo
Region: Tuscany, Michelin Map: 563

The Regency, facing out to a park in the most exclusive residential area, is one of Florence's finest luxury hotels and a welcome haven in the overcrowded tourist scene. Gracious hospitality comes naturally to owner Amedeo Ottaviani (also of the Lord Byron in Rome) and his philosophy that every guest should be treated with the best possible personal attention goes hand in hand with the intimate ambiance of the hotel, a former private home. Upon arrival guests are warmly greeted by resident manager, Lara, and invited into one of the cozy English-style sitting rooms richly appointed with fine antiques and paintings, floral-patterned carpeting, and exquisite fabrics in warm red tones. Beyond are two intimate, formal dining rooms, where the house chef is praised for his innovative creations based on Tuscan specialties incorporating the region's top-quality ingredients. The larger glassed-in dining area looks out over the exceptionally lush courtyard garden where romantic candlelit dinners are served in the summer months. Comfortable bedrooms and suites are spread among the top floors and a separate building connected to the main villa. They are uniquely appointed with white furnishings reproduced from original Tuscan antiques, patterned carpeting, and contrasting wall fabrics. Each has its own refurbished marble bathroom. The concierge is on hand to organize museum and concert reservations, and guides.

❄ 🍽 ⚙ ☕ 💳 ☎ 🐕 🚻 @ W ⛾ P 🍴 🚭 📷 ⚲ 🎣 👥 🐎 🍇

HOTEL REGENCY
Owner: Amedeo Ottaviani
Piazza Massimo D'Azeglio, 3
Florence, (FI) 50121, Italy
Tel: (055) 24 52 47, Fax: (055) 23 46 735
25 Rooms, Double: €275–€560
10 Suites: €740–€970
Open: all year, Credit cards: all major
10-minute walk to the city center
Region: Tuscany, Michelin Map: 563

If you are looking for a hotel in Florence that offers both a fabulous location and reasonably priced, pleasant rooms, the simple Relais Uffizi is for you. The double wood doors of the ancient building are located on the Chiasso del Buco, a quaint narrow back street accessed through an ancient arch from the Chiasso de' Baroncelli, off the Piazza della Signoria. Upstairs in the main reception lounge, the gracious owner, Elisabetta Matucci, or one of her friendly assistants will give you a warm welcome. Because there are so few rooms and the hotel is family-managed, guests are known by name and made to feel like friends. Nothing is contrived or overly sophisticated: instead there is an informal, comfortable ambiance. The heart of the hotel is the lounge where large windows look down upon the famous Piazza della Signoria with its statues and outdoor cafes. From this marvelous perch, you can relax in quiet comfort and enjoy all the drama and activity of Florence unfolding just below you. Although this is a simple hotel with remarkably low rates, no deluxe hotel in Florence can surpass this view of Florence. A maze of hallways leads to the individually decorated guestrooms. They vary in shape and size (number 3 with a canopy bed is especially spacious), but all are attractive in decor and have some antique furnishings. Best of all, they are immaculately clean and offer all the basic amenities.

RELAIS UFFIZI
Owner: Elisabetta Matucci
Chiasso de' Baroncelli/Chiasso del Buco, 16
Florence, (FI) 50122, Italy
Tel: (055) 26 76 239, Fax: (055) 26 57 909
13 Rooms, Double: €160–€250
2 Suites: €220–€270
Open: all year, Credit cards: all major
Overlooking Piazza della Signoria
Region: Tuscany, Michelin Map: 563

The Torre di Bellosguardo is a romantic historic villa nestled on the shelf of a hill with an unsurpassed view of Florence. Below the enormous castle-like home, the tiled rooftops, steeples, towers, and domes of the city seem like a fairyland at your fingertips. It is not surprising that the setting of the Torre di Bellosguardo is so breathtaking: it was chosen by a nobleman, Guido Cavalcanti (a friend of Dante), as the most beautiful site in Florence. The villa is owned today by Amerigo Franchetti who takes great pride in his stunning home and, with a passion for perfection, is restoring the villa to its original glory. The spacious austere guestrooms with views are decorated in authentic period antiques and vary in size as they would in a private home with few frills. Other rooms include frescoed ballroom, Orangerie, and upstairs loggia terrace. The most splendid features of the hotel are its incredible setting and meticulously groomed botanical garden, which highlights a swimming pool set on a terrace overlooking Florence, Brunelleschi cupola and all. In summer lunch is served by the swimming pool, otherwise breakfast is the only meal available. For dinner, you must wind down a narrow twisting road to go to a restaurant. If you want to walk into Florence, ask about the "secret" path—a short cut down the hill to the city (15 minute walk). Down a level through an underground tunnel a small pool, sauna and steam room.

TORRE DI BELLOSGUARDO
Owner: Amerigo Franchetti
Via Roti Michelozzi, 2, Florence, (FI) 50124, Italy
Tel: (055) 22 98 145, Fax: (055) 22 90 08
8 Rooms, Double: €290*
7 Suites: €340–€390*
*Breakfast not included: €20
Poolside lunch in summer, light dinners on request
Open: all year, Credit cards: all major
5-minute drive to city center
Region: Tuscany, Michelin Map: 563

The pristine grey-white Villa Vedetta, originally a private home is the only accommodation positioned right at Florence's most famous panoramic viewing point, the Piazzale Michelangelo. Brunelleschi's unmistakable dome dominates the scene and can be privately enjoyed from the hotel's garden with swimming pool and large Jacuzzi area, from the expansive terrace, and from most guestrooms. A trendy Michelin star restaurant within the villa, Onice, under the guidance of Chef Andrea Accordi, presents artistic, innovative Tuscan-based cuisine and a vast wine list. Eight stylish guestrooms in a contemporary vein have all the trimmings expected of a luxury property and are appointed in light grays, and accented with touches of cherry red, satin peach, or celestial blues. Modern bathrooms are done in marble with mosaic trims. The main sitting areas are freshly appointed with striped sofas and modern artwork. But what guests really rave about is the attentive staff, always willing and ready to assist with warmth and knowledge. A variety of interesting theme stays involving shopping, art or Chianti wineries make your stay more complete. Easy shuttle to the city center available upon request. *Directions:* From A1 autostrada, exit Firenze Sud. Turn right in Via Enrick de Nicola and continue along the river, until you reach bridge Ponte S. Niccole. At the light turn right over the bridge, and enter in Viale Michelangelo. Continue for 1km. Hotel is on the right.

VILLA LA VEDETTA
Manager: Samuel Porreca
Via Michelangelo 78
Florence, (FI) 50125, Italy
Tel: (055) 68 16 31, Fax: (055) 65 82 544
18 Rooms, Double: €449–€1099*
*Breakfast not included: €40
Open: all year, Credit cards: all major
History Traveller, Relais & Châteaux
3 km from Florence center
Region: Tuscany, Michelin Map: 563

The Bencista is a real find for the traveler looking for a congenial, unpretentious, family-run hotel near Florence that has charm and yet is reasonably priced. The villa, romantically nestled in the foothills with a bird's-eye view of Florence, is owned and managed by the Simoni family who are always about, personally seeing to every need of their guests. Simone Simoni speaks excellent English, and on the day of my arrival he was patiently engrossed in conversation with one of the guests, giving him tips for sightseeing. Downstairs there is a jumble of sitting rooms, bars, and parlors, each decorated with dark Victorian furniture. Upstairs are the bedrooms, which vary in size, location, and furnishings. Some are far superior to others. Many people return year after year to their own favorite room. During the season, reservations should be made well in advance, especially for a room with a view over Florence, as the hotel is beautifully located for sightseeing in both Florence and Tuscany. (If you do not have a car, you can take the bus that runs regularly into Florence from the top of the road every 20 min.) Two meals (breakfast and a choice of lunch or dinner) are included in the price. One of the outstanding features of the pensione is its splendid terrace where guests can enjoy a sweeping panorama of Florence.

PENSIONE BENCISTA
Owner: Simone Simoni
Florence–Fiesole, (FI) 50014, Italy
Tel & Fax: (055) 59 163
32 Rooms, Double: €120–€430*
4 Suites: €460*
*Includes breakfast & dinner
Closed: Dec to Feb, Credit cards: MC, VS
8 km NE of Florence
Region: Tuscany, Michelin Map: 563

Fiesole, a small town tucked in the green wooded hills above Florence, has long been a favorite of ours. Staying here gives you the best of both worlds—you can enjoy the peacefulness of the countryside while being just a short ride away from Florence. If you are looking for ultimate luxury, nothing can compete with the Villa San Michele, but the Hotel Villa Fiesole offers a delightful alternative for those on a more conservative budget. You can easily spot the Villa Fiesole, set just above the road as it loops up the wooded hillside. Originally a private mansion, the Villa Fiesole was converted into a delightful small hotel in 1995, being equipped with all the finest modern amenities but keeping the overall ambiance of an exquisite home. In this part of the hotel, the rooms vary somewhat in size because of the nature of the building. A new wing has been added and the construction, although obviously recent, was done in excellent taste so that it blends in beautifully with the original villa. Here the rooms are almost identical in size and furnishings. Each is especially spacious and decorated in a most appealing way, using tones of rich blue and whites, giving an overall ambiance of refined good taste. The hotel does not have a formal restaurant but, in addition to breakfast, a light lunch, dinner, and simple buffet supper are available for guests. The Florence bus #7 stops in front of the villa every 20 minutes until 6 pm.

HOTEL VILLA FIESOLE
Manager: Simone Taddei
Via Beato Angelico, 35
Florence–Fiesole, (FI) 50014, Italy
Tel: (055) 59 72 52, Fax: (055) 59 91 33
32 Rooms, Double: €130
4 Suites: €430–€460
Meals for hotel guests only
Open: all year, Credit cards: all major
8 km NE of Florence
Region: Tuscany, Michelin Map: 563

It would be difficult to find another hotel with as many attributes as the Villa San Michele—in fact, almost impossible. How could you surpass a wooded hillside setting overlooking Florence, a stunning view, gorgeous antiques, impeccable management, gourmet dining, and, as if this were not enough, a building designed by Michelangelo. The Villa San Michele was originally a monastery dating back to the 15th century and occupied by Franciscan friars until Napoleon turned it into his headquarters. The adaptation of its rooms and public areas to today's standards has been made without affecting the ambiance of serenity and history. Most of the rooms are in the historical building and have been recently renovated and redecorated with taste and somber elegance. Eighteen junior suites are located in the Italian garden and three suites in the Limonaia, once the greenhouse for storing lemon plants during the winter. All have sweeping views of Florence and the Arno Valley. The lounges, dining rooms, terraces, and gardens are also exquisite. Meals can be enjoyed either in the elegant dining room or on a lovely veranda that stretches along the entire length of the building. A panoramic swimming pool has been built on a secluded terrace above the hotel. Now a permanent cooking school, the Villa San Michele School of Cookery offers a wide range of gastronomic courses.

VILLA SAN MICHELE
General Manager: Luca Finardi
Via Doccia, 4
Florence–Fiesole, (FI) 50014, Italy
Tel: (055) 56 78 200, Fax: (055) 56 78 250
21 Rooms, Double: €950–€1100
25 Suites: €1300–€3200
Open: Apr to Nov, Credit cards: all major
History Traveller
7 km NE of Florence
Region: Tuscany, Michelin Map: 563

Nestled in a small village in the foothills of the Alps, you'll find one of our favorite hotels, the very special Villa Abbazia, situated across from a picturesque 12th-century abbey. When you enter into the 17th-century palazzo—which is graced by fine antiques, Oriental carpets, lovely fabrics, and bouquets of fresh flowers—the Zanon family welcomes you as if you were a friend in their own home. All of the palazzo's bedrooms and suites are stunning. Each guestroom has been splendidly decorated and exudes the ambiance of an English country manor. Meticulous care and tender love has gone into every tiny detail, including the fresh flowers and individual breakfast china, which reflects the color scheme of each room. In addition to the bedrooms in the Palazzo, there are four beautiful suites in the magnificently restored 19th-century, Liberty-style villa across the garden. The Abbazia is surrounded by excellent places to dine, including its own restaurant, La Corte, where one can find delicious foods typical of the region in a pleasant and intimate environment. The Villa Abbazia is located in a region rich in medieval villages and Palladian villas, most appealing for lovers of art and architecture. The historic towns of Asolo and Vittorio Veneto are nearby.

❄ ☕ 🍴 ⛲ 💳 ☎ 🐕 @ W Y P 🍴 ✍ 🚶 👣 🐎 ⚓ 💃

VILLA ABBAZIA
Owner: Zanon family
Via Martiri della Liberta
Follina, (TV) 31051, Italy
Tel: (0438) 97 12 77, Fax: (0438) 97 00 01
12 Rooms, Double: €230–€320, 6 Suites: €350–€500
Restaurant closed Sundays
Open: all year, Credit cards: all major
Relais & Châteaux
90 km S of Cortina, 60 km NW of Venice
Region: Veneto, Michelin Map: 562

Staying in the Albani hills just south of Rome is an excellent alternative to the higher-priced accommodations in the city—the area offers easy public transportation, proximity to both airports, and picturesque towns, lakes, and gardens. Frascati is best known for its wine and many restaurants, which Romans invade on weekends. The Hotel Flora stands out among the choice of smaller hotels. Formerly a private residence, the turn-of-the-last-century gray-and-white pristine villa has a courtyard and surrounding garden where breakfast is served in the summer months. The best rooms, a variety of doubles, junior suites, and suites, are spacious, with terraces and high ceilings. These are on the upper floors, while the rest are in a newer building next door. The polished decor throughout is neoclassical, with black-and-white marble floors and bathrooms, and antique furnishings, and the guestrooms include many amenities as well as air conditioning. Top-floor rooms have balconies with nice views. To the right of the reception area guests enjoy a comfortable lounge and bar. Sightseeing in the vicinity includes lakes Nemi and Albano, the gardens of Ninfa and Villa Aldobrandini, and Rocca di Papa. A shuttle service is available for transfers to and from airports and the metro station (€58 for two). *Directions:* Exit from Rome's GRA ring road at Via Tuscolana and continue straight to Frascati. Hotel signs are posted in the town.

❄ ☕ 🛷 ♨ CREDIT ☎ 🐕 ♿ @ W ♈ P 🍴 🚭 🖼 🔑 ⚓ 🧍 👫 🏇 ⚓ 🍇 🍸

HOTEL FLORA
Owner: Barbante Family
Viale Vittorio Veneto, 8
Frascati, (RM) 00044, Italy
Tel: (06) 94 16 110, Fax: (06) 94 16 546
34 Rooms, Double: €135–€200
3 Suites: €190–€290
Open: all year, Credit cards: all major
19 km south of Rome
Region: Lazio, Michelin Map: 563

The Castello di Spaltenna is a charming hotel, nestled within an ancient feudal hamlet in one of the prettiest parts of Tuscany's glorious Chianti wine region. From the castle with its fortified monastery and adjacent church adorned by an 11th-century bell tower, you can look out in every direction to a blissful scene of rolling hills, valleys, and woodlands dotted with castles and medieval villages. Although deluxe in every detail, the hotel reflects its heritage with beamed ceilings, thick walls, stone floors, and watchtowers. The decor too pays tribute to the past with handsome old oil paintings, priceless tapestries, gorgeous Persian carpets, handmade wrought-iron beds, and splendid antique furniture. A wonderful feature of the hotel is its restaurant, Il Pievano, situated in the centuries old hall of the Castello di Spaltenna. The heart of the hotel is its internal courtyard. When the weather is mild, guests enjoy fine dining here in a fairy-tale setting created by softly illuminated candles, tables dressed with fine linens, fresh flowers, and for a romantic touch, a harp playing in the background. On a terrace below the castle guests can relax after a day of sightseeing and enjoy an exceptionally beautiful, large swimming pool. A final touch is an indoor pool, which is part of the resort's deluxe spa facility. *Directions:* From Gaiole in Chianti, follow signs to the castle.

※ ➡ 🍴 CREDIT ☎ 🏋 @ 🍸 P ⫫ 🌺 ≈ 🚶 🖼 🐕 👫 🏇 🍇

CASTELLO DI SPALTENNA
Manager: Guido Conti
Gaiole in Chianti, (SI) 53013, Italy
Tel: (0577) 74 94 83, Fax: (0577) 74 92 69
38 Rooms, Double: €230–€540
Closed: Feb & Mar, Credit cards: all major
50 km S of Florence, 30 km N of Siena
Region: Tuscany, Michelin Map: 563

L'Ultimo Mulino

When dreaming of Tuscany, one usually envisions sweeping fields of vineyards and gentle hills dotted with olive trees. L'Ultimo Mulino has a totally different type of setting, in a heavily wooded nook by a small stream. This small hotel was originally a medieval olive mill and the antique millstone in the lounge stands testament to the hotel's colorful past, as do many architectural features, including 13 dramatic brick arches, which form a vaulted ceiling in the lounge. The primary color scheme throughout is white and blue—seen in the sofas and also in the dining room in the cushions and the table linens and china. The guestrooms all have a rustic ambiance, appropriate to the old mill, with wrought-iron headboards used throughout. The price of the rooms depends upon the size and the amenities. The least expensive rooms are fairly small but those in the upper category are large, and several have their own private terrace. The bathrooms are especially nice, and many have the added luxury of Jacuzzi tubs. All the rooms have air conditioning, direct-dial phones, mini-bars, good lighting by the beds, and satellite televisions. One of the most pleasant features of the hotel is a 20-meter swimming pool built into a terrace above the hotel. *Directions:* From Radda in Chianti, take the road for Gaiole and Siena. About 5 km from Radda, turn left at the sign to L'Ultimo Mulino. The hotel is about midway between Radda and Gaiole.

L'ULTIMO MULINO
Manager: Massimo Rossinelli
Localita: La Ripresa di Vistarenni
Gaiole in Chianti, (SI) 53013, Italy
Tel: (0577) 73 85 20, Fax: (0577) 73 86 59
12 Rooms, Double: €160–€230
1 Suite: €260–€300
Meals for hotel guests (Tues-Sun)
Closed: mid-Nov to mid-Mar, Credit cards: all major
50 km S of Florence, 30 km N of Siena
Region: Tuscany, Michelin Map: 563

Tenuta Gangivecchio is far off the beaten path. Not only will you discover a jewel of a small inn, but the adventure of finding Gangivecchio leads you through Sicily's beautiful Madonie region. The Tornabene family began by converting a room in their home (a 13th-century Benedictine monastery of great character) into a restaurant, serving a set-menu lunch based upon fresh produce from the farm. The excellence of the simple yet delicious meals soon brought guests from as great a distance as Palermo, a two-hour drive away. Happily for the traveler who loves to stay in the countryside, the enterprising Tornabene family have now renovated the stables of the monastery into ten tastefully decorated guestrooms, appealing in their simplicity, with rustic red-tile floors, fresh whitewashed walls, hand-loomed scatter rugs, dark-wood accents, rough-hewn beamed ceilings, attractively framed old prints on the walls, and sweet cotton floral bedspreads. Delicious home-cooked meals are served to guests in a pretty dining room on the ground floor of the inn. Plan to arrive on a weekend for a lunch prepared by Signora Wanda and her daughter Giovanna, served in the dining room of the monastery. *Directions:* Drive east through Gangi on S.S. 120. Just outside of town turn right at a signpost for Gangivecchio. Go about 1 km and turn left at the tiny yellow sign. Continue 5 km up the hill and the Tenuta Gangivecchio is on your right.

≌ ⚞ 🖭 ☎ @ P ⫪ ≈

TENUTA GANGIVECCHIO
Owner: Paolo Tornabene
C. da Gangivecchio
Gangivecchio, (PA) 90024, Italy
Tel & Fax: (0921) 68 91 91
8 Rooms, Double: €90–€114
Closed: Jul, Credit cards: MC, VS
130 km SE of Palermo, 127 km NW of Catania
Region: Sicily, Michelin Map: 565

La Foresteria Serego Alighieri is on a working farm producing wine and olive oil. Only a discreet brass sign on the gate hints at any commercialism, yet it is indeed a fabulous place to stay. Each reasonably priced guestroom is a one- or two-bedroom apartment with a well-equipped kitchen, charming living room, and a large bathroom tiled in local marble. The decor throughout reflects tasteful, elegant simplicity—whitewashed walls set off country antiques, and comfortable sofas are upholstered in Venetian pure-cotton fabrics in green and cream stripes. Soft green is repeated in the pretty cotton drapes and bedspreads. It is not surprising that La Foresteria has been developed with such love and meticulous care to maintain the estate's authentic charm—the present owner, the gracious Count di Serego Alighieri, is the 20th generation to own the property! Family records indicate the first ancestor to own the land was the poet Dante's son, who purchased the estate in 1353. This vast farm was almost doomed at the end of World War II when the retreating armies had orders to destroy it. As a forestalling tactic, the present count's father invited the commanding officers to a magnificent party. Perhaps it was the abundance of the excellent wines served, but happily the officers forgot their orders. To celebrate this miracle of the saving of the town, every April the local townspeople make a pilgrimage to the estate to celebrate mass—followed, of course, by a little wine.

LA FORESTERIA SEREGO ALIGHIERI
Owner: Count Pieralvise di Sergo Alighieri
Via Stazione, 2
Gargagnago, (VR) 37020, Italy
Tel: (045) 77 03 622, Fax: (045) 77 03 523
8 Apartments: €313 daily, €1648 weekly
Closed: Jan, Credit cards: all major
18 km NW of Verona
Region: Veneto, Michelin Map: 562

The Grand Hotel a Villa Feltrinelli, snuggled on the shore of romantic Lake Garda just steps from the tiny, picturesque village of Gargnano, is an incredible property. This fairy-tale villa—painted in muted cream and peach-colored stripes accented by a jaunty tower and turreted roof—is so appealing it makes you smile from first glance. It was built as a private home for the Feltrinelli family, who made their fortune in lumber. The building had been long neglected when Bob Burns became captivated by its romantic charm and for three years poured unrestricted love and money into meticulously returning the mansion to its original glory. Talented artisans worked around the clock restoring gorgeous murals, stained-glass windows, handsome paneling, massive chandeliers, and splendid floors. Although this is a super-luxurious, exquisite jewel of a hotel, the ambiance exudes the warmth and friendliness of a private home. There is hardly a hint of commercialism: guests are warmly welcomed at the door; registration is discreetly accomplished in the guestroom; the mini-bar is stocked with complimentary drinks; suitcases are unpacked (if the guest so desires) and whisked away to storage; laundry and dry cleaning are complimentary; drinks in the bar can be signed for on the honor system. For quality and sumptuous accommodations, the Villa Feltrinelli is an incredible value. *Directions:* Located at the north end of Gargnano.

※ ☕ ⚓ 💳 ☎ 🏨 @ W Ⓨ P ⑪ ≋ ⛴ ⛱ 🏃 🚶 🐎 ⛵ 🍷

GRAND HOTEL A VILLA FELTRINELLI
Manager: Markus Odermatt
Gargnano, Lake Garda, (BS) 25084, Italy
Tel: (0365) 79 80 00, Fax: (0365) 79 80 01
21 Suites: €800–€4000
Closed: Nov to Mar, Credit cards: all major
History Traveller
140 km E of Milan, 78 km W of Verona
Region: Lombardy, Michelin Map: 561

Hotel du Lac, an intimate, family-managed hotel in the colorful, tiny village of Villa di Gargnano, is very special. If you want an elegant hotel decorated with opulent fabrics and ornate furnishings, this would not be your cup of tea. But for genuine hospitality, superb lakefront setting, and spotlessly clean, attractive rooms at very reasonable prices, the Hotel du Lac is a real winner. From the moment we walked in and met the charming young owner, Valerio Arosio, I knew this would be a special hotel. The reception and sitting areas as you enter are simply decorated with modern, nondescript furnishings. In contrast, the bedrooms are unexpectedly attractive for such moderately priced accommodations. Each has a lovely antique headboard and a sweet, simple charm. There is satellite TV and free Internet connections in all the rooms and the bathrooms are modern and even have hairdryers. Splurge and ask for one of the bedrooms with a terrace and view of the lake. When the weather is warm, most meals are served outside. However, there is an attractive dining room with windows on three sides capturing views of the lake. Unfortunately, the hotel does not have private parking, however they can suggest public parking lots in the area. *Directions:* Villa di Gargnano is located just south of Gargnano. The hotel is in the center of town.

HOTEL DU LAC
Owner: Valerio Arosio
Via Colletta, 21
Gargnano, Lake Guarda, (BS) 25084, Italy
Tel: (0365) 71 107, Fax: (0365) 71 055
11 Rooms, Double: €94–€134
Restaurant closed Mondays
Open: Mar to Nov, Credit cards: MC, VS
140 km E of Milan, 78 km W of Verona
Region: Lombardy, Michelin Map: 561

The Hotel Villa Giulia is an outstanding small hotel just on the edge of the quaint, colorful, medieval village of Gargnano. It has a prime location: not only lakefront, but also surrounded by large, park-like grounds. The main house, reminiscent of a quaint Victorian villa, sits center stage with a tree-studded lawn stretching down to a terrace overlooking the lake. In the garden is a wonderful swimming pool tucked in under the frame that in days gone by was used to protect the precious lemon trees that are so famous in this part of Italy. Some of the guestrooms are located in the main villa, others in two separate renovated buildings on the property, but they all share the facilities in the main house. Here you find a parlor with an old-fashioned appeal and a spacious dining room with super views of the lake. The guestrooms in this original villa are my favorites, especially rooms such as 7 or 17, which have stunning views. In addition to its attractive rooms, great Italian cooking, and outstanding location, the Hotel Villa Giulia has another ingredient that makes it even more special—it is run by your sweet and charming hostess Barbara, who took over the management of the hotel a few years ago from her aunt. The hotel has been lovingly redecorated and is a wonderful choice for accommodations along the ever-so-romantic Lake Garda. *Directions:* Located on the north edge of Gargnano.

HOTEL VILLA GIULIA
Owner: Bombardelli family
Viale Rimembranza, 20
Gargnano, (BS) 25084, Italy
Tel: (0365) 71 022, Fax: (0365) 72 774
23 Rooms, Double: €220–€330
1 apartment: €1100 weekly
Open: Easter to Oct, Credit cards: all major
140 km E of Milan, 78 km W of Verona
Region: Lombardy, Michelin Map: 561

The gracious Segre family warmly welcomes guests to their elegant country home/hotel located on the upper half of the Riviera north of Genoa. The property is immersed in the soft green landscapes and right next door to one of Italy's most popular golf courses. From the main gate up the lane on the left-hand side is an inviting pool while the entrance to the inn with its large front window sits to the right. Most of the 32 guestrooms with balconies are within the new three-story wing attached to the main house and overlook the surrounding gardens and golf course. Guestrooms and the many common rooms including large living room and breakfast room, are appointed with crisp floral fabrics and accented with antiques and paintings. Guests can dine at one of the hotel's three restaurants. Il Rosmarino is a gourmet restaurant which combines fresh local produce with regional seafood recipes, accompanied by a vast selection of wines. Il Bistrot offers the best Ligurian cuisine and La Piscina is a casual pool-side restaurant open for lunch. Excursions in the area include the more undiscovered coastline going towards the French border, as well as Genoa and its newly developed pier area with aquarium and restaurants, or the classic Riviera with highlights such as enchanting Portofino. *Directions:* Exit autostrada A10 at Albenga and follow signs for Garlenda and La Meridiana for a total of 9 km.

HOTEL LA MERIDIANA
Owner: Segre Family
Via ai Castelli
Garlenda, (SV) 17033, Italy
Tel: (0182) 58 02 71, Fax: (0182) 58 01 50
12 Rooms, Double: €240–€300,* 15 Suites: €420*
*Breakfast not included: €22
Open: Easter to Nov, Credit cards: all major
Relais & Châteaux
90 km W of Genoa
Region: Liguria, Michelin Map: 561

L'Ostelliere is part of a new breed of farm countryside accommodation offering a high level of comfort and service in a sophisticated ambiance. The restored 18th-century farmhouse complex holds 28 very spacious bedrooms, each individually appointed with a mix of creatively restored country antiques from Spain, Italy and England. They harmonize nicely with the earth tone color schemes, contemporary artwork, plank wood floors and stone walls, contrasted with red accents in pillows and fine fabrics. Besides the hotel, there is a gourmet restaurant, La Gallina, and a prestigious winery, Villa Sparina, combined to form the Monterotondo Resort. Pristine vineyards, spread about the 300-acre property composed of hills and woods, produce a variety of grapes. The magnificent wine cellars just underneath the hotel can be toured. Meals are served outside overlooking the vineyards, or in the lofty brick dining room, once a hay barn. In the evening, lighting is obtained by hidden spots and candlelight, creating a magical ambiance. Taking advantage of the location between the Ligurian Riviera and Piedmont countryside, the very capable chef pulls together the best of both regions and creates innovative dishes enhanced by the superb choice of wines. A super professional staff is on hand to suggest itineraries in the area. *Directions:* Exit autostrada A7 at Serravalle Scrivia and follow for Serravalle, then turn for Monterotondo. After passing the church in town, turn right at sign for Ostelliere.

L'OSTELLIERE   New
General Manager: Marisa Giuliano
Frazione Monterotondo 56
Gavi, (AL) 15066, Italy
Tel: (0143) 60 78 01, Fax: (0143) 60 78 11
15 Rooms, Double: €150–€250
13 Suites: €220–€650
Open: all year, Credit cards: all major
25 km south of Alessandria, 25 km N of Genova
Region: Piedmont, Michelin Map: 561

The story goes that two hundred years ago a wealthy merchant from Genoa fell in love with a Chinese woman and had his extravagant seaside residence built in oriental style. This romantic air lingers at the Cavaliere family's Villa Pagoda, an intimate hotel with plenty of attractive features. The whimsical six-tiered villa is full of character and charm due to its irregular-shaped architecture and one can just imagine the glamorous parties that were held in the main salon with enormous Murano chandelier, grand piano and polished Carrara marble floors. Antiques and precious artwork, including an impressive collection of small Mirò lithographs, decorate the stairways of the home with its 18 bedrooms and junior suites of various dimensions. The most desirable ones are the sea-view rooms at the very top. Almost all rooms now have renovated bathrooms and parquet floors. Surrounding the villa is a lush park and garden stretching down to the sea where the town's elevated 2-kilometer promenade with spectacular views is reached. Il Roseto is the name of the restaurant which serves gourmet seafood in the large dining room opening up to the garden with outdoor seating. A second more intimate dining room upstairs is where a delectable buffet breakfast is served. From here you are conveniently based to tour several interesting local museums, the restored historic center of Genova, Portofino and Cinque Terre areas.

❄ ⚞ 💳 ☎ 🐕 🏨 @ W Ⓨ P 🍴 🚭 ≋ 🖼 ⌔ 🏌 ⚓ 🏃 👫 🏄

*ROMANTIK HOTEL VILLA PAGODA   **New***
Owner: Alessandro Cavaliere
Via Capolungo, 15, Genova–Nervi, (GE) 16167, Italy
Tel: (010) 37 26 161, Fax: (010) 32 12 18
13 Rooms, Double: €155–€265*
4 Suites: €290–€650*
*Breakfast not included: €14.50
Open: all year, Credit cards: all major
Romantik Hotels
Near Portofino-Italian Riviera, 18 km E of Genova
Region: Liguria, Michelin Map: 561

The Frascati hillside wine area just south of Rome is an alternative to staying in the city. Before opening its doors in 1997, the 16th-century Villa Grazioli undertook ten years of tedious restoration work—it was imperative to conserve the architecture, grounds, and the many important frescoed ceilings by G.P. Pannini. After the restoration it was transformed into a splendid hotel under the strict regulations of the Ministry of Historical Buildings. The spacious reception area and four inviting frescoed sitting rooms on the first floor remind us that this was once a private residence. Ten spacious double rooms and two suites are offered right in the villa off the impressive galleria—a head-spinning vaulted hall completely frescoed from floor to ceiling, overlooking the front garden. The remaining more standard rooms are located across the garden in what was originally the lemon-tree greenhouse, all decorated conservatively with antiques and rich fabrics and offering all the modern amenities. An underground tunnel connects the two buildings. The four formal, high-ceilinged dining rooms have an enormous terrace taking in the surrounding park, Italian gardens, and a spectacular panoramic view over Rome. The hotel has a shuttle service to Frascati or the local train station. *Directions:* From the GRA (the circle road around Rome) exit onto the N21/22. Go south to Grottaferrata. At the end of town, a sign to the left marks the way to the hotel.

PARK HOTEL VILLA GRAZIOLI
Manager: Francesco Ceribelli
Via Umberto Pavoni, 19
Grottaferrata, (RM) 00046, Italy
Tel: (06) 94 54 001, Fax: (06) 94 13 506
58 Rooms, Double: €200–€330
2 Suites: €450–€560
Open: all year, Credit cards: all major
History Traveller, Relais & Châteaux
20 km south of Rome
Region: Lazio, Michelin Map: 563

Gubbio is one of Umbria's many jewels: a small, wonderfully intact medieval town that presses against the wooded hillside. A not-to-be-missed sight in Gubbio is the Piazza Grande, considered to be one of the boldest examples of medieval town planning, and facing onto this awesome masterpiece is the Relais Ducale. Gazing from the square, you would hardly know that a hotel is secreted within the building, but you will notice a large, open, stone passageway. Enter here and climb up the stairs through a tunnel-like corridor where you will emerge into a little lane. Continue on until you come to a hotel sign by the gate on a stone wall. Ring the bell for entrance and suddenly the hotel reveals itself with a charming inner garden courtyard off which you find the discreet reception office. The hotel, once the guest quarters for the Ducale Palace, has been sleekly renovated, but impressive features of its past are seen throughout with massive thick walls, high vaulted ceilings, and stone archways. On the fourth level of the hotel there is a romantic garden with one side enclosed by a carved stone balustrade, where you can gaze out to a beautiful panoramic view. Fine antique furniture is used for accent, handsome oil paints adorn the walls, and Oriental carpets brighten the floors. The pretty guestrooms have a sedate, refined decor, showing an effort to preserve the aristocratic aura of the hotel's heritage. All guestrooms have LCD TVs and Internet access.

❄ 🍽 ☕ ✏ 🍵 CREDIT ☎ 🐕 🏠 @ 🍷 🍴 🖼 ⚒ ♿ 🏃 👫 🐎 🍇

RELAIS DUCALE
Owner: Rodolfo Mencarelli
Via Ducale, 2
Gubbio, (PG) 06024, Italy
Tel: (075) 92 20 157, Fax: (075) 92 20 159
32 Rooms, Double: €155–€275
Open: all year, Credit cards: all major
54 km NW of Assisi, 92 km E of Arezzo
Region: Umbria, Michelin Map: 563

La Posta Vecchia, a spectacular villa nestled on the edge of the ocean just north of Rome's airport, was the home of the late John Paul Getty. There are 19 bedrooms (mostly suites) tucked into a stunning mansion secluded by manicured gardens artfully designed to emphasize the ruins of the Pompeii-like villa. The magic starts from the moment you ring the bell at the gated entrance—the gate swings open, you drive through a vast park, and suddenly, the storybook villa comes into view. Within the mansion, priceless antique furniture, statues, and fine fabrics richly adorn the rooms, creating an opulent, tasteful splendor in the lounges and the guestrooms. The dining room is exquisite, but even more romantic is to dine on balmy evenings on the terrace perched above the ocean. When Getty was installing the magnificent pool in the northern wing, he discovered the foundations of a Roman villa—thought perhaps to be the weekend retreat of Julius Caesar. Getty, who was profoundly interested in archaeology, spared no expense to preserve this antiquity. These Roman ruins are now encompassed by the lower level of the home and guests can view the splendid mosaic floors, walls, and pottery—displayed as if in a living museum. La Posta Vecchia is expensive, but a once-in-a-lifetime experience. *Directions:* Exit the A12 at Ladispoli and follow signs to town. La Posta Vecchia is in Palo Laziale, 2.2 km south of Ladispoli.

LA POSTA VECCHIA
Manager: Alessio Minetto
Ladispoli, Palo Laziale, (RM) 00055, Italy
Tel: (06) 99 49 501, Fax: (06) 99 49 507
19 Rooms, Double: €590–€1550
Open: Mar 19 to Nov 14, Credit cards: all major
Relais & Châteaux
25 km N of Rome airport
Region: Lazio, Michelin Map: 563

Cinque Terre is the name given to five villages (Monterosso, Riomaggiore, Vernazza, Manarola, and Corniglia) that are built into the mountainous coast of Liguria. Several of these picturesque villages are accessible only by foot or train. There are several choices of places from which you can explore these tiny fishing hamlets, one of these being the modest, rather dated resort of Levanto. The Hotel Stella Maris is a simple, two-star hotel, but it exudes warmth and caring, and is recommended to the traveler who is looking for a reasonably priced place to stay and who values hospitality rather than decorator-perfect accommodation. Not that the hotel is lacking in character: it is located on the second floor of a 17th-century palazzo and remnants of its past grandeur remain. Many of the bedrooms feature high, elaborately frescoed ceilings and handsome antique beds. I think my favorite is number 4, an especially inviting room with a romantic wooden, French-style headboard. Supper is served by candlelight in the intimate and elegant dining room under the frescoed ceiling. Breakfast and dinner are included in the room rate. Although only a little English is spoken, Renza and Alexandro exude a merry warmth that is sure to touch your heart. A fresh basket of fruit is given with the Junior and Superior suites.

HOTEL STELLA MARIS
Owners: Renza & Alexandro Italiani
Via Marconi, 4
Levanto, (SP) 19015, Italy
Tel: (0187) 80 82 58, Fax: (0187) 80 73 51
5 Rooms, Double: €160–€240*
3 Suites: €300–€370*
*Includes breakfast & dinner
Closed: Nov, Credit cards: all major
83 km SE of Genoa, 36 km NW of La Spezia
Region: Liguria, Michelin Map: 561

Lucca is an outstanding walled town—truly one of Italy's jewels. If you want to visit Lucca, but prefer staying in the countryside, just a ten-minute drive away sits the sumptuous Locanda L'Elisa, a pretty, deep-lavender villa with white trim peeking out from the trees. The hotel has the appearance of a private home and, happily, this intimate, homelike quality remains even after you step inside where you are warmly greeted. As you look around, it is obvious that this was previously the residence of a wealthy family. Fine antiques, splendid paintings, and luxurious fabrics combine to create a mood of refined elegance. All of the guestrooms are individually decorated, but exude a similar old-world ambiance created with dark woods and opulent materials. The walls are richly covered in damask fabrics that color-coordinate with the draperies and bedspreads. However, the mood changes dramatically in the appealing dining room, found in a glass-enclosed conservatory. During the day, sunlight streams in through the windows and guests can enjoy both excellent cuisine and a view of the trees, green lawn, and colorful, well-tended beds of flowers. In this same garden you find a refreshing swimming pool. The Locanda L'Elisa is a very special luxury hideaway with a gracious warmth of welcome. *Directions:* Take the A11 to Lucca then take N12r (not 12) toward Pisa. Soon after leaving Lucca, watch for a sign on the left for Locanda L'Elisa.

LOCANDA L'ELISA
Owner: Alessandro Del Grande
Via Nuova per Pisa, 1952 (S.S. 12B1S)
Massa Pisana
Lucca, (LU) 55050, Italy
Tel: (0583) 37 97 37, Fax: (0583) 37 90 19
10 Rooms, Double: €210–€390*
*Breakfast not included: €16
Closed: Jan, Credit cards: all major
4.5 km S of Lucca on N12r, 65 km W of Florence
Region: Tuscany, Michelin Map: 563

It was welcome news to hear that a small deluxe hotel had opened in the historical center of Lucca, one of our favorite medieval walled cities. After years of meticulous restoration, the 12th-century Palazzo Alexander first opened for guests in 2000. Your gracious host and creator of this small inn is Mario Maraviglia, who welcomes guests as friends with hardly a hint of commercialism—there isn't even a hotel sign in front—and his team shares his philosophy. To the left of the marble-floored reception foyer is an ornate, intimate breakfast room and bar, set with small tables and fancy, gold-embellished chairs. Two huge chandeliers enhance the dark, handsome, beamed ceiling. As well as the elevator, a wonderful, very old stone staircase, illuminated by a stained-glass skylight, leads up to the guestrooms, each named after a famous Italian opera. The bedrooms are furnished with antique reproduction furniture in an ornate Venetian style. All the rooms have mini-bars, hairdryers, TVs, direct-dial phones, and elegant marble bathrooms. If you want to splurge, ask for "Tosca" which has a romantic little terrace tucked in the rooftop. At the moment there are only a few rooms, but the building next door has been purchased and soon there will be ten additional suites. *Directions:* The hotel has a parking lot nearby and you can drive through the pedestrian zone to the hotel. Ask for a diagram on how to reach the hotel.

❄ ☕ 🛷 CREDIT ☎ ♨ @ ⛾ P 🖼 ⚖ 🚶 🍇

PALAZZO ALEXANDER
Owner: Mario Maraviglia
Via Santa Giustina, 48
Lucca, (FI) 55100, Italy
Tel: (0583) 58 35 71, Fax: (0583) 58 36 10
13 Rooms, Double: €120–€270
Open: all year, Credit cards: all major
70 km W of Florence, in historic center
Region: Tuscany, Michelin Map: 563

The Luz family bought and restored this lovely turn-of-the-last-century villa across from the lake more than 30 years ago. It retains its Liberty-style decor (1890s) throughout the several sitting and dining rooms with high, frescoed ceilings, stained-glass and lead windows, and ornate chandeliers. The reception area has an old-fashioned wooden bar with leather stools, velvet sofas and armchairs, Oriental carpets, and an enormous stone fireplace. Bedrooms upstairs vary in size (single, double, or suite) and are in keeping with the general decor of the accommodation. Many amenities are offered such as air conditioning and hydro jet baths in suites. A garden surrounds the villa where in the summer months tables and umbrellas are set up for dinner or buffet breakfast. Gracious Signora Renate runs the show, assisting her guests with various itineraries around the lake area. Guests have access as well to the Luz family's other lakefront hotel, with its alternative restaurant, park, and swimming. This place exudes old-world charm. *Directions:* Luino is halfway up the eastern side of the lake and the hotel is easily found right in town.

CAMIN HOTEL LUINO
Manager: Signora Renate Loeur
Viale Dante, 35
Luino, Lake Maggiore, (VA) 21016, Italy
Tel: (0332) 53 01 18, Fax: (0332) 53 72 26
13 Rooms, Double: €150–€300
Restaurant closed Mondays
Open: Feb to Dec 20, Credit cards: all major
100 km NW of Milan, 20 km S of Lugano
Region: Lombardy, Michelin Map: 561

Whether you are cutting straight across Italy from Rome to the Adriatic Sea and need a halfway stop, or want to explore the center of the Abruzzo region, the Hotel Sole is certainly the best bet in town. The prim solar-colored residence dating to the 19th century has been completely renovated into a pleasant and efficient hotel on a quiet square a block from the main street with its cathedral and shops. A spacious, rather standard reception area with striped upholstered sofas greets guests. All 51 rooms have been given a classic décor and outfitted with many modern amenities including internet in rooms. Right within the hotel is the city's most acclaimed restaurant, "Locanda del Moro" elegantly appointed, where the buffet breakfast is also served. L'Aquila is surrounded by mountains, nature parks, and ski resorts with majestic Gran Sasso, the highest peak of the Alpennines, being the focal point. The city features two ancient churches from the 12th century, a 19th-century theater, and a curious fountain with 99 spouts each with a different sculpted face representing the 99 castles and villages of this territory in that historical period. *Directions:* The Hotel Sole is centrally located only few minutes from all the major attraction in L Aquila.

HOTEL SOLE   New
Manager: Tullia Taglianetti
Largo Silvestro dell'Aquila, 4
L'Aquila, (AQ) 67100, Italy
Tel: (0862) 22 551, Fax: (0862) 40 43 32
51 Rooms, Double: €125–€210
Open: all year, Credit cards: all major
110 km NE of Rome, 104 km W of Pescara
Region: Abruzzo, Michelin Map: 563

The Biohotel Hermitage is truly a gem—a beautiful chalet-style inn with an incredible mountain setting. It is located on the outskirts of Madonna di Campiglio, a popular resort that bustles with activity both in summer and winter. To reach the hotel, you pass through Madonna di Campiglio and continue beyond the lake to a secluded paradise where the hotel nestles on a wooded plateau overlooking an astounding, unobstructed view of the Dolomites that rise in jagged granite peaks just across the valley. One rarely finds such pristine beauty. Adding perfection to the scene is the Maffei family who has showered their guests with hospitality for over a hundred years. Your current hosts, Barbara and Marcella, along with their parents, Edda and Giacomino Maffei, and their dog, Luce, continue the tradition of cordiality, hospitality, and love of nature that was handed down to them from their grandparents. Although the hotel has grown over the years and exudes a sophisticated elegance, it still maintains a splendid, inviting, country ambiance. The interior of the hotel is as attractive as the exterior with cozy wood paneled rooms, cute wood alpine chairs with carved hearts, pretty country fabrics, and porcelain tile fireplaces. Charm, country-cozy décor, and quality are obvious throughout. In winter there is a shuttle to take guest to the slopes. *Directions:* Ask the hotel for directions.

BIOHOTEL HERMITAGE
Owner: Maffei Family
Via Castelletto Inferiore 69
Madonna di Campiglio, (TN) 83084, Italy
Tel: (0465) 44 15 58, Fax: (0465) 44 16 18
15 Rooms, Double: €190–€380*
10 Suites: €260–€600*
*Includes breakfast & dinner
Closed: May, Oct and Nov, Credit cards: all major
88 km W of Bolzano, 214 km NW of Milan
Region: Trentino-Alto Adige, Michelin Map: 562

Clinging to the steep hillside above the beautiful coast of Basilicata, Maratea is a charming village of very old colorful houses and narrow cobbled streets. As the road loops ever-upward through the town, you soon come to the Locanda delle Donne Monache, carved into the rocky slope next to the tiny parish church of St. Maria. Originally a nunnery dating back to the early 1700s, the convent has been transformed into a deluxe small hotel. The exterior—salmon-colored stuccoed walls with white trim and rustic heavy-tiled roof—blends well with other houses in the village. Inside, the color scheme continues with sky-blue added for accent. The bedrooms are tucked throughout the hotel, each taking advantage of its special vista. The largest guestrooms are designated as suites. Number 9 is especially interesting, with a dramatic bathtub carved into the rocks and a pretty view out over the tiled rooftops. The most outstanding feature of the hotel is its garden where, located on the upper terrace next to the small church, a swimming pool seems to float in the air, romantically suspended above the jumble of village rooftops. Overlooking the garden, on balmy summer evenings, guests enjoy superb meals outside under the stars. The quiet serenity must have appealed to the nuns so long ago. *Directions:* Follow the road up to Maratea following signs for Centro Storico. In the main square you will see signs pointing to the hotel.

LA LOCANDA DELLE DONNE MONACHE
Manager: Vincenza Lamagna
Via Carlo Mazzei, 4
Maratea, (PZ) 85046, Italy
Tel: (0973) 87 61 39, Fax: (0973) 87 62 03
27 Rooms, Double: €200–€500
Open: Apr to Oct, Credit cards: all major
220 km S of Naples, 5 km W of Maratea
Region: Basilicata, Michelin Map: 564

The sienna-and-cream-colored, Liberty-style Villa Cheta Elite is located on the main coastal road just south of Acquafredda. A steep path winds up through the garden to the hotel, which has a series of tall French doors opening onto a shaded terrace where glimpses of the sea can be seen through the flowers and the trees. The hotel retains the genuine warmth and charm of a private home, without any hint of the formal commercialism of a hotel. Throughout there is a comfortable lived-in, old-fashioned elegance. Stefanie, the exceptionally gracious young owner, personally supervises every detail in the operation of her small hotel and welcomes one and all as personal guests. Each bedroom is charmingly decorated using family antiques. One of my favorites, room 44, is an exceptionally pretty, spacious, corner room. When the weather is balmy guests eat dinner on the terrace whose white wrought-iron tables are prettily set with hand-embroidered linens and bouquets of flowers from the garden. The home-cooked meals are outstanding—we highly recommend you request the meal plan. If you prefer small, family-owned hotels to the sophisticated glamour of resort-style hotels along this magical coast of southern Italy, the Villa Cheta Elite will definitely win your heart. *Directions:* 9 km north of Maratea on S18.

❄ ☕ ✀ ♨ 💳 ☎ 🏠 @ W Ⴤ P 🍴 🖼 ⚿ ⊥ 🚶 🏇 ⚓ 🎭

ROMANTIK HOTEL VILLA CHETA ELITE
Owner: Stefanie Aquadro
Via Timpone, 46, Acquafredda
Maratea, (PZ) 85041, Italy
Tel: (0973) 87 81 34, Fax: (0973) 87 81 35
18 Rooms, Double: €155–€270
Open: Apr to Oct, Credit cards: all major
Romantik Hotels
1 km S of Acquafredda, 210 km S of Naples
Region: Basilicata, Michelin Map: 564

One of our favorite recommendations along the southern coast of Italy is the Santavenere Hotel, an ideal stopping point if you are driving south to Sicily. However, don't just consider it as a place to spend the night en route—the Santavenere is so special you will want to linger and use it as a base to explore this lovely niche of Italy. The hotel, built in 1956, is perfectly positioned on a promontory above the sea, affording unsurpassed views of the gorgeous, sparkling, turquoise water. Although the hotel is of contemporary construction, its interior radiates an old-world charm combined with a nautical flair. The living room is elegant, but not stuffy—comfortable slipcovered chairs and sofas form cozy conversation nooks, while fine antiques and beautiful ship models lend further charm. The guestrooms too are extremely attractive in their decor and, best of all, each has its own terrace or balcony with a view of the sea or the park. The property is very large and in the meticulously groomed gardens there are gorgeous displays of flowers and lush lawns. Here you find a beautiful swimming pool from which a path leads to the edge of the cliff and then loops down through a fragrant pine forest to the sea where guests can swim in the crystal-clear water. *Directions:* Take the coastal highway N18 to Maratea. Do not go into the town, but instead follow signs for the porto and Fiumicello, then for the hotel.

SANTAVENERE HOTEL
Manager: Biagio Sisca
Fiumicello
Maratea, (PZ) 85040, Italy
Tel: (0973) 87 69 10, Fax: (0973) 87 76 54
38 Rooms, Double: €280–€700
Open: all year, Credit cards: all major
220 km S of Naples, adjacent to Maratea Porto
Region: Basilicata, Michelin Map: 564

The more adventurous traveler will be greatly rewarded with a stay at the Eremo, a 15th-century convent-turned-inn near the sea, conveniently located for exploring the baroque cities of Ragusa, Noto, and Modica. The noble Nifosi family restored the historic building with the desire of offering unique accommodation to travelers. The combination of professions in the family (antique collector, architect, and chef) made the project a natural. The typical baglio fortress with white-stone courtyard dominates the flat plain. An arched reception area was once part of the church and is striking with its contrast of white stone walls and black tiled floors, guarded by a knight in armor. The refined decor throughout is soothingly simple, in keeping with the building's medieval origins, and bedrooms, fashioned from friars' cells, are appointed with wrought-iron beds, white bedspreads, and antique armoires. Particular attention has been given to the traditional Sicilian cuisine, accompanied by a long list of Sicilian wines and served in either what was once the vaulted refectory or the crypts below. Fascinating itineraries are organized by boat, bike, jeep, or even by the owner's private plane, including overnight trips to the islands or Tunisia. Shuttle service is available from cities or airports. *Directions:* From N115, turn southwest toward the coast. 7.5 km before Marina di Ragusa, turn right and follow the signs to the Eremo della Giubiliana.

EREMO DELLA GIUBILIANA
Manager: Salvatore Mancini
S.P. per Marina di Ragusa Km 7.5
Marina di Ragusa, (RG) 97100, Italy
Tel: (0932) 66 91 19, Fax: (0932) 66 91 29
13 Rooms, Double: €250–€820
Open: all year, Credit cards: all major
On the southern coast of Sicily
Region: Sicily, Michelin Map: 565

If you are looking for a centrally located luxury accommodation with personalized service and all the trimmings, you have made the right choice at Relais Villa San Martino. The once private residence has been transformed by one of Italy's most prominent restorers of art, Martino Solito, into an intimate, tasteful and very efficient accommodation with 21 comfortable bedrooms and suites, an attractive wellness center, and a top-rated restaurant with impressive wine list. Although in close proximity to the main road, the peach-colored typical rectangular-shaped villa faces towards the back countryside and lush surrounding gardens where the swimming pool and a second guesthouse is situated. Soft color choices throughout the common areas and bedrooms along with the many windows facing out to terraces bestows the place with light, light and more light. Antique pieces adorn classic bedrooms all enhanced by fabulous custom-made brocades and damasks in shades of beige, gold, olive, and dusty rose. Mosaic bathrooms have special features such as double sinks, or hyrojet tubs. Besides a rich buffet breakfast or light lunch poolside, don't miss out on an exquisitely-prepared meal at the Duca di Martina restaurant, truly an exceptional culinary experience. Easy day trips are made to historic Martina Franca, Locorotondo, Ostuni, Alberobello and the land of the characteristic conical "trulli" houses. *Directions:* From Martina Franca follow for Taranto and after 3 km turn left at hotel entrance.

RELAIS VILLA SAN MARTINO   **New**
Manager: Claudio Felix Gherardini
Via Taranto 59 - Zona G
Martina Franca, (TA) 74015, Italy
Tel & Fax: (080) 48 05 152
15 Rooms, Double: €240–€370
6 Suites: €490–€790
Open: all year, Credit cards: all major
75 km SW Bari, 2 km W Martina Franca
Region: Apulia, Michelin Map: 564

The intense, untouched beauty of the Marittima area is gradually drawing attention away from the more popular northern areas of Tuscany, and the Villa Il Tesoro is a prime example of this trend. At first sight, "refreshingly diverse" comes to mind. The Swiss family Guldener, owners of this 300-acre property just 14 km from the seaside, have put their personal mark in the overall concept and detail of this sophisticated country resort. Within the traditional, preserved architecture of a group of stone farmhouses, the décor is contemporary and minimalist in line with the color, space, and nature of the surrounding soft hillsides adorned with olive groves and vineyards. Perfection reigns; from the stunning main sitting room completely open to the mesmerizing landscapes, to the wine bar, the attractive dining room, the circular swimming pool, and the impeccable grounds. With the idea that luxury is space, all similarly appointed guestrooms are true suites with living areas of varied dimensions, with striped zebra chairs and fluffy cloud-like white beds. "Il Fiore del Tesoro" restaurant chef Massimo Mammano serves an artful array of mouth-watering dishes inspired by the four seasons and authentic gastronomic culture of the Mediterranean. *Directions:* From the E80 coastal highway, exit at Follonica Est (or Scarlino from the south) and follow to Massa Marittima. Before the town, pass through Valpiana and turn left at signs for the villa.

※ ☕ ⚒ ♨ 🆑 ☎ 🐕 @ ⛾ P ⋔ ≈ 🖼 🐾 ⅋ ♿ 🚶 🍇

VILLA IL TESORO
Owner: Guldener Family
Localita: Valpiana
Massa Marittima, (GR) 58024, Italy
Tel: (0566) 92 971, Fax: (0566) 92 97 60
20 Rooms, Double: €205–€360
Closed: Jan 9 to Feb 9, Credit cards: all major
56 km NW of Grosseto, 58 km NW of Siena
Region: Tuscany, Michelin Map: 563

Matera is a large, modern city, but within it lies a secret treasure—a sunken "city within a city" that is hidden from view until the moment you are upon it. When you arrive, follow signs that say "Sassi", an ancient city of haunting beauty below the modern Matera, a site so extraordinary that it is on the UNESCO World Heritage list. Here you find an amazing labyrinth of twisting streets and houses built within the hillside that seem totally unreal. It is no wonder that Mel Gibson chose this timeless locale when filming his movie, "The Passion of Christ." The Sassi Hotel makes an ideal base for exploration, since it is built within a series of stone houses right in the old city. This is not a luxury hotel; but a simple, very special place to stay with a friendly staff that strives to please, pleasant and spacious guestrooms, private bathrooms, and awesome views. In addition to its reception area and lounge, there is a cozy bar, breakfast room, and even a tiny conference room. The hotel steps down 5 levels from the street with a stone staircase connecting various houses, within which the bedrooms are found. Many of these have a cave-like ambiance (like the other buildings in the city); since, in ancient times, the houses began as caves. Each of the bedrooms has its own personality. My favorite is 602, a memorable suite with a terrace snuggled in the rooftops and an incredible view. *Directions:* Ask for detailed directions when making reservations.

SASSI HOTEL
Owner: Raffaele Cristallo
Via San Giovanni Vecchio 89
Matera, (BA) 75100, Italy
Tel: (0835) 33 10 09, Fax: (0835) 33 37 33
26 Rooms, Double: €90–€120
Open: all year, Credit cards: all major
140 km W of Brindisi, 65 km S of Bari
Region: Apulia, Michelin Map: 564

Alexander Ortner's grandfather bought this shooting lodge in 1954 and over the years the family has expanded it to become the smallest four-star hotel in Merano. It really deserves accolades, for it is a simply delightful hotel, hospitably run by the Ortners, with the most spectacular views across the vineyards of the Merano Valley. This gorgeous view is the focus of the vine-covered terrace and in warm months a table is prepared for guests both here and in the dining room so that they always have a choice of where to dine. The set dinner menu ranges from five to seven courses (with a choice of main course), depending on the season and what is fresh and available (the executive chef has received numerous awards). Select one of the estate's wines to accompany the meal. Relax by the pool in the shade of the old apple trees or sunbathe au natural on the secluded deck. The hotel was renovated in 2005 and a wellness and beauty spa were added and now most rooms are two-room suites with balconies and splendid views, large enough for a family of four. I was very struck by the variety of nationalities among the guests. The hotel also has an award-winning restaurant. *Directions:* Take the Merano Sud exit from the new Bolzano-Merano road, follow signs for Hafling for 4 km, then turn right towards Labers. Follow this road for 5 km to the hotel.

HOTEL CASTLE FRAGSBURG
Owner: Ortner family
Via Fragsburger Strasse, 3
Merano–Labers, (BZ) 39012, Italy
Tel: (0473) 24 40 71, Fax: (0473) 24 44 93
20 Rooms, Double: €280–€330
12 Suites: €300–€380
Closed: Nov 12 to Mar 19, Credit cards: MC, VS
Relais & Châteaux
28 km NW of Bolzano, 150 km N of Verona
Region: Trentino-Alto Adige, Michelin Map: 562

The warmth of welcome at the Hotel Oberwirt is incredible. The entire staff set new standards for the meaning of graciousness—they pamper guests like long-lost friends. And, as for the owner, Josef Waldner, he is without a doubt one of the most charming hosts in the world. He is never "behind the scene" but rather in evidence from morning to night, chatting with his guests and overseeing that every detail of the hotel is faultless. But, it is not only hospitality that makes the Romantik Hotel Oberwirt so remarkable. Everything about the hotel is perfect: it is located in a pretty little village; the décor is outstanding; the amenities are positively highest quality, the bedrooms are beautiful, the swimming pool lovely, and the spa and indoor pool quite wonderful. It is amazing to realize that the hotel dates back to the 16th century and has been in the Waldner family since 1749. In addition to the hotel, the family owns apple orchards and breeds magnificent Haflingers, some of the most beautiful horses in the world with their golden color set off by glorious creamy mane. Although the hotel rings of elegance and sophistication, there is nothing stuffy or ostentatious. Quite the opposite. There is a home-like charm throughout. You cannot help but fall in love with this superb hotel. *Directions:* From the Bolzano-Merano highway, take the Marling exit. Follow signs to the town center. The hotel is located on the left, beyond the church.

ROMANTIK HOTEL OBERWIRT
Owner: Josef Waldner
St-Felix-Weg 2
Merano–Marling, (BZ) 39020, Italy
Tel: (0473) 22 20 20, Fax: (0473) 44 71 30
27 Rooms, Double: €135–€260
22 Suites: €200–€440
Closed: mid Nov to end of Mar, Credit cards: all major
Romantik Hotels
31 km NW of Bolzano, 152 km N of Verona
Region: Trentino-Alto Adige, Michelin Map: 562

The Four Seasons opened its doors in 1993 to well-deserved rave reviews and instant success. The hotel (whose origins date back to a 15th-century convent) is superbly set in Milan's fantasy shopping area whose rich selection of chic designer boutiques is unrivaled anywhere in the world. For sightseeing, just a comfortable stroll through quaint cobbled streets brings you to La Scala Theatre, the Galleria, and the stunning Duomo. The hotel is an oasis of refined, understated elegance and restful tranquility. You enter into what was originally the chapel, now a spacious, refreshingly uncluttered room decorated in muted tones of beiges and creamy whites. Fresh flowers abound, enhancing vaulted ceilings, fine contemporary furnishings, fragments of stunning frescoes (uncovered during renovation and meticulously restored), and accents of museum-quality antiques. Unfortunately, there is not enough space on this page to go into greater detail about the hotel. In essence, the two restaurants are superb, the inner courtyard garden lovely, the guestrooms have every conceivable convenience, the linens are the finest. No expense was spared to pamper the guest—as an example, the marble walls, floors, and even mirrors in the bathrooms are heated so that no fog will collect. The icing on the cake is the caring staff who pamper you shamelessly.

FOUR SEASONS HOTEL MILANO
Manager: Vincenzo Finizzola
Via Gesù, 6/8, Milan, (MI) 20121, Italy
Tel: (02) 77 088, Fax: (02) 77 08 50 00
Toll Free: (800) 332-3442 USA
118 Rooms, Double: €680–€815,* 41 Suites: €850–€8300*
*Breakfast not included: €34–€36
Open: all year, Credit cards: all major
History Traveller
Heart of Milan, close to shopping & sightseeing
Region: Lombardy, Michelin Map: 561

In the first edition of our guide to Italy, the Grand Hotel et de Milan was featured as our favorite hotel in Milan. There is no hotel in Milan more richly imbued with tradition. Dating back to 1863, it is located only two blocks from La Scala Theatre and has been "home" for many of the world's most famous artists, including Giuseppe Verdi who composed some of his operas while living here. From first glance you are immediately enveloped in a romantic mood of the past. The heart of the hotel is the spacious lounge, gently illuminated by a large domed skylight, with cream-colored wood paneling, marble floor accented by Oriental carpets, comfortable sofas and chairs, potted palms, and a marble fireplace completing the elegant scene. Beyond the lounge there is a nostalgic, old-fashioned bar whose mirrored walls and elegant drapes form the perfect backdrop for afternoon tea or a post-theater drink. The hotel's Don Carlos restaurant (named after one of Verdi's operas) continues the romantic theme with dark-green fabric walls almost covered with pictures of famous artists who have performed at La Scala. As you would expect, the guestrooms too are superbly decorated with fine furniture, lovely fabrics, and many antiques.

GRAND HOTEL ET DE MILAN
Manager: Antonio Cailotto
Via Manzoni, 29, Milan, (MI) 20121, Italy
Tel: (02) 72 31 41, Fax: (02) 86 46 08 61
72 Rooms, Double: €617–€731*
23 Suites: €789–€1475*
*Breakfast not included: €35
Open: all year, Credit cards: all major
Abitare La Storia
Heart of Milan, 2 blocks from La Scala
Region: Lombardy, Michelin Map: 561

The Hotel de la Ville is a gem of a hotel. The location just couldn't be more perfect—a few minutes' walk takes you to La Scala, the spectacular Duomo, or to the Galleria, Milan's romantic glass-domed shopping arcade. The exterior, a modern glass-and-stone façade, doesn't prepare you for the interior, which exudes a cozy, old-world charm. You enter into a lovely reception area, softly illuminated from a domed skylight. Just off the reception is a cozy lounge in a color scheme of rich green and gold. An intimate cherry-paneled bar is tucked in one corner, discreetly available for afternoon tea or an aperitif. The ambiance is one of genteel, old-world elegance. The individually decorated guestrooms all boast of the same quality: the walls are covered with elegant Italian silk fabric that color-coordinates with the fabric on the beds and draperies. All rooms have modernized bathrooms, beautifully tiled with marble in tones of beige, cream, or green. The hotel's L'Opera Restaurant is well known for its regional cuisine and vintage wine cellar. Other wonderful features of the hotel are the rooftop swimming pool and fitness center. The son and daughter of the founder, the late Count Bocca, continue his tradition of excellence and the finest hospitality. *Directions:* From the central ring road take the Corso Venezia to Piazza S. Babila, the Corso Matteotti to the Piazza Meda, and the Via Hoepli to the hotel.

HOTEL DE LA VILLE
Manager: Fausto Simone
Via Hoepli, 6
Milan, (MI) 20121, Italy
Tel: (02) 87 91 311, Fax: (02) 86 66 09
109 Rooms, Double: €360–€770
1 Suite: €793
Open: all year, Credit cards: all major
Heart of Milan, between the Duomo & La Scala
Region: Lombardy, Michelin Map: 561

In a city where standardized business hotels and high rates abound, the Regency remains a rare alternative. Although not located in the tourist center of the city, it is an easy solution for those with a car who are coming or going north to the Malpensa airport. In a residential area, the historic building dating back to the late 1800s, was once the residence of a noble family. The whimsical castle-like architecture style, known as Coppedè after the architect/sculptor's name, complete with turrets, corner tower and columns certainly stands out among the gray buildings of the city. The warmth and character is identified upon entering with the reception area looking out over a courtyard where guests can sit and read the morning paper. Two colorful lounges are adorned with family crests and stained-glass skylights, and include working fireplace, bar and comfortable armchairs. These areas lead to the sunny-colored dining room where a buffet breakfast is served. The 71 bedrooms spread out on the five upper floors have efficient marble bathrooms, patterned carpet carpeting, floral wall paper and all four-star amenities. The top floor rooms have mansard beamed ceilings, another rarity in modern Milan. A helpful staff at the desk can assist with restaurant suggestions, touring logistics, and other needs. *Directions:* One block north of Piazza Firenze.

HOTEL REGENCY
Manager: Lorenzo Magni
Via G. Armondi 12
Milan, (MI) 20155, Italy
Tel: (02) 39 21 60 21, Fax: (02) 39 21 77 34
71 Rooms, Double: €280–€350
Open: all year, Credit cards: all major
Central locations near the fairgrounds
Region: Lombardy, Michelin Map: 561

It is only logical that Milan, Italy's trend-setting capital of fashion and design, be one of the first to boast a seven-star hotel, the Town House Galleria. It is uniquely housed center stage in the Galleria, Milan's romantic, 19th-century shop-lined atrium. One side of the Galleria opens to the breathtaking Cathedral; the other side leads to La Scala Theater, another of Milan's gems. The hotel is accessed from the back street side through a courtyard with exterior glass elevator and potted palms. The guestrooms on the top two floors look out to the interior of the Galleria. Details of the Galleria's colorful mosaic floors, façades adorned with statues, boutiques, and cafés can also be privately viewed from the large corner window of the intimate restaurant. The hotel is appointed in contemporary design style with an occasional antique piece, parquet oak floors, designer fabrics and linens. The aim here is to create an exclusive home ambiance with someone personally looking after your every need. That someone is the well-versed butler, who in order to be able to recommend places to guests, has personally tested all suggestions. Whatever the whim, it can be taken care of here, whether it be a private nanny, a Bentley with driver, massage treatments, or any other service offered by the group of international luxury partners of the hotel. Luckily the group has two other properties in the city with the same concept but at a more reasonable rate.

❄ CREDIT ☎ 🛗 @ W Y P ⊓ 🖼 🐾 ⊺ 🏃 ⛷ ⛵

TOWN HOUSE GALLERIA
Manager: Claudia Milati
Via Silvio Pellico 8
Milan, (MI) 20121, Italy
Tel: (02) 89 05 82 97, Fax: 0(2) 89 05 82 99
24 Suites: €800–€4000*
*Breakfast not included: €30
Open: all year, Credit cards: all major
Within the Galleria
Region: Lombardy, Michelin Map: 561

For exploring the southeastern region of Sicily, indulging in Sicilian Baroque architecture and delectable local cuisine, Modica, the city of 100 churches, is definitely a highlight. This fascinating area is getting well-deserved attention also because the past five years have brought about a wave of updated accommodations. Your top choice in Modica is undoubtedly the Palazzo Failla, the historic 18th-century home of the gracious Failla family who recently had the entire building restored, preserving hand-made painted ceramic tile floors, black volcanic stone floors, wrought iron pieces, decorative vaulted frescoes, and heirloom antique furniture. Ten period bedrooms with high ceilings are found on the upper floor reached by elevator or the main staircase from reception, each individually appointed as in a private home. Off to the right of the main hall is the highly rated La Gazza Ladra restaurant, with experienced chef Accursio Craparo in command. Artistically presented dishes are based on traditional Sicilian recipes. The stylish ambiance of the immaculate white dining room has black and white checked floors, crisp white table linens, antique credenzas, and a wine list of 400 labels. To the left of the main reception hall is the Blandini bar where a cappuccino is served in the morning, tea in the afternoon or an aperitif with the locals at twilight. *Directions:* Via Blandini is situated in the center of Modica Alta, one block from the S. Teresa church.

PALAZZO FAILLA
Owner: Paolo Failla Family
Via Blandini 5
Modica, (RG) 97015, Italy
Tel: (0932) 94 10, Fax: (0932) 94 10 59
10 Rooms, Double: €135–€200
Open: all year, Credit cards: all major
On the southern coast of Sicily, center of Modica
Region: Sicily, Michelin Map: 565

The Villa Beccaris is just the sort of charming inn we search for and is especially welcome in a region where there are surprisingly few of its breed. The Langhe wine country southeast of industrial Turin is characterized by gently rolling hillsides covered with endless rows of vineyards and dotted with enchanting ancient villages and fortified castles. Monforte is one such village and the 18th-century Villa Beccaris is found just outside its ancient walls. The individually decorated bedrooms are spread about the main villa, two attached wings forming the inner courtyard, and a separate adjacent guesthouse. The owners of the inn are all local industrialists and wine producers who have striven to retain a distinct aura of romance and elegance. A private home ambiance is created with precious antiques throughout bedrooms, with Oriental carpets, parquet floors, stenciled walls and ceilings, fine linens, portrait paintings, and elegant chandeliers. The golden breakfast room with antique bar and original wood floors leads out to the flower-laden courtyard to one side and to the surrounding park with enormous oak trees to the other. The garden reveals a curved swimming pool and picturesque views over the ancient village. Downstairs is the original vaulted wine cellar, which serves as a lounge area for guests in the evenings. *Directions:* From the main square follow signs for Roddino, taking the first left up the Via Fracchia to the inn.

❄ ☕ ✄ CREDIT ☎ 🏠 ⛲ @ W Y P ≈ ⌂ ⛷ 🏃 🚶 🐎 ⛷ 🍇

VILLA BECCARIS
Manager: Federica Giachino
Via Bava Beccaris, 1
Monforte d'Alba, (CN) 12065, Italy
Tel: (0173) 78 158, Fax: (0173) 78 190
23 Rooms, Double: €160–€210
1 Suite: €280–€350
9 Apartments: €180 daily, €800 weekly
Open: all year, Credit cards: all major
60 km SE of Turin
Region: Piedmont, Michelin Map: 561

Il Melograno is a rarity: a small, luxury hotel that is truly managed by the family, creating a warmth and cordiality seldom found in a hotel of this sophistication. Camillo Guerra oversees every detail of his hotel, ably assisted by his children. White walls enclose the large property whose core is a stunning, white, 16th-century fortified farmhouse, which for many years was the holiday retreat of the Guerra family. In 1985, Signor Guerra (an antique and fine-art dealer from Bari) decided to expand his home-away-from-home into a hotel. Taking meticulous care to preserve the hundreds of ancient olive trees, he built a series of superbly furnished guestrooms clustered in white Moorish-style buildings facing intimate patios. The original farmhouse now houses the reception, romantic bar, beautiful dining room, and various intimate lounges. Throughout, everything is decorated in antiques. Cheerful floral slipcovered chairs and Oriental carpets accent stark white walls and floors. One of the inner patios is a fragrant small orange grove, watered by an ancient stone irrigation system. Breakfast is served on the poolside terrace overlooking the pomegranate and fig trees. Il Melograno makes an excellent, luxurious base for exploring the fascinating Apulia region of southern Italy. The hotel also has a lovely spa with indoor pool. *Directions:* Located just west of Monopoli on the road to Alberobello. As you head toward Alberobello, there is a sign to the hotel on the right.

IL MELOGRANO
Manager: Roberta Guerra
Contrada Torricella, 345
Monopoli, (BA) 70043, Italy
Tel: (080) 69 09 030, Fax: (080) 74 79 08
37 Rooms, Double: €300–€470
Open: mid-Mar to mid-Jan, Credit cards: all major
Relais & Châteaux
On the heel of Italy, 70 km NW of Brindisi
Region: Apulia, Michelin Map: 564

La Peschiera is owned by the Guerra Family, proprietors of Il Melograno, a deluxe hotel built within a 16th-century farmhouse tucked in among ancient olive trees just outside of Monopoli. In order to provide access to the sea, a minivan started shuttling Il Melograno guests to a nearby a beach area where they could relax overlooking the water. Soon a restaurant was opened to provide more services. Then guestrooms were added and, thus, a "sister" hotel evolved called La Peschiera. The name is appropriate, since the property had been used as a fish hatchery since the 18th century. Today, the fresh water pools have been converted into seven swimming pools, ranging from one absolutely enormous pool down to smaller ones, each with a different water temperature. The pools are utilized in a program of massage and beauty treatments using seawater. The guestrooms all have two spacious terraces, one facing the swimming pool and the other facing the sea, which rolls up against the rocks just in front of the terraces. The rooms are attractively decorated and have large bathrooms (the suites have two bathrooms). The hotel owns a small adjacent beach, but this is a rocky area of the coast; so the most appealing place to swim is in the hotels' seven pools. The restaurant is wrapped on three sides by picture windows, but the favorite place to dine is on a large, wooden terrace that extends to the edge of the water. *Directions:* On the coastal road south of Monopoli.

❄ ☕ 🚴 CREDIT ☎ Y P ⍊ ❀ ≈ 🧍 🏠 ♿ ⛵ 🧍 🏄

MONOPOLI LA PESCHIERA HOTEL
Owner: Guerra Family
C. da Losciale
Monopoli, (BA) 70043, Italy
Tel & Fax: (080) 80 10 66
9 Rooms, Double: €570–€1000
2 Suites: €920–€1600
Open: Apr to Nov, Credit cards: all major
On the heel of Italy, 70 km NW of Brindisi
Region: Apulia, Michelin Map: 564

The general trend in hotel accommodation today is to offer guests services of a wellness center whether it is simply massage or a full-fledged spa. The Grotta Giusti satisfies the latter having the advantage of thermal waters which fill one of two large swimming pools. The hotel is located next to Montecatini Terme, in what was once the private 19th-century retreat of the poet, Giuseppe Giusti, and where Giuseppe Verdi was frequently a guest. Classic-styled, very comfortable bedrooms are dispersed among the original stone home and the more recently-built wing with spacious reception, series of sitting rooms, elegant frescoed salon, cigar room and full bar. Rooms of various sizes have white marble bathrooms and junior suites have a direct line to the thermal waters. The spacious veranda dining room looking out to the surrounding gardens offers a regular menu featuring Tuscan specialities or tailor-made meals for those following one of the many programs. Treatments of all types are available on the long list of anti-stress therapies ranging from classic to oriental techniques. What sets this place apart from the rest is not only the historic residence with natural thermal waters but the extraordinary grotta situated below the hotel, where guests sit in total silence and benefit from the natural detoxing steam emanating from the earth. A deserved break from intense touring!

❋ ☕ ✂ 🅒 ☎ 🏠 🛗 🕴 W Ⴅ P 🍴 🚭 ☘ ≋ 🖼 ⛷ 🕴 🕺 🍇

GROTTA GIUSTI NATURAL SPA RESORT   **New**
Manager: Antonio Niccoli
Via Grotta Giusti, 1411
Monsummano Terme, (PT) 51015, Italy
Tel: (0572) 90 771, Fax: (0572) 90 77 200
57 Rooms, Double: €360–€680*
*Includes breakfast & dinner
Open: all year, Credit cards: all major
30 km W of Florence
Region: Tuscany, Michelin Map: 563

Montagnana is an exceptionally picturesque medieval village with walls that are still intact, punctuated by 24 towers. However, it is not only the appeal of this cute town that attracts visitors. People also come from afar to dine at the Ristorante Aldo Moro, drawn by its fabulous food and beautiful dining rooms where tables are set with fine linens and bouquets of fresh flowers. Happily, the Ristorante Aldo Moro also has guestrooms, so you do not need to worry about driving "home" after a splendid meal with fabulous wines. The guestrooms are all attractively decorated and offer all the modern amenities such as air conditioning, mini-bars, and satellite TVs. Bedrooms are all similar in decor, with traditional-style furnishings. Suites are larger, but the standard rooms are quite spacious enough, so no need to splurge. The public lounges are also most appealing, with antique furnishings that lend a lovely, old-world, sedate elegance. Behind the hotel there is a small garden where guests are welcome to sit and relax. It is no wonder that this is such a superior hotel—it is a family-run operation, with the Moro family always present, overseeing both the restaurant and the hotel with great care for quality. *Directions:* Exit the A13 at Monselice and take the N10 west to Montagnana. Via Marconi is a small street off the piazza.

HOTEL RISTORANTE ALDO MORO
Owner: Moro family
Via Marconi, 27
Montagnana, (PD) 35044, Italy
Tel: (0429) 81 351, Fax: (0429) 82 842
34 Rooms, Double: €96–€112*
*Breakfast not included, Restaurant closed Mondays
Closed: mid-Jul to mid-Aug, Credit cards: all major
85 km SW of Venice, 57 km S of Padova
Region: Veneto, Michelin Map: 562

The Castelletto di Montebenichi is an enchanting small castle in a tiny, storybook-perfect, medieval village perched on a hilltop in Tuscany, romantically facing a miniature plaza enclosed by a circle of homes built into the old tower walls. This is a sturdy, stone building with a crenellated roof, arched windows, and a row of colorful coats of armor stretching across the top. Inside, it seems as if you are truly stepping back in time—the renovation has been so carefully accomplished that you don't realize any changes have been made (until you see the modern bathrooms). All the fabulous murals have been restored and the floors and beamed ceilings reflect the rich patina of age. The furnishings, too, reflect another era with rich fabrics, beautiful light fixtures, lovely oil paintings, and many fine antiques. Your exceptionally personable hosts, Marco Gasparini and Arnaldo Soriani, want their guests to feel like friends. Everything possible is done to create this ambiance, including an open bar where guests can fix themselves refreshment whenever they want. Breakfast is served in a charming, sunny room with arched windows on three sides. There are also cozy lounges, a stunning library, a swimming pool, a gym with indoor Jacuzzi, and a sauna. This is a non-smoking hotel. No children under 14. *Directions:* Midway between Siena and Arezzo. From the A1, exit at Valdarno and follow signs for Montevarchi, Bucine, Ambra, and then Montebenichi.

CASTELLETTO DI MONTEBENICHI
Owners: Marco Gasparini & Arnaldo Soriani
Montebenichi, (AR) 52020, Italy
Tel: (055) 99 10 110, Fax: (055) 99 10 113
9 Rooms, Double: €240–€330
Open: Apr to Nov, Credit cards: all major
History Traveller
26 km NE of Siena
Region: Tuscany, Michelin Map: 563

The Villa Zuccari, the childhood home of owner Paolo Zuccari, opened its doors in 2005 to guests. With the admirable success of their other nearby hotel, San Luca in Spoleto, it was natural that he and his gracious wife, Daniela, decided to transform the spacious pink villa into a small hotel. The back side of the villa is attached to the small town, while the front looks out over the garden, swimming pool and outlying fields. The main hall leads past the reception area, two cozy vaulted living rooms to the main dining room with its original terracotta tiled ceiling and sun-colored walls. Genuine local recipes are savored here with special attention given to the use of locally grown products. Individually styled bedrooms are found on the ground and first floors. While one daughter oversees the hotel in Spoleto, the other daughter, an architect, supervised the renovation project. Comfortable rooms are purposely on the large size, have antique furnishings and feature terraces or garden patios. Each bathroom has been created with a different combination of marble patterns, many with both bathtub and separate shower. A separate house in the garden can be rented for 8-10 guests. Before a full day of touring Umbria from this centrally located spot, a full breakfast awaits guests in the trellis-painted bar and breakfast room. *Directions:* From the Spoleto-Perugia highway S.S. 3 exit at Trevi/Montefalco and follow signs to Madonna della Stella/Montefalco for 4 Km.

VILLA ZUCCARI
Owners: Daniela & Paolo Zuccari
Località San Luca
Montefalco, (PG) 06036, Italy
Tel: (0742) 39 94 02, Fax: (0742) 39 91 94
31 Rooms, Double: €110–€240
3 Suites: €210–€350
Open: all year, Credit cards: all major
3km east of Montefalco, 30km SW of Perugia
Region: Umbria, Michelin Map: 563

Il Borghetto Country Inn is an absolute dream, an idyllic hideaway in one of the most enchanting areas of Tuscany. It is owned by the Cavallini family who originally bought a farmhouse in the heart of the exquisite Chianti district to use as a family weekend retreat. When the adjacent farmhouse came on the market, they bought it too, restored it to perfection, and opened a tiny hotel. What makes this small inn so special is that it is a family operation. The father, Roberto Cavallini, watches over the operation from Milan, his son, Antonio, is the on-site manager, and the charming daughter, Ilaria, ably helps out. Guests have their own intimate, beautifully decorated lounge, which also serves as the breakfast room (in warm weather breakfast is served outside on the lovely terrace). Rosie Cavallini did all the decorating and every detail is of superb quality with beautiful fabrics, original paintings, abundant displays of fresh flowers, Oriental carpets, and fine antiques. But the best I've saved for last—a sweeping vista of olive groves and vineyards that produce extra virgin olive oil, Chianti Classico and Merlot wine. Tours and wine tasting in the cellar are available, as well as on-site cooking courses which include food and art tours in Florence, Siena and the surrounding countryside. *Directions:* Leave the Florence-Siena expressway at Bargino. Exit, turning right, and then almost immediately, turn up the hill toward Montefiridolfi. 2.6 km after the exit, Il Borghetto is on your right.

IL BORGHETTO COUNTRY INN
Owner: Cavallini family
Via Collina S. Angelo, 23
Montefiridolfi, (FI) 50020, Italy
Tel: (055) 82 44 42, Fax: (055) 82 44 247
6 Rooms, Double: €100–€160
2 Suites: €200–€240
Open: Mar to Nov, Credit cards: MC, VS
17 km S of Florence
Region: Tuscany, Michelin Map: 563

La Chiusa, nestled in the hills of Tuscany southeast of Siena, is an old stone farmhouse whose restaurant is so well known that guests come from far and wide to enjoy the meals where everything is fresh, homemade, and delicious. Dania and Umberto Lucherini are the gracious owners and Dania is the talented chef. Almost all the vegetables, olive oil, meats, wines, and cheeses come either from the inn's own farm or from those nearby. The original wood-burning oven still stands in the courtyard in front of the inn, emitting delicious aromas of freshly baking bread. The dining room is large and airy, with an uncluttered simple elegance enhanced by windows overlooking rolling hills. When the weather is balmy, meals are also served on the back terrace, which is ideally positioned to capture a sweeping view. The emphasis here is definitely on the exquisite meals, but there are also bedrooms for guests who want to spend the night. Like the dining room, the guestrooms are perfectly in keeping with the ambiance of the old farmhouse, lovely in their rustic simplicity yet with every modern convenience. In addition to the standard guestrooms, there are some deluxe suites—one even has an olive press in the bathroom! *Directions:* From the highway A1, take the "Val di Chiana" exit. Turn left and follow the signs that lead to Torrita di Siena and then Pienza. About 7 km past Torrita di Siena turn left toward Montefollonico.

LA CHIUSA
Owner: Lucherini family
Via della Madonnina, 88
Montefollonico, (SI) 53040, Italy
Tel: (0577) 66 96 68, Fax: (0577) 66 95 93
15 Rooms, Double: €230–€350
3 Suites: €500
Restaurant closed Tuesdays
Closed: Christmas week, Credit cards: all major
60 km S of Siena, 10 km NW of Montepulciano
Region: Tuscany, Michelin Map: 563

The tiny medieval village of Montegridolfo, nestling on the crown of a gentle hill, seems too perfect to be real—everything looks fresh and new and all the buildings homogeneous. At first it is a bit confusing because every picture-perfect little restaurant, shop, and boutique has the same buff-colored brick façade, pretty red geraniums out front, and white embroidered curtains peeking behind brown-shuttered windows. Yes, the village is real, but was totally reconstructed at one time as one development. The Albergo Palazzo Viviani, a part of this renovation, is a hotel converted from a noble palace and still retains the charm of a private home. The living room with its honey-colored walls, oil paintings, opulent drapes, open fireplace, and handsome antique furnishings is extremely attractive. Upstairs are eight elegant, luxurious guestrooms. The most dramatic is the Affreschi suite, with gorgeous frescoes on the walls, ornately painted ceiling, and, best of all, windows on three sides letting light stream into the room. In a separate building in the garden there are more rooms, each named for a flower. These guestrooms are less expensive, but although smaller than those in the Palazzo, are nicely decorated. There are also five suites and thirty rooms in various buildings around town. *Directions:* Leaving Bologna, take A14 towards Ancona. Exit at Cattolica. Follow signs for San Giovanni, then to Saludecio, and then to Montegridolfo.

ALBERGO PALAZZO VIVIANI
Manager: Stefano Ugolini
Montegridolfo, (RN) 47837, Italy
Tel: (0541) 85 53 50, Fax: (0541) 85 53 40
53 Rooms, Double: €140–€420
Open: all year, Credit cards: all major
35 km NW of Rimini
Region: Emilia-Romagna, Michelin Map: 562

La Dionora is a delightful hotel just outside the walled town of Montepulciano, one of Tuscany's jewels. This appealing small inn, made of tan stone and accented by brown shutters, has a stunning location, crowning a gentle hill with a 360-degree view. As far as the eye can see there are rolling hills covered with forests, fields of sunflowers, olive groves, and, in the distance, the sweet walled village of Pienza. As you approach, it is obvious that this is a well cared for, beautifully managed property. Everything is absolutely meticulous, from the perfectly tended flower beds to the lovingly decorated bedrooms. Three of the guestrooms are located upstairs in the farmhouse with windows that capture the splendid view. The other rooms, each with a private terrace, are in a similar one-story stone building just steps away. All have Tuscan-style antiques enhanced by Ferragamo fabrics and fireplaces. Breakfast is served in the garden in a most attractive stone "winter garden" with arched glass walls on four sides through which the sunlight streams in. Also in the garden is a beautiful swimming pool. Dinner is served by request during the summer season. Maria Teresa Cesarini, the friendly owner, is ably assisted by Giulio D'Antonio and they are perfect hosts who are very familiar with Tuscany and can help with planning your day. *Directions:* Take N146 from Montepulciano toward Pienza. After 3 km, turn left at the sign for La Dionora.

❄ ☕ ✄ ☕ 💳 ☎ @ W P 🚭 🌿 ≈ 🖼 ⚓ 🎋 🏃 🐎 🍷

LA DIONORA
Owner: Mrs. Maria Teresa Cesarini
Via Vicinale di Poggiano
Montepulciano, (SI) 53040, Italy
Tel: (0578) 71 74 96, Fax: (0578) 71 74 98
4 Rooms, Double: €330
2 Suites: €360–€380
Closed: Dec 8 to mid-Feb, Credit cards: all major
65 km S of Siena, 4 km W of Montepulciano
Region: Tuscany, Michelin Map: 563

Montorio makes an excellent base for exploring Tuscany and Umbria: spacious, guestrooms; glorious setting; spectacular views; cooking facilities; large modern bathrooms; and moderate prices. This 15th-century stone farmhouse is perched on a hill surrounded by olive groves, vineyards, and towering cypress trees. The views are awesome with nothing to disturb the mood of serenity except perhaps for the song of birds and the ringing of church bells. The beautiful walled town of Montepulciano is nearby and from the terrace of Montorio you can also see the charming Renaissance church of San Biagio. The inn is self-catering which means that each room has its own kitchenette and, unlike a hotel, there is not a manager on site so you need to arrive between 4–7 pm when someone is there to check you in. Some self-catering properties do not have daily maid service and charge for utilities, but the Montorio has daily maid service (except on Sunday) and includes all utilities (except in winter when heating costs are added). Each of the suites has a kitchen or kitchenette and is tastefully decorated with pleasingly simple Tuscan-style, antique furniture. Centuries-old trees and flowers cascading from terracotta pots embellish the delightful terrace. *Directions:* Just on the north edge of Montepulciano, on the road to Pienza.

MONTORIO
Owner: Stefania Savini
Strada per Pienza, 2
Montepulciano, (SI) 53045, Italy
Tel: (0578) 71 74 42, Fax: (0578) 71 56 35
5 Apartments: €120–€180 daily
*Breakfast not included
Minimum Stay Required: 3 nights
Open: Feb 1 to Dec 15, Credit cards: MC, VS
65 km S of Siena
Region: Tuscany, Michelin Map: 563

The romantic, ochre-colored, 17th-century Villa Poggiano is truly a gem. The Savini family bought the abandoned mansion, which nestles on a wooded hillside near the charming walled city of Montepulciano, and have tenderly restored it to its original splendor. An intimate, cozy parlor with comfortable chairs grouped around an open fireplace, a sweet breakfast room, and two enormous suites are on the first floor. A wide staircase leads to four more beautiful rooms. There are also three delightful suites in a separate brick building facing a sweeping panorama of the countryside. The tasteful decor creates a warm, homelike ambiance. Throughout the villa, everything is on a grand scale with handsome fireplaces, sumptuous bathrooms, gorgeous antique furniture, exceptionally spacious rooms, and ornate chandeliers. The villa faces an idyllic Tuscan countryside with olive trees dotting the gentle hillside. Behind the villa is a thick forest with romantic paths meandering through the woodlands. There is also an enormous travertine swimming pool with a granite wall on one side embellished with a large sculpture, while on the other side, lounge chairs are set on a wide terrace outlined by very old cypress trees. The warmth of welcome by Stefania and her charming mother is so genuine you will never want to leave. *Directions:* Take the N146 from Montepulciano toward Pienza and after about 2 km, turn left at the sign for Villa Poggiano.

※ ◼ ⚞ CREDIT ☎ @ W ⏐ P ⊘ ❀ ≈ 🖼 🏃 🏃🏃 🐎 ❦

VILLA POGGIANO
Owner: Stefania Savini
Via di Poggiano, 7
Montepulciano, (SI) 53045, Italy
Tel: (0578) 75 82 92, Fax: (0578) 71 56 35
14 Rooms, Double: €210–€320
Open: Apr to Nov, Credit cards: MC, VS
Abitare La Storia
65 km S of Siena, 2 km W of Montepulciano
Region: Tuscany, Michelin Map: 563

Tucked in the gentle Tuscan hills, Monteriggioni is a stunning sight. You will be captivated from afar at your first glimpse: the romantic town crowning the hilltop with its circular stone wall, punctuated by tall towers, still intact. If you have come just to sightsee, you must park your car below the town, but if you are one of the lucky ones who have a reservation at the Hotel Monteriggioni, drive through the portal in the wall to the hotel, which is located at the far end of the little square. It is hard to believe that this lovely small hotel, now so beautiful, used to be a stable. It took three years for the present owners to achieve the miracle you see today. Michela Cagnazzo, the owner, is responsible for the decoration and her taste is faultless. White walls, handsome antique furniture, white slipcovered sofas, and bouquets of fresh flowers create a fresh, appealing country ambiance. The guestrooms are also charming, with the same style of decor as the public rooms. Behind the hotel there is a terrace where breakfast is served, weather permitting. Just beyond is a small swimming pool tucked in the garden with a serene backdrop of the old moat, now filled with olive trees, and the stone walls of the town. The hotel has no restaurant but the Ristorante Il Pozzo next door offers authentic Tuscan cooking, and there are other restaurants nearby. It is a delightful hotel that does credit to a charming village. *Directions:* From the S2 at Monteriggioni, follow signs to the town.

HOTEL MONTERIGGIONI
Owner: Michela Gozzi Cagnazzo
Monteriggioni, (SI) 53035, Italy
Tel: (0577) 30 50 09, Fax: (0577) 30 50 11
12 Rooms, Double: €200–€240
Closed: Jan 7 to end-Feb, Credit cards: all major
15 km NW of Siena, 55 km S of Florence
Region: Tuscany, Michelin Map: 563

If you are looking for deluxe accommodations along the popular Cinque Terre, the Hotel Porto Roca comes closest to filling the bill. A narrow lane leads up the wooded hillside from Monterosso al Mare to the hotel, which is splendidly located on a cliff overlooking the sea. Only taxis are allowed up this road but the hotel will pay the fare from and back to the public car park. The lobby is one very large, all-purpose room with the reception desk as you enter, the guest lounge in the middle, and a bar at the far end. The room has almost a medieval look with dark furniture, large oil paintings, one wall of stone, ornately upholstered sofas and chairs, and, to top it all off, two regal knights standing in suits of armor. The dining room is one level up and has a wall of windows overlooking the sea. However, when the weather is warm, meals are served outside where white wrought-iron tables are set on a delightful terrace overlooking Monterosso al Mare and the sea. Throughout the spacious property there are many secluded nooks where guests can relax, but the most popular place is a terrace perched above the cliffs where lounge chairs are arranged to capture the view. *Directions:* From the A12, exit at Carrodano and follow signs to Levanto. From Levanto follow signs up the hill toward Monterosso al Mare. After the tunnel, turn right at the sign to Monterosso Fegina and go down the hill to Monterosso where there is a large public car park.

HOTEL PORTO ROCA
Manager: Guerrina Arpe
Via Corone, 1, Cinque Terre
Monterosso al Mare, (SP) 19016, Italy
Tel: (0187) 81 75 02, Fax: (0187) 81 76 92
43 Rooms, Double: €170–€295
1 Suite: €350–€500
Minimum Stay Required: 3 nights
Open: mid-Mar to Nov, Credit cards: all major
30 km N of La Spezia, 94 km SE of Genoa
Region: Liguria, Michelin Map: 561

Constantly in search of places to stay in the increasingly popular Cinque Terre, we were pleased to receive a letter from one of our readers highly praising the Hotel Villa Steno and its gracious owners, Matteo and Carla. We are pleased to confirm her impressions of the Villa Steno, a simple yet most appealing small, family-run hotel with a tranquil location just above Monterosso. The hotel, an attractive, mustard-yellow villa accented by green shutters, offers guests a warm welcome. Usually Matteo or his sweet wife, Carla, is at the reception desk to greet you (you might also see their adorable daughter, Chiara). The heart of the hotel is the breakfast room where there is also a small guest sitting area. Here modern furnishings made of blond wood and sunlight streaming in through large windows create a pleasing mood. A hearty buffet breakfast includes fantastic pastries baked fresh each morning by Matteo's father. The guestrooms are simply furnished, but fresh and impeccably clean. Each of the bedrooms has a modern bathroom, and except for two, all of the guestrooms have either a balcony or a private terrace. Matteo's brother, Marco, owns another hotel, the Pasquale, located in the center of the village. Both hotels were started by their enterprising grandfather, Pasquale, and his wife, Fortunata. *Directions:* Ask Matteo to send you his excellent instructions.

HOTEL VILLA STENO
Owners: Carla & Matteo Pasini
Via Roma, 109, Cinque Terre
Monterosso al Mare, (SP) 19016, Italy
Tel: (0187) 81 70 28, Fax: (0187) 81 73 54
16 Rooms, Double: €150–€190
Open: Mar to Nov, Credit cards: all major
30 km N of La Spezia, 94 km SE of Genoa
Region: Liguria, Michelin Map: 561

La Locanda del Capitano is a tiny inn romantically tucked in the historic center of a medieval, picture-perfect walled village perched on a hilltop overlooking a serene, gentle, Umbrian landscape. The hotel is at heart a restaurant, which has quickly gained well-deserved publicity for the outstanding quality of the kitchen but, luckily for guests, there are also a few bedrooms. The guestrooms are small, but sweetly decorated in an appropriately simple, country style. All have pretty wrought-iron headboards with floral paintings hand-done by a local woman. The choice guestrooms are the two with a small terrace tucked up amongst the ancient tiled rooftops. La Locanda is the creation of your charming hosts, Carmen and Giancarlo Polito, who decided at the tender ages of 26 and 27 to begin their life together in the countryside and discovered in a newspaper ad the perfect site for their inn, a centuries-old stone house in the idyllic town of Montone. As soon as they saw the house, their hearts were won. Carmen and Giancarlo are wonderful with their guests, and even organize tours for a minimum of seven people into the countryside for truffle hunting during the season. *Directions:* Heading north from Perugia on the E45, take the Montone exit. The hotel is just a block from the town square.

LA LOCANDA DEL CAPITANO
Owners: Carmen & Giancarlo Polito
Via Roma, 7
Montone, (PG) 06014, Italy
Tel: (075) 93 06 521, Fax: (075) 93 06 455
10 Rooms, Double: €130
Closed: Jan 10 to Feb 10, Credit cards: all major
39 km N of Perugia
Region: Umbria, Michelin Map: 563

In recent years Naples has launched a badly-needed clean-up campaign for its neighborhoods and monuments. Although there certainly has been improvement, it remains a litter-strewn and chaotic yet ultimately fascinating metropolis. Your best bet for safety and easy access to sights is to stay in the city center and the Chiaja is an excellent choice within a slim selection of charming hotels. Close to the San Carlo Theater and the main shopping street of Via Toledo, the pedestrian-only Via Chiaia is lined with shops and restaurants. Entering through an inner courtyard, the hotel's entrance is one flight up where an inviting reception area and living room greet guests. The sun-colored breakfast room is just off this main area and 27 rooms of various sizes are found down a hall which wraps around the courtyard on this same floor as well as an additional six rooms on the floor above. A former residence of a noble family, the new owners strived to maintain the same ambiance even though they completely renovated it with updated amenities. Each room has original turn-of-the-last-century antique pieces and different tones in the matching bedspreads and draperies, tiled floors and floral wallpaper. Sparkling new bathrooms have an occasional jacuzzi tub. A friendly and efficient staff await guests and assist with city itineraries or logistics to the islands of Capri, Ischia or Procida. *Directions:* The hotel is just off the Piazza del Plebiscito.

❄ ☕ ⚒ 💳 ☎ 🐕 🏨 @ W Ⴤ P 🖼 ⚓ 🧍 🚶 🏇 ⚓ 🍇

CHIAJA HOTEL DE CHARME
Manager: Massimo Taurmino
Via Chiaja 216
Naples, (NA) 80121, Italy
Tel: (081) 41 55 55, Fax: (081) 42 23 44
14 Rooms, Double: €110–€165
14 Suites: €145–€205
Open: all year, Credit cards: all major
In the heart of town
Region: Campania, Michelin Map: 564

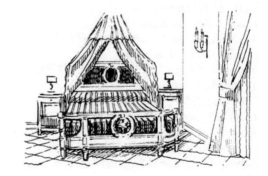

The Costantinopoli 104 is a gem— a charming small, boutique hotel in the historic heart of Naples. From the hotel, you can explore most of the city on foot, including (four blocks away) the breathtaking Museo Archeologico Nazionale. What a pleasure to come home after a day of sightseeing to a secluded hideaway, and be warmly welcomed like a friend. When your hosts (the gracious Santoro family) purchased the villa, it was originally going to be their home; but luckily for you and me, they decided to convert it into a small hotel. The villa is approached through huge doors that face onto the Via Santa Maria di Costantinopoli. You ring a bell for entry, and find yourself in a large, rather drab courtyard. But don't be discouraged; continue straight ahead, then turn left, and you come to a small gate. Once again, ring the bell. When the gate opens, you unexpectedly discover a beautiful, secret garden with manicured beds of flowers and a pretty swimming pool. At one end of the property is a handsome 19th-century villa, enhanced by a Liberty stained-glass window. Within, the ambiance is one of a private home, delightfully lacking the commercialism of a large hotel. The décor is fresh and pretty with refined taste shown throughout. Every detail displays quality and loving care. The standard bedrooms are moderate in size. If you want more space, request a junior suite such as 104. *Directions:* Difficult to navigate to by car. Buy a detailed map.

COSTANTINOPOLI 104
Owner: Clelia Santoro
Via Santa Maria di Costantinopoli 104
Naples, (NA) 80138, Italy
Tel: (081) 55 71 035, Fax: (081) 55 71 051
13 Rooms, Double: €220–€230
5 Suites: €250–€255
Open: all year, Credit cards: all major
History Traveller
Historic center near Piazza Bellini
Region: Campania, Michelin Map: 564

If you prefer a classic, luxury hotel with all the amenities, the Grand Hotel Santa Lucia in the historic part of Naples makes an excellent choice. It is one of the most outstanding of the several grand old hotels that line the Via Partenope, a charming boulevard that wraps around the colorful waterfront. White trim and balconies facing the sea accent this dignified, classic, eight-story building. What makes the hotel especially appealing is its location overlooking the Santa Lucia harbor (abounding with fancy yachts), the Borgo Marinari (a tiny ancient fishing hamlet now filled with colorful restaurants), and the Castel dell'Ovo (a dramatic historical fortress that juts into the sea directly in front of the hotel). You enter into a spacious, ornate lobby with mirrored walls, marble columns, 18th century style furnishings, Murano glass chandeliers, and 17th century paintings. The staff, in morning coats, enhances the ambiance of elegance. Although there is an air of formality, the welcome is extremely gracious. The guestrooms are beautifully furnished in a traditional style with everything of fine quality. If you want to splurge, the deluxe rooms and suites facing the sea are larger than the standard rooms, and also offer superb views. If money doesn't matter, the huge Presidential Penthouse Suite, with a private terrace on the top floor, is incredible. *Directions:* The hotel is directly across from the Castel dell'Ovo (a major landmark).

GRAND HOTEL SANTA LUCIA
Owner: Antonio Melchiorre
Via Partenope, 46
Naples, (NA) 80121, Italy
Tel: (081) 76 40 666, Fax: (081) 76 48 580
96 Rooms, Double: €265–€1700
Open: all year, Credit cards: all major
Historic center on waterfront
Region: Campania, Michelin Map: 564

Sardinia's lovely beaches and inlets of turquoise water are outstanding, but not to venture inland from the coast means missing wonderful scenery and rich archaeological sites. The perfect solution is to combine the two—after a holiday by the sea, plan to stay for several days at the Hotel Su Gologone. Here you can experience all the best the countryside has to offer: delightful rural landscape, rustic country charm, excellent meals featuring Sardinian specialties, and even sightseeing excursions. The Hotel Su Gologone is set in a high valley among gently rolling hills dotted by grazing sheep. Adding drama to the tranquil scene is a backdrop of granite mountains whose jagged peaks reach to the sky. The exterior of the hotel exudes a country charm with stark white walls accenting Mediterranean-blue shutters and doors, red-tiled roof, and flowers, flowers, flowers. Inside, the ambiance of a country hotel is set from the moment you enter the lobby. All of the furnishings have a rustic flair with the extensive use of local handicrafts including hand-woven rugs, pretty fabrics, and simple wooden furniture. Although there are 65 guestrooms, the hotel seems much smaller because many of the rooms are in small cottages scattered about the property. Although the room rate is amazingly low, the Su Gologone offers the amenities of a resort hotel with a pool, tennis, mini-golf, excursions, bikes, horseback riding, and a spa.

✳ ☕ 🏃 ♨ CREDIT ☎ 🏠 🏋 @ ⅄ P ⅋ ❀ 🏊 🏃 🖼 ⟁ 🚶 🏇 ⚓ 🍇

HOTEL SU GOLOGONE
Manager: Luigi Crisponi
Sorgente Su Gologone
Oliena, Sardinia, (NU) 08025, Italy
Tel: (0784) 28 75 12, Fax: (0784) 28 76 68
65 Rooms, Double: €175–€440
Open: Christmas & Mar to Nov, Credit cards: all major
6 km NE of Oliena
On road to Dorgal, Island of Sardinia
Region: Sardinia, Michelin Map: 566

The island-like promontory of Argentario, facing the islands of Giglio and Giannutri, has always been a favorite seaside haven for Romans. Located on a narrow strip of land connecting Argentario to the mainland is the quaint town of Orbetello. Here you find a charming small hotel, the San Biagio, built within a private residence dating back to 1851. The Magnosi family restored the palazzo, creating the feeling of a nobleman's home, not only in the rich furnishings, but also with the many original architectural features of the palazzo itself. Some of these wonderful features include the arched entrance hall that leads to a small courtyard where breakfast is served, the high-ceilinged rooms with ornate moldings and frescoed borders, and the central staircase leading up to the richly appointed guestrooms that are in the main house, each of which has a luxurious marble travertine bathroom. The family's antique pieces collected throughout Europe adorn the intimate sitting rooms as well as the pretty bedrooms. The addition of 28 rooms in an adjacent building, with informal restaurant, wine bar, indoor swimming pool and spa was finished in 2006. Although the San Biagio offers no views in a seaside location, it provides top-level accommodation at exceptional comparable rates. *Directions:* From the SS1 Aurelia N1, exit at Orbetello and go to the historic center. Facing the church (duomo), Via Dante is the street on its left side.

SAN BIAGIO
Owner: Gianfranco Magnosi family
Via Dante, 40
Orbetello, (GR) 58015, Italy
Tel: (0564) 86 05 43, Fax: (0564) 86 77 87
40 Rooms, Double: €200–€250
8 Suites: €250–€350
Open: all year, Credit cards: all major
Center of Orbetello, 160 km N of Rome
Region: Tuscany, Michelin Map: 563

Orta San Giulio is unbelievably picturesque and one of the most romantic places to dine here is the Albergo Ristorante Leon d'Oro, whose owners, the Ronchetti family, have another small, reasonably priced hotel, La Contrada dei Monti, in the middle of the village. This 16th-century building has been lovingly renovated, with great care taken to preserve the original architectural features such as arches, wood beams, exposed stone walls, and wrought-iron fixtures, but adding all the modern comforts such as tiled bathrooms, telephones, and satellite TVs. The intimate reception area has a charming sitting area with splendid arched ceiling embellished with fresco paintings, a fireplace flanked by prettily upholstered chairs, and a handsome tiled floor highlighted by the family coat of arms. The overall ambiance is one of exceptional quality and charming, refined elegance. The core of the hotel is a central courtyard where breakfast is served on warm days. When it is chilly, guests use a sweet breakfast room with a beamed ceiling. The guestrooms are also attractive, with lovely fabrics that color-coordinate with the bedspreads and draperies. Bedrooms are all very similar in decor, but the color scheme varies with each floor. *Directions:* Leave your car in the public parking area and walk into town. Turn left at Via Contrada dei Monti to the hotel on your right.

LA CONTRADA DEI MONTI
Owner: Ronchetti family
Via Contrada dei Monti, 10
Orta San Giulio, Lake Orta, (NO) 28016, Italy
Tel: (0322) 90 51 14, Fax: (0322) 90 58 63
17 Rooms, Double: €110–€160
Open: all year, Credit cards: all major
84 km NW of Milan Malpensa airport
Region: Piedmont, Michelin Map: 561

From the moment you see the Villa Crespi, perched on a hillside overlooking Lake Orta, you can't help chuckling at this elaborate, gingerbread castle that looks straight out of the Arabian Nights. And see it you will, for its minaret with an onion dome ending in a pointed needle stretches up above the trees and is visible from far away. The mansion is quite incredible: the façade is embellished with colorful tiles in fancy designs and further enhanced by elaborately carved stonework and Moorish-style arched windows. Inside, the mood continues with an entry hall that soars many stories high and walls lavishly covered with carved stone. This ambiance of opulence is maintained throughout with gorgeous inlaid wood floors, walls covered with brocade fabric, crystal chandeliers, and ceilings richly adorned by fancy plaster designs. This fairy-tale castle, dating back to 1800s, is the creation of Benigno Crespi, a very wealthy cotton producer who, during his travels to Persia, became fascinated with the romantic palaces he visited. Over the years, poets, kings, and princesses have graced its halls, but now the villa is a deluxe small hotel welcoming paying guests who come to enjoy wonderful food at the 2 Michelin-stars restaurant, sleep in elegant bedrooms, and enjoy the splendid park-like grounds with a view of the lake behind the hotel. The hotel also has a full fitness center. *Directions:* From the north, you will see the hotel on your right as you approach town.

VILLA CRESPI
Manager: Cinzia Primatesta
Via G. Fava, 18
Orta San Giulio, Lake Orta, (NO) 28016, Italy
Tel: (0322) 91 19 02, Fax: (0322) 91 19 19
6 Rooms, Double: €200–€300
8 Suites: €250–€600
Restaurant closed Tues & Wed for lunch
Closed: Jan to mid-Mar, Credit cards: all major
84 km NW of Milan, 1 km E of Orta San Giulio
Region: Piedmont, Michelin Map: 561

The town of Orvieto, just off the main expressway between Rome and Florence, is one of the most picturesque of all the Umbrian hilltowns. This small city is perched on the top of a hill—an intriguing sight that can be viewed from many kilometers away. Less than a ten-minute drive south of Orvieto is a 12th-century Gothic abbey that has been converted into a hotel where you can stay surrounded by the romantic ruins of yesteryear. Although there is a commercial air to La Badia, the reception is caring and friendly. The manager, Ettore Pelletti, has been with the hotel for over 20 years, as has the chef, so, as you can see, there is a real continuity of management. Although this is not a cozy, small hotel, you are bound to enjoy the setting, the pool, the old-world ambiance, and the food. The dining room is one of the most attractive rooms in the hotel. It has an enormous, high-vaulted stone ceiling, wrought-iron fixtures, heavy wooden beams, eye-catching copper accents, and, at one end, a cavernous fireplace complete with a roasting spit. The standard bedrooms, although not large or with inspired decor, are comfortable and many have a stunning view up to the town of Orvieto. If you want to splurge, ask for one of the romantic suites, which have much prettier furnishings. In the meadows behind the monastery there is a lovely pool. *Directions:* From Orvieto, follow signs for Viterbo. The hotel is 4 km south of Orvieto.

LA BADIA
Owner: Contessa Luisa Fiumi
Orvieto, (TR) 05019, Italy
Tel: (0763) 30 19 59, Fax: (0763) 30 53 96
27 Rooms, Double: €220–€280
Restaurant closed Wednesdays
Closed: Jan & Feb, Credit cards: all major
Abitare La Storia
4 km S of Orvieto, 115 km N of Rome
Region: Umbria, Michelin Map: 563

With a rich history dating back to the 16th century, the Hotel Palazzo Piccolomini in the historic center of Orvieto, an incredible, walled city perched atop a high hill, was once home to the wealthy Piccolomini family. At the end of the 1980s the palace was rescued from neglect and after many years of restoration, opened in 1999 as a hotel. In the entrance some of the original architectural features remain, accented by a few pieces of antique furniture, but overall the mood is contemporary. From the reception hall, a flight of steps leads up to a large lounge where the frescoed ceiling again attests to the hotel's glamorous past. However, the room that most portrays the age of the building is the breakfast room in the cellar. It has a giant stone pillar supporting a coved ceiling, an ancient well tucked in a corner, and a carefully preserved medieval stone staircase leading to secret places far below. The standard bedrooms are moderate in size and well equipped in the style of a modern hotel with good lighting, writing desks, satellite TVs, mini-bars, air conditioning, and hairdryers. The hotel sits on a corner facing the small Piazza Ranieri and from here it is a delightful stroll through picturesque little squares to Orvieto's crown jewel, the stunning, not-to-be-missed cathedral. *Directions:* From the A1, exit at Orvieto and follow signs to the center. When the road splits, take the road to the right. Follow signs to the hotel.

HOTEL PALAZZO PICCOLOMINI
Manager: Roberto Mazzolai
Piazza Ranieri, 36
Orvieto, (TR) 05018, Italy
Tel: (0763) 34 17 43, Fax: (0763) 39 10 46
29 Rooms, Double: €154–€280
Open: all year, Credit cards: all major
4 km S of Orvieto, 115 km N of Rome
Region: Umbria, Michelin Map: 563

A convenient stopover while heading either north or south along the main artery—the A1 autostrada—is the Villa Ciconia inn. Located below the historical center of Orvieto, in the newer commercial outskirts, the property maintains its tranquil setting thanks to the fortress of trees protecting the 16th-century stone villa. The first floor includes reception area, breakfast room, and two large high-ceilinged dining rooms. These latter, with their somber gray-stone fireplaces, tapestries, heavy dark-wood beams, and subdued-color frescoes depicting allegorical motifs and landscapes, give the place a medieval castle's air. The 12 air conditioned bedrooms on the second floor are appointed either in appropriate style, with antique chests and wrought-iron beds, or with more contemporary furnishings (lower rates) and all the amenities of the four-star hotel that this is. Most rooms are quiet and look out onto the 8 acres of woods behind the villa. There are also two enormous beamed sitting rooms on this floor for guests and a beautiful new swimming pool. The restaurant has a solid reputation for creating excellent Umbrian specialties. Manager Anna Elena Petrangeli is always on hand to assist guests. *Directions:* Exiting from the autostrada, turn right towards Orvieto and right again where marked Arezzo, Perugia, passing under the tollway. The Ciconia is just after the river on the left-hand side of the road.

VILLA CICONIA
Owner: Petrangeli family
Via dei Tigli 69
Orvieto, (TR) 05019, Italy
Tel: (0763) 30 55 82, Fax: (0763) 30 20 77
12 Rooms, Double: €160–€170
Restaurant closed Mondays
Open: all year, Credit cards: all major
In the historic center of town, 115 km N of Rome
Region: Umbria, Michelin Map: 563

A dear friend and world traveler highly recommended Masseria Montelauro, giving rave reviews regarding its serene, harmonious ambiance, attentive staff, and exquisite candlelit meals served under the pergola. We also were immediately captivated by the elegant simplicity of this countryside property near the sea. White is the prominent color: on the exterior façade of the ex-monastery, the white-washed walls of bedrooms, the fabrics on the bedspreads, sofas, and cushions. This clean and cool effect is pleasantly complemented by the natural sandy-colored stone walls and floors which contrast with black wrought iron beds and bedside lanterns. Spacious vaulted bedrooms on both ground and first floors have independent entrances and look out either to the front gardens or to the courtyard with inviting borderless pool backed by olive trees. Sleek bathrooms have the amenities of a luxury accommodation. A fresh country breakfast is served in the stone-walled arched dining area or on the outdoor patio. Proprietor, Elisabetta Massaro, and her daughter, Mercedes, have created a discreet and sophisticated hideaway capturing the essence of the Salento area while doing a number on the senses. Enjoy the surrounding landscapes by car, boat, bike or horseback. *Directions:* Take the SS 613 highway south from Brindisi for Lecce and follow for Maglie, then after Otranto exit at Uggiano La Chiesa turning left at signs for Montelauro.

MASSERIA MONTELAURO   **New**
Owner: Elisabetta Massaro
S.P. Otranto-Uggiano
Otranto, (LE) 73028, Italy
Tel: (0836) 80 62 03, Fax: (0836) 80 10 01
26 Rooms, Double: €160–€325
1 Suite: €245–€365
Open: Apr to Oct, Credit cards: all major
35 km SE of Lecce, 80 km S of Brindisi
Region: Apulia, Michelin Map: 564

As you travel down to the most southern tip of the heel of Italy in the area south of Lecce known as Salento, you will no doubt make a stop in the charming seaside village of Otranto of ancient origins. To be able to capture the true essence of this timeless spot, linger a few days to at the Palazzo Papaleo where you will be treated like honored house guests. The family residence within the historic center of town, adjacent the 11th-century cathedral, has been passed down to granddaughter, Francesca, a direct descendant of the aristocratic Papaleo family. She and her amiable French husband, Marc-André, have taken on the challenge of offering high-level hospitality and service in an area just starting to develop in tourism. The ancient palazzo has been completely renovated, producing 9 modernly-equipped bedrooms with many amenities and mosaic tiled bathrooms. Two suites have a vaulted frescoed ceiling and loft and other rooms have an occasional antique piece or small balcony. Breakfast is served in the formal living room or up on the rooftop garden where you have a full circle view of the port, enjoyed also from a hydro jet tub (massages and steam room also available). Super informed hosts are intent on providing all possible services plus assistance on local itineraries from boat tours, wine or olive oil tastings, excursions to Lecce and smaller towns. Take the time to explore this fascinating area of Puglia! *Directions:* Located in the heart of Otranto.

HOTEL PALAZZO PAPALEO   **New**
Owner: Paolo Maniglio
Via Rondachi, 1
Otranto, (LE) 73028, Italy
Tel: (0836) 80 21 08, Fax: (0836) 80 51 29
9 Rooms, Double: €200–€370
2 Suites: €320–€490
Open: all year, Credit cards: all major
35 km SE of Lecce
Region: Apulia, Michelin Map: 564

Elba is a beautiful small island, easily accessible in one hour by car ferry from Piombino. After exploring Tuscany, or while en route along the coast heading north from Rome, you will find that Elba makes a delightful stopover where you can happily spend several days relaxing and exploring the island's many pretty inlets and picturesque fishing villages. The Hotel Villa Ottone is idyllically nestled in a tranquil park and has its own private beach (there is also a swimming pool). The original part of the hotel is a romantic villa (which belonged to Signor Di Mario's grandfather) facing directly onto the sea. If you want to splurge, ask for a deluxe room in the villa. Some of the guestrooms are located in an attractive building that also houses the reception area and the dining room, while more guestrooms are found in a separate wing nestled amongst the trees. The furnishings throughout are tasteful and everything is immaculately maintained. Be sure to visit the bar, which has a stunning ceiling of intricate plasterwork and lovely frescoes. In high season you need to take the modified American plan (MAP), which includes breakfast and either lunch or dinner and there is a three-night minimum. However, this is no problem as the food is very good and beautifully served. Villa Ottone is a hotel with great personality, overseen with meticulous attention to detail by the gracious Signor Di Mario.

HOTEL VILLA OTTONE
Owner: Di Mario family
Localita: Ottone
Ottone, Isola di Elba, (LI) 57037, Italy
Tel: (0565) 93 30 42, Fax: (0565) 93 32 57
75 Rooms, Double: €165–€320*
*Includes breakfast & lunch or dinner
Open: May to Oct, Credit cards: all major
11 km SE of Portoferraio
Region: Tuscany, Michelin Map: 563

If you want to stay in the heart of Palermo, the Centrale Palace Hotel has an absolutely superb location—on one of Palermo's most colorful main streets with the city's prime sightseeing targets just steps away. Within minutes you can be at the spectacular cathedral, the museums, or the theater. However, it is not location alone that makes the Centrale Palace so special—this well-run, friendly hotel would be a winner anywhere. The building dates back to the 17th century, at which time it was the home of a noble family. Its grand past is still alive in the soaring ceilings, beautiful polished tile floors, marble columns, ornate chandeliers, frescoed ceilings in the conference rooms, handsome mirrors, fine oil paintings, and many precious antiques. The attractive guestrooms maintain the old-world ambiance with traditional furnishings and color-coordinating fabrics. One of the most endearing features of the hotel is its lovely roof garden overlooking the city where dinner is served in warm weather. Palermo is such an impossibly congested metropolis that our suggestion is to pick up a rental car as you leave the city. However, if you do drive, ask the hotel to send you directions, then mark the location on your map. Happily, once you arrive, the receptionist will have a porter take your car to their parking area. This, I assure you, is a blessing. The hotel has plans underway to add more bedrooms in the near future.

❄ ☕ ⚗ 🍵 CREDIT ☎ 🛗 🏋 @ ⚲ P 🍴 ❦ 🐾 ♿ ⚓ 🏇 🍇

CENTRALE PALACE HOTEL
Manager: Pietro Cascino
Corso Vittorio Emanuele, 327
Palermo, Sicily, (PA) 90134, Italy
Tel: (091) 33 66 66, Fax: (091) 33 48 81
104 Rooms, Double: €240–€327
Open: all year, Credit cards: all major
On the northern coast of Sicily
Region: Sicily, Michelin Map: 565

An alternative stay in the fascinating city of Palermo is the Hotel Principe di Villafranca. The hotel is located just outside the city's center in a more residential area with street-level shops. The basic, modern façade of the hotel can throw one off at first, however, this first impression vanishes immediately upon entering and viewing the interior of the hotel. You are now in a elegant and very charming accommodation, similar to that of a private home. To the left of the foyer (which leads to a sitting room with fireplace, library, and dining room) is the reception area with a stairway ascending to the thirty-four guestrooms on the floor above. A décor including Sicilian antiques, paintings, Oriental carpets, and coordinated draperies in warm, hunter green and mustard yellow creates an inviting ambiance. Very comfortable guestrooms are classically appointed with soft, peach walls, parquet floors with distinctive details, locally crafted marble bathrooms, and fine linen sheets. The restaurant, "Il Firriato", serves fine Sicilian fare. A small fitness center is also available. *Directions:* The hotel is located two blocks south of Piazza Castelnuovo (Via Dante) and a 15-minute walk to the center of the city. A private garage is available.

HOTEL PRINCIPE DI VILLAFRANCA
Manager: Licia Guccione
Via G. Turrisi Colonna, 4
Palermo, Sicily, (PA) 90141, Italy
Tel: (091) 61 18 523, Fax: (091) 58 87 05
34 Rooms, Double: €220–€280
Open: all year, Credit cards: all major
On the northern coast of Sicily
Region: Sicily, Michelin Map: 565

The Villa Le Barone was once the home of the famous Tuscan Della Robbia family, whose beautiful terracottas are still seen throughout Italy. It was restored after the First World War by Marchesa Maria Bianca Viviani Della Robbia as a wine estate and later converted into a deluxe boutique hotel by her granddaughter, Duchessa Franca Visconti. Now her cousins, Conte Corso Aloisi and his wife, are the owners. They frequently live in the villa, greet guests and ensure that the impeccable standards and taste prevail. Staying at the Villa Le Barone is very much like being the guest in a private, elegant home set in the gorgeous Tuscan hills in front of the San Leolino abbey. The lounges are especially inviting, beautifully furnished with charming, family antiques. There are 28 guestrooms, all of which vary in size with modern tiled bathrooms and are individually decorated. Rooms are in the main villa or in renovated cottages and barns. Some have their own terrace. The tennis court has a breathtaking view over the Chianti hills and there is a lovely swimming pool, romantically set on a terrace looking over the vineyards and rose garden. Wonderful little hideaways are found secluded in the park-like setting where guests can find a quiet nook to read or just to sit and soak in the beauty of the surrounding hills. Dinner is served in the restaurant, which formerly housed the winery. *Directions:* From the center of Panzano, follow signs to the hotel.

❄ 🍵 🛎 CREDIT ☎ @ W P ≈ 🏌 🖼 🍴 🏃 🐎 🍇

VILLA LE BARONE
Owners: Count & Countess Aloisi de Larderel
Via San Leolino, 19
Panzano in Chianti, (FI) 50020, Italy
Tel: (055) 85 26 21, Fax: (055) 85 22 77
29 Rooms, Double: €230–€400,* 1 Suite: €300–€400*
*Includes breakfast & dinner
Open: all year, Credit cards: all major
Abitare La Storia
31 km S of Florence, 6 km S of Greve
Region: Tuscany, Michelin Map: 563

Relax in the countryside just 6 kilometers from the bustling city of Verona at the exquisite Villa del Quar where you can enjoy excellent accommodations, gourmet dining (two Michelin stars), and the warmth and charm of a family-managed hotel. The gracious owner, Leopoldo Montresor, is a talented architect who spared no expense to assure that his renovations resulted in an estate exuding charm and taste. The Montresors live in one wing of the villa, conveniently close for Evelina Acampora-Montresor, who manages the hotel. The property has been in the Montresor family for many generations—ever since Leopoldo's great-great-great-grandfather won the land in a game of cards at the casino in Venice in the early 1800s. Your heart will be captivated from the moment you pass the family chapel and enter the reception lounge, elegantly decorated with finely upholstered sofas in warm shades of pinks and mellow yellows. Sunlight floods the room through a wall of windows, which open onto an inviting side terrace where guests dine in warm weather. There is also a superb 16th-century wine cellar and a most attractive beamed-ceilinged winetasting room where meals are served elegantly on tables set with fine linens. The guestrooms are equally appealing and furnished in antiques. A large swimming pool is set enchantingly in a meadow with vineyards stretching almost to the edge of the pool, where a gazebo bar is at guests' disposal.

HOTEL VILLA DEL QUAR
Owners: Evelina & Leopoldo Montresor
Via Quar N12, Pedemonte, (VR) 37020, Italy
Tel: (045) 68 00 681, Fax: (045) 68 00 604
18 Rooms, Double: €240–€390
10 Suites: €425–€850
Open: mid-Mar to Jan, Credit cards: all major
History Traveller
Relais & Châteaux
6 km N of Verona, 22 km E of Lake Garda
Region: Veneto, Michelin Map: 562

The Castel Pergine is a storybook castle hotel perfect for the budget-minded tourist. No need to forfeit romance, for even though the Castel Pergine is good value for money, it has a fabulous location dominating a hilltop above the town of Pergine. The Castel Pergine is more famous as a restaurant than a hotel—the dining room has an engaging medieval decor, gorgeous views, and good food. When Verena and Theo Schneider-Neff came from Switzerland and took over the hotel, they made many improvements, including installing a state-of-the-art kitchen. They also upgraded the bedrooms and added snug showers to some of them. Keep in mind that this is a budget hotel, so don't expect luxurious accommodations. And, be sure to request one of the superior guestrooms with a private bathroom. The accommodations range from rather simple to comfortably charming, the more expensive having en-suite showers, handsome wooden paneling, and country-style furnishings. Room 27, a corner room, is especially pretty, but the beds are shorter and narrower than in the other superior rooms. The Castel Pergine is a real bargain and its secluded hilltop setting is definitely a winner. *Directions:* Exit the autostrada at Trento Nord and follow signs for Padova to Pergine. Exit for Pergine centro. At the first roundabout take the first exit, and at the second roundabout take the second exit. After 800 meters, turn left at the chapel. Don't go into the center of Pergine.

CASTEL PERGINE
Managers: Verena & Theo Schneider-Neff
Pergine, (TN) 38057, Italy
Tel: (0461) 53 11 58, Fax: (0461) 53 13 29
21 Rooms, Double: €108–€150*
*Includes breakfast & dinner
Restaurant open daily in high season
Open: Easter to Nov, Credit cards: all major
10 km E of Trento, 2.5 km E of Pergine
Region: Trentino-Alto Adige, Michelin Map: 562

A truly classic hotel with old-world charm, the 120-year-old Brufani Palace was once two hotels sitting back to back in the main piazza of Perugia's historic center. Joined together like Siamese twins, the hotel has been recently restored to its original splendor with, of course, double of everything, including many spacious sitting rooms, two bars, a restaurant, and enormous formal breakfast room. Unlike many newly restored accommodation, obvious effort has been made to retain its old-fashioned flavor while updating amenities and maintaining a five-star level. Carpeted bedrooms are spacious and elegantly appointed with antiques, gilded mirrors, and marble bathrooms, most with lovely views over historic Perugia or the Umbrian countryside. Guests can choose from standard doubles, suites and junior suites with high ceilings, or cozy beamed mansard rooms. All guests can enjoy the full 360-degree views from the highest point in the city, the Brufani's rooftop terrace. Another unique feature of this hotel is the swimming pool down in the original cantinas with brick vaulted ceilings. Etruscan relics were found while digging and now the glass-bottom pool proudly displays this discovery! The hotel also has a gym and sauna. Step out of the hotel and you are right on the main street of charming Perugia. *Directions:* Follow hotel signs up to the historic center to the Piazza Italia. Hotel staff will take care of parking.

HOTEL BRUFANI PALACE
Manager: Enrico Costa
Piazza Italia, 12
Perugia, (PG) 06100, Italy
Tel: (075) 57 32 541, Fax: (075) 57 20 210
94 Rooms, Double: €330*
*Breakfast not included: €32
Open: all year, Credit cards: all major
History Traveller
Center of Perugia, 40 km W of Cortona
Region: Umbria, Michelin Map: 563

The sleepy village of Solomeo, located between Perugia and Lake Trasimeno, had been almost completely abandoned until a well-known cashmere company bought and restored most of the town to its original charm, using the individual houses and apartments for offices and workshops. Pier Luigi Cavicchi, an import/export consultant, and his friendly wife Donatella (who runs the family's farm) inherited a turn-of-the-last-century villa, located right in the heart of town. Pier Luigi (who had spent many happy summers at the villa) and his wife thoroughly renovated the property and opened it as an inn. Their wish was to maintain the original character of the beloved residence while adding all possible amenities (including air conditioning). The result is a compact and quaint hotel that has it all. The 12 English-style country bedrooms are named after flowers and this theme is followed through in stenciled borders, bedspread fabrics, and bathrooms. Preserved stencil work on walls and ceilings in the entrance, tea room, and upstairs sitting room were done by the same artist who decorated the town's church across the street. The bright breakfast room downstairs has stone walls and beams and leads to terraces overlooking the countryside where a garden, swimming pool, exercise room, meeting room, and four garden bedrooms are situated. In the immediate area are a golf club and horseback-riding facilities. The hotel is 10 km outside of Perugia in Solmeo.

LOCANDA SOLOMEO
Owners: Pier Luigi & Donatella Cavicchi
Piazza Carlo Alberto dalla Chiesa, 1 Loc. Solomeo
Perugia, (PG) 06070, Italy
Tel: (075) 52 93 119, Fax: (075) 52 94 090
12 Rooms, Double: €105–€135, 1 Suite: €130–€170
Restaurant by reservation only
Closed: Christmas week until mid-Jan
Credit cards: all major
10 km W of Perugia
Region: Umbria, Michelin Map: 563

I am such a romantic that, as the boat chugged across Lake Maggiore from Stresa to the medieval fishing village of Isola dei Pescatori (Fisherman's Island) and I saw the Hotel Verbano with its reddish-brown walls, dark-green shutters, and tables set on the terrace overlooking the lake, my heart was won—completely. To accommodate the many people who clamber off the excursion boats each day to visit this picturesque island, the hotel has a large dining room with arched windows overlooking the lake. However, when the weather is warm, the favorite place to dine is outside on the idyllic terrace overlooking nearby Isola Bella (Beautiful Island). In the evening, when most of the tourists have departed, the terrace becomes even more romantic—particularly with a full moon reflecting on the rippling water. The food is excellent, featuring fish fresh from the lake. The 12 bedrooms, all with a lake view, are delightful, with high ceilings, wooden floors, and modern bathrooms. Several have balconies and three share a large terrace. *Directions:* Exit the A26 at Stresa and follow signposts for the waterfront where you take the public ferry to Isola dei Pescatori (the ferry is much cheaper than the private water taxis).

HOTEL VERBANO
Owners: Alberto & Roberto Zacchera
Via Ugo Ara, 2
Pescatori, Isola dei, Lake Maggiore, (VB) 28838, Italy
Tel: (0323) 30 408, Fax: (0323) 33 129
12 Rooms, Double: €165–€185
Open: all year, Credit cards: all major
Abitare La Storia
80 km NW of Milan, ferry from Stresa
Region: Piedmont, Michelin Map: 561

The new breed of small luxury boutique hotels has made important strides in Italy and the Hotel Ai Capitani, the first of its kind on Lake Garda, is a prime example. Fifteen contemporary suites named after composers are housed in a 300-year-old building in the center of the historic part of town, evidence of which is visible in the pastel frescoes cleverly preserved and visible on each floor and within some guestrooms. Prominent decorating colors feature black, brown, and beiges, giving a sleek, contemporary look that is emphasized by beds frames lined with soft leather, satin parquet floors, high-tech lighting and tiled bathrooms plus all possible amenities. Giorgio Lecchi, chef of the small restaurant, Il Ramo, has a daily menu of regional dishes and lake fish choices served up in the luminous dining room. A second restaurant across the way is a trendy spot for locals. Being at the base of the lake, you have easy access to the Veneto region including Verona, Vicenza and the Palladian villas The hotel, in the capable hands of manager Gianni Mannai, offers many special services to distinguish it from other luxury hotels such as: helicopter transfers, luxury car rental, boat excursions on the lake to charming villages (using the hotel's own vessel Falstaff), transfers to the nearby golf course, and complete spa services within the hotel premises. *Directions:* From the A4 autostrada Milano-Venezia exit at Peschiera del Garda and follow for center of town.

❄ 🚴 💳 ☎ ♨ @ 🍸 P 🍴 ❀ 🖼 ⚓ 🚶 👣 🏄

HOTEL AI CAPITANI
Manager: Gianni Mannai
Via Castelletto, 2/4
Peschiera Sul Garda, (VR) 37019, Italy
Tel: (045) 64 00 782, Fax: (045) 64 01 571
15 Rooms, Double: €390–€1320*
*Breakfast not included
Open: all year, Credit cards: all major
In the center of Peschiera
Region: Veneto, Michelin Map: 561

Nestled in the tranquil Tuscan countryside between two enchanting hilltop villages (Pienza and Monticchiello) is another jewel, L'Olmo. You cannot help instantly losing your heart to this very special little hotel. It has the warmth and intimacy of a bed and breakfast, yet the service and amenities rival those of the finest deluxe hotel. This bit of paradise is owned by the Lindo family. A few years ago they left the bustling city of Turin and bought a beautiful 16th-century stone house, which they lovingly restored to perfection, down to the smallest detail, preserving original terracotta floors and wood-beamed ceilings. With superb taste and guests' comfort in mind, five suites were created and appointed with antique chests, locally made wrought-iron beds, and pretty floral fabrics for color. Each has its own travertine marble bathroom and two have a fireplace. There is also a two bedroom, two bath apartment which is great for families. Francesca and her mother Loredana, your exceptionally charming hostesses, tend to guests in a warm and highly professional manner. Downstairs are two cozy sitting rooms leading out to the stone courtyard with tables and flower pots. A full buffet breakfast or gourmet candlelit dinner—upon request—is served in the luminous dining room. Lunch and dinner are also served in the romantic garden pergola. *Directions:* From Pienza drive south, after 6 km turn left to Monticchiello. Follow signs for L'Olmo on your right.

L'OLMO
Owners: Francesca & Loredana Lindo
Monticchiello
Pienza, (SI) 53020, Italy
Tel: (0578) 75 51 33, Fax: (0578) 75 51 24
5 Rooms, Double: €180–€280
1 Apt, Double: €300
Dinner upon request
Open: Apr 1 to Nov 15, Credit cards: all major
6 km S of Pienza
Region: Tuscany, Michelin Map: 563

The Relais Il Chiostro is idyllically snuggled inside the stone walls of Pienza, a medieval hilltop village that is one of Tuscany's most perfect jewels. The hotel is built within a stunning 15th-century monastery; a heritage immediately apparent when you step through the massive arched wood doors into an exceptionally beautiful small cloister. The hushed courtyard is framed by a colonnade of marble columns linked by stone arches. The restaurant and the various lounges and sitting rooms occupy the ground floor. Upstairs there are 37 attractive, individually decorated guestrooms with splendid frescoed ceilings featured in some of the suites. The choice rooms overlook the beautiful Tuscan countryside, but views from the other rooms are also delightful—overlooking either the garden cloister or the ancient tiled rooftops of Pienza. One of the most outstanding features of the hotel is its spectacular location. Perched above the valley, the hotel takes full advantage of its position with a terrace garden (where meals are served when the weather is warm) which stretches to the edge of the wall where guests can enjoy an incredible panoramic view of Tuscany at its finest. On a terrace below, a large swimming pool nestles in another garden. *Directions:* Located one block from the main square, Piazza Pio II.

HOTEL RELAIS IL CHIOSTRO DI PIENZA
Manager: Massimo Cicala
Corso Rossellino, 26
Pienza, (SI) 53026, Italy
Tel: (0578) 74 84 00, Fax: (0578) 74 84 40
37 Rooms, Double: €120–€290
Closed: Jan 7 to Mar 20, Credit cards: all major
52 km SE of Siena
Region: Tuscany, Michelin Map: 563

In a small city near the coast, not far from the charming town of Lucca and the popular town of Pisa, you will find the Albergo Pietrasanta. Although "albergo" suggests a simple hotel, this small, deluxe property does not fit that definition. Located in the center of Pietrasanta, the building dates back to the 17th century when it was the home of the prestigious and wealthy Barsanti Bonetti family. There is a sophisticated, understated elegance throughout the hotel and a mood of luxury is set as you enter the lobby. To the right of the spacious foyer are two splendid lounges which exude the ambiance of a private home, with pastel walls, soft lighting, comfortable chairs grouped around a handsome fireplace, polished terrazzo floors, beautiful paintings, and bouquets of fresh flowers. The far end of the lounge opens through arched doors into one of the hotel's most special features, a romantic garden courtyard, part of which is enclosed in glass to create a "winter garden" where a bountiful breakfast is served each morning. Forming one wall of the courtyard is a separate building, formerly the stables, which has been renovated to house additional deluxe accommodations. As would be expected, guestrooms reflect the same subdued, sophisticated good taste as the public rooms. *Directions:* From the A12, exit at Versilia-Forte dei Marmi and follow signs to Pietrasanta. In town follow signs to the hotel. The hotel is 20 km from Pisa Airport.

❄ ✦ ☕ 💳 ☎ 🐕 🛗 ♟ @ W Y P ⬚ ♿ ✈ ♞ 🚶 🍇

ALBERGO PIETRASANTA
Manager: Barbara Pardini
Via Garibaldi, 35
Pietrasanta, (LU) 55045, Italy
Tel: (0584) 79 37 26, Fax: (0584) 79 37 28
19 Rooms, Double: €300–€400*
2 Suites: €580–€850*
*Breakfast not included: €20
Closed: Nov 20 to Mar 1, Credit cards: all major
35 km NW of Lucca, 105 km NW of Florence
Region: Tuscany, Michelin Map: 563

For years there was no outstanding place to stay in Pisa, but all that changed dramatically in March 2003 when Maria Luisa Bignardi opened her deluxe, small boutique hotel (her family's home since the 1500s) within a few minutes' stroll of Pisa's stunning Piazza dei Miracoli. The Hotel Relais dell'Orologio is truly exceptional in every way—it exudes romance and offers refined comfort, staff to cater to your every whim, a perfect location, gourmet dining, fine wines, lovely decor, and, best of all, the genuine warmth of your elegant, charming hostess. It took eight years of love, imagination, and hard work to restore the long-neglected mansion to its former grandeur and now every detail exudes good taste, understated grandeur, and the highest quality. The furnishings are beautiful, with family heirlooms used in the intimate lounge and in the well-decorated guestrooms, each of which enjoys fine fabrics, excellent linens, quality mattresses, and marble bathrooms. The standard guestrooms are small, so if you prefer more space, we suggest one of the junior suites. In the evening, gourmet meals are served at the hotel's charming restaurant Lady Hallett's Bar, offering typical Tuscan food and featuring the hotel's own wines, olive oils and fresh vegetables. The Hotel Relais dell'Orologio is truly a gem. *Directions:* Take the North Pisa exit from the A12. When you get into town, follow well-marked signs to the hotel.

❄ ☕ ✄ 💳 ☎ 🐎 ♨ @ W Y P 🍴 🚭 🖼 ⚐ ♿ 🛁 🕺 🏇 🍇

HOTEL RELAIS DELL'OROLOGIO
Owner: Maria Luisa Bignardi
Via della Faggiola 12-14
Pisa, (PI) 56126, Italy
Tel: (050) 83 03 61, Fax: (050) 55 18 69
16 Rooms, Double: €280–€720
2 Suites: €680–€850
Open: all year, Credit cards: all major
History Traveller
77 km W of Florence
Region: Tuscany, Michelin Map: 563

It is difficult to find a hotel in Rome with windows thick enough to keep out the ever-present buzz of traffic. Less than an hour's drive from the city, the Borgo Paraelios offers an ideal solution: a luxurious country villa immersed in the lovely Tuscan-like hills of Sabina. This splendid villa is filled to the brim with elegant antiques, rich, warm-colored tapestries, and period paintings. It is a masterpiece harmonizing old and new, with antique terracotta tile floors, stone fireplaces, beamed ceilings, and antique doors from castles brought here and cleverly incorporated into the building. The soft, less impressive bedrooms styled in tune with the countryside theme, look out over the lush garden where guests can breakfast on private patios. Meandering through the main living room, two libraries, and billiard room, one has the sense of having been invited to the country home of nobility for a weekend of absolute peace and tranquility. Transportation to and from Rome is available for a charge. When you return from the city, (40-minute train ride) enjoy an excellent meal served in the frescoed formal dining room or take advantage of the hotel's many amenities: 9-hole golf course (closed for 2008 season), indoor and outdoor pools, tennis court, small beauty center. *Directions:* Exit A1 at Soratte/Ponzano and go towards Stimigliano. At end of road turn right for Poggio Mirteto, after 4 km turn left for Terni on S.S.313, the hotel gate is just on the left.

❄ ☕ 🎿 [CREDIT] ☎ 🐕 ♿ 🏋 P ¶ 🚭 ☘ ≈ 🎿 🐕‍🦺 🎯 🏇

BORGO PARAELIOS
Owner: Andrea Salabé family
Localita: Valle Collicchia
Poggio Catino, (RI) 02040, Italy
Tel: (0765) 26 267, Fax: (0765) 26 268
18 Rooms, Double: €300–€390
Open: all year, Credit cards: all major
Relais & Châteaux
45 km NE of Rome, 2 km N of Poggio Mirteto
Region: Lazio, Michelin Map: 563

Gennarino a Mare is primarily a restaurant—one of the best known in Ponza both for its seafood specialties and its prime location right on the waterfront. It even has a large deck that stretches out over the water, built upon wooden pilings. Gennarino a Mare is a favorite place to dine, especially in summer when boats of all shapes and sizes dock at the adjacent pier and the merry yacht set comes to eat and drink. The restaurant has hosted many of the world's rich and famous, so there's no telling who might be sitting at the next table. It is no wonder the restaurant is so popular: as you enjoy dinner, you can watch the reflection of the fishing boats shimmering in the water and, behind them, the gaily painted houses of Ponza stepping up the hill like brightly painted blocks. Owner Francesco Silvestri was born in the same house where the restaurant now stands. The 12 simple bedrooms, located on the floors above the restaurant, are all decorated similarly with colorful matching drapes and bedspreads setting off white walls. Although small, each room has its own little step-out balcony with a romantic view. Remember, Gennarino a Mare is basically a restaurant, but a real winner for a simple, reasonably priced place to stay in Ponza. *Directions:* Take either the ferry or hydrofoil from Anzio to Ponza. The hotel is on the opposite side of the port, so it is best to take a taxi.

GENNARINO A MARE
Owners: Tilla & Francesco Silvestri
Via Dante, 64
Ponza, (LT) 04027, Italy
Tel: (0771) 80 071, Fax: (0771) 80 140
12 Rooms, Double: €180–€290
Open: all year, Credit cards: all major
Island of Ponza, ferry from Anzio
Region: Lazio, Michelin Map: 563

For those desiring a taste of life on one of Italy's twenty-odd islands, Ponza ranks high on the list. This small, informal fishing village, its pastel-colored houses hugging the hillside with rocky shores and splendid, emerald waters, is a favorite summer destination of Romans. Two hours from the city (one to Anzio, another on the hydro jet boat), it is a perfect, quick getaway. The Grand Hotel Santa Domitilla, named after the island's patron saint, opened as the answer to a need for a high-level accommodation, in contrast to the more spartan, pensione-type accommodation of the island. The guestrooms are freshly appointed with hand-painted colored tiles, all with patios or terraces, although just a handful have sea views. (A common, rooftop terrace and suites with patios provide ample sea views for all.) In the heart of the island, the hotel offers a peaceful retreat. It is nestled in a lush garden with two small swimming pools, fresh and seawater, one having two access points into a natural rock cave! Mediterranean-styled rooms in three buildings surround the noteworthy seafood restaurant, Il Melegrano, with its tropical bamboo pergola, a large entrance lounge, two bars, and a beauty center. Personally run by owner Signora Domitilla (the sister of Franco at Gennarino al Mare), the experienced hospitality is warm and personalized. *Directions:* Take the hydro jet boat from Anzio (www.alilauro.it), and be met at the port by the hotel shuttle.

GRAND HOTEL SANTA DOMITILLA
Manager: Paolo Greca
Via Panoramica
Ponza, (LT) 04027, Italy
Tel: (0771) 80 99 51, Fax: (0771) 80 99 55
46 Rooms, Double: €300–€700
Open: all year, Credit cards: all major
Island of Ponza, ferry from Anzio
Region: Lazio, Michelin Map: 563

The Pitrizza is a tiny jewel of a hotel located on the Emerald Coast of the island of Sardinia—the playground of the Aga Khan and the jet set of the world. From the moment you enter through the front gate, marked only with a discreet sign, you are in a world of tranquility and absolute beauty. There is a central clubhouse that has a beautiful lounge, a delightful dining room with hand-hewn wooden chairs, a card room, and a bar. A small, protected patio extends from the dining room where meals are served when the weather is warm. French doors from the lounge open onto the terrace, which leads down to a most unusual swimming pool, cleverly designed into the natural rock. Once in this outstanding pool, you have the impression that you are swimming in the sea, not a pool, because the water level matches that of the bay. The bedrooms are all spacious and beautifully decorated—everything is of the very finest quality. They are tucked away in small cottages whose sod roofs covered with flowers blend into the landscape. The two magnificent Presidential Suites each have a private pool and a breathtaking bay view. If your idea of a vacation is a frenzy of activity and things to do, then the Pitrizza is definitely not for you. There are no planned activities—only lovely peacefulness, gourmet food, a beautiful pool, a spa, and a delightful small white-sand beach. Although extremely expensive, the Pitrizza is truly special and lives up to every expectation.

HOTEL PITRIZZA
Manager: Pierangelo Tondina
Porto Cervo, (SS) 07020, Italy
Tel: (0789) 93 01 11, Fax: (0789) 93 06 11
55 Rooms, Double: €1460–€2960*
*Includes breakfast & dinner
Open: May to Sep, Credit cards: all major
NE tip of Island of Sardinia
Region: Sardinia, Michelin Map: 566

Sardinia is a large island, making it difficult to settle in just one place and visit all the sights. Therefore, we felt it important to find a hotel for those who want to explore the area around Alghero. After looking without success for a charming place to stay in the city, we chose the Hotel El Faro, a large hotel built in the 1950s and refurbished in 2004, situated 12 kilometers away on the tip of a small peninsula at the Bay of Nymphs. A historic stone tower, Normanna, and a lighthouse mark the strategic spot. The hotel, too, sports a mock lighthouse, a symbol of its namesake, "El Faro." The white-stuccoed hotel spreads out over the Mediterranean peninsula and because there is water on three sides, many of the guestrooms have a sea view (and a balcony from which to enjoy it). Some of the vistas are more spectacular than others, so ask for a room in front overlooking the bay, such as number 159 or one of its neighbors. The mattresses are a bit soft for our taste, but the large bathrooms are topnotch, and the furniture attractive in typical Sardinian style. On large terraces situated below the hotel are sun decks. The first terraced deck leads to the inside of the hotel where there is a restaurant and indoor swimming pool. A lower terrace, snuggled into the rocks, features a larger pool for adult swimmers. The ambiance is of a modern, first-class resort-style hotel, similar to those you find in this category around the world, and a friendly, well-kept place to stay.

HOTEL EL FARO
Manager: Patrizia Sechi
Porto Conte, (SS) 07041, Italy
Tel: (079) 94 20 10, Fax: (079) 94 20 30
92 Rooms, Double: €190–€420
24 Suites: €262–€920
Minimum Stay Required: 3 nights
Open: May to end of Sep, Credit cards: all major
12 km from Alghero, Island of Sardinia
Region: Sardinia, Michelin Map: 566

The Il Pellicano (one of Italy's most idyllic hotels) has been cleverly designed in the traditional villa style and, although not old, looks as though it has snuggled on its prime hillside position overlooking the Mediterranean many years. The façade is stucco, painted a typical Italian russet and set off by a tiled roof. Vines enwrap the building, further enhancing its appealing look. You enter into a spacious, attractive lobby where the sun streams through the windows enhancing the white walls, terracotta floors, and wood-beamed ceilings. The sophisticated and refined ambiance continues with comfy sofas, antique accents, and enormous displays of fresh flowers enlivening every conceivable nook and cranny. The overall impression is one of light and color—and impeccable taste. Beyond the reception area is a spacious terrace where chef Antonio Giuda (one Michelin star) prepares elaborate seafood menus, served outdoors overlooking the dramatic bay and islands. From the terrace, a lawn dotted with cypresses, olive trees, and umbrella pines extends down the hillside to a heated-seawater pool romantically perched at the cliff's edge. From the bluff, both steps and an elevator access a pier at the water's edge. Off the stairs, a large terrace with lounge chairs and mats for sunning has been built into the rocks. The hotel also has a complete spa, tennis courts, boutique, conference room and beauty salon. Exquisite.

❄ ☕ 🎿 ♨ 💳 ☎ 🛗 🍽 @ 🍸 P 🍴 🚭 🌺 🏊 🏃 🖼 ⛳ ⚓ 🎣 🏇 🚤 🍇

IL PELLICANO
Manager: Francesca Tozzi
Localita: Sbarcatello
Porto Ercole, (GR) 58018, Italy
Tel: (0564) 85 81 11, Fax: (0564) 83 34 18
49 Rooms, Double: €470–€1602
Open: Apr to Oct, Credit cards: all major
Relais & Châteaux
160 km N of Rome, 4.5 km S of Porto Ercole
Region: Tuscany, Michelin Map: 563

Standing proudly on the cliffs overlooking one of Italy's most spectacular coastlines are the remains of a 13th-century Spanish watchtower. The tower has been cleverly incorporated into, and stands as the dramatic symbol for, the Hotel Torre di Cala Piccola, which shares a beautiful small promontory (called Cala Piccola) with luxurious private villas discreetly hidden behind high walls. The hotel looks as though it too might be a private home. The first part of the hotel you see (which houses the informal reception area, lounge, and bar) is a sienna-toned building with red-tiled roof and green shutters, snuggled among silvery olive trees and flowering oleanders. The moderately sized, nicely decorated guestrooms are not in the main building, but instead share romantic stone cottages. Some of the accommodations are designated as one-room apartments with a divider creating a separate sitting area. However, these are a bit cut up and I much preferred the regular doubles. The cottages are strategically placed on the property to capture the view. And what a view! High cliffs drop precipitously down to the sea, forming a series of coves where the rich blue water of the Mediterranean dances in the sunlight. Also capturing this absolutely stunning vista are a lush lawn where, during the summer, dinner is served and, on a lower terrace facing the island of Giglio, a dramatic swimming pool, which seems to almost float high above the sea.

HOTEL TORRE DI CALA PICCOLA
Manager: Stefania Marconi
Cala Piccola - Porto Santo Stefano
Porto Santo Stefano, (GR) 58019, Italy
Tel: (0564) 82 51 11
50 Rooms, Double: €190–€380
Closed: Nov to Feb, Credit cards: all major
On the coast, 10 km SW of Porto Santo Stefano
Region: Tuscany, Michelin Map: 563

The pearl of the Ligurian Riviera, exclusive and intimate, Portofino is known as the living room of the rich and famous. Top name brand boutiques, pastel-colored houses, outdoor café dining, and a small harbor holding magnificent yachts are backed by a mountain falling into the sea. Tucked away from the mainstream is the sleekly restored San Giorgio boutique hotel which compensates for its position facing away from the sea with super comfortable and quiet rooms, a long list of special services and personalized hospitality. The owner has personally overseen the redecorating of the home, attractively appointed in cream and beige tones contrasted with black and white features such as the Ardesia marble used in bathrooms. Common areas and hallways have a modern sculpture in bronze as the focus. The 18 rooms, ranging from smaller doubles to suites, feature many modern amenities and extras including the finest in bed linens. On the upper floor is the breakfast room where a buffet is offered at any hour of the morning and can be served also outside on the terraced garden behind the hotel. A second hotel has been purchased set in a nearby cove, which offers guests the option of an excellent seafood restaurant and use of the private beach area. Private boats are arranged for tours of the Cinque Terre villages or the abbey of San Fruttuoso as well as ground tours of Genova with its marvelous palazzos and squares.

❄ ☕ CREDIT ☎ ⛊ W Ⴤ P 🚭 🖼 ♿ ⛵ 🏌 👫 ⚓

*HOTEL SAN GIORGIO   **New***
Manager: Giovanni Caprino
Via Del Fondaco 11
Portofino, (GE) 16034, Italy
Tel: (0185) 26 991, Fax: (0185) 26 71 39
16 Rooms, Double: €300–€440
2 Suites: €540–€810
Open: all year, Credit cards: all major
35 km E of Genoa
Region: Liguria, Michelin Map: 561

Ask any experienced traveler to name one of the most picturesque harbors in the world, and tiny Portofino, with its cluster of colorful houses reflecting in the turquoise sea, is always right on top of the list. However, this adorable town has only a few places to stay, so it was with great excitement that we learned that one of our all-time favorite hotels, Hotel Splendido (a dazzling jewel on the hillside overlooking Portofino), was opening an extension in the center of town. As would be expected, this new facility rates only superlatives. Everything is done in excellent taste and the quality in every detail is supreme. The ambiance and refined decor is much like its "sister" hotel on the hill, with a similar elegantly serene color scheme. There is a fresh quality throughout, with gleaming hardwood floors, light-colored wood furnishings, and rich fabrics. Nothing is heavy or formal—a rsophisticated yet more informal ambiance prevails. The food also is of the same superb standards as the Splendido, with fresh seafood meals served either in a charming dining room or outside on the terrace overlooking the harbor in the hotel's restaurant, Chuflay. If you want to be at the heart of the action of picturesque Portofino, especially if you enjoy watching the glamorous yachts pull into the harbor, the Splendido Mare makes an excellent choice. An added bonus: you can use all of the facilities at the Splendido, which is just a pleasant walk or hotel shuttle bus ride away.

❄ ☕ ✂ 💳 ☎ 🛗 🏌 @ W Y P 🍴 🚭 ❀ ≈ 🖼 ⚓ ⛵ 🚶 🏃 🐎 🌊

SPLENDIDO MARE
General Manager: Ermes De Megni
Via Roma, 2
Portofino, (GE) 16034, Italy
Tel: (0185) 26 78 02, Fax: (0185) 26 78 07
10 Rooms, Double: €650–€990
6 Suites: €1200–€2400
Open: Apr to Oct, Credit cards: all major
37 km E of Genoa
Region: Liguria, Michelin Map: 561

Located up a winding, wooded road high above the town of Portofino, the super-deluxe Hotel Splendido sits majestically above the beautiful blue Mediterranean, overlooking the boats moored in Portofino's lovely harbor. Stretching across the front of the hotel is a magnificent flower-laden terrace—a favorite choice of guests who enjoy dining outside with an incredible vista of the sea. As would be expected in such a world-class hotel, the food is outstanding and artfully served. Leading from the hotel are romantic little pathways where you can stroll through the wooded grounds and stop along the way at strategically placed benches to enjoy incomparable views. For those who would like more serious exercise, on a terrace below the hotel is an enormous swimming pool, while located in the lush tropical gardens to the left of the hotel are tennis courts and a gym. The luminous public spaces are charming, with comfortable chairs covered with floral prints and fresh flowers galore. Every detail is perfect and in excellent taste. The bedrooms too are lovely and decorator-perfect, many with balconies affording a truly splendid view of Portofino. The suites on the second floor of the hotel are spectacular: The most magnificent being the Presidential Suite with two large bathrooms, two elegant living areas, and four terraces overlooking Portofino. A private speedboat is available for excursions. The Splendido is without a doubt one of the most special resorts in Italy.

❄ ☕ ✈ 💳 ☎ 🛗 ☂ @ W ♈ P ⑪ ❀ ≋ 🎿 🖼 ⛳ ⚓ ⚘ 👥 ⚓

HOTEL SPLENDIDO
General Manager: Ermes De Megni
Salita Baratta, 16
Portofino, (GE) 16034, Italy
Tel: (0185) 26 78 01, Fax: (0185) 26 78 06
26 Rooms, Double: €880–€1450
34 Suites: €1500–€4200
Open: Apr to Nov, Credit cards: all major
37 km E of Genoa
Region: Liguria, Michelin Map: 561

The intimate Buca di Bacco won our hearts immediately—not that it is super elegant or grandly deluxe, but it possesses all the ingredients that make a hotel very, very special. It has an unbeatable location directly on the beach in the center of Positano, charming decor, excellent food, and spectacular views and—most important of all—radiates a graciously warm welcome. It is no wonder that the hospitality is so genuine: the Rispoli family has been catering to guests for three generations. Grandfather Rispoli emigrated to the United States years ago but his heart longed for his beautiful Positano, so when he saved enough money he returned and bought a property right on the beach where he opened a restaurant with guestrooms. From the moment you enter, you will be impressed by the tasteful decor. The lobby has a tiled floor in a beautiful green, yellow, and white design. The greens and yellow are picked up in the various fabrics used throughout. Salvatore Rispoli is often at the front desk, but the entire family is busy behind the scenes. Salvatore's sister is responsible for the glorious flower arrangements, while Carla and Nicodemo Rispoli are often in the kitchen overseeing the excellent meals. Almost all of the rooms have either a balcony or a terrace with a view. If you really want to splurge, ask for the most deluxe room, number 10, an exceptional corner room with an enormous terrace and the best view in Positano.

BUCA DI BACCO
Owner: Rispoli family
Via Rampa Teglia, 4
Positano, (SA) 84017, Italy
Tel: (089) 87 56 99, Fax: (089) 87 57 31
47 Rooms, Double: €200–€265
7 Suites: €305–€420
Closed: Nov to Mar, Credit cards: all major
Amalfi Coast, 55 km S of Naples
Region: Campania, Michelin Map: 564

The Marincanto is a classic hotel in Positano which in the 1960's, even though being very understated, had such illustrious guests as Jackie Onassis and Grace Kelly, among other stars. A complete renovation in the past years has brought this charming place up to par with the top choices in town offering those famed views out over the cliffside town to the sea. It is certainly the coast's best kept secret. From the main street level all you can see is the parking area and a small entrance leading to the elevator which takes you down to the main reception area. Everything that epitomizes the coast is found here in one open and airy space: light, the turquoise sea, colorful ceramic tiles, spotless white interiors, and flowers bursting out of vases everywhere. The breakfast terrace is a dream with potted lemon trees and crisp white linens and more views where light meals are served. Each sun-laden room has its own private terrace from which to take in the sunset over the sea or breakfast. A private beach below the hotel reached by many steps is another privileged feature along with its perfect location on the main street of Positano.

HOTEL MARINCANTO　　***New***
Owner: Giuseppe Vespoli
Via Cristofo ro Colombo, 50
Positano, (SA) 84017, Italy
Tel: (089) 87 51 30, Fax: (089) 87 55 95
57 Rooms, Double: €170–€260
Closed: Nov to Apr, Credit cards: all major
Amalfi Coast, 55 km S of Naples
Region: Campania, Michelin Map: 564

For those who want to stay in the heart of the colorful fishing village of Positano, the Palazzo Murat, a charming, family-run hotel, makes an excellent choice. It is superbly located—surrounded by shops and only steps down to the beach. The hotel consists of two parts: the original building (a 200-year-old palace) plus an attached new wing that stretches to the side. The palace has a faded-pink patina whose charm is accented by wonderful arched alcoves, intricately designed windows, and magenta bougainvillea clinging to the walls and cascading from the wrought-iron balconies. The entrance to the hotel is through a sun-drenched patio, a favorite gathering spot for guests. In the evening, tables are beautifully set on the patio where guests can dine under the stars with the scent of jasmine perfuming the air. Within, the old-world feeling is maintained with tiled floors, white walls, and formal settings of antique sofas and chairs. My favorite bedrooms are the five upstairs in the palace section: especially appealing are those with shuttered French doors opening onto small balconies that capture a view of the bay. All the rooms are comfortable and have television, radio, and mini-bar. The hotel has its own boat that takes guests for excursions along the coast six times a week. *Directions:* Follow signs from the center of the village (located in the pedestrian area).

HOTEL PALAZZO MURAT
Owner: Attanasio family
Via dei Mulini, 23
Positano, (SA) 84017, Italy
Tel: (089) 87 51 77, Fax: (089) 81 14 19
30 Rooms, Double: €255–€455
Restaurant open for dinner only
Open: Mar to Jan, Credit cards: all major
Amalfi Coast, 55 km S of Naples
Region: Campania, Michelin Map: 564

A wonderful newcomer on the Amalfi Coast is the super-serviced and romantic Punta Regina hotel, located in the heart of Positano with terraces and views that make it difficult to leave this romantic spot. The current owners, the Russo family, had the four-story white palazzo totally refurbished, incorporating many amenities. It is obvious that they had two specific goals foremost in mind: guests' comfort and accessibility to the fabulous coastal views on every possible occasion. The 18 generously proportioned bedrooms are primarily junior suites and larger suites, some having gorgeous terraces larger than the room itself, with Jacuzzis hidden among lush Mediterranean gardens. Elegantly appointed bedrooms in soft-peach or olive tones have antique furnishings, rich fabrics, and luxurious marble and tiled bathrooms, all using the best-quality local materials and craftsmen available. The top terrace with head-spinning views in every direction has a gazebo where breakfast is served if not in the guestrooms—on terraces, of course! It is an easy walk to shops, restaurants, and the beach where the ferry for Capri departs. *Directions:* From the main coastal road, take Via Pasitea down into Positano. The hotel is on the left-hand side at the beginning in the first residential section of town.

PUNTA REGINA
Manager: Benedetta Russo
Via Pasitea, 224
Positano, (SA) 84017, Italy
Tel: (089) 81 20 20, Fax: (089) 81 23 161
18 Rooms, Double: €195–€315
2 Suites: €345–€390
Closed: Nov to Mar, Credit cards: all major
Amalfi Coast, 55 km S of Naples
Region: Campania, Michelin Map: 564

The spectacular, family-run Il San Pietro di Positano is claimed to be one of the most beautiful, deluxe hotels in the world. It is—there is no question about it. From the moment you approach the hotel, class is evident: no large signs; no gaudy advertising; just an ancient chapel along the road indicates to the knowledgeable that an oasis is hidden below the hill. After parking in the designated area near the road, you take an elevator, which whisks you down to the lounge and lobby. You walk out of the elevator to a dream world—an open, spacious oasis of sparkling white walls, tiled floors, colorful lounge chairs, Oriental rugs, antique chests, flowers absolutely everywhere, and arches of glass through which vistas of greenery and sea appear. To the right is a bar and to the left is a marvelous dining room—again with windows of glass opening to the view, but with the outdoors appearing to come in, with the walls and ceilings laced with plants and vines. The bedrooms too seem to be almost a Hollywood creation—more walls of glass, bathrooms with views to the sea, and balconies on which to sit and dream. If you can tear yourself away from your oasis of a bedroom, an elevator will whisk you down the cliff to the small terrace at the water's edge. If all this sounds ostentatious, it isn't. It is perfect. *Directions:* Follow the coastal highway south from Positano. Soon after town a chapel on your right marks the entrance to the hotel.

❄ ☕ 🚐 🎫 ☎ 🐕 ♿ 🍴 @ W Ⓨ P 🍴 🚭 ❀ 🏊 ⚲ 🏛 ⚓ 🚶 🏇 🚤 🎿

IL SAN PIETRO DI POSITANO
Owners: Virginia Attanasio Cinque & Sons
Via Laurito, 2, Positano, (SA) 84017, Italy
Tel: (089) 87 54 55, Fax: (089) 81 14 49
40 Rooms, Double: €420–€600
21 Suites: €600–€1200
Minimum Stay Required: 3 nights
Open: Mar 20 to Nov 2, Credit cards: all major
Relais & Châteaux
Amalfi Coast, 55 km S of Naples
Region: Campania, Michelin Map: 564

Le Sirenuse is a superb luxury hotel tucked in the picturesque ancient fishing village of Positano. It is no wonder that so many writers and artists have been attracted to this colorful town of brightly hued houses clinging to the precipitous hillside as it drops down to its own small bay. And it is also no wonder that so many of these famous people have found their way to the oasis of Le Sirenuse, a favorite hideaway for discerning travelers seeking discreet, understated elegance. From the moment you enter the hotel lobby the mood is set with fresh white walls, tiled floors, oil paintings on the walls, accents of antiques, and an abundance of colorful flowers everywhere. The hotel is built on terraces cut into the hillside and so almost all the rooms capture a wonderful view out over the quaint rooftops and the tiled domed cathedral to the shimmering blue waters of the bay. It is only a short walk through the perpendicular streets until you are on the beach. The dining room has walls of glass that allow the maximum enjoyment of the vista below, but most diners prefer the splendor of eating outdoors on the terrace, surrounded by flowers and views of the sea. On another level of the hotel there is a swimming pool. The hotel also has a spa and its own parking area (rare for Positano). *Directions:* Located near the center of town, on the right side of the road as you drive up the hill.

❄ ☕ ⛷ ♨ 💳 ☎ 🚻 🍴 @ Υ P ⊪ ❧ ≈ ⚓ 🚶 ⛵ 🍇

LE SIRENUSE HOTEL
Manager: Antonio Sersale
Via C. Colombo, 30
Positano, (SA) 84017, Italy
Tel: (089) 87 50 66, Fax: (089) 81 17 98
63 Rooms, Double: €500–€900
Open: all year, Credit cards: all major
History Traveller
Amalfi coast, 55 km S of Naples
Region: Campania, Michelin Map: 564

The Villa Franca, with a commanding position overlooking the sea, is one of Positano's classic villas transformed into a well-priced hotel. The management is extremely friendly and there is an immediate warmth and charm as soon as you walk into the redesigned and redecorated villa. The Russo family wanted to create an attractive full-service hotel combined with the friendliness and service of a small inn, and it is just that. The fresh Mediterranean decor is most appealing, with royal-blue slipcovered armchairs, a profusion of plants, lacquered terracotta vases, white-tiled floors and walls, and arched windows everywhere, so that you don't miss the mesmerizing views of the sea for a second. The two restaurants, one by the pool and the other by the bar, serve excellent local cuisine. The bedrooms follow the same cheerful theme with colorful ceramic-tiled floors, cream bedspreads with green-and-yellow-striped trim and exquisite views. On the rooftop is a swimming pool with a 360-degree view over the world's most beautiful coastline. Guests also enjoy a sauna, massage room, and solarium. *Directions:* Follow the road into Positano and the hotel is on the left.

HOTEL VILLA FRANCA
Owner: Mario Russo
Viale Pasitea, 318
Positano, (SA) 84017, Italy
Tel: (089) 87 56 55, Fax: (089) 87 57 35
28 Rooms, Double: €210–€390
Minimum Stay Required: 3 nights
Open: Apr to Nov, Credit cards: all major
Amalfi Coast, 55 km S of Naples
Region: Campania, Michelin Map: 564

The Hotel Villa Odino makes an excellent option for hotel accommodation when visiting Venice—especially if you prefer to return to the tranquility of the countryside in the evening. The hotel is about a kilometer from the train station where a 20-minute journey brings you into the heart of the city. However, it isn't just its convenience to Venice that makes the Villa Odino such an excellent choice—this jewel of a little hotel would be a winner anyway. The handsome mansion, built in the gentle countryside on the banks of the River Sile, dates back to 1563 when it was a residence for emissaries of the Bishop of Torcello. The mansion has been meticulously restored by the charming Pasini family (including three lovely daughters) who personally manage the hotel, showering attention on their guests. One daughter, beautiful Enrica, showed us around the attractively decorated home. Every detail exudes loving attention, with fresh flowers everywhere and each room individually decorated in an appealing, homelike way. All of the guestrooms are spacious and have large modern bathrooms. My favorite rooms are those in a separate wing facing the pool, each of which has French doors opening onto a private terrace. *Directions:* Take A4 north from Venice and exit at Quarto d'Altino. After leaving the motorway, turn left. At the first intersection, turn right, follow the river to the hotel.

HOTEL VILLA ODINO
Manager: Enrica Pasini
Via Roma, 146
Quarto d'Altino, (VE) 30020, Italy
Tel: (0422) 82 31 17, Fax: (0422) 82 32 35
24 Rooms, Double: €130–€190
6 Suites: €210–€350
Closed: Dec 23 to Jan 6, Credit cards: all major
25 km NE of Venice, 15 km SE of Treviso
Region: Veneto, Michelin Map: 562

The Relais Vignale is a superb small hotel idyllically located in the heart of the Chianti wine region. It enjoys the enviable honor of having the best of both worlds—it feels as if you are secluded in the countryside, yet you are right in Radda, one of Tuscany's most picturesque towns. It was the manor house of a large Chianti estate, which still produces fine wines. The hotel sits on the main street, but magically, the back of the hotel opens onto a gorgeous, pristine view of rolling hills laced with vineyards and dotted with olive trees. Some of the guestrooms are in the main manor while others, which also have lovely views, are just across the street. The guestrooms and cozy lounges are tastefully decorated with antiques. Care has been taken in the restoration to preserve many of the enticing architectural features of the manor such as heavy beams, arched hallways, decorative fireplaces, and painted ceilings. Behind the hotel, meticulously kept gardens lead down the hillside to a romantic wisteria- and jasmine-covered terrace where guests enjoy breakfast, or dinner under the stars, with an incredible view. Another bonus of this fine hotel is the heated swimming pool, overlooking the vineyards. The hotel also has a wine shop with free tastings of products of the estate.

❄ ☕ ✄ ▣ ☎ 🛗 @ W Y P ⫲ ⊘ ≈ 🖼 🏃 🚶 🐎 🍇

RELAIS VIGNALE
Manager: Monica Bernetti
Via Pianigiani, 15
Radda in Chianti, (SI) 53017, Italy
Tel: (0577) 73 83 00, Fax: (0577) 73 85 92
34 Rooms, Double: €215–€260
5 Suites: €350–€385
Open: Mar 21 to Nov 2, Credit cards: all major
In the heart of Chianti, 52 km S of Florence
Region: Tuscany, Michelin Map: 563

Coming from a generations-old tradition in the restaurant business, it was only natural that brothers Antonio and Giuseppe open a hotel for their loyal clients within the fascinating historic Baroque centre of Ragusa (called Ibla). Their Locanda Don Serafino is located on a narrow stone street of this Unesco World Heritage site. You enter into an intimate reception with a lounge to one side and a breakfast/bar room to the other. White sofas and white bedspreads fit in well with wood floors, armoires and stone walls, purposely giving guestrooms a look in tune with the house, All have modern blue bathrooms and are scattered on different levels of the house, several with an independent entrance directly from the street. Five larger doubles have features such as a luminous corner bedroom or a turquoise-tiled tub set back under a stone arch. Within easy walking distance is their refined gourmet restaurant with the same name, an award-winning establishment within an ancient stone building originally the horse stables of the adjoining palazzo. The enoteca has an impressive wine list with over 700 prestigious labels. Their second restaurant is open only during the summer at the hotel's private beach at Marina di Ragusa. *Directions:* From Catania take the SS 514 Catania-Ragusa, exit Ragusa Ovest and follow signs to historic center of Ragusa, Ibla. The Via XI Febbraio street is just off of Via del Mercato circling the center.

ROMANTIK HOTEL LOCANDA DON SERAFINO
Owners: Antonio & Giuseppe La Rosa Family
Via XI Febbraio, 15
Ragusa Ibla, (RG) 97100, Italy
Tel: (0932) 22 00 65, Fax: (0932) 66 31 86
10 Rooms, Double: €150–€170
5 Suites: €200
Open: all year, Credit cards: MC, VS
Romantik Hotels
Historic Center of Ragusa, Ibla
Region: Sicily, Michelin Map: 565

Divine, exquisite, blissful are some of the words that come immediately to mind in describing the Hotel Caruso, reopened in 2005 after a much talked about multi-million dollar renovation project. No detail disappoints even the most discerning of travelers. It joins an elite club of top hotels in the world. An historic hotel offering accommodation since 1893, the perched position with its mesmerizing sea and mountain views has captured the attention of the many illustrious guests. The variety of double rooms and suites (all with balconies, terraces or private gardens) have tiled floors and are appointed in soft cream colors which do not distract the eye from the main attraction: the clear blue sea below. While some pieces are original antiques, the rest have been made exclusively for the hotel in traditional Neapolitan style. The elegant 18th-century frescoed salon with fireplace and vaulted ceiling leads to a long arcade bar where piano music is played nightly. Traditional meals are served in the Caruso restaurant. However, when the weather permits, preferred seating is outdoors in the enchanting garden at the Belvedere. The pièce de résistance is without a doubt the infinity swimming pool lined with white columns, precariously hanging cliff side. Ravello is a dream of a location and the Caruso fits right into that dream. As an added bonus. the hotel offers boat excursions of the Amalfi coast. *Directions:* Drive up to Ravello and to hotel's front door.

HOTEL CARUSO
General Manager: Franco Girasoli
Piazza San Giovanni del Toro 2
Ravello, (SA) 84010, Italy
Tel: (089) 85 88 01, Fax: (089) 85 88 06
24 Rooms, Double: €780–€1000
24 Suites: €1320–€3190
Open: Apr to Nov, Credit cards: all major
7 km W of Amalfi, 64 km S of Naples
Region: Campania, Michelin Map: 564

The Hotel Palumbo is a 12th-century palace, owned since 1875 by the Vuilleumier family. The location is perfect—high in the clouds overlooking terraced vineyards and beyond to the brilliant blue Mediterranean, which dances in and out of the jagged rocky coast. The romance begins when you enter the richly hued, ceramic-tiled lobby with its ancient atrium of arched colonnades, green plants flowing from every nook, masses of fresh flowers, and gorgeous antiques. Each small corner is an oasis of tranquility, from the intimate bar to the cozy antique-filled tiny lounges. There is a lovely dining room with a vaulted ceiling and a stunning painting by Guido Reni, but usually meals are served on the terrace, which perches like a bird's nest in the sky. Wherever you dine, the food is excellent. There is a stunning garden with a Jacuzzi in the rear featuring a vine-covered terrace overlooking the Amalfi coast. Another tiny patio capturing both the sun and the view is tucked onto the roof of the villa. There are only 21 bedrooms—the size varies since this was an old villa, but all are individually decorated and have their own charming personality. A few guestrooms are located in a nearby annex. There is villa down by the sea where you can enjoy sunbathing and swimming. The Hotel Palumbo exudes a romantic ambiance and a wealth of old-world character. *Directions:* Located on the upper edge of town. Ask for directions to the hotel garage.

HOTEL PALUMBO
Manager: Marco Vuilleumier
Via S. Giovanni del Toro, 16
Ravello, (SA) 84010, Italy
Tel: (089) 85 72 44, Fax: (089) 85 81 33
17 Rooms, Double: €600–€800
4 Suites: €950
Open: all year, Credit cards: all major
66 km S of Naples, 6 km N of Amalfi
Region: Campania, Michelin Map: 564

The Villa Cimbrone is not only a hotel: its gardens are one of Ravello's most famous attractions. The tourist office proclaims, "The Villa Cimbrone—essence of all the enchantment of Ravello—hangs like a swallow's nest on the cliffs." The villa is reached by a delightful ten-minute walk from Ravello's main square (the signs are well marked to this favorite sightseeing prize); then, once you pass through the gates, the villa and its magnificent gardens open up like magic. The gardens are truly superb—if you have ever received a postcard from Ravello, chances are it showed the view from the terrace of the Cimbrone. Most dramatic of all is the belvedere with its stately Roman statues accenting the dazzling sea view. Luckily, this gorgeous villa is also a charming, intimate hotel. The rooms are of museum quality with furniture fit for a king. The hotel is even further enhanced with a splendid swimming pool and a beautiful restaurant. Before being purchased by the present owners, the Vuilleumier family, this fabulous villa was the prized possession of an English lord, who, toward the end of World War II, landed with the Allied troops in Salerno. Somehow he was able to find a jeep, and wound up the twisting road to see once again his beloved villa once again. *Directions:* Because its gardens are open to the public, the hotel is signposted from the center of town. (Pedestrian-only area.)

❄ ☕ 🛵 💳 ☎ 🛗 👤 @ W 🍷 🍴 🏊 🚶 🏞 🕊 ⚓ 🚶🚶 🐎

VILLA CIMBRONE
Manager: Giorgio Vuilleumier
Ravello, (SA) 84010, Italy
Tel: (089) 85 74 59, Fax: (089) 85 77 77
17 Rooms, Double: €305–€800
2 Suites: €720–€950
Open: Apr to Nov, Credit cards: all major
66 km S of Naples, 6 km N of Amalfi
Region: Campania, Michelin Map: 564

The northeastern corner of Italy, south of Venice, offers such splendid cities as Ferrara, Mantova, Rovigo, and Ravenna. Ravenna has gained worldwide recognition for its stunning gold and brightly-colored mosaics preserved from Byzantine times and shown off in eight of the city's churches and basilicas. Since the city is surrounded by flat marshland, most people get around by bike, which makes its historical center a pleasant place to walk. Accommodation is limited, so it was a great discovery to come across the Albergo Cappello, a truly unique hotel. After the death of one of Italy's foremost industrialists who had spent great sums of money on restoring the 14th-century palazzo, it was purchased and turned into a charming hotel. In order to give the exquisite property back to the citizens of Ravenna, the owners came up with the concept of a cultural center/art gallery/restaurant/hotel. The two double rooms and five suites are located on the upper floors off a frescoed hall where artwork is displayed. The guestrooms are purposely decorated in minimalist style, using contemporary lighting and soft hues so as not to distract from the original architectural features. Light lunches are served in the cantina, while dinners are served out in the courtyard. This is not a hotel in the standard sense with a 24-hour front desk—front door keys are provided so guests can let themselves back in after dinner.

❄ ☕ 🧹 CREDIT ☎ 🐕 ⚑ @ Υ P ‖ 🚭 ⛷ ♿ ⊥ 🕴 🚶 🏇 ⚓ 🍇

ALBERGO CAPPELLO
Owner: Filippo Donati
Via IV Novembre, 41
Ravenna, (RA) 48100, Italy
Tel: (0544) 21 98 13, Fax: (0544) 21 98 14
7 Rooms, Double: €160–€200
Open: all year, Credit cards: all major
In the heart of Ravenna, 136 km NE of Florence
Region: Emilia-Romagna, Michelin Map: 562

The Villa Rigacci is a picture-perfect example of a 15th-century Tuscan villa with its creamy-white stucco façade, thick walls, heavy red-tile roof, green-shuttered windows, and beautiful gardens. The Pierazzi family takes great care to see that all the guests receive their personal attention and are made to feel "at home." In summer, after a day of sightseeing, guests relax in the back garden where a large pool, surrounded by lounge chairs and umbrellas, stretches out on a terraced lawn. Inside, handsome family antiques adorn the sitting rooms and library. The chef specializes in traditional Tuscan cuisine, and from October to March cooking courses are organized. The dining room is especially lovely, but in summer guests usually choose to enjoy their meals outside on the terrace. Each bedroom is individually decorated with very appealing country-style antiques accented by lovely fabrics—creating rooms that blend beautifully with the old-world ambiance of the villa. Although the surrounding area is not as pristinely rural as some parts of Tuscany, once you enter into the beautiful grounds (highlighted by cypress, pine, and olive trees) you enjoy a serene setting and accommodations with charm. *Directions:* From Florence go south on the A1. Take the Incisa exit. Turn right to Matassino. At the second roundabout turn left toward Vaggio. Pass Vaggio. Go toward San Giovenale. After crossing a bridge, the hotel is about 100 m on your right.

❄ ☕ 🏃 ♨ CREDIT ☎ 🏠 🏋 @ ⅄ P 🍴 🚭 🏊 🖼 🐕 🕺 🚶 🏇 🍇

VILLA RIGACCI
Owners: Kirsten & Federico Pierazzi
Loc. Vaggio, 75
Reggello–Vaggio, (FI) 50066, Italy
Tel: (055) 8656718, Fax: (055) 86 56 537
28 Rooms, Double: €95–€165
5 Suites: €145–€185
Open: all year, Credit cards: all major
30 km SE of Florence, 5 km SW of Reggello
Region: Tuscany, Michelin Map: 563

With a prime position in the heart of medieval Reggio Emilia, the Hotel Posta exudes great character and charm. Though dating back to the 13th century, the property became an inn in 1515, making it one of the oldest hotels in Italy. In days of yore, the huge front doors swung open to let travelers enter for the night, along with their horses which were also fed and cared for. The hotel has been meticulously renovated, preserving its rich heritage, including a handsome 14th-century assembly hall. This stunning room—with its soaring ceiling, heavy beams, and beautiful frescoed walls depicting coats of arms—is now used for banquets, weddings, and conferences. The quaint lacquered furniture in the lounge and cute bar with festooned painted angels came from a 19th-century confectionery shop. The guestrooms are all individually decorated with attractive furniture including some antiques and pretty coordinating fabrics on the curtains and bed coverings. If you want more space, request one of the junior suites. If you really want to splurge, ask for 120, a gorgeous corner suite with beautiful furnishings and both windows and bed opulently draped with blue-and-white fabric. Another choice is to ask for one of the rooms in the back of the hotel overlooking the spectacular Piazza Prampolini—these are great fun (top floor rooms have a small balcony). *Directions:* From the A1, take the Reggio exit. When you reach town, follow signs to Hotel Posta.

❄ ☕ 🛎 CREDIT ☎ 🛗 🍴 @ W Y P 🖼 🔔 🏃 🐎 🍇

HOTEL POSTA
Manager: Umberto Sidoli
Piazza del Monte 2, Reggio Emilia, (RE) 42100, Italy
Tel: (0522) 43 29 44, Fax: (0522) 45 26 02
38 Rooms, Double: €150–€215
9 Suites: €230–€280
Closed: 2 weeks in Aug & Christmas
Credit cards: all major
Abitare La Storia
65 km NW of Bologna, 29 km SE of Parma
Region: Emilia-Romagna, Michelin Map: 562

The Villa Luppis property, with its rich historical past, was originally an 11th-century monastery restored in 1500 after a devastating war and bought by the Luppis family in 1800. In order to be able to maintain the vast estate, Stefania and Giorgio Ricci Luppis opened its doors as a hotel in 1993. Their intention was to maintain the flavor of their original home by keeping the family's period antiques and precious paintings intact. The effect is true old-world charm that surrounds you within the beamed dining room with enormous fireplace, various frescoed sitting rooms, and arched front hall overlooking the garden. Bedrooms and suites within two wings of the villa are in theme with matching bedspreads and draperies, antique pieces, gilded mirrors, and stenciled bordered or beamed ceilings. On-site activities include a swimming pool and tennis courts, and bikes for touring the surrounding park are offered. The excellent restaurant, where Chef Antonino Sanna works wonders with fresh seafood, organizes a three- to five-day cooking school and wine lessons with wine expert Moreno Romano—the classes even include visits to local cantinas and cheese producers. A variety of fascinating local itineraries are suggested to the Villas of Palladio on the Brenta canal, or to the Pordenone, Udine, and Gorizia castles. A shuttle is available daily to/from Venice (40 minutes). Transportation to/from Marco Polo airport is available on request.

❄ ☕ 🎿 ⛷ 💳 ☎ 🐕 🛗 👤 @ ☂ P ⅋ 🏊 🎣 🚣 ⛱ 🎽 🐎 🎿 ⛷ ⚓

VILLA LUPPIS
Owners: Stefania & Giorgio Ricci Luppis
Via S. Martino, 34
Rivarotta–Pasiano, (PN) 33080, Italy
Tel: (0434) 62 69 69, Fax: (0434) 62 62 28
39 Rooms, Double: €220–€275
11 Suites: €260–€330
Open: all year, Credit cards: all major
15 km SW of Pordenone, 40 km NE of Venice
Region: Friuli-Venezia Giulia, Michelin Map: 562

The recently opened Villa Matilde, ancestral summer residence of the noble Bocca family, maintains its original aura of an 18th-century patrician villa. Located at the edge of a small village halfway between Turin and the Alps, the villa is on the main road to town, hidden among the chestnut trees in the front park. Original tiled floors, frescoed salons and library, domed main hall with balcony have been preserved. Twelve of the bedrooms are actually within the historic home on the two upper floors, each individually appointed with antiques, chandeliers, parquet floors and rich fabrics and bed linens, while the remaining newer rooms are divided between the ex-orangerie and a restored farmhouse, all part of the rural complex accessed by an inner brick courtyard. Adjacent to the guesthouse is a swimming pool, tennis court and small spa center. The gourmet restaurant concentrating on regional recipes has been created from the original horse stalls directly off the main reception area where a very helpful staff is on duty to assist guests. A country-style buffet breakfast is served in a dainty front parlor. This northern section of the Piedmont region is well-known for its excellent food and fine wines and has the strategic advantage of being near the Turin with its myriad of cultural events, the castle area south of Aosta, and the Mont Blanc. *Directions:* From Turin take the A5 north to Aosta, exit Romano Canavese and follow to town. Hotel is well marked.

RELAIS VILLA MATILDE
Manager: Marzia Giussani
Viale Marconi 29
Romano Canavese, (TO) 10090, Italy
Tel: (0125) 63 92 90, Fax: (0125) 71 26 59
30 Rooms, Double: €243–€357
13 Suites: €432–€487
Open: all year, Credit cards: all major
35 km from Torino
Region: Piedmont, Michelin Map: 561

The Hotel Barocco is a full service refined hotel with a friendly and intimate ambiance. The location is excellent—although the address is shown as being on the busy Piazza Barberini with its famed Triton fountain, the entrance, marked by a row of potted shrubbery, is discreetly tucked around the corner. You enter into an intimate lobby where there is no frenzy of activity, just a reception counter tended by a gracious staff headed by cordial manager, Franco, happy to assist you whether it is with reservations for dinner or transportation to the airport. Beyond the reception area is a lounge which opens onto a small bar. The decor features a series of murals depicting scenes of Rome, below which the walls are covered with a rich cherry wood. The breakfast room, where a full buffet is served, has the same decor with scenes of Rome on the wall. The guestrooms on six floors have great city views or balconies (all similar in decor, but different in size) continue the same classic look, with travertine bathrooms, reproduction paintings, and an abundant use of cherry wood in the built-in headboards, wainscoting, desks, and bedside tables. Cream, wine red color themes, as well as deep-blue matching drapes and bedspreads, accent the wood trim giving a sophisticated, refreshing, almost nautical look. The rooms are a good size, but seem larger by the placement of enormous wall mirrors behind some beds. Several new suites, one with rooftop terrace, have been added.

❄ ☕ 🍴 💳 ☎ 🐕 🛗 @ 🍸 P 👤 🐎

HOTEL BAROCCO
Manager: Franco Caruso
Via della Purificazione 4
Piazza Barberini, 9
Rome, (RM) 00187, Italy
Tel: (06) 48 72 001, Fax: (06) 48 59 94
41 Rooms, Double: €199–€350
5 Suites: €300–€600
Open: all year, Credit cards: all major
Heart of city, facing Piazza Barberini
Region: Lazio, Michelin Map: 563

The recently refurbished Bernini Bristol is back in splendid form and part of the competing group of top accommodation in Rome. First and foremost it boasts one of the most spectacular rooftop restaurants in the city with a full 360-degree view. The original hotel façade dating to 1874 was radically transformed under the Mussolini regime while the interiors retain the ambiance of a grand hotel. At the foot of the Via Vento right in front of one of Bernini's masterpieces, Triton's fountain. This luxury hotel does not overlook a thing when it comes to guest service, regardless of size. Of course hospitality is nothing new to the Bocca family, proprietors of nine other grand hotels throughout Italy. The spacious open salon leading from the reception area with its austere architecture and squared-travertine pillars, has been softened with enormous antique hanging tapestries, comfortable armchairs, chandeliers and soft lighting. A wide variety of room types are offered, between either the new, minimalist modern look or the more classic style with contrasting brocaded draperies, and bedspreads, gilded mirrors, patterned carpeting, silk flock on walls and timeless Carrara marble bathrooms. Many of the suites on the upper floors enjoy the same stunning views as the restaurant. Among many services and features is a new spa, SINA Wellness Club, with a variety of treatments and services.

HOTEL BERNINI BRISTOL
Manager: Lorenzo Vivalda
Piazza Barberini, 23
Rome, (RM) 00187, Italy
Tel: (06) 48 89 31, Fax: (06) 482 42 66
127 Rooms, Double: €449–€515*
*Breakfast not included: €15–€30
Open: all year, Credit cards: all major
In the heart of town
Region: Lazio, Michelin Map: 563

The splendid Duke Hotel is run by brother-sister team Marco and Rosa Visocchi, who learned the art of hospitality from their father and grandfather. They have integrated high standards and attention to detail and quality in the daily running of The Duke Hotel, located in the Villa Borghese area. The hotel offers free limousine service to view the sights of Rome. The polished reception area leads to a cozy reading room and the heart of the hotel, the Polo Lounge and bar area with its colorful celestial-blue stained-glass skylight, fireplace, and English-club ambiance. The hotel's I Duchi Restaurant offers exquisite cuisine and immecible service in this luxurious setting. The polished and elegant classical style of decor continues throughout the luminous bedrooms, all renovated with parquet floors, LCD TVs, and wireless Internet. Some rooms have balconies or terraces. The extraordinary feature of this hotel is its customized guest care including twice-daily maid service, free courtesy shuttle service to the city center, museum and concert ticketing, tour guides, transfers, and immediate response to guests' every need including broadband connection. The hotel is a few minutes walk from the Renzo Piano's Parco della Musica, and is a meeting place for performers and customers of this concert hall, the largest in Europe. The Duke is a sponsor and supporter of all the major cultural events in Rome ensuring hotel guests have privileged access to the most exclusive events in town.

❄ ☕ ⚗ 💳 ☎ ⚌ @ ⅄ P ⑪ ♿ 🚶 🐎

THE DUKE HOTEL
Owners: Marco & Rosa Visocchi
Via Archimede, 69
Rome, (RM) 00197, Italy
Tel: (06) 36 72 21, Fax: (06) 36 00 41 04
78 Rooms, Double: €410–€465
14 Suites: €605–€1385
Open: all year, Credit cards: all major
Parioli neighborhood near Villa Borghese
Region: Lazio, Michelin Map: 563

The magnificent Hotel Hassler stands out as Rome's premier deluxe hotel—still family-owned and managed by the Wirth family. Its location at the top of the Spanish Steps is unsurpassed: the majority of Rome's monuments and chic boutiques are close by, and for guests who want to explore Villa Borghese Park, complimentary bikes are available. The fact that the proprietor, Roberto Wirth, is on the premises shines forth: you almost feel like a guest in a private palace. When the Hassler was renovated, Astrid Wirth, Roberto's wife, even tracked down the old-established manufacturer who was able to reproduce the original fabrics for the walls. The decorating theme is classical with hues of warm reds and ochres prevailing, the same rich colors used in many palazzi across Rome. At the heart of the Hassler is a romantic inner garden courtyard, a delightful oasis with stone walls laced with vines, a fountain, statues, flowers, cozy little tables, and a bar. The panoramic restaurant at the Hassler is also spectacular, boasting one of the finest views and cuisine in Rome: the entire panorama of the city surrounds you as you dine. All of the guestrooms are splendid, but if money is no object, reserve one of the magnificent suites, some with enormous terraces and a view so spellbinding that you will never want to leave this splendid hotel. Dining is available also at the elegant Salone Eve or at the Palm Court Garden—or at the nearby Hassler owned Aroma del Palazzetto restaurant.

HOTEL HASSLER
Manager: Roberto E. Wirth
Trinita dei Monti, 6
Rome, (RM) 00187, Italy
Tel: (06) 69 93 40, Fax: (06) 69 94 16 07
98 Rooms, Double: €580–€3400*
*Breakfast not included: €33–€45
Open: all year, Credit cards: all major
At the top of the Spanish Steps
Region: Lazio, Michelin Map: 563

It just was not enough to have already created two top notch boutique hotels with fabulous locations, now the Di Rienzo brothers have launched their latest delight, Inn at the Roman Forum. Zeroing in on two critical features, key location with views and ambiance, the inn is not only just around the corner from the Roman Forum but literally has a piece of the forum within its premises! On a quiet and picturesque street of the characteristic Monti neighborhood, the peach-colored 15th-century residence, has been transformed into an intimate, luxury accommodation full of very unique surprises. Enter the front doorway as would a resident Roman and meet your host in the reception sitting room. Continue to the back and turn back time as you enter a cave-like space complete with columns, statues and other artifacts of this section of the Trajan Roman marketplace. Back to reality, the individually-styled "classic meets ethnic" bedrooms are distributed on the three upper floors with every imaginable amenity and designer bathrooms. The next surprise comes as you enter the sophisticated top floor lounge with fireplace, where breakfast is served either in or outside on the front rooftop terrace with superb glimpses over cupolas and tiled roofs to the Palatine hill. The final triumph of this awe-inspiring place are the two back bedrooms on this same floor which open out to a walled-in garden complete palm trees. Not simply a stay, but an experience.

INN AT THE ROMAN FORUM
Owner: The Di Rienzo Family
Via degli Ibernesi, 30
Rome, (RM) 00187, Italy
Tel: (06) 691 90 970, Fax: (06) 454 38 802
14 Rooms, Double: €290–€650
Open: all year, Credit cards: all major
Between Via Cavour and Corso Fori Imperiali
Region: Lazio, Michelin Map: 563

The Inn at the Spanish Steps is divine. Surprisingly, there are few exceptional accommodation choices in the historic center, but this property, half a block from the world's most famous staircase, is truly remarkable. The dream of the Di Rienzo brothers, owners of several large hotels in Rome, was to create an intimate, almost club-like ambiance with all the trimmings for a few privileged guests in an unbeatable location. So they took over an historical, 17th-century private residence (Hans Christian Andersen lived here for years), striving to maintain its origins as a home. The inn now offers a minuscule reception room on the ground floor, 24 bedrooms spread out among the three upper floors, and a marvelous rooftop garden where guests can have an ample buffet breakfast or sunset drink, either in the cozy veranda or out on the flower-laden terrace, complete with bird's-eye view of the steps and the fashionable Via Condotti. Doubles are divided into two categories: superiors at the back and luxury doubles and junior suites at the front. Rooms with wood floors and antique furnishings include every possible amenity. Upholstered walls and coordinated drapes accent frescoed or beamed ceilings. There is even a 3-bedroom penthouse suite with breathtaking views and 24-hour butler service. Guests who remain more than three nights receive the bonus of an airport transfer or guided tour of the city. Nothing else compares.

THE INN AT THE SPANISH STEPS
Manager: Gaetano Lauro
Via dei Condotti, 85
Rome, (RM) 00187, Italy
Tel: (06) 69 925 657, Fax: (06) 67 86 470
24 Rooms, Double: €300–€990
Open: all year, Credit cards: all major
At the Spanish Steps
Region: Lazio, Michelin Map: 563

A fine exemplification of superlative hospitality, distinguished host, Amedeo Ottaviani, also the owner of the luxurious Regency Hotel in Florence, offers guests every imaginable service. The former patrician villa with pristine white exterior is hidden away on a cobblestone street in the city's most exclusive residential neighborhood near the Villa Borghese park. The peaceful but central location and highly personalized guest care are the successful ingredients in creating the intimate ambiance of a private home. An inviting lounge and library, just beyond the reception area, are decorated in line with the entire hotel in sleek art-deco style with lacquered black pieces and gold or red accents in carpeting, drapes, and upholstery all set off by stark white walls. The host's delightful private collection of portrait paintings displayed throughout softens the ambiance. Sumptuous bedrooms and suites on three top floors have the same attention to detail, with vintage marble bathrooms and views over stately villas and a lush park. Downstairs is the attractive, club-like Salotto bar and lounge, where you can enjoy light lunches and winetastings from the award-winning cellars. Not to be missed is a meal at the elegant restaurant, Sapori del Lord Byron, highly praised by the Wine Spectator, the house chef creates his renowned dishes with total respect to traditional Italian cuisine and ingredients. A courtesy shuttle to town is available.

❄ ☕ 🧳 CREDIT ☎ 🛗 @ W ♈ P 🍴 🚭 🖼 ⟲ 🚶 🐎

HOTEL LORD BYRON
Owner: Amedeo Ottaviani
Via G. de Notaris, 5
Rome, (RM) 00197, Italy
Tel: (06) 32 20 404, Fax: (06) 32 20 405
27 Rooms, Double: €275–€560
5 Suites: €815–€1100
Restaurant closed Sun to non-residents
Open: all year, Credit cards: all major
On the edge of Villa Borghese Park
Region: Lazio, Michelin Map: 563

Just off the Popolo Square on the Via del Babuino with its many exclusive boutiques and antique shops is the intimate Hotel Piranesi. The residence, known as Palazzo Nainer, dates to 1820 and was designed by the renowned architect Giuseppe Valadier, who filled Rome with his elegantly-designed buildings. It was bought and completely refurbished by the Cesari family, renown producers of fine linens and fabrics, whose elegant store is right next door. The location could not be better at walking distance to the Spanish Steps, and neither could the high-quality attention and service offered by its very competent staff, lead by manager Patrizia. A "boutique" hotel in style, it has 32 bedrooms of varying size with marble bathrooms, the most desirable being those on the top floors with private terraces. Richly furnished rooms with all amenities are smartly decorated in soothingly soft yellow hues with antique armoires and desks, and accented, as throughout the entire hotel, with Piranesi etchings of Rome. Sunset drinks can be served up on the marvelous rooftop terrace looking up to the Borghese Gardens, and Roman rooftops, and terraces. An extensive breakfast buffet is served in the luminous yellow breakfast room near the small reception area. Other facilities include a fitness room, sauna and solarium, garage nearby, and car rental and driver service. Delightful.

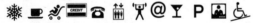

HOTEL PIRANESI
Manager: Alessandro Cesari
Via del Babuino, 196
Rome, (RM) 00187, Italy
Tel: (06) 32 80 41, Fax: (06) 36 10 597
32 Rooms, Double: €198–€520
Open: all year, Credit cards: all major
Just steps away from the Piazza del Popolo
Region: Lazio, Michelin Map: 563

A new alternative in the area of St Peter's Basilica right within the Vatican City walls is the Residenza Paolo VI, special because of its unique position right at the edge of one of the world's most famous monuments. This seemingly modern building from the façade is actually of ancient origins, evident in sculpted Roman columns preserved within walls at the entrance. A small front courtyard leads to the main door and elevator which takes you past Vatican office spaces and photos of past Popes to the third floor reception area. The classical music playing sets the calm mood of the place and half of the bedrooms are lined down two narrow hallways with white tiled floors, reminiscent of the monk's cells from times past. New guestrooms are classically appointed with reproduction antiques, oriental rugs and chandeliers. The 29 rooms are concentrated on the two upper floors with the corner junior suites having privileged views through Bernini's colonnade to the Basilica's impressive façade. A wood-paneled breakfast room on the top floor offers a buffet in the morning as well as light meals, but the best feature is the rooftop terrace lined with 6 small tables, which overlooks a larger private terrace with fountain and potted palms. At this height, the view reaches the top of the colonnade straight out to the cupola, magnificently illuminated at night, for a superb close-up look at the sculpted details of Michelangelo's masterpiece.

RESIDENZA PAOLO VI
Manager: Annamaria Molinari
Via Paolo VI 29
Rome, (RM) 00193, Italy
Tel: (06) 68 48 70, Fax: (06) 68 67 428
29 Rooms, Double: €230–€290
Open: all year, Credit cards: all major
Left-hand side of St Peter's Square
Region: Lazio, Michelin Map: 563

The Splendide Royal is one of the emerging new boutique-style hotels on Rome's hotel scene. After a complete renovation of this classic 19th-century palazzo on the border of the Borghese Park and a few blocks away from the Via Veneto, the hotel now offers luxury accommodation. The doors just recently opened to travelers wishing the retro style of a grand hotel, yet the personalized attention of a smaller scale establishment. Guests are greeted in the elegant foyer, with its Murano chandeliers, white patterned marble floors, gold-framed portraits, and half bust statues. Suites, junior suites, and deluxe doubles are distributed among four floors. The top floor boasts one of Rome's more exclusive rooftop restaurants, the formal one Michelin star "Mirabelle", with its enchanting views over the famous landmarks, city rooftop gardens, and characteristic tiled roofs and cupolas. A lovely, buffet breakfast is served hotel guests in a lower, enclosed terrace. Many of the guestrooms enjoy this same privileged view and some suites have private terraces. The ultra-sumptuous décor of the guestrooms have been designed to deliberately contrast the minimalist trend. Red, royal blue, and gold brocade draperies and bedspreads, elaborate gilded mirrors, antique pieces, paintings, and patterned carpeting are incorporated with the latest of modern conveniences. *Directions:* Borders the Villa Borghese Park, three blocks from the Spanish steps.

HOTEL SPLENDIDE ROYAL
Manager: Silvio Catalano
Via di Porta Pinciana 14
Rome, (RM) 00187, Italy
Tel: (06) 42 16 89, Fax: (06) 42 16 88 00
68 Rooms, Double: €290–€1800*
*Breakfast not included: €32
Open: all year, Credit cards: all major
Three blocks from the Spanish Steps
Region: Lazio, Michelin Map: 563

When it comes to the expression "room with a view" you couldn't possibly make a better choice than this super-deluxe property. The Di Rienzo family of the Inn at the Spanish Steps decided to go one step further and refurbished in high style the penthouse apartment on the corner of the Piazza di Spagna and Via Condotti. With this address need we say more? The ambiance is of pure privacy and privilege with the choice of taking over the entire apartment or one of the four deluxe rooms: two doubles, suite, and junior suite. Each room, some with a small balcony, looks directly over the world's most famous staircase with a heart-stopping view over the entire square. A full-time butler is at the complete disposal of guests and can also provide a walking tour of the historical city. In addition, a driver or chef can be hired upon prior arrangement. A sleek and contemporary sitting area in earth tones with accents in black, same décor as the rooms, looks directly out to the flower-laden terrace where breakfast is served overlooking your neighbors' terraces—the likes of Bulgari, Valentino and Gucci. Although this is an 18th-century palazzo, the apartment has been outfitted with all the latest technology including hanging plasma televisions, high-speed Internet connection and automatic temperature control. A one-of-a-kind indulgence, spacious and luxurious marble bathrooms are the icing on the cake.

THE VIEW AT THE SPANISH STEPS
Manager: Gaetano Lauro
Via dei Condotti, 85
Rome, (RM) 00187, Italy
Tel: (06) 69 925 657, Fax: (06) 67 86 470
4 Rooms, Double: €390–€3500
1 Suite: €1000–€3000
Open: all year, Credit cards: all major
Region: Lazio, Michelin Map: 563

Accessed by a steep, winding road, the 18th-century rectangular Palazzo Terranova, which dominates the northern Tiber valley and seemingly all of Umbria, is softened by surrounding terraced gardens filled with roses, lavender, cascading geraniums, and magnolia trees. This stylish country house was lovingly restored back to life by an English family some years ago and is filled with precious antiques and paintings from England and Italy. The current owners continue this passion for beauty and art in this tranquil, Italian countryside setting. Each masterpiece of a bedroom, with its stenciled and painted designs, holds some enchanting feature and, just as in the creation of a painting, utmost attention has been given to color scheme, composition, and lighting. Most of the rooms have king-sized wrought-iron beds, soft linens and stunning views. The restuarnt is open to guests for lunch and dinner with meals being prepared using fresh, seasonal ingredients, hightlighting the special dishes of the area. There is a scenic pool taking advantage of views and spa treatments available.   Delightful staff is on hand to satisfy any whim. *Directions:* From the E45 Perugia-Cesana, exit Promano. Pass through Cinquemiglia. Turn left at the roundabout, direction Trestina. At the three-way intersection; take the middle road, direction Morra. This road takes you through Bivio Lugnano and Badia Petroia to arrive in Ronti. Drive through village, turning left at T-intersection, up hill for 2.2 km.

PALAZZO TERRANOVA
Manager: Valentina Morriconi
Localita: Ronti near Morra
Ronti, (PG) 06010, Italy
Tel: (075) 8570083, Fax: (075) 8570014
10 Rooms, Double: €290–€680
Closed: Jan & Feb, Credit cards: all major
80 km N of Perugia
Region: Umbria, Michelin Map: 563

A favorite summer retreat of Romans (located 100 km south of the city) is the stretch of dunes and beach along the coast from Sabaudia to the Circeo mountain cascading into the sea. The area is a national park with Mediterranean flora and fauna, and has a unique feature of four small lakes that line the shore. Right on one of these wood-lined lakes (just outside of Saubadia) is where the Il San Francesco hotel has been resurrected from a 40-year-old building that is immersed in a lush park. Elena Daneo, owner of the Hotel Fontana in Rome (featured in our B&B guide), has tastefully and comfortably appointed the 27 guestrooms that are divided between the two floors of the prim white edifice with deluxe doubles offering terraces overlooking the lake. A spacious suite has a large terrace, superb views and features two bathrooms. The soft decor with prevalent colors of beige and creams is decidedly colonial, working well with the naturalistic ambiance of sea, lake and woods. During the summer months a shuttle takes guests to a reserved portion of the long stretch of beach where a chaise lounge and umbrella await them. Lunch and dinner are served everyday in the hotel's own restaurant, featuring traditional local dishes based on fresh seafood and local specialties. Extra indulgences include steam room and indoor hydro jet pool plus a boat for taking tours on the lake. *Directions:* From Rome follow the S.S.148 Pontina south to Saubadia.

IL SAN FRANCESCO
Manager: Elena Daneo
Via Caterattino
Sabaudia, (LT) 04016, Italy
Tel: (0773) 51 59 51, Fax: (0773) 51 23 80
25 Rooms, Double: €160–€275
2 Suites: €450
Open: all year, Credit cards: all major
100 km south of Rome on coast
Region: Lazio, Michelin Map: 430

It is difficult to imagine an alternative to staying on the spectacular Amalfi coast, but all doubts were washed away as we approached the charming Oasi Olimpia Relaisi. Whether it be the bend-over-backwards hospitality or the incredible views one has from the terraces of the prim white villa, the place is exceptional in all aspects. The whole staff, along with owner Salvatore, discreetly make sure guests have all they need and much more. Eleven spacious and elegant bedrooms—most are junior suites with balconies or terraces—have five-star amenities. The place breathes pure romance whether you are dining candlelight in the excellent restaurant with white tablecloths and fresh flowers, or under the wisteria-laden pergola among ancient olive trees. The chef prepares delectable local dishes with a personal flair, and also runs the cooking school in a separate wing built off the main kitchen. A shuttle takes guests to Sorrento or to the beach. After a day of touring, the swimming pool set under towering umbrella pines awaits you, and there you can sip an aperitif while watching the sunset. *Directions:* From Naples, follow the coastal road towards Sorrento. Before reaching Sorrento, turn left at Meta and follow up over the mountain to other side of the gulf and turn right towards Sant' Agata through town up to the Oasi. Avoid arrival on Friday or Saturday evenings when traffic is at a standstill.

❄ ☕ ✗ ♨ ▦ ☎ ⌂ ⅏ @ W Ⴤ P ⫙ ☺ ≈ ⋏ ▣ ♿ ⚓

OASI OLIMPIA RELAIS
Owner: Salvatore Insigne
Via Deserto, 26
San Agata, (NA) 80064, Italy
Tel: (081) 80 80 560, Fax: (081) 80 85 214
6 Rooms, Double: €240–€320
5 Suites: €345–€485
1 Apartment: €1000 weekly
Open: all year, Credit cards: all major
7 km from Sorrento and Positano
Region: Campania, Michelin Map: 564

The Villa Il Poggiale is an intimate, elegant boutique hotel. This traditional Tuscan country villa dating to the Renaissance period has had such illustrious proprietors as noble families Corsini, Martini, and Ricasoli-Rucellai, and has been in the Vitta family for the past 50 years. Brothers Johanan and Nathanel have brought the family residence back to its former glory, transforming it from a private country home to an exclusive inn, with no expense spared on beauty, comfort and modern conveniences. On the ground floor you find the splendidly decorated grand main salon plus another smaller one off which three of the generous bedrooms and suites with antique furnishings and lovely new bathrooms are found. Soft-peach, olive-green, and pale-yellow color schemes are displayed in fine fabrics used for bedspreads, draperies, and upholstery. Other frescoed bedrooms upstairs are nicely spaced apart by three additional sitting rooms, the most desirable being those away from the main road. A full buffet breakfast featuring homemade cakes and local specialties is served in the garden terrace, which leads down to the swimming pool with its extraordinary views of the picture-perfect Tuscan landscape. This is a luxurious villa where you will feel like guest in a private home. May to October a traditional Tuscan buffet dinner is also offered. *Directions:* Drive through San Casciano following signs for Empoli. After 2 km, Villa Il Poggiale is on the left.

VILLA IL POGGIALE
Owners: Johanan & Nathanel Vitta
Via Empolese, 69, Val di Pesa
San Casciano, (FI) 50026, Italy
Tel: (055) 82 83 11, Fax: (055) 82 94 296
8 Rooms, Double: €130–€150
8 Suites: €195–€240
2 Apartments: €300-€1,100 daily
Closed: Feb, Credit cards: all major
17 km S of Florence
Region: Tuscany, Michelin Map: 563

The luxurious Villa Mangiacane with its combination historic home, worldly décor, and high-tech amenities is, in a word, magnificent. Owner Glynn Cohen returned from years in South Africa and purchased the 15th century estate which encompasses 600 acres of surrounding land dedicated to the production of Chianti Classico wines and extra virgin olive oil. The stately villa once the residence of the Machiavelli family, is assumed to be the architectural work of Michelangelo. The eight sumptuous bedrooms and suites can be rented separately or as a full house rental and are elegantly appointed with priceless antiques and artwork, finest fabrics and linens, and designer bathrooms. Besides grand but comfortable salons, dining room, library, wine cellars, terraces, swimming pool, and gym, spectacular Renaissance views are awarded at every window. In fact the home was designed on the same axis as the Duomo cathedral in Florence with the long driveway, villa entrance and exit to the back frescoed loggia, all perfectly aligned to frame the famous cupola through a pathway cut in the hilltop woods. Truly amazing. A full staff caters to your every whim and the remaining 18 spacious rooms were added in 2006 in the adjacent house complex. *Directions:* Exit A1 at Firenze Certosa, go straight towards Tavarnuzze. Pass Tavernuzze, drive over a the small bridge named "Scopet" on your right. At the first stop turn right and drive 50 m to the hotel.

VILLA MANGIACANE
Manager: Silvia Piazzini
Via Faltignano 4
San Casciano, (FI) 50026, Italy
Tel: (055) 82 90 123, Fax: (055) 82 90 358
26 Rooms, Double: €250–€2500
Open: all year, Credit cards: all major
10 km south of Florence
Region: Tuscany, Michelin Map: 563

Italy abounds in well-equipped spas concentrated around its many thermal water sources, yet the one at Fonteverde truly stands out among the rest. While most four and five star hotels now feature some kind of a wellness center, we added the Hotel Fonteverde for its combination of awesome setting, historic Medicean palazzo, and full-fledged Italian-style spa. The guestrooms, classically appointed and full of amenities, are spread about the original 17th-century home and an attached modern duplicate. A full buffet breakfast is served in the courtyard or indoors, while dinners are presented in an elegant restaurant highlighting fine local products: Porcini mushrooms, Pienza cheese, Brunello wine and Chianina meat. A spacious bar and lounges open out to a large terrace taking in a sweeping vista of the entire untouched valley with its occasional Tuscan farmhouse. This same view is savored from within one of the many thermal pools; one has its own circuit of hydro-jets created for specific body parts. This is a gorgeous lesser-known area of Tuscany called the Val d'Orcia with Mount Amiata looming on the horizon and many interesting medieval towns to explore. *Directions:* Exit Autostrada A1 from the north at Chiusi-Chianciano; then follow first signs for Sarteano, then San Casciano dei Bagni to the hotel.

HOTEL FONTEVERDE
Manager: Antonio Politi
Località Terme 1
San Casciano dei Bagni, (SI) 53040, Italy
Tel: (0578) 57 241, Fax: (0578) 57 22 00
66 Rooms, Double: €330–€560
14 Suites: €690–€1340
Open: all year, Credit cards: all major
90 km SE of Siena, 158 km N of Rome
Region: Tuscany, Michelin Map: 563

The Rosa Alpina hotel is an oasis of luxury, comfort, and elegance in the very heart of the majestic Dolomite mountains. Although San Cassiano dates back to 1780, this ski and summer resort has seen growing popularity. The Pizzininis were a fundamental part of the development of the area and besides running the hotel in the pre-World War II years, they built the first ski lift and power plant for the village. For three generations the Pizzinini family has dedicated itself to the art of hospitality and performs this art with extreme naturalness, warmth, and efficiency, which is seemingly innate to the people in this Val Badia area. Although presenting a simple, typical chalet-style exterior from the street, the hotel expands to the side and back with mountain views and private gardens. Rooms and suites reflect the colors of surrounding nature, with primarily soft-cream hues accented with meadow greens and rust reds. The hotel incorporates many special features such as four restaurants, one with a two stars Michelin rating. Here chef Norbert Niederkofler works wonders based on regional recipes and leads off-season cooking classes. Daniela Pizzinini directs the full-spa center. *Directions:* Exit from the A22 at Val Gardena and drive through Ortisei, Selva, Corvara, and La Villa to San Cassiano. The Rosa Alpina is on the main road in town.

ROSA ALPINA
Owner: Paolo Pizzinini
Strada Micura de Ru, 20, Dolomites
San Cassiano in Badia, (BZ) 39030, Italy
Tel: (0471) 84 95 00, Fax: (0471) 84 93 77
21 Rooms, Double: €280–€580
8 Suites: €370–€730
Open: Jan to Mar & Jun to Oct, Credit cards: all major
Relais & Châteaux
29 km W of Cortina, 6 km SE of Badia
Region: Trentino-Alto Adige, Michelin Map: 562

Finding the appealing Golf Hotel brought us an unexpected bonus: we discovered a niche of Italy that hugs the border north of Trieste, an absolutely gorgeous region of wooded hills, rolling fields, and vineyards. The Castello Formentini, superbly positioned on a hillock overlooking the countryside, has belonged to the Counts of Formentini since the 16th century. For many years there has been a restaurant within the castle, serving excellent meals and a medieval banquet on select Saturdays. Just outside the castle walls, one of the historic buildings of the castle complex has been converted into a small, charming luxury inn. The attractive, gracious owner, Isabella Formentini, says that all of the magnificent antique furnishings in the hotel are family heirlooms: in fact, she says the furniture is more valuable than the castle. Everything is authentic, even the wonderful prints and paintings. From the intimate lobby to each of the spacious guestrooms, everything is decorator-perfect and exudes a delightful country-manor ambiance. Only four of the rooms are within the castle, but all guests can stroll through the gate and into the castle grounds where the swimming pool lies invitingly in the shaded lawn. Guests also enjoy a tennis court. The hotel is open in the winter for groups of 10 to 20 persons.

GOLF HOTEL
Owner: Contessa Isabella Formentini
San Floriano del Collio, (GO) 34070, Italy
Tel: (0481) 88 40 51, Fax: (0481) 88 40 52
15 Rooms, Double: €160–€220
Open: Mar to Nov, Credit cards: all major
40 km N of Trieste, 7 km N of Gorizia
Region: Friuli-Venezia Giulia, Michelin Map: 562

Without a doubt, San Gimignano is one of the most picturesque places in Tuscany: a postcard-perfect hilltop village punctuated by 14 tall towers. During the day, the town bustles with activity, but after the busloads of tourists depart, the romantic ambiance of yesteryear fills the cobbled streets. For the lucky few who spend the night, there is a jewel of small inn, the Hotel L'Antico Pozzo. What a pleasure to see a renovation with such excellent taste and meticulous attention to maintaining the authentic character of the original building. The name of the hotel derives from an antique stone well (pozzo), which is softly illuminated just off the lobby. The fact that only the most affluent families could afford the luxury of a private well indicates that this 15th-century townhouse was once a wealthy residence. A timeworn stone staircase leads up to the air conditioned bedrooms, tucked at various levels along a maze of hallways. Each one of the quietly elegant rooms has its own personality with thick stone walls, terracotta floors, and beautifully framed antique prints, plus satellite television. One of my favorites, number 20, has the palest of pastel-peach-colored walls, windows opening onto the terrace, and a fabulous domed ceiling painted with ancient Roman designs. Number 14 is also outstanding—a very large room with a canopy bed. Another advantage of L'Antico Pozzo is that this is a long time family-run hotel.

HOTEL L' ANTICO POZZO
Manager: Emanuele Marro
Via San Matteo, 87
San Gimignano, (SI) 53037, Italy
Tel: (0577) 94 20 14, Fax: (0577) 94 21 17
18 Rooms, Double: €120–€180
Open: all year, Credit cards: all major
55 km SW of Florence, 38 km N of Siena
Region: Tuscany, Michelin Map: 563

San Gimignano is one of the most fascinating of the medieval Tuscany hilltowns. As you approach, this looks like a city of skyscrapers: come even closer and the skyscrapers emerge as 14 soaring towers—dramatic reminders of what San Gimignano must have looked like in all her glory when this wealthy town sported 72 giant towers. Most tourists come just for the day to visit this small town, but for those lucky enough to be able to spend the night, San Gimignano has a simple but very charming hotel, La Cisterna. The hotel is located on the town's main square and fits right into the ancient character of the surrounding buildings with its somber stone walls softened by ivy, arched shuttered doors, and red-tile roof. Inside La Cisterna, the medieval feeling continues with lots of stone, vaulted ceilings, leather chairs, and dark woods. The bedrooms are not fancy, but pleasant, and some have balconies with lovely views of the valley. Renovations added air conditioning and satellite TV (for European channels and CNN). La Cisterna is probably more famous as a restaurant than as a hotel and people come from far and wide because not only is the food delicious, but the dining rooms are delightful. Especially charming is the dining room with the brick wall, sloping ceiling supported by giant beams, and picture windows framing the gorgeous hills of Tuscany.

🛏️ 🛒 💳 ☎ ⛲ @ W P 🍴 🖼️ ♿ 🚶 👫 🏇 🍇

LA CISTERNA
Owner: Salvestrini family
Piazza della Cisterna, 24
San Gimignano, (SI) 53037, Italy
Tel: (0577) 94 03 28, Fax: (0577) 94 20 80
50 Rooms, Double: €90–€145
2 Suites: €120–€150
Restaurant closed Tue & lunch on Wed
Open: Mar 14 to Jan 6, Credit cards: all major
55 km SW of Florence, 38 km NW of Siena
Region: Tuscany, Michelin Map: 563

We instantly fell in love with Il Borro and decided that this gorgeous property would be perfect for those who want to nestle into Tuscany for a week or more in a "home away from home." Il Borro is owned by Ferruccio Ferragamo and managed by Leonardo Utari. This isn't your normal hotel at all—it is a huge estate with vineyards, walnut groves, olive trees, woodlands, and pastures. For such a vast property (1755 acres), it is amazing that there are only twenty-four suites, accommodating from two to six persons. Each has a bedroom (or bedrooms), kitchen, and living room. A wide variety of accommodations is offered: fourteen of the suites are in three houses nestled in the countryside, twelve are in individual cottages in the hamlet of Borro, and the last, a romantic, secluded little mill, stands by the river. My favorites are the twelve cottages in Borro, an adorable village with a cluster of enchanting stone buildings facing onto narrow, cobbled, pedestrian-only streets. This hamlet, reached by a beguiling stone bridge, is a real town with its own tiny plaza, artisan shops, boutiques, church, cobbler, goldsmith, restaurant, delicatessen and wine bar. Here, the twelve guest cottages are tucked among the villagers' homes. No matter where you stay, the decor and accommodations are outstanding, and in the off season prices drop dramatically. *Directions:* When you reach the town of San Giustino Valdarno, follow signs to Il Borro.

IL BORRO
General Manager: Leonardo Utari
San Giustino Valdarno, (AR) 52024, Italy
Tel: (055) 97 70 53, Fax: (055) 97 70 55
24 Rooms, Double: €200–€420
Open: all year, Credit cards: all major
60 km W of Florence
Region: Tuscany, Michelin Map: 563

This very special historic residence was once the summer villa of the Grand Duke of Tuscany, attracted to the bucolic countryside between Pisa and Lucca with its natural thermal waters. They are the same theraputic waters enjoyed by Etruscans, Ancient Romans and nobility of Europe in later years up to today. Meticulous attention has been given to the restoration of this splendid palazzo, perserving high vaulted ceilings covered with frescoes, as presented in the main salon as well as in many of the sumptuous bedrooms and suites. Several rooms are bi-level with the loft bedroom elevated giving a closer look at the pastel-hued frescoes. Fine fabrics, linens, marble bathrooms and the latest amenities available are featured in all. Fine meals are served in the main dining room while aperitifs can be taken out on the terrace lined with potted lemon trees. A steep hillside backs the property with trails which take guests up to the terrace for views to the leaning tower. If this weren't already enough to satisfy the most demanding of guests, the hotel has its own adjoining full-fledged spa, a luxurious haven offering a long list of treatments ranging from traditional, oriental and ayurvedic. Summer packages can include treatments and tickets to the Puccini Opera Festival. *Directions*: Exit at Lucca Est from the A11 autostrada then follow the signs for Terme di San Giuliano. After 10 km you enter the town of San Giuliano Terme, here follow the signs to "Terme".

BAGNI DI PISA NATURAL SPA RESORT   *New*
Manager: Paolo Gutta
Largo Shelley, 18
San Guiliano Terme, (PI) , Italy
Tel: (050) 88 501, Fax: (050) 88 50 401
51 Rooms, Double: €310–€390*
8 Suites: €460–€600*
*Includes breakfast and dinner
Open: all year, Credit cards: all major
10 km NW of Pisa, 60 km W of Florence
Region: Tuscany, Michelin Map: 563

Staying at the Villa Arceno is truly like staying with friends in a sumptuous Italian villa. Although a luxurious property with stunning decor and impeccable service, the hotel exudes the warmth and charm of a small inn. The manager, Gualtiero Mancini, makes everyone feel at home. The mood of grandeur is set as you approach by a seemingly endless private road that winds through lovingly tended vineyards to a classic, three-story, ochre-colored villa. At one time the summer home of royalty, this 17th-century Palladian villa has been masterfully restored, both outside and within. The public rooms are more like lounges in a private home with a sophisticated, yet comfortable, elegance. The individually decorated guestrooms in the main villa are gorgeous—even the standard rooms are enormous and splendidly decorated. All the rooms are so outstanding it is difficult to choose, but I think my favorites are suites 104 and 204, both with sweeping vistas of vine-covered fields. Reveling in the utter peace and quiet, go sightseeing in nearby Siena, explore the wonders of Tuscany, or enjoy the hotel's bicycles, swimming pool, tennis court, and (best of all) the park. Here you can stroll for hours along romantic lanes shaded by rows of cypress trees or meander on paths through the forest, passing almost-hidden statues, to an idyllic, secluded lake. The hotel is being renovated and is set to open March 2009 with a lovely new spa. *Directions:* Ask hotel for directions.

RELAIS VILLA ARCENO
Manager: Gualtiero Mancini
San Gusmè, (SI) 53010, Italy
Tel: (0577) 35 92 92, Fax: (0577) 35 92 76
16 Rooms, Double: €345–€525
Open: Apr to mid-Nov, Credit cards: all major
22 km NE of Siena, 9 km NW of Castelnuovo
Region: Tuscany, Michelin Map: 563

If you are looking for a place to stay in the heart of Tuscany that is moderately priced, yet does not sacrifice one ounce of charm or quality of accommodation, the family-run Hotel Belvedere di San Leonino is unsurpassable. Ceramic pots of geraniums, trellised grapevines, and climbing roses soften and add color to the weathered stone buildings, which were originally a cluster of 15th-century farmers' cottages. Off the central patio area you find a small reception area, a blandly decorated living room, and an attractive dining room with tiled floors, rustic beamed ceiling, and appropriately simple wooden tables and chairs. When the weather is warm, meals are served outside in the garden. Because the rooms are tucked into various parts of the old farmhouses, they vary in size and shape. They also differ in decor, but all have an antique ambiance with wrought-iron headboards, beautiful old armoires, and pretty, white curtains. What adds the icing to the cake is the setting of the Belvedere, nestled in the very heart of the Chianti wine region, surrounded by stunning scenery—in every direction you look there are idyllic, sweeping vistas of rolling hills dotted with vineyards, olive groves, and pine forests. Hotel Belvedere is conveniently located only a short drive from the freeway.

HOTEL BELVEDERE DI SAN LEONINO
Manager: Signora C. Orlandi
San Leonino, (SI) 53011, Italy
Tel: (0577) 74 08 87, Fax: (0577) 74 09 24
29 Rooms, Double: €100–€156*
*Breakfast not included: €7
Open: mid-Mar to mid-Nov, Credit cards: all major
16 km N of Siena, 65 km S of Florence
Region: Tuscany, Michelin Map: 563

Villa Giona is a dream—a private, historic residence-turned-accommodation. The cordial Saletti family has meticulously restored and maintained all the original architecture and has run it firsthand, creating an aura of hospitality in the home of friends. The impressive, 16th-century stately villa, surrounded on all sides by vast, open lawns accented with lemon vases and ancient statues, is complete with the characteristic "barchessa" wings and holds six, very spacious guestrooms. Each of the non-smoking guestrooms on the upper two floors has the amenities of a five-star hotel plus some unique feature, whether it be the mansard beamed rooms on the top floor, the high-ceilinged rooms (one with private terrace) on the upper, noble floor, or the one and two bedroom apartments in a separate tower across the manicured vineyards. Breakfast is a country buffet complete with fresh breads and cakes, offered on the upper loggia overlooking the enchanting garden. In Veneto wine country (Villa Giona is the home of the prized Allegrini wines) and halfway between lovely Verona and Lake Garda, the villa is also where Giuliano Hazan conducts his weeklong cooking courses. *Directions:* Exit A22 at Verona Nord. Follow signs towards Valpolicella and San Pietro Incariano. After 10 kms turn right at roundabout and head towards San Pietro. Pass through San Floriano. When you reach Pedemonte, turn right for Cengia, then after 1 km, turn left for the Villa.

VILLA GIONA
Owners: Paolo & Caterina Saletti
Via Cengia, 8
San Pietro in Cariano, (VR) 37029, Italy
Tel: (045) 68 55 011, Fax: (045) 68 55 010
13 Rooms, Double: €170–€380
4 Suites: €250–€460
1 Apartment: €370 daily, €1200 weekly
Open: all year, Credit cards: all major
19 km N of Verona, 18 km E of Lake Garda
Region: Veneto, Michelin Map: 562

The Residence San Sano is a very special small hotel in San Sano—a picturesque hamlet in the center of the Chianti wine-growing region. We were charmed by the hotel, which is incorporated into a cluster of 16th-century stone houses. A cozy dining room serves guests excellent meals featuring typically Tuscan-style cooking. Each of the bedrooms is delightfully furnished in antiques and each has a name incorporating some unique feature of the hotel, the name evolving from the time during reconstruction when each room was remembered by its special feature. One is called the Bird Room: here birds had claimed the room for many years and had nested in holes that went completely through the wall. With great imagination, the holes were left open to the outside, but on the inside were covered with glass. Another room is named for a beautiful, long-hidden Romanesque window that was discovered and incorporated into the decor and another for an antique urn uncovered during renovation. The hotel has upgraded the property with a beautiful swimming pool and several spacious new light and bright rooms with private terraces overlooking the garden and vineyards. This is a wonderful country house dipped in history.

HOTEL RESIDENCE SAN SANO
Owner: Maurizio Amabili
San Sano, (SI) 53010, Italy
Tel: (0577) 74 61 30, Fax: (0577) 74 61 56
15 Rooms, Double: €130–€200
Meals for hotel guests only (closed Sun)
Open: mid-Mar to Feb, Credit cards: all major
60 km S of Florence, 9 km S of Radda
Region: Tuscany, Michelin Map: 563

The marvelously scenic Langhe wine country, rivaling Chianti but without all the tourists, was in dire need of an upscale property in a historical residence and the San Maurizio fulfilled the void nicely. This super inn poised up on a hill looking over vineyards and olive groves has undergone a courageous and lengthy restoration. Originally a Cistercian monastery, the massive U-shaped building around a lovely rose garden has 31 elegantly appointed rooms (most are suites), created from the monks' cells, each equipped with all amenities and technological conveniences. Many architectural features have been enhanced including soaring ceilings with frescoes, original wood or brick floors, arched doorways, plus a chapel and vaulted wine cellars dating to the 17th century. Guests can lounge in one of a series of grand sitting rooms, appointed with antiques, Oriental carpets, and gold-framed paintings, or outdoors in the surrounding gardens with walks. The formal restaurant with Michelin star, of renowned chef Guido di Costigliole, and run by Lidia Alciati e Luca Zecchin, concentrates on the best regional cuisine, accompanied of course by the rich selection of local wines. Outings on horseback, golf, and guided historical visits of castles and wineries can be organized. A swimming pool and full spa are right on the premises. *Directions:* From San Stefano Belbo, follow signs for Valdivilla. After 2 km turn right at the inn's sign.

❄ ☕ 📇 ☎ 🏨 @ ♈ P 🍴 🚭 🌺 ≈ 🖼 ⌂ ⅃ 👤 🚶 🐎 🍇 ⚓

RELAIS SAN MAURIZIO
Manager: Cesare Pavese
Localita: San Maurizio, 39
San Stefano Belbo, (CN) 12058, Italy
Tel: (0141) 84 19 00, Fax: (0141) 84 38 33
21 Rooms, Double: €240–€435,* 9 Suites: €380–€550*
*Breakfast not included: €20
Open: Mar to Nov, Credit cards: all major
Relais & Châteaux
22 km SE of Asti
Region: Piedmont, Michelin Map: 561

The 16th-century Locanda San Vigilio has been in Count Guarienti di Brenzone's family for over 400 years. This small hotel, nestled next to a miniature private peninsula stretching into the lake, that in days of yore offered shelter to fishing boats, has a prime location directly on Lake Garda. If you want to see and be seen by the rich and famous, choose the glamorous Villa d'Este on Lake Como as your hub, but if you desire utter tranquility, the Locanda San Vigilio makes a good choice. Here you will find understated luxury, nothing commercial at all. Only a small sign marks the tree-lined entrance just a few kilometers north of the town of Garda. The entrance to the hotel also serves as access for a public park and at first you might think you have the wrong turn, but tell the attendant at the gate that you have a reservation at the hotel and he will let you pass. The lane runs through century old cypress trees to the parking area for the Locanda. After parking your car in the designated area, you walk past the family's private villa and then down a path to the hotel, a sturdy stone building so close to the water that waves gently lap the walls. The dining room is especially inviting and if you are lucky, you can dine at one of the cozy tables overlooking the lake. The guestrooms hidden away on the grounds vary in size, some being much more spacious than others. The prize bedrooms are the more expensive ones upstairs with windows overlooking the lake.

LOCANDA SAN VIGILIO
Owners: Agostino & Guarienti di Brenzone
Lake Garda
San Vigilio, (VR) 37016, Italy
Tel: (045) 72 56 688, Fax: (045) 72 56 551
11 Rooms, Double: €270–€600
3 Suites: €500–€890
Open: Mar to Dec, Credit cards: AX, VS
History Traveller
154 km W of Venice, 3 km N of Garda
Region: Veneto, Michelin Map: 562

One of the most unspoiled scenic areas of western Sicily is the northernmost point west of Palermo, San Vito Lo Capo, which is part of the Zingaro Natural Reserve Park. The town is an informal summer resort that attracts many tourists mainly in the months of July and August. Otherwise, the sleepy town (its one main street lined with seafood restaurants, stores and ancient church) is at one's entire disposal. The only hotel right on the beach is the Capo San Vito. A seemingly anonymous, modern building from the exterior, one is surprised upon entering it. Owner Paolo Graziano has remodeled the hotel and has created a soft, zen-like ambiance, using warm earth tones complimenting the crystal, turquoise sea surroundings. The reception area and halls have colorful, hand-painted tiled floors. New and comfortable guestrooms are found on three floors, most with balconies looking out to the rocky cliff and beach. The rooftop wellness center offers a variety of new age treatments, as well as hydro jet pool, sauna, steam bath, gym, and a lounge area with soothing sea views. The popular restaurant stretches out from the main dining area in two directions on the beach, immersed in palms, with rattan furniture. It has a very tropical feel and is lovely at night when all is by candlelight. *Directions:* Exit the A29 autostrada from Palermo at Castellamare del Golfo and follow signs to the hotel.

❄ ☕ ⚙ 💳 ☎ 🐕 ⛪ 🏋 @ ⛉ P 🍽 🚭 ❀ 🖼 ♿ ⚓ ⛵

HOTEL CAPO SAN VITO
Owner: Paolo Graziano
Via San Vito, 1
San Vito Lo Capo, Sicily, (TP) 91010, Italy
Tel: (0923) 97 21 22, Fax: (0923) 97 25 59
36 Rooms, Double: €180–€380
Open: all year, Credit cards: all major
On the northern coast of Sicily
Region: Sicily, Michelin Map: 565

Hotel Baita Fiorita is tucked high in the village of Santa Caterina Valfurva, a well-known mountain resort. One of its stars is the Olympic downhill champion, Deborah Compagnoni, whose family owns the Hotel Baita Fiorita. The hotel, an attractive chalet-style building with window boxes overflowing with geraniums, is located in the center of town. From the moment you step inside, you know that this small hotel is imbued with the warmth and caring of the owners. Country antiques throughout are enhanced by pretty fabrics, bouquets of fresh flowers, sweet embroidered curtains, mellow-with-age paneled walls, polished wood floors, and porcelain fireplaces. The walls abound with photos and trophies of Deborah's ski accomplishments, along with those of her brothers who are also renounced skiers and mountaineers. Deborah's mother, Adele Compagnoni, prepares wonderful meals featuring fresh produce and highlighting regional specialties. There is a main dining room on the ground level, plus a second dining area on a lower level that oozes even more old-world charm. The guestrooms are each individual in décor but all exude a cozy, alpine ambiance with paneled walls, pretty curtains, hand-made cushions and puffy down comforters. Each room is named for a flower and Deborah hand-painted a plaque for each door with the appropriate flower. *Directions:* From Tirano drive north on SS38 to Bórmio and follow signs to Santa Caterina Valfurva.

ROMANTIK HOTEL BAITA FIORITA
Owner: Compagnoni Family
Via Frodolfo 3
Santa Caterina Valfurva, (TN) 23030, Italy
Tel: (0342) 92 51 19, Fax: (0342) 92 50 50
22 Rooms, Double: €130–€260
Closed: May, Oct & Nov, Credit cards: all major
Romantik Hotels
25 km E of Bolzano, 120 km N of Verona
Region: Lombardy, Michelin Map: 562

The refreshingly unspoiled village of Santa Maria di Castellabate hugs the sea at the southern tip of the Bay of Salerno. Just steps away from this cluster of colorful houses and brightly painted fishing boats, the Palazzo Belmonte nestles in utter tranquility within its own 5-acre park, hidden behind high stone walls. There is not even a discreet sign at the massive gates to hint that you have arrived at a hotel. The palazzo is the estate of your charming host, Prince Belmonte, who opens both his home and heart to guests. Amazingly, the property has remained in the prince's family since it was built in the 17th century as a hunting lodge where the kings of Italy and Spain came to play. The magic begins the moment you enter through the vaulted portal into the central stone-walled courtyard where the scent of jasmine, roses, and honeysuckle perfumes the air. Prince Belmonte has his private residence on the top floor of the palazzo that also houses 21 guestrooms. Our favorite accommodations are the 30 new luxurious rooms (all with terrace or balcony) tucked in among the trees in the palace's lovely park. A path through the garden leads to a beautiful swimming pool and beyond to a small "secret" gate which leads down to the palazzo's private sandy beach. Dinner is often served on the terrace—to dine by candlelight under the stars by the sea is truly memorable. Meals are for guests only.

PALAZZO BELMONTE
Manager: Angela Wilkinson
Santa Maria di Castellabate, (SA) 84072, Italy
Tel: (0974) 96 02 11, Fax: (0974) 96 11 50
53 Rooms, Double: €260–€445
8 Suites: €330–€580
Meals for hotel guests only
Open: May to Nov, Credit cards: MC, VS
History Traveller
72 km S of Salerno, on S edge of town
Region: Campania, Michelin Map: 564

Santa Maria di Castellabate is a picturesque village hugging the sea at the southern tip of the Bay of Salerno. I fell in love with this exceptionally colorful, unspoiled fishing hamlet several years ago. Villa Sirio is an ancient villa from 1904 located in the historic center right on the sea. Alfonso and Rosalinda Tortora restored the building and opened in 1997 as a charming, small hotel. They are fantastic hosts who treat their guests as friends, extending their hearts to all who come through the door. The handsome building is painted a rich yellow with white trim around the windows. The mood is set as you enter the intimate reception area where oil paintings decorate the walls and give a welcoming, homelike ambiance. The color scheme throughout is a happy one and all the guestrooms are lovingly decorated in fine taste. The rooms facing the sea are in pretty hues of blue and yellow and have a balcony, while those facing the village are in green and yellow. What fun to sleep with the waves lapping beneath your window. You can enjoy the clear sea while sunbathing on the hotel's private beach. The food is excellent and served in a beautiful dining room under a coved ceiling with giant arches. From June to September you can eat on the sea reef terrace by candlelight. The Tortora's son, Andrea, and his American wife, Alessandra, run the restaurant.

HOTEL VILLA SIRIO
Managers: Andrea & Alessandra Tortora
Via Lungomare de Simone, 15
Santa Maria di Castellabate, (SA) 84048, Italy
Tel: (0974) 96 10 99, Fax: (0974) 96 05 07
15 Rooms, Double: €130–€280
Open: May to Oct, Credit cards: all major
72 km S. of Salerno, in center of village
Region: Campania, Michelin Map: 564

Having heard about a lovely little chalet tucked among the pines high in the Italian Alps near the French border, I was beginning to wonder what awaited me as the road wound through the ski town of Sauze d'Oulx with its unattractive jumble of modern concrete ski hotels. However, the road soon left the resort town and continued as a track, twisting higher and higher into the mountains until suddenly Il Capricorno came into view, nestled in the forest and surrounded in winter by ski runs. This is a wonderful place to enjoy a skiing holiday or perfect for summer walking along mountain trails. Just as you enter the hotel there is a tiny bar and, beyond, a cozy dining room enhanced by dark wooden chalet-style chairs, rustic wooden tables, and a stone fireplace with logs stacked neatly by its side. The bedrooms, too, are simple but most pleasant, with dark-pine handmade furniture, neat little bathrooms, and, for a lucky few, balconies with splendid mountain views. However, the greatest assets of this tiny inn are the owners, Mariarosa and Carlo Sacchi. Carlo personally made most of the furniture and will frequently join the guests for skiing. Mariarosa is the chef, a fabulous gourmet cook. *Directions:* Exit the A32 at Oulx (signpost Sauze d'Oulx) and follow the road up into the mountains and through the town. In winter you are collected by snowmobile from the town.

IL CAPRICORNO
Owners: Mariarosa & Carlo Sacchi
Les Clotes
Sauze d'Oulx, (TO) 10050, Italy
Tel: (0122) 85 02 73, Fax: (0122) 85 00 55
7 Rooms, Double: €190–€220*
*Includes breakfast & dinner
Open: Dec to May & mid-May to mid-Sep
Credit cards: VS
2 km E of Sauze d'Oulx, 60 km W of Turin
Region: Piedmont, Michelin Map: 561

The Masseria San Domenico opened its doors to guests in 1996. Not that the building is new—quite the contrary—the lovely old farmhouse (masseria) dates back to the 15th century. The age is immediately reconfirmed as you drive up to the hotel—both sides of the lane are bordered by groves of centuries-old olive trees with thick gnarled trunks and silvery-green leaves. Typical of the region, the large farm complex has a Moorish look, with white walls gleaming in the sunlight. However, the fact that this is no longer a rustic farm is quickly apparent: an enormous, lake-like swimming pool lies snuggled next to the hotel; there are two tennis courts; the food is outstanding; the beautifully decorated guestrooms are all spacious, with large tiled bathrooms, marble floors, crisp-white walls, cheerful drapes and matching bedspreads. The sea is 500 meters from the hotel and some of the rooms capture the bright blue of the Adriatic sparkling in the sun across an expanse of olive trees. It is also the source of the purified seawater used in their thalassotherapy spa. The hotel also offers an 18-hole golf course with a brand new 15-room guest house. The Masseria San Domenico makes the perfect choice if you are looking for a hotel offering every amenity, yet so superbly managed that you feel like a pampered guest in a small, family-run hotel. *Directions:* On the coastal road, about 2 km south of Savelletri di Fasano.

❄ ☕ 🍴 💳 ☎ 🛗 🍽 @ W ♈ P 🍴 🚭 🌸 🏊 🎿 🏞 ♿ ⚓ 🚶 🥾

MASSERIA SAN DOMENICO RESORT
Manager: Viola Melpignano
Savelletri di Fasano, (BR) 72010, Italy
Tel: (080) 482 77 69, Fax: (080) 482 79 78
36 Rooms, Double: €330–€638
10 Suites: €610–€2530
Closed: Jan 10 to Mar 10, Credit cards: all major
History Traveller
On the heel of Italy, 56 km NW of Brindisi
Region: Apulia, Michelin Map: 564

Hotels seem more special when the owners are on the premises. This is the atmosphere at the Masseria Torre Coccaro, which is owned by the Muolo family, who has lived in Apulia for generations. Already owners of two large, modern hotels in nearby Monopoli, they bought a beautiful, old, white-washed Masseria (a large olive-producing farm) with a 16th century watchtower and transformed the property into a luxurious hotel. The Muolo's gracious son, Vittorio, manages the hotel with warmth and efficiency—nothing seems too much trouble for his guests' comfort. Although there are only 34 rooms, the hotel has a large swimming pool, two restaurants, a cooking school, fitness room, private chapel, wine tasting, 9 holes of golf on-site, conference rooms, a spa with indoor pool that is tucked within an ancient cave, horseback riding, yoga classes, a private beach (a short distance away), and an excursion boat. The hotel is located in a serene farm area that close to the sea. The guestrooms are each uniquely decorated and offer every comfort. Only two rooms are within old caves that were discovered on the property. If you want something really special, ask for the suite that has its own huge private, walled courtyard complete with private swimming pool. However, you don't need to splurge on a suite, my favorite are the standard rooms. *Directions:* Signposted on the coastal road as you drive south from Savelletri di Fasano.

❄ 🍽 🌿 ☕ 💳 ☎ 🏠 🛎 @ W Y P ♨ 🌿 🏊 🎿 📷 🐕 ⛱ 🏋 🚶 🐎 🍇

MASSERIA TORRE COCCARO
Owner: Vittorio Muolo
C. da Coccaro, 8
Savelletri di Fasano, (BR) 72010, Italy
Tel: (080) 48 29 310, Fax: (080) 48 27 992
34 Rooms, Double: €270–€495
5 Suites: €384–€1310
Open: all year, Credit cards: all major
On the heel of Italy, 56 km NW of Brindisi
Region: Apulia, Michelin Map: 564

At just 28 km north of Genoa and close to the autostrada continuing to Milan is the sleepy town of Savignone with the 16th-century Palazzo Fieschi sitting right in its main square. The Caprile family has taken over the hotel in 1997, continuing a tradition of offering home-like hospitality to travelers since 1856 when the original proprietors, Count Fieschi rented out rooms. The sensation of stepping back in time is encountered upon entering the large gray-tiled reception area with atrium and potted plants which continues down a hall straight back to a bar and out to the spacious lawn, fountain and gardens with ancient trees overlooking the town. To the right of the wide stone staircase leading up to the 22 bedrooms on the upper two floors is a frescoed dining area where travelers stopover from either Milan or Genova for an excellent regional meal (no one can miss the pesto sauce or gnocchi) prepared by the owners. No two of the old-fashioned style bedrooms are alike either in size or décor which counts mostly on a mix of country antiques from the late 1800s. New bathrooms are plain and functional and restoration work on rooms left either original brick floors or were completely modified with new tiled floors. Daughter, Sara, is on hand to suggest classic Riviera or off the beaten track itineraries. *Directions:* Exit from the autostrada A7 at Busalla and follow the S.S.35 past the industrial area to Savignone.

PALAZZO FIESCHI
Owners: Simonetta & Aldo Caprile
Piazza della Chiesa 14
Savignone, (GE) 16010, Italy
Tel: (010) 93 60 063, Fax: (010) 93 68 21
24 Rooms, Double: €90–€190
3 Suites: €100–€200
Open: Mar 1 to Dec 24, Credit cards: all major
28 km N of Genova
Region: Liguria, Michelin Map: 561

The Maremma, an intensely scenic area in the coastal foothills of southern Tuscany, offers a wealth of sightseeing possibilities: walled villages, Etruscan ruins, archaeological sites, and marvelously unspoiled landscapes. The congenial Pellegrini family converted a 200-year-old stone farmhouse into a hotel and over the years, into a veritable country resort. The "Castagneta" restaurant is the heart of the inn and has tables set in a beamed-ceilinged room filled with sunlight from large French doors opening onto a panoramic terrace where meals are served on warm days. A real bonus are the delectable typically local meals: including hearty soups and pastas coupled with fine regional wines. Learn the kitchen's secrets firsthand by participating in the cooking classes. The singles and some double bedrooms are found in the main house while a group of new and spacious guestrooms including four suites have been added in two nearby annexes, comfortably appointed with wrought iron beds, artisan-made furnishings and many amenities. There is also a full spa offering a variety of oriental philosophy based treatments, indoor heated salt-water pool, sauna, and outdoor pool. Down the hill from the hotel you find the equestrian center where horses are groomed each day for guests, ready for countryside excursions. Plenty to keep one happy here. *Directions:* From Scansano, take S.S. 322 towards Manciano. The hotel is on the right after 3 km.

ANTICO CASALE DI SCANSANO
Owners: Massimo Pellegrini & family
Loc. Castagneta
Scansano, (GR) 58054, Italy
Tel: (0564) 50 72 19, Fax: (0564) 50 78 05
28 Rooms, Double: €130–€190
4 Suites: €195–€260
14 Apartments: €550–€1250
Minimum Stay Required: One week minimum in Aug
Open: all year, Credit cards: all major
Region: Tuscany, Michelin Map: 563

The Villa Soranzo Conestabile is a splendid, three-story, 16th-century mansion that was built as a summer residence by one of the wealthiest Venetian families who were direct descendants of the powerful Doge, Giovanni Soranzo (the genius who originated the concept of Venice as a great sea power). Although located in the center of Scorzè, a small agricultural and commercial town, the house is secluded within its own 3-hectare park, which is especially romantic with a small pond, a stream, lovely gardens, centuries-old trees, and seven spectacular magnolias, which must be some of the largest in the world. Today the Villa Soranzo Conestabile is owned by the Martinelli family. The property was bought by the grandfather whose restaurant in Cortina was a favorite hangout for Hemingway (notice the wonderful old photos of Hemingway and Granddad on the wall). My favorite guest room, number 2, is a spacious, high-ceilinged corner room with antique furniture and windows capturing lovely views of the park. If you are on a budget, choose one of the less expensive bedrooms on the top floor. Although smaller and less grand, they are also decorated with antiques and are very attractive (my favorite is number 18). The Villa Soranzo Conestabile is an excellent value, especially when compared with hotel prices in Venice. It is possible to commute to the city center by the frequent bus service from in front of the house (a 45-minute trip).

✳ ☕ ✗ 💳 ☎ 🐾 @ P ⑪ ⚒ ⚓ 🏃 🐎 ⛷ 🎿

VILLA SORANZO CONESTABILE
Owner: Martinelli family
Via Roma, 1
Scorzè, (VE) 30037, Italy
Tel: (041) 44 50 27, Fax: (041) 58 40 088
20 Rooms, Double: €140–€200
Restaurant open Mar to Oct, Mon to Fri
Open: all year, Credit cards: all major
24 km NW of Venice
Region: Veneto, Michelin Map: 562

This is one of the most scenic areas of the Dolomites and Sesto is one of the most attractive of the mountain towns. Just beyond town you find the delightful Berghotel Tirol, a lovely hotel built in typical Dolomite chalet style. Inside, the tasteful decor continues the delightful Alpine style, with one lovely room with beams and light-pine furniture leading to another. However, the special features of the Berghotel Tirol are its marvelous location on the hillside looking over this lovely valley with towering mountains as a backdrop and the warmth of welcome from Kurt Holzer, his wife Resi, and their son Walter. Many of the rooms have large balconies, which capture the view and the warmth of the mountain sun. The adjacent "residence" has lovely apartments (for two to four persons) with tiny kitchens, which can be rented for weekly stays or on a half-board basis. A network of trails in every direction tempts everyone into the crisp mountain air. When you return at night to the hotel, it is rather like a house party: table-hopping is prevalent as guests share their day's adventures. Below the hotel are a fitness center with sauna, panoramic swimming pool, whirlpool, and massage rooms, a children's room with billiards and football, and a large parking garage. *Directions:* Arriving in Sesto from S. Candido, go through town to the suburb of Moos where you turn left for the hotel.

BERGHOTEL TIROL
Owner: Holzer family
Sexten
Sesto, (BZ) 39030, Italy
Tel: (0474) 71 03 86, Fax: (0474) 71 04 55
46 Rooms, Double: €140–€280*
*Includes breakfast & dinner
Open: Christmas to Easter & late May to Oct
Credit cards: none
2 km SE of Sesto toward Moos, 44 km NE of Cortina
Region: Trentino-Alto Adige, Michelin Map: 562

When you wake up at the Hotel Helvetia and look out your window at the tiny crescent bay where colorful houses reflect in the still waters and fishing boats bob in the harbor, you might think for a moment you are in Portofino. Sestri Levante is not quite as picture-perfect—but almost—and here you will find less congestion and much more reasonable prices. In the beautiful section called Baia del Silenzio sits a jewel of a small hotel, the Helvetia, pressed snugly into the hillside, at the far end of the bay with a stunning view. This appealing small hotel is not fancy or pretentious, but just exactly right, and its prices provide an exceptional value. The decor is bright and pretty, with a few antiques for accent and masses of fresh flowers. All the rooms have been renovated and have excellent modern bathrooms. Opt for one of the lovely deluxe rooms with a view of the sea and a balcony—these are worth every penny. The final touch of perfection to this delightful establishment is that the owners, Signor and Signora Pernigotti, personally manage the property. *Directions:* Exit the A12 at Sestri Levante, following signs to the town center. At the roundabout in the center of town, go around the circle and take the road that runs along the park. Turn left when you come to the beach, left in front of the white church with tall columns, then immediately left again. At this point, follow signs to Hotel Helvetia.

HOTEL HELVETIA
Owner: Signor L. Pernigotti
Via Cappuccini, 43
Sestri Levante, (GE) 16039, Italy
Tel: (0185) 41 175, Fax: (0185) 45 72 16
21 Rooms, Double: €150–€200
6 Suites: €160–€230
Open: Mar to Nov, Credit cards: all major
34 km SE of Portofino, 59 NW of La Spezia
Region: Liguria, Michelin Map: 561

The Grand Hotel Continental Siena, an elegant small hotel that opened in early 2002, is one of the most exciting properties to come on the scene in Siena in many years. Although there are lovely places to stay on the periphery, there has never been an outstanding hotel in the heart of Siena, within steps of all of its fabulous sights. To say that this need for an exceptional property has now been fulfilled is an understatement: the Grand Hotel Continental Siena is an absolute dream and would be a sensation anywhere in the world. Located just off the Piazza del Campo, the building dates back to 1600 when it was designed as a magnificent palace for the noble Chigi family. After years of labor by countless artisans, the palace has been returned to its original splendor. The grandeur and opulence of the rooms are breathtaking. Fine fabrics, exquisite furnishings, and priceless antiques create a setting of unsurpassed grandeur. At the heart of the palace a central courtyard, protected by a glass roof, allows the sunlight to fill the hotel with sunshine. Off the courtyard the various parlors and ballrooms are gorgeous. A sweeping, wide staircase leads upstairs to the sumptuous bedrooms and suites, some of which feature magnificent, museum-quality, frescoed ceilings.

GRAND HOTEL CONTINENTAL SIENA
Manager: Giuseppe Artolli
Banchi di Sopra, 85
Siena, (SI) 53100, Italy
Tel: (0577) 56 011, Fax: (0577) 56 01 555
51 Rooms, Double: €440–€590*
12 Suites: €685–€1580*
*Breakfast not included: €28
Open: all year, Credit cards: all major
In heart of Siena, steps from Piazza del Campo
Region: Tuscany, Michelin Map: 563

Siena is a fascinating walled, hilltop city filled with a wealth of fabulous museums, intriguing squares, and breathtaking churches. If you want to stay within walking distance of the all the major sights and your budget precludes a splurge at the deluxe Grand Hotel Continental, the Palazzo Ravizza pensione makes an excellent choice. The brick exterior of the hotel looks quite plain but inside, the beauty of this once-grand 17th-century palace is immediately revealed. Belonging to the same family for 200 years, the mansion exudes the warmth of a home, with an intimate parlor, card room, music lounge, cozy bar, handsome ceiling frescos, old family portraits, and fresh flowers on polished antique tables. The Palazzo Ravizza is a simple hotel and some of the fabrics show a well-worn look, but overall it is well kept and appealing and for the price, it is an excellent choice. The individually decorated bedrooms vary in size, but all are furnished with antiques, down comforters, and have flat screen TVs. The choice rooms are those that overlook the back garden—I especially liked rooms 14 and 11. The most outstanding feature of the Ravizza is its splendid large garden. This is the heart of the hotel where guests can enjoy a meal or cold drink at one of the tables on the terrace or relax on one of the benches strategically placed for capturing a sweeping view of the Tuscany hillside. *Directions:* Near the Porta San Marco gate. Ask hotel for exact directions.

❄ ☕ 🍴 CREDIT ☎ Y P 🍴 🖼 🐾 👫 🏇 🍇

PALAZZO RAVIZZA
Owner: Francesco Grottanelli
Pian dei Mantellini, 34
Siena, (SI) 53100, Italy
Tel: (0577) 28 04 62, Fax: (0577) 22 15 97
30 Rooms, Double: €180–€270
Open: all year, Credit cards: all major
15-minute walk to Piazza del Campo
Region: Tuscany, Michelin Map: 563

The Locanda dell'Amorosa, a charming small hotel with great warmth and excellent management, makes a super base for exploring Tuscany and Umbria. From the Locanda dell'Amorosa it is an easy drive to such sightseeing delights as Siena, Pienza, Orvieto, Todi, and Assisi. The Locanda dell'Amorosa is actually a tiny town located a few kilometers south of Sinalunga. You approach along a cypress-lined road that cuts through fields of grapes. Park your car and enter through the gates into the walled 14th-century medieval village where you are greeted by an enormous courtyard with its own little church—exquisite inside with its soft pastels and its lovely fresco of the Madonna. A rustic wine bar next to the church features a selection of the estate's wines and can provide guests a light meal when the restaurant is closed. On the right side of the courtyard are the stables, which have been converted to a stunning restaurant whose massive beams and natural stone-and-brick walls are tastefully enhanced by arched windows, thick wrought-iron fixtures, and wooden tables. The guestrooms, located in a separate building, are tastefully appointed with a few antiques and matching bedspreads and draperies. The rest of this tiny village spreads out behind the main square and the buildings are used for the production of wine. *Directions:* Exit the A1 at Sinalunga. Just before town turn left toward Torrita. After 2 km, the hotel is on your right.

❄ ☕ ✒ ♨ 💳 ☎ @ ⅋ P 🍴 ≈ 🖼 🛎 🐎 🍇 🍷

LOCANDA DELL'AMOROSA
Managers: Carlo Citterio & Alessandra Chervatin
Sinalunga, (SI) 53048, Italy
Tel: (0577) 67 72 11, Fax: (0577) 63 20 01
27 Rooms, Double: €248–€660
Restaurant closed Mon & lunch on Tues
Closed: Jan 7 to Mar 6, Credit cards: all major
History Traveller
110 km S of Florence, 40 km SE of Siena
Region: Southern Tuscany, Michelin Map: 563

Caol Ishka features contemporary interiors within a traditional older building with a fusion of Italian design in a classic Sicilian farmhouse setting. The Gaelic name given by Irish co-owner Gareth, means "sound of water" being on the bank of the river Anapo right beside Fiume Ciane nature reserve. The twin pink-colored houses seen from the main road coming from Siracusa are surrounded by an open lawn and garden. On the premises is the Zafferano Bistrot appointed in minimalist style with grey walls and simple hanging spotlights over tables so as not to distract from the artful regional seafood dishes with a twist. Tables out on the patio overlook the inviting infinity-edge pool. Ten guestrooms are divided between the two homes, six of which are accessed directly from the exterior and have private wood decks. One different from the other, the rooms have many surprising aspects between high design furniture, artwork, decorative lighting, and latest trend bathrooms with exposed stone walls and wood floors as a base. Emanuela is on hand to make suggestions with itineraries of Sicily's scenic southern tip (water taxi to Ortigia, canoe rental for river). *Directions:* Head south on the ss115, Via Elorina from Siracusa 3 km. The hotel is on your right hand side. Siracusa, a Unesco World Heritage site, seems like a dreary modern town until you reach the historic center called Ortigia with a newly restored square highlighting Baroque architecture.

CAOL ISHKA
Manager: Ermanuela Marino
Via Elorina, Contrada Pantanelli
Siracusa, Sicily, (PA) 97100, Italy
Tel: (0931) 69 057, Fax: (0931) 68 561
10 Rooms, Double: €190–€280
Closed: Jan 15 to Feb 14, Credit cards: all major
5 km S of Siracusa
Region: Sicily, Michelin Map: 565

Although often missed by tourists, Syracuse has a fascinating ancient center located on the island of Ortigia, where the Greeks founded the city of Siracusa. However, you hardly realize you are on an island since it is linked to the modern town by just a short bridge. This historic old part of Siracusa is definitely where you want to be and, without a doubt, the Grand Hotel Ortigia Siracusa is the place you want to stay. The hotel has a ideal setting: across the street from the dock where colorful fishing boats are pulled up and just a pleasant stroll away from the beautiful Duomo, the Piazza Archimede, and the Temple of Apollo. The Grand Hotel Siracusa, housed in a handsome yellow building with white trim, has a pleasing old-world ambiance. Inside, you are greeted by an old-fashioned elegance with marble columns, marble floors, high ceilings, potted plants, portraits on the walls, huge Venetian-glass chandeliers, and accents of antique furniture. The bedrooms are tastefully decorated with traditional-style furniture, pretty, muted wallpapers, and color-coordinating bedspreads and draperies. Ask for one of the rooms with a view to the sea—it is fun to look out your window and watch the fishing boats reflecting in the clear blue water. A glass-enclosed elevator takes you up to the attractive rooftop restaurant where you dine romantically in front of walls of windows overlooking the waterfront and the town.

❄ ☕ 🏂 ☕ 💳 ☎ 🛗 @ W Ⓨ P 🍽 ⚓ ⚓ ⚓ 🍇

GRAND HOTEL ORTIGIA SIRACUSA
Manager: Andrea Corso
Viale Mazzini, 12
Siracusa, Sicily, (SR) 96100, Italy
Tel: (0931) 46 46 00, Fax: (0931) 46 46 11
58 Rooms, Double: €230–€298
Open: all year, Credit cards: all major
On the eastern coast of Sicily
Region: Sicily, Michelin Map: 565

What a sense of impending grandeur you experience as you wait for the giant iron gates of the Villa Cortine Palace to swing open. Inside, the road winds and curves impressively past fountains and statues, flower gardens and mighty trees, until it reaches the summit where the Villa Cortine Palace majestically reigns. This beautifully situated villa has been expanded so that it now boasts a new section, which appears to have more than doubled the original size. Throughout the hotel, the guestrooms are undergoing well-deserved renovation. The newly upgraded rooms have much more charm than those that still retain the rather dated rattan furniture. Some of the rooms are in the original part of the villa, which is to the left as you enter the lobby. This section displays a truly old-world grandeur with incredibly ornate furniture, soaring ceilings, and stunning paintings. What leaves absolutely nothing to be improved upon are the gardens—they are awe-inspiring. The villa is surrounded by graveled walkways that wind in and out amongst the fountains, ponds, statues, and glorious rose gardens, all overlooking the lovely Lake Garda. A path leads down to the lake where there is a private pier for swimming. The hotel also has a swimming pool and tennis court.

VILLA CORTINE PALACE HOTEL
Manager: Roberto Cappelletto
Lake Garda
Sirmione, (BS) 25019, Italy
Tel: (030) 99 05 890, Fax: (030) 91 63 90
48 Rooms, Double: €460–€640
6 Suites: €640–€680
Minimum Stay Required: 3 nights
Open: Mar 28 to Oct 15, Credit cards: all major
On Lake Garda, 35 km W of Verona
Region: Lombardy, Michelin Map: 561

Located about an hour's drive south of Milan's Linate airport, the Locanda del Lupo makes a convenient stop if you plan to drive directly south toward Florence. Soragna is a sleepy little town in the countryside whose main point of interest is a walled, medieval fortress. Around the central plaza, buildings of great character are interspersed with modern construction. The Locanda del Lupo, built in the 18th century by the noble Meli Lupi family, is just a block off the plaza and easy to find. The inn is best known as a gourmet restaurant: there is a series of beautiful dining rooms with gleaming copper hanging from whitewashed walls, terracotta floors, dark-beamed ceilings, antique clocks, and 17th-century oil paintings. To the left of the reception area is a cozy bar and, beyond, a formal living room furnished in antiques. A flight of stairs leads to the guestrooms whose old-world ambiance is enhanced by beamed ceilings, tiled floors, and thick walls. Each bedroom is individually decorated and exudes a refined, country-house atmosphere. Authentic antique furnishings (including fine wooden chests and wrought-iron bedsteads) impart a feeling of quality. *Directions:* From the Milan-Bologna A1 expressway, take the Fidenza exit and follow signs to Soragna. Go to the central square (Piazza Garibaldi) where you find Via Garibaldi running off the square.

❄ 🍴 ☕ CREDIT ☎ 🐕 🛗 @ W Y P 🍴 🖼 ⚓ 👪 🏃 🐎 🍇

LOCANDA DEL LUPO
Manager: Enrico Dioni
Via Garibaldi, 64
Soragna, (PR) 43019, Italy
Tel: (0524) 59 71 00, Fax: (0524) 59 70 66
46 Rooms, Double: €114–€139*
1 Suite: €169–€210*
*Breakfast not included: €8
Open: all year, Credit cards: all major
100 km S of Milan, 118 km N of Bologna
Region: Emilia-Romagna, Michelin Map: 562

If the idea of staying in an extraordinary medieval fortress that crowns a spectacular hilltown far off the beaten path appeals, you will fall in love with the Hotel della Fortezza—it is an absolute jewel. This tiny hotel is in a splendid part of Tuscany called Maremma, little known to the casual tourist, but well worth exploration. There are many walled villages in the hills that lie between Orvieto and the coast, all beckoning you to drive within their walls, but one of the most beautiful of all is Sorano. The town is nestled into a pocket of the hill, a jumble of ancient stone and stucco buildings that form a striking architectural design, and crowning the top of the town is the imposing Orsini Fortress. You enter through an impressive gate, cross a stone bridge over what was once a moat, then pass through a tower gate and into the fortress where you find the hotel. This is not a deluxe hotel nor does it pretend to be, but the interior is extremely appealing, with the guestrooms decorated with great taste, appropriate to the charm of the building. Almost all of the bedrooms have a breathtaking view of the town and beyond to the densely wooded hills. Number 16 is an especially attractive corner room, larger than most, with handsome antique headboards and windows on two sides. However, even the smaller rooms have sensational views. This area is well known for its many walking trails. *Directions:* In Sorano, look for signs to the Fortezza Orsini.

HOTEL DELLA FORTEZZA
Manager: Luciano Caruso
Piazza Cairoli, 5
Sorano, (GR) 58010, Italy
Tel: (0564) 63 20 10, Fax: (0564) 63 32 09
15 Rooms, Double: €120–€200
Closed: Jan & Feb, Credit cards: all major
160 km NW of Rome
Region: Tuscany, Michelin Map: 563

Perched on a bluff with a sweeping view of the sea, the deluxe Grand Hotel Excelsior Vittoria exudes a charming, refined, old world grandeur. Since the hotel was built in 1834, it has been continuously owned by the Fiorentino family, who are still involved with the day by day management, making this property especially outstanding. The owner's wife, Lidia Fiorentino, personally oversees the decorating, carefully blending the finest of modern amenities without sacrificing the appealing antique ambiance. The hotel is composed of three villas overlooking the sea that are enhanced by a lovely 5-acre garden, complete with orange grove and swimming pool—the setting is so tranquil that you would hardly know you are in the heart of Sorrento. A large terrace at the edge of the bluff is a favorite place for guests to relax, soaking in the beautiful view and watching the action of the ferry boats which are constantly gliding in and out of the Marina Piccola—the harbor just below the hotel. There are two dining rooms. A popular choice on balmy evenings is the Bosquet where guests dine on the terrace under the stars with a splendid view of the Bay of Naples. The most treasured restaurant is the opulent Vittoria, a stunning dining room with a spectacular frescoed ceiling. The tradition of frescoed ceilings and walls has been nurtured with a resident artist who is constantly at work. Guests can be pampered at the hotel's luxurious spa.

GRAND HOTEL EXCELSIOR VITTORIA
Owner: Fiorentino family
Piazza Torquato Tasso, 34
Sorrento, (NA) 80067, Italy
Tel: (081) 87 77 111, Fax: (081) 87 71 206
98 Rooms, Double: €275–€550
23 Suites: €485–€1900
Open: all year, Credit cards: all major
History Traveller
48 km S of Naples, 250 km S of Rome
Region: Campania, Michelin Map: 564

La Taverna Etrusca is in an intriguing, picturesque, little-known part of Tuscany called Maremma, where you find ancient towns with very old stone houses, wrapped by dense green woodlands, tucked into the landscape. Throughout this region, hiking, biking, and horseback riding are popular ways to discover the countryside. Etruscan ruins are found everywhere, making this an especially interesting area to explore. This property's emphasis is not as a hotel, but rather as a restaurant. It's housed in a rustic stone building situated in the center of a tiny village that seems to be suspended in time. The restaurant, which specializes in traditional Tuscan and Maremman dishes, faces onto a tiny piazza where a stone church, topped by a whimsical bell tower, sits at one end. Within, the restaurant abounds with medieval allure. High ceilings are enhanced by wood beams and huge stone archways divide the room into romantic dining areas. When the weather is mild, meals are also served outside on the terrace. Many dining guests never realize that there are also a few hotel rooms upstairs. These are small and simply decorated, but are very nice for the price. *Directions:* Located in the center of the village, facing the piazza.

LA TAVERNA ETRUSCA
Manager: Luciano Caruso
Piazza del Pretorio 16
Sovana, (GR) 58010, Italy
Tel: (0564) 61 61 83, Fax: (0564) 61 41 93
7 Rooms, Double: €90–€130
Restaurant closed Wednesdays
Closed: Jan & Feb, Credit cards: all major
95 km SE of Siena
Region: Tuscany, Michelin Map: 563

It was love at first sight as I drove up the long graveled road through forest and vineyard and suddenly caught my first glimpse of the Borgo Pretale, a tiny cluster of weathered stone buildings nestled next to their medieval watchtower. My first impression was more than justified—this small inn is truly paradise. There are absolute serenity and beauty here with nothing to mar the perfection. Civilization seems far away as the eye stretches over a glorious vista of rolling hills forested with oaks, juniper, and laurel, interspersed with square patches of vineyards. But although this small village is seemingly remote, it is only a short drive south of Siena, thus a perfect hideaway from which to enjoy the magic of Tuscany. The rooms in the tower are showplaces of fine country antiques and splendid designer fabrics, blended together with the artful eye of a skilled decorator. Every piece is selected to create a sophisticated yet rustic elegance. The rooms in the surrounding cottages are furnished in a more "country" style, though maintaining standards of elegance and comfort. The lounge beckons guests to linger after dinner by the roaring fire. A path leads to a groomed tennis court and farther on to a swimming pool on a hillside terrace. NOTE: The closest town on most maps is Rosia, which is about 5 kilometers southeast of Borgo Pretale. To reach the hotel, go through Rosia and follow signs to Borgo Pretale.

BORGO PRETALE
Manager: Daniele Rizzardini
Sovicille, (SI) 53018, Italy
Tel: (0577) 34 54 01, Fax: (0577) 34 56 25
27 Rooms, Double: €205–€215
7 Suites: €235
Open: Apr to Nov, Credit cards: all major
18 km SW of Siena on Rte 73
Region: Tuscany, Michelin Map: 563

As you twist up the steep, narrow road from Spoleto toward Monteluco, you will see on your left an appealing, ochre-colored villa. The setting looks so fabulous that you will hope this is your hotel. It is, and you won't be disappointed. The Eremo delle Grazie is an astounding property—truly a living museum, with history simply oozing from every nook and cranny. The property has been the home of the Lalli family for many years, but its roots hark back to the 5th century when a small grotto where religious hermits came to live occupied the site. The grotto still exists, but now serves as a wine cellar behind the bar. From its humble beginnings the importance of this grotto grew, becoming so well known that one of Italy's important cardinals, Camillo Cybo, lived here (his bedroom is now one of the guestrooms). The cardinal enjoyed his comfort so instead of residing in the small damp grotto, he slept in a lovely bedroom, which he had painted to look like a cave. One of my favorite places in Eremo delle Grazie is the tiny, incredibly beautiful, vaulted chapel with beautifully preserved 15th-century paintings of the life of Mary. Another favorite is the splendid terrace with a sweeping view of the glorious Umbrian landscape. According to Signor Lalli, Michelangelo was once a guest here. In his letter to Vasari, Michelangelo wrote that he left part of his heart at Eremo delle Grazie—as you will, too.

EREMO DELLE GRAZIE
Owner: Professor Pio Lalli
Spoleto, Monteluco, (PG) 06049, Italy
Tel: (0743) 49 624, Fax: (0743) 49 650
6 Rooms, Double: €190–€210
4 Suites: €230–€320
Open: all year, Credit cards: all major
Abitare La Storia
3.5 km E of Spoleto, 124 km N of Rome
Region: Umbria, Michelin Map: 563

The walled hill town of Spoleto is a must on any trip to Umbria. What Spoleto has that is so outstanding is its Bridge of Towers (Ponte delle Torri), an absolutely awesome feat of engineering. Built in the 13th century on the foundations of an old Roman aqueduct, this bridge, spanning a vast crevasse, is supported by ten Gothic arches that soar into the sky. The Hotel Gattapone (a mustard-yellow building with dark-green shutters) is built into the hillside and provides a box-seat location to admire this architectural masterpiece. As you enter, there is a cozy reception area. To the left is a bright, sunny lounge with modern black-leather sofas, a long black-leather bar, very pretty deep-blue walls, large pots of green plants, an antique grandfather clock, and, best of all, an entire wall of glass which provides a bird's-eye view of the bridge. To the right of the reception area, steps sweep down to another bar and lounge where breakfast is served. This room is even more starkly modern, with deep-red wall coverings. The newer wing of the hotel houses the superior-category bedrooms, each with a sitting area and large view windows. In the original section of the hotel the bedrooms are smaller, but also very attractive and every one has a view. Although most of the hotels in this guide have more of an antique ambiance, the Gattapone is highly recommended—a special hotel offering great warmth of welcome and superb vistas.

HOTEL GATTAPONE
Owner: Dr. Pier Hanke Giulio
Via del Ponte, 6
Spoleto, (PG) 06049, Italy
Tel: (0743) 22 34 47, Fax: (0743) 22 34 48
15 Rooms, Double: €140–€230
Open: all year, Credit cards: all major
130 km N of Rome, 48 km S of Assisi
Region: Umbria, Michelin Map: 563

Le Logge di Silvignano, a stunning castle of creamy-beige stone, embraces one side of a tiny 12th-century village with a population of about 85 people tucked high in the hills north of Spoleto. It is not surprising to learn the building was originally a strategic lookout to guard against enemy attack since the setting is breathtaking, with a sweeping view of the narrow valley far below. Although termed a "castle" the structure is not in the least foreboding, but rather a splendid edifice with a handsome, open, arched gallery supported by ornately carved, octagonal pillars stretching across the front. There are six beautiful, individually decorated suites, all extremely attractive with medieval stone floors accenting handsome furniture which is either antique or handcrafted locally of wood or wrought iron. The fine bed linens and fabrics are woven locally from the Montefalco looms. A huge terrace, magically transformed into a romantic, manicured garden enhanced by fragrant, colorful roses, spreads in front of the castle to the edge of the bluff. Although Le Logge would be a winner by any standards, it is the genuine warmth and charm of your lovely hosts that make a stay here so outstanding. For dinner, guests can prepare a light meal in their own kitchenette or dine in a local restaurant. The hotel has a beautiful pool with views of the valley and a club house where guests can relax or dine upon reservation. *Directions:* Ask for detailed driving instructions.

LE LOGGE DI SILVIGNANO
Owners: Diana & Alberto Araimo
Frazione Silvignano, 14
Spoleto, (PG) 06049, Italy
Tel: (0743) 27 40 98, Fax: (0473) 27 05 18
5 Rooms, Double: €120–€180
1 Apartment: €600 weekly
Closed: Nov 10 to Mar 31, Credit cards: all major
130 km N of Rome, 35 km S of Assisi
Region: Umbria, Michelin Map: 563

Spoleto is always a favorite with tourists, not only during the music festival (end of June until mid-July), but throughout the year. Due to its popularity, there used to be a shortage of charming places to stay within the walled city but happily that problem was solved with the opening of the Hotel San Luca in 1995. The family-owned San Luca is a splendid small hotel—very polished, very sophisticated, yet exuding great personal warmth and friendliness. Built within a 19th-century tannery, the hotel (which is painted yellow and has a traditional red-tiled roof) only hints at its past. The renovation has been so extensive that much of what you see today is of new construction, but the ambiance is old world. From the moment you enter, there is a fresh, luminous atmosphere with pastel walls reflecting light streaming in through large arched windows opening onto a central courtyard. The reception lounge is especially appealing, with comfortable chairs upholstered in cheerful peach fabric grouped around a large fireplace and a few choice antiques adding greatly to the homelike feeling. A pair of canaries in an antique birdcage repeats the color scheme. The spacious, pastel-colored, completely soundproofed guestrooms are all equally attractive and well equipped with lots of closets, excellent lighting, and large, exceptionally modern bathrooms. And the surprise is that the price for such high quality is amazingly low.

❄ ☕ ✀ ☕ 🖩 ☎ 🏠 ⛲ @ W Ⓨ P 🚭 🖼 🔔 🐾 ♿ 🚶 🐎 ⛺

HOTEL SAN LUCA
Manager: Daniela Zuccari
Via Interna delle Mura, 21
Spoleto, (PG) 06049, Italy
Tel: (0743) 22 33 99, Fax: (0743) 22 38 00
33 Rooms, Double: €110–€240
2 Suites: €210–€300
Open: all year, Credit cards: all major
In historic city center
130 km N of Rome, 48 km S of Assisi
Region: Umbria, Michelin Map: 563

Italy abounds with romantic places to stay, but none can surpass the outstanding beauty of the Villa Milani. This stunning property, on a hill overlooking Spoleto, just about has it all: enchanting architecture, breathtaking 360-degree view, splendid decor, gorgeous antiques, and owners who shower their guests with kindness. The villa was built in 1880 by one of Rome's most famous architects, Giovanni Battista Milani, the grandfather of your hostess Giovanna Milani Capobianchi. Milani obviously poured both his talent and heart into his countryside retreat, embellishing his home with splendid ceilings, fireplaces, columns, marble statues, romantic gardens, and ancient Roman artifacts. The result is splendid. The current owners lived for many years in Rome then changed their lifestyle completely and moved to Spoleto, where they tenderly restored the home to its original splendor, adding beautiful bathrooms to each bedroom and a fantastic pool, perched on a terrace looking out to the soft wooded hills of Umbria. Giovanna must have inherited some of her grandfather's talent, for she has decorated each room to perfection. The smallest room is also the most romantic, located in the tower with windows on four sides. *Directions:* On S.S.3, coming from the north turn right at the second exit; while coming from the south, turn left at the first exit (opposite the Monteluco road). At the first intersection turn left and go uphill following signs to the villa.

VILLA MILANI
Owners: Giovanna & Luigi Capobianchi
Localita Colle Attivoli, 4
Spoleto, (PG) 06049, Italy
Tel: (0743) 22 50 56, Fax: (0743) 49 824
11 Rooms, Double: €190–€640
Meals for hotel guests only
Open: all year, Credit cards: all major
3 km E of Spoleto, 124 km N of Rome
Region: Umbria, Michelin Map: 563

With a glorious, unobstructed view to the sea, the Hotel Belvedere can definitely lay claim to one of the prime positions in the picturesque town of Taormina. Of course this location is not just luck because, undoubtedly, the site was carefully chosen when the Belvedere (one of the first hotels in town) was constructed at the turn of the last century. The gentleman who originally built the hotel is the grandfather of the present owners—a continuity that adds greatly to the care and warmth of welcome given to the guests. From first glance, the hotel is immediately appealing—a pale ochre-colored villa laced with ivy and accented by wrought-iron balconies. Flowers abound on the walkways and a romantic garden terraces down below the hotel, providing quiet shady nooks for guests to enjoy the view. On one of the lower terraces, a large swimming pool is practically hidden by a lush blanket of shrubs, shade trees, and towering palms. This cool oasis is a favorite gathering spot for guests, and although there is no formal restaurant, light refreshments including pasta, sandwiches, and cold drinks are available by the pool. The lounges of the hotel are pleasantly decorated with contemporary furniture accented by some family antiques. The guestrooms are modern, with built-in beds. However, it is not the decor that captures the hearts of guests who return each year, but rather the friendliness of the staff, the gorgeous gardens, and superb setting.

❄ ☕ ⚷ [CREDIT] ☎ 🐾 ♿ @ P 🍴 🚭 ≈ 🖼 ♿ ⛵ 🏌 👤 🐴 🏄

HOTEL BELVEDERE
Owners: Serena & Christian Pecaut
Via Bagnoli Croci, 79
Taormina, Sicily, (ME) 98039, Italy
Tel: (0942) 23 791, Fax: (0942) 62 58 30
47 Rooms, Double: €110–€380
Poolside snack bar open daily
Open: mid-Mar to Nov, Credit cards: MC, VS
On the eastern coast of Sicily
Region: Sicily, Michelin Map: 565

There is no doubt that the Timeo is the shining star of Taormina. Its location alone is worth special mention, being positioned just under the main attraction of Taormina's historical center, the Greek-Roman amphitheater, dramatically illuminated at night. Since there is no street traffic it is a particularly peaceful spot as well. The discreet entrance and reception lead to the veranda living room, with parquet floors and highlighted by selected antiques. A cozy winter-garden bar with painted trellis is found off a long hallway lined with windows leading to the restaurant. Two contrasting dining rooms, one with arches and original dark mahogany panels and the other luminous and airy with surrounding full-length windows, are where exquisite meals based on fresh seafood are served. The true center of the hotel is the expansive terrace which all the common rooms overlook, divided into outdoor dining area and sitting areas with plump wicker sofas from which to enjoy the breathtaking sea views. An elegant, neoclassical style prevails throughout the bedrooms, which are situated above and below the main building and in the adjacent peach-colored villa, most with terraces or balconies. A shuttle to a private beach is provided. Since our last visit the hotel restored an annex building now called the Villa Flora which allowed them to add 30 rooms. *Directions:* Follow signs to the Teatro Greco—the hotel is on the way.

❄ ☕ ☕ 💳 🏠 ☎ 🐕 ♿ 🍴 @ W Y P 🍴 ✱ 🏖 ⚓ ✈ 🎋 🐎 ⚓

GRAND HOTEL TIMEO
Manager: Pierangelo Fondina
Via Teatro Greco, 59
Taormina, Sicily, (ME) 98039, Italy
Tel: (0942) 23 801, Fax: (0942) 62 85 01
43 Rooms, Double: €340–€580
40 Suites: €427–€1735
Open: all year, Credit cards: all major
On the eastern coast of Sicily
Region: Sicily, Michelin Map: 565

After a partial facelift, the San Domenico Palace, one of Italy's most famous historic hotels and a Karen Brown favorite in the past, has returned to the guide after a four years' absence during which it changed hands several times. It remains one of the most classic hotels in Italy, and we welcome it back. The monumental 15th-century monastery was converted into a hotel in the late 1800s and has catered to many illustrious guests for over a century. It's mix of various epochs is exemplified in the ancient 17th-century entrance and courtyard and the Renaissance inner cloister. 105 guestrooms are well-distributed between the main building; "antico convento", originally where the monks' cells were; and the noble style villa, "grand hotel", where high-ceilinged rooms on the top floor have large terraces. Guestrooms are tastefully appointed in warm mustard and burgundy tones with grand antiques and face out to the sea and majestic Etna volcano. The formal Italian gardens are marvelous—overflowing with rare flowers of every color, climbing bougainvillea vines, and palm trees. A swimming pool area where light lunches are served is located at the very back of the garden. Among the many common rooms is a cozy bar with fireplace (originally the monks' refectory) Les Bougainvillèes Restaurant offering traditional and Sicilian cuisine, and Principe Cerami, the hotel's gourmet restaurant which has been awarded one Michelin star. *Directions:* In the center of Taormina.

SAN DOMENICO PALACE HOTEL
Manager: Paolo Moreggio
Piazza San Domenico, 5
Taormina, Sicily, (ME) 98039, Italy
Tel & Fax: (0942) 61 31 11
105 Rooms, Double: €290–€900
7 Suites: €630–€2300
Open: all year, Credit cards: all major
On the eastern coast of Sicily
Region: Sicily, Michelin Map: 565

With the success of their hotel Villa Ducale, Rosaria and Andrea Quartucci did not hesitate to open a second accommodation right in the center of town. The 1920s castle-like stone villa overlooking the sea, underwent an ambitious restoration in 2007. Passionate travelers themselves, Andrea and Rosaria, with a flair for decorating and details, compiled a list of their own personal preferences and transferred their ideas into reality at Villa Carlotta. The main reception area leads down a hall to the first set of rooms, all with terraces and sea views, many amenities, and a soft contemporary style enhanced by the warm color schemes selected for each individual room. On the opposite side of the hall is a large tavern with evidence of the stone Byzantine catacombs recently discovered, while a rear door offers access to the surrounding gardens and swimming pool. Perched on the top floor is the veranda rooftop breakfast room with spectacular views and the same super buffet breakfast as the Villa Ducale, unanimously proclaimed the best in town. Besides the many interesting sights in Taormina (10 min walk), suggested by the personable staff, a shuttle is available to the private beach. *Directions:* Exit at Taormina from the autostrada A18. After the toll station keep to your right in the direction of Taormina Mazzaro and follow the coastal road for 2.5 km. Turn right for Taormina centro onto Via Luigi Pirandello. After 2 km you'll see the Villa entrance.

VILLA CARLOTTA
Owners: Rosaria & Andrea Quartucci
Via Pirandello 81
Taormina, Sicily, (ME) 98039, Italy
Tel: (0942) 62 60 58, Fax: (0942) 23 732
23 Rooms, Double: €150–€300
5 Suites: €250–€500
Open: all year, Credit cards: all major
Center of Taormina
Region: Sicily, Michelin Map: 565

The Villa Ducale's superlative reputation has been earned thanks to the passionate hospitality of its owners, Rosaria and Andrea Quartucci. Originally Rosaria's childhood home, its 15 romantically-styled rooms and suites are within two houses, divided by the street. A winding road takes you up past the center of town to a residential area that offers memorable views. If you are able to tear yourselves away from Villa Ducale's comfortable, very attractive rooms (each appointed with Sicilian solar color palette, local artisan work, antiques, and fine linens) you will be rewarded with a sumptuous buffet breakfast on the flower-laden terrace featuring a variety of home-prepared specialties to satisfy any taste. Try to concentrate on this feast while gazing over the steep hillside sweeping down to the open sea and back up to the towering Etna volcano looming to the right. Most rooms have a terrace and all have sea-views of either the northern or southern coastline. The very friendly staff assists with the many convenient services offered, including free Internet access, private mini van shuttle to the town center or down to the private beach. Don't miss a chance to walk down to town on the walking path with head-spinning views right over the sea, Teatro Greco, and more. *Directions:* Exit at Taormina from autostrada A18. Follow 2 km for center city, and continue towards Castelmola until you see the yellow villa on the left-hand side of the road.

VILLA DUCALE
Owners: Rosaria & Andrea Quartucci
Via Leonardo da Vinci, 60
Taormina, Sicily, (ME) , Italy
Tel: (0942) 28 153, Fax: (0942) 28 710
12 Rooms, Double: €130–€270
5 Suites: €250–€450
Open: all year, Credit cards: all major
1 km from center of Taormina
Region: Sicily, Michelin Map: 565

The Villa Sant'Andrea is a four-star deluxe hotel snuggled along a tiny bay that lies below Taormina, our favorite, very old, Sicilian town, which has a breathtaking position on a cliff above the sea. A cable car (within an easy walk of the hotel) can swiftly whisk you up the hill to Taormina to see its splendid Greek theater, browse through the quaint streets, or have lunch in a trattoria. Then, when your excursion is over, you can take the cable car back to the tranquility of the beautiful Villa Sant'Andrea, which exudes the ambiance of an English home—which is not surprising as the hotel was originally built in 1830 as a private residence for a wealthy English family. Of course, the building has been added onto over the years, but it still has an intimate appeal. Commanding a superb waterfront setting, the villa is built in levels that step down the hill, ending right on a private beach where, surrounded by palm and banana trees, the hotel has its own section with lounge chairs reserved exclusively for guests. On a level just above the beach there is a charming terrace—a favorite nook for breakfast. The decor of the public rooms has a refined, homelike elegance with many lovely antiques and period paintings. Good taste also prevails in the guestrooms, some of which have a lovely view of the sea, enhanced by the dramatic rocks that jut above the clear blue waters. *Directions:* On S114, the road that runs along the sea below Taormina. Exit at Taormina and follow 5 km to Mazzaro.

VILLA SANT'ANDREA
Manager: Giovanni Nastasi
Via Nazionale, 137
Taormina, Sicily, (ME) 98030, Italy
Tel: (0942) 23 125, Fax: (0942) 24 838
78 Rooms, Double: €248–€462
7 Suites: €400–€730
Open: Apr 7 to Nov 3, Credit cards: all major
On the eastern coast of Sicily
Region: Sicily, Michelin Map: 565

The road to the Pensione Stefaner winds up a tiny mountain valley in the heart of the Dolomites. The road is spectacular. As we rounded the last curve before San Cipriano (St. Zyprian), the valley opened up and there spread before us was a sweeping vista of majestically soaring mountains. Across soft-green meadows painted with wildflowers and dotted with tiny farm chalets soared an incredible saw-toothed range of gigantic peaks. A tiny church with a pretty steeple added the final touch of perfection to the already idyllic scene. There are many places to stay in this region—none are glamorous resorts, but generally small, family-run pensions. One of our favorites is the Pensione Stefaner, an attractive, chalet-style hotel with flower-laden balconies—easily found as it is on the main highway through town. There is a smattering of antiques, but most of the furniture is new. The hotel is efficiently and warmly managed by the attractive Villgrattner family. Mathilde is a gracious hostess and her husband Georg creates wonderful home-cooked meals for the guests (everyone also loves their friendly German Shepherd). The simple bedrooms (very '60s in their decor) all have en suite shower rooms, and some have balconies with mountain views. *Directions:* From the Verona-Brennero autostrada, exit at Bolzano Nord and follow signs for Tires. Go through town to San Cipriano and the Pensione Stefaner is on your left.

PENSIONE STEFANER
Owners: Mathilde & Georg Villgrattner
(San Cipriano)
Tires, (BZ) 39050, Italy
Tel: (0471) 64 21 75, Fax: (0471) 64 23 02
18 Rooms, Double: €98–€132*
*Includes breakfast & dinner
Meals for hotel guests only
Closed: mid-Nov to mid-Dec, Credit cards: VS
NE Italy in Dolomites, 17 km E of Bolzano
Region: Trentino-Alto Adige, Michelin Map: 562

Crowning the top of a small hill near the enchanting walled village of Todi (which you can see in the distance), the Relais Todini has a breathtaking, 360-degree view of wooded hills, soft valleys, manicured fields, vineyards, and tiny villages. You will be captivated at first sight of this charming, 14th-century stone hotel with architectural roots going back to the Etruscan-Roman period. Although built of rustic, tan-colored stone, there is nothing rustic about this hotel. From the moment you walk through the manicured gardens and into the beautiful frescoed lobby, you are surrounded by elegance and luxury. You register at an intimate table rather than a hotel-like counter before being shown to your room. All the guestrooms are beautifully decorated and the suites are especially opulent, with fine antique furniture and lush fabrics. The public rooms are also handsomely furnished, particularly the dining room with its tall-back chairs upholstered in tapestry and charming chandeliers embellished with clusters of grapes. One wall has windows of glass that open out to a terrace and beyond to a large swimming pool. On the estate tennis, biking, walking, swimming and a gorgeous health and body center with Turkish baths are just a few of the options available to guests. *Directions:* From Rome, take the A1 north, exit at Orte. Follow E45 toward Perugia. Exit at Casigliano-Collevalenza and follow signs toward Todi. Turn left Rosceto Scalo to the hotel.

RELAIS TODINI
Manager: Clementi Paolo
Collevalenza
Todi, (PG) 06050, Italy
Tel: (075) 88 75 21, Fax: (075) 88 71 82
12 Rooms, Double: €180–€360
Restaurant open Thu to Sun
Open: all year, Credit cards: all major
7 km SE of Todi, 45 km S of Perugia
Region: Umbria, Michelin Map: 563

The elegant Le Tre Vaselle is located in Torgiano, a small wine village not far from Assisi. The interior reflects the ambiance of a graceful country manor with sophisticated furnishings and exquisite taste displayed in every detail. The hotel belongs to the Lungarotti family who are famous for their production of superb wines and who own all of the vineyards surrounding Torgiano for as far as the eye can see. Excellent meals, accompanied by fine Lungarotti wines, are served in the beautiful dining room. The guestrooms are attractively decorated and offer every amenity of a deluxe hotel, including wireless Internet. Le Tre Vaselle also has outstanding conference rooms furnished in antiques with adjacent dining rooms. The Lungarotti family has thought of everything—to keep the wives happy while their husbands are in meetings, with a new spa and cooking classes are sometimes offered. Other diversions include an outdoor swimming pool, an indoor pool with whirlpool, a sauna, a gym, and even a small outdoor amphitheater. The Lungarottis also have a private wine museum that would be a masterpiece anywhere in the world. Not only do they have an incredible and comprehensive collection of anything pertaining to wine throughout the ages, but the display is a work of art. If you are interested in the production of wine, the museum alone would be worth a detour to Le Tre Vaselle. *Directions:* The hotel is well marked in the center of town.

❄ ☕ ⚗ ☕ 💳 ☎ 🛗 🏋 @ W ⚘ P 🍴 ❦ ≈ 🛥 🏹 🐎 ❦

LE TRE VASELLE
Owner: Lungarotti family
Via Garibaldi, 48
Torgiano, (PG) 06089, Italy
Tel: (075) 98 80 447, Fax: (075) 98 80 214
60 Rooms, Double: €215–€240
13 Suites: €280
Open: all year, Credit cards: all major
17 km SW of Assisi, 158 km N of Rome
Region: Umbria, Michelin Map: 563

The Hotel Gardesana, housed within a grand 15th-century building, is a treasure: an intimate, family-managed, lakeside hotel, romantically snuggled above the colorful inner harbor of Torri del Benaco, a delightful fishing village which is so incredibly picturesque that it looks like a stage set. The four-story, rich-salmon-colored building has an arched portico stretching across the front and a rustic terracotta roof. You step inside into a pleasingly decorated lounge and reception accented by antiques and bouquets of fresh flowers. One floor up is the dining room with doors opening onto a wisteria-clad terrace, which looks across the tiny harbor with its colorful bobbing boats reflecting in the water to the impressive turreted walls of the medieval castle. The scene oozes romance but, best of all, the food is superb (the restaurant has earned many honors). The comfortable guestrooms are decorated in a traditional style and, like the rest of the hotel, reflect the refined good taste of the owners. All of the bedrooms are nice with new marble bathrooms, but request one with a view of either the harbor or the lake and, if you want to really splurge, see if one of the rooms with a balcony is available. The Hotel Gardesana is not an opulent, super-deluxe hotel, but is instead a wonderful, friendly place to stay in one of Italy's quaintest towns. *Directions:* In the center of Torri del Benaco on the west side of Lake Garda.

HOTEL GARDESANA
Owners: Annalisa & Giuseppe Lorenzini
Piazza Calderini, 20
Torri del Benaco, Lake Garda, (VR) 37010, Italy
Tel: (045) 72 25 411, Fax: (045) 72 25 771
34 Rooms, Double: €100–€170
Minimum Stay Required: 3
Closed: Nov, Credit cards: all major
150 km W of Venice, 73 km S of Trento
Region: Veneto, Michelin Map: 562

The stunning Hotel Panta Rei opened in the summer of 2004 on the splendid Golfo di Santa Eufemia. It is not surprising the hotel is so outstanding, as it was designed by the talented architect, Adolfo Salabé, who also built and owns two other hotels: the Porto Pirgos (just a few kilometers away) and the Borgo Paraelios (just north of Rome). Each of these three hotels has its unique personality, yet each exudes the same fine quality and awesome décor throughout. The Hotel Panta Rei is snuggled on a pristine, pine-dotted hillside that drops steeply down to the sea. A path winds through the forest down to the waterfront. You come first to an open-air restaurant and bar where guests dine with a glorious view. A swimming pool nestles in the heart of the property. Some of the guestrooms overlook the swimming pool. These are in pastel-hued buildings that reflect the style of the local fishermen's cottages. The remaining guestrooms, tucked amongst the pines below the swimming pool, are not in colorfully painted buildings like the others, but instead have exteriors that are neutral in tone, and blend so cleverly into the woods that they are almost invisible from below. These are my favorites because you feel like you are perched in a birdhouse, high in the trees. All of the guestrooms have large windows and doors opening onto view terraces or decks. All are furnished in antiques, appropriate in ambiance to a rustic fisherman's home.

❄ ☕ ✂ CREDIT ☎ ♈ P ⫪ ≈ 🖼 ⚓ 🧍 🏇 🚣

HOTEL PANTA REI
Owner: Adolfo Salabé
Località: Marina di San Nicola
Parghelia, Tropea, (CZ) 89861, Italy
Tel: (0963) 60 00 00, Fax: (0963) 60 17 21
21 Rooms, Double: €180–€290*
*Includes breakfast & dinner á la carte
Open: May to Oct, Credit cards: all major
4 km E of Tropea, Southern Italy-near tip of toe
Region: Calabria, Michelin Map: 564

When the Porto Pirgos first opened its doors to guests in 1999, it redefined the meaning of luxury. A refined, intimate elegance reigns supreme, with cozy nooks, comfortable chairs, soft lighting, awesome antiques, bouquets of fresh flowers, wrought-iron fixtures, beamed ceilings, thick walls, oil paintings, gorgeous antiques, and richly hued Oriental carpets accenting antique terracotta floors. Adding to the romance are the sea views framed by every window. You cannot help falling in love with this superb small hotel built on a slope of a hill that stretches down to a pristine white-sand beach gently lapped by the crystal sea. Built upon the foundations of a private villa, the hotel today continues to exude the ambiance of an exquisite, fine home. The guestrooms are also furnished with antiques and, like the rest of the hotel, everything is of the highest quality and good taste. A large swimming pool is set in the garden by the hotel and a second pool nestles under towering pine trees next to the beach. Breakfast and dinner are included in the price of the room and not only is the food exceptionally delicious, but the setting is outstanding. The main dining room has a stunning mosaic floor that looks as if it came right out of an old Roman villa. When the weather is balmy, guests eat out on the terrace where, as the sun sets and the stars begin to appear, you can see the volcano of Stromboli on the horizon.

PORTO PIRGOS
Manager: Caterina Messina
Localita: Marina di Bordila
Parghelia
Tropea, (VV) 89861, Italy
Tel: (0963) 60 03 51, Fax: (0963) 60 06 90
18 Rooms, Double: €280–€520
4 Suites: €308–€640
Open: mid-May to Oct, Credit cards: all major
5 km E of Tropea, Southern Italy–near tip of toe
Region: Calabria, Michelin Map: 564

Although Marco Tonazzi (a professional skier for 20 years) lives in Vail, Colorado, with his beautiful wife and two little girls, he frequently returns to the hamlet of Valbruna in to the northeast corner of Italy where he learned to ski as a child. He so loved this picturesque, traditional village, majestically-framed by the Julian Alps, that he, along with two brothers and a group of life-long friends, bought a long-neglected property. Working with a skilled architect, they totally renovated the building and created a charming, chalet-style hotel. It opened in 2002 and is a real gem. This is not an elaborate, sumptuous hotel, but rather a small, cozy, country village inn brimming with personality and unsurpassed, old-fashioned hospitality. The bar, which is the heart of the inn, is "home" to all the locals who gather here each day for a glass of wine, a cup of coffee, or just to chat. On the ground floor there is a pretty dining room, a cozy breakfast room with antique paneling, and a library with a collection of rare books on mountaineering and history. Each guestroom is unique in décor and size, but all are extremely inviting and ooze top notch quality in every detail. If you want to splurge, ask for the Jof Fuart—a large, attractively decorated guestroom with a fireplace, beamed ceiling, and a dazzling view of the mountain peaks. *Directions:* Driving from Venice on the A23, take the Valbruna exit. The inn is in the center of town.

VALBRUNA INN
Manager: Marco Tonazzi
Via Alpi Giulie 2
Malborghetto
Valbruna, (UD) 33010, Italy
Tel: (0428) 66 05 54, Fax: (0428) 66 05 59
13 Rooms, Double: €90–€190
Closed: Nov & 2 weeks in Apr, Credit cards: all major
80 km N of Udine, 120 km N of Trieste
Region: Friuli-Venezia Giulia, Michelin Map: 562

Sicily's coastlines are dotted with ancient stone buildings called "Tonnara", once important tuna fishing centers. The Tonnara Bonagia, built in the 17th century on the northwestern tip of Sicily, is an example of one that has been transformed into an international, seaside resort. This is scenic and undeveloped coast going from the point of San Capo di Vito following along to the port city of Trapani. The towering, hilltop town of Erice looms slightly inland, and the stunning temple and amphitheatre of Segesta are a half hour away. The vast hotel complex mixes old and new quite well; maintaining the original, fortress stone walls complete with lighthouse and immense, brick courtyard where there are shops, a restaurant, and the reception office; while a modern building has been introduced for the twenty rooms with terraces looking out to the bay. Rooms are pleasantly decorated in subtle tones with standardized furnishings, with suites that have seaviews in three directions. Besides an excellent seafood restaurant, "La Muciara", and a bar overlooking the small port to one side and the inner courtyard to the other; there is an enormous, seaside swimming pool, tennis court, and diving center for guests. The Tonnara is an excellent alternative to the more simple hotels the area offers. Area tours can be prearranged with the efficient staff. *Directions:* 9 km from Trapani, from the Palermo-Trapani highway exit at Valderice. Follow signs to Bonagia.

❄ ☕ 🏄 💳 ☎ 👫 🏋 ✗ ⓟ 🍴 🚭 🏊 🚶 🖼 ♿ ⛱ 🛥

TONNARA DI BONAGIA
Manager: Enzo Marrocco
Piazza Tonnara, 1
Bonagia
Valderice, Sicily, (TP) 91010, Italy
Tel: (0923) 43 11 11, Fax: (0923) 59 21 77
102 Rooms, Double: €188–€584
Open: Apr to Oct, Credit cards: all major
On the northern coast of Sicily
Region: Sicily, Michelin Map: 565

The moderately priced Stella d'Italia is located in San Mamete, a tiny, picturesque village nestled along the northern shore of Lake Lugano, just a few minutes' drive from the Swiss border. Mario and Dolores Ortelli are the most cordial of hosts and son Franco, the fourth generation of the family runs the Stella d'Italia with his wife Melania. The heart of the hotel is a 17th-century villa with thick-walled rooms, painted ceilings, and large French windows opening to views of the lake. The same panoramic lake view is enjoyed by all the guestrooms. Equally spacious rooms are found in the wing renovated in 1999—these have not only space and views but also terraces and top-of-the-line bathrooms. Quite the nicest feature of the hotel is the superb little lakefront garden—a green lawn, fragrant flowers, lacy trees, and a romantic vine-covered trellised dining area make this an ideal spot for wiling away the hours. Steps lead down to a small pier from which guests can swim. Another interesting feature for golf enthusiasts is that there are several golf courses within an easy drive of the hotel—one of these (near the town of Grandola) is among the oldest in Italy. The ferry dock for picking up and dropping off passengers is adjacent to the hotel. *Directions:* From Lugano (Switzerland) head east towards St. Moritz. Cross the border in Valsolda and San Mamete is the next village. Park beside the hotel.

❄ ☕ 🛷 CREDIT ☎ 🏠 👪 P 🍴 🖼 ⚓ 👤 👫 🚴 🏄

STELLA D'ITALIA
Owner: Ortelli family
Valsolda San Mamete, Lake Lugano, (CO) 22010, Italy
Tel: (0344) 68 139, Fax: (0344) 68 729
34 Rooms, Double: €125–€160
Open: Apr to Oct, Credit cards: all major
8 km E of Lugano, 100 km N of Milan
Region: Lombardy, Michelin Map: 561

Wandering through the narrow streets as one does in Venice, we happened upon this delightful hotel on a small canal facing the SS Apostoli square. The gracious owner, Mariella Bozzetto, proudly showed us this exceptionally beautiful brick palazzo, home in the 12th century to one of the most powerful men in Venice, the Doge Marino Falier. Mariella, a talented architect, designed the hotel conversion with a passion for detail and the final result is stunning. You enter into a small entry hall with peach and cream colored walls softly illuminated by Murano glass wall sconces, an inlaid marble floor, and large oil paintings of old Venice. Upstairs you find the main room set with small tables where a rich buffet breakfast is served each morning with fine linens, fresh flowers, and lovely silverware. The guestrooms, splendid with brocaded draperies, color-coordinating fabric walls, and bedspreads in soft green, rose or burgundy hues, have all the modern enhancements, including TVs, air conditioning, hairdryers, and wireless Internet connections. Each room is individual in décor, yet has the same elegance without being overdone. If possible, splurge on the suite—more expensive, but one of the best values in Venice. It is splendidly decorated with rich fabrics, romantic canopy bed, Oriental carpet on hardwood floor, bathroom with Jacuzzi tub, and a little balcony overlooking the canal. This hotel is a great bargain for the quality and service received.

❄ ☕ 🍽 💳 ☎ @ W Y P 🚭 🖼 ♿ 🚶 ⛷ 🍇

HOTEL ANTICO DOGE
Owner: Mariella Bozzetto
Cannaregio, 5643
Venice, (VE) 30121, Italy
Tel: (041) 24 11 570, Fax: (041) 24 43 660
20 Rooms, Double: €90–€235
1 Suite: €240–€360
Open: all year, Credit cards: all major
Vaporetto stop: Ca d'Oro
Region: Veneto, Michelin Map: 562

Brothers Alessio and Nicola natives of the island of Murano, brought home their worldly experience in tourism and have created a very unique hotel. With all the comforts and amenities of a grand hotel but with the intimacy and care of a private home, the hosts welcome sophisticated travelers who are searching for something beyond the usual choice. In the four-story completely renovated historic home on a side canal facing the imposing church of Santa Maria della Salute, five deluxe theme rooms (king beds) were created using classic Venetian elements as the base (damask fabrics, Murano chandeliers, speckled marble floors) but with a contemporary mood. The general colors applied are somber beige, browns, black and grays, but with certain surprises as the Doges corner room, done completely in red with gold accents. Individual designer bathrooms have been created for each room with one having its own terrace. A second terrace for general use is appointed in Moroccan style with tables for an outdoor breakfast and lounges piled with colorful cushions. All rooms feature complimentary wireless Internet, CD/DVD players with DVD library, and free soft drinks in the minibar. Breakfast is served in the beamed dining room with chandelier and big arched windows overlooking the private landing dock. Straight across from San Marco, the area near the Guggenheim museum has galleries, good restaurants and, especially, peace and quiet.

CA MARIA ADELE
Owners: Alessio & Nicola Campa
Dorsoduro 111
Venice, (VE) 30123, Italy
Tel: (041) 52 03 078, Fax: (041) 52 89 013
12 Rooms, Double: €300–€455
2 Suites: €450–€675
Open: all year, Credit cards: all major
Vaporetto stop: Salute
Region: Veneto, Michelin Map: 562

In the category of luxury boutique hotels in Venice, the Ca'Nigra emerges as a true winner. The Feron family purchased the 17th-century palazzo just across from their established hotel Ai Due Fanali, in our B&B guide, and brought back to life one of Venice's most interesting properties. Centrally set on the Grand Canal in a quiet residential area, the striking burgundy home has two large, walled-in, arbored rose gardens and is lined on two sides by water. In fact you can pull your private boat right into a covered dock. With a sophisticated and more demanding traveler in mind, attention was given to the most modern technology available while enhancing the innate historic value of the residence. Walk right into the clean and contemporary main lobby with glass and lucite desk looking out to the side canal and up to 22 individually appointed junior suites with designer bathrooms, which blend the contemporary with the more classic Venetian style (Murano glass, speckled marble and mother of pearl floors, patterned parquet, damask fabrics) and accents of the Orient, so prevalent in the city's historic past. The triumph is the loggia suite with bottle-glass windows and bed facing out to the Grand Canal. Among the many common spaces are the upstairs beamed and frescoed living room with fireplace, modern courtyard breakfast room/bar and terrace overlooking the garden. Personalized services and amenities abound. A fascinating hotel.

CA'NIGRA LAGOON RESORT
Owner: Stefania Stea
Santa Croce 927
Venice, (VE) 30135, Italy
Tel: (041) 27 50 047, Fax: (041) 24 48 721
22 Rooms, Double: €180–€750
Open: all year, Credit cards: all major
Vaporetto stop: Riva Di Biaso
Region: Veneto, Michelin Map: 562

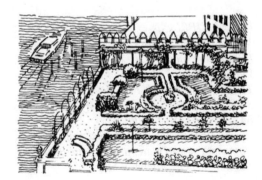

The Hotel Cipriani was founded by the late Giuseppe Cipriani, who during his lifetime became a legend in Venice. This beloved man, who founded the internationally famous Harry's Bar in Venice, had a dream of building an extraordinary hotel within easy reach of St. Mark's Square and yet far enough away to guarantee seclusion and peace. He bought 3 acres on the island of Giudecca and with the financial assistance of some of his prestigious friends he accomplished his dream—an exquisite Venetian palace-style hotel. Considered one of the finest luxury accommodations in the world, it is also the only hotel with a tennis court and swimming pool with magnificent gardens in Venice proper. The splendor continues inside where the lounges are tastefully decorated in whites and beiges and the bedrooms are large and elegant. In addition to the many guestrooms and junior suites, there are sixteen luxurious bedrooms with butler service (some with a private garden overlooking St. Mark's Square), located next door in the renovated Palazzo Vendramin. With all this, and the addition of the new Casanova Beauty and Wellness Center, you truly have the best of all worlds at the exquisite Cipriani—a deluxe resort yet only minutes from the heart of Venice in the private launch that waits to whisk you any time of the day or night to St. Mark's Square. Excellent cuisine is served at the Fortuny Ristorante, or the more casual Cip's Club.

HOTEL CIPRIANI
Manager: Giampaolo Ottazzi
Isola della Giudecca, 10
Venice, (VE) 30133, Italy
Tel: (041) 52 07 744, Fax: (041) 52 03 930
34 Rooms, Double: €850–€1450
64 Suites: €1850–€6800
Open: April to Nov, Credit cards: all major
Vaporetto stop: Zitelle, also private dock
Region: Veneto, Michelin Map: 562

This perfectly delightful small hotel with street or canal-side entrances, exudes the charm and elegance of the 15th century when it was built as the private mansion of a wealthy Venetian. The location is superb—in the historical heart of Venice, only 100 meters from Saint Mark's Square, yet on a quiet canal where the gentle singing of gondoliers will lull you to sleep at night. When redoing the hotel, the Polo Family spared no expense to ensure that every detail is of the highest quality and that the furnishings reflect the grandeur of Venice. Adept manager Andrea Doria not only takes an intense personal interest in the hotel's perfection but also welcomes guests as friends. All of the bedrooms with marble bathrooms are decorated in classic Venetian style, with similar decor in each: damask fabric walls, matching draperies, speckled marble floors, antique-style furnishings, and, in the rooms with high ceilings, Murano glass chandeliers. Just the colors of the fabric-covered walls vary from one delightful room to the next. Much smaller than the others, but especially romantic is a room tucked under the rafters with its own little rooftop terrace. Downstairs there is a comfortable bar area and breakfast room with faux window and painted scenes of Venice. For other meals, a limitless number of restaurants are just steps away. The hotel has ten additional rooms next door in the Locanda Remedio, plus three nicely decorated one and two-bedroom suites.

HOTEL COLOMBINA
Owner: Polo Family
Calle del Remedio-Castello, 4416
Venice, (VE) 30122, Italy
Tel: (041) 27 70 525, Fax: (041) 27 76 044
33 Rooms, Double: €180–€440
Open: all year, Credit cards: all major
Vaporetto stop: San Zaccaria, also private dock
Region: Veneto, Michelin Map: 562

The Hotel Flora is reached down a tiny lane, just off one of the main walkways lined with elegant boutiques to St. Mark's Square: a secluded hideaway, protected from the bustle of the city yet conveniently close to all the action. At the end of the tiny alley the doors open into a small lobby, beyond which is an enchanting small garden, an oasis of serenity with white wrought-iron tables and chairs surrounding a gently tinkling fountain. Potted plants, small trees, and lacy vines complete the idyllic scene. The hotel encloses the garden on three sides. Doors open from the garden to a little bar and the double breakfast room/salon where an Internet point has been set up. The public areas are Victorian in mood with dark furniture and red velvet fabrics. The individually appointed bedrooms vary greatly in their size and decor, some being quite small, but all have carefully chosen antique furnishings and Victorian-style wallpaper covers many of the walls lending a definite old-world ambiance. Gracious owner Signor Romanelli, personally sees that his guests are well taken care of, as well as longtime reception manager and native Venetian, Giovanni. The Hotel Flora is a true favorite of many travelers to Venice. Although it is a relatively simple hotel, the it is a rare find for those who want a relatively inexpensive place to stay in the heart of Venice that combines a superb location, genuine warmth of welcome and service, and innate charm.

HOTEL FLORA
Owner: Ruggero Romanelli
Calle Larga 22 Marzo, 2283/a
Venice, (VE) 30124, Italy
Tel: (041) 52 05 844, Fax: (041) 52 28 217
44 Rooms, Double: €185–€260
Open: all year, Credit cards: all major
Vaporetto stop: Vallaresso
Region: Veneto, Michelin Map: 562

If you love opulent elegance, and if cost is of no consequence to you, the Gritti Palace is an excellent choice for your hotel accommodation in Venice, as it has always been for royalty and the elite from around the world. The location is superb—just a short walk from St. Mark's Square yet far enough removed to miss the city's noise and summer mob of tourists. With careful planning, you can be entirely insulated in a private and very special world from the moment you arrive until you reluctantly depart. Whether you take a private motor launch from the airport or the Piazzale Roma, you can descend stylishly at the deluxe little private pier in front of the hotel where porters will be waiting to whisk you to your luxurious room. All at a price, of course. The Gritti Palace is very expensive—but then what would you expect when staying in the 15th-century palace of the immensely wealthy Venetian Doge, Andrea Gritti? The Gritti Palace has a charming flower-laden terrace directly on the bank of the Grand Canal where you dine in splendor and watch the constant stream of boat traffic passing by. The lobby and lounge areas open off the terrace and are grandly decorated with precious antiques and works of art. Following suit are the finely appointed bedrooms where privileged that have canal views are awarded with a 24-hour one-of-a-kind show. The Gritti Palace also offers week-long cooking courses by renown chef of the Club del Doge restaurant.

HOTEL GRITTI PALACE
Manager: Massimo Feriani
Campo Santa Maria del Giglio, 2467
Venice, (VE) 30124, Italy
Tel: (041) 79 46 11, Fax: (041) 52 00 942
*91 Rooms, Double: €589–€3692**
**Breakfast not included: €50*
Open: all year, Credit cards: all major
Vaporetto stop: Santa Maria del Giglio or private dock
Region: Veneto, Michelin Map: 562

Torcello is a tiny, sleepy island about 50 minutes from Venice by boat. For those who want to be close to Venice yet feel worlds away, the Locanda Cipriani Torcello is a superb, romantic hideaway owned by the Cipriani family. Your charming host, Bonifacio Brass, still remembers his famous grandfather who founded the Locanda and one of the world's most renowned pubs, Harry's Bar in Venice. The magical Locanda Cipriani Torcello is above all popular among knowledgeable gourmets as a fantastic restaurant. Many arrive every day from Venice just to dine, and then depart, never knowing that this restaurant also has exceptionally charming guestrooms. A simple farmhouse from the exterior, it has been renovated with great charm and exudes a understated elegance with beautiful country antiques and fresh flowers. You enter into a rustic, cozy dining room, but when the weather is warm, most guests prefer to dine outside on the beautiful terrace overlooking the beautifully manicured gardens that in summer offer a fantasy of color as well as the striking church and bell tower of Torcello. There are only five bedrooms—all are delightful and decorated in a simple, charming decor. Many famous guests have already discovered this oasis, including Ernest Hemingway, a friend of Cipriani's, who came here for inspiration to write two novels. I think you will share his belief that the Locanda Cipriani Torcello is a very special place.

※ ⬛ ✄ ⚬ CREDIT ☎ @ W Y P ⑪ ⚓ ⚓ 🚶 ⚓

LOCANDA CIPRIANI TORCELLO
Manager: Bonifacio Brass
Isola Torcello
Venice, (VE) 30142, Italy
Tel: (041) 73 01 50, Fax: (041) 73 54 33
9 Rooms, Double: €230–€330
Restaurant closed Tue
Closed: Jan 5 to Feb 10, Credit cards: all major
Island location, Vaporetto stop: Torcello
Region: Veneto, Michelin Map: 562

Named after the famous musician, Antonio Vivaldi, the Locanda Vivaldi, a charming hotel that reflects its rich heritage as a 16th-century palace, sets a mood of refined elegance from the moment you leave behind the busy waterfront. There is no formal counter bustling with people waiting to check in. Instead, guests sit in quiet comfort in front of an antique table to register. The reception area extends to a most appealing small lounge similar to a cozy living room in a private home: slipcovered sofas, a stunning antique desk, a handsome mirror, and bouquets of fresh flowers create a refined, understated elegance. One side of the lounge opens to a romantic garden with tables, and at the other end of the room is an intimate bar and breakfast room in peach hues. An elevator takes one up to the 27 guestrooms decorated in classic Venetian style: Fabric-covered walls, handsome headboards with ornate gilt trim, and matching bedspreads and draperies create an old-world elegance. Beautiful marble bathrooms have either hydro jet showers or bathtubs. The more expensive rooms have lagoon views and, if you want to splurge, the finest room also has a small balcony. Another bonus of the hotel is that on the third floor you find a terrace where light meals are served that captures a stunning view of Venice. If you arrive by private boat, you enter the hotel through a side garden. The hotel also owns the building beyond the garden and has added three more bedrooms.

LOCANDA VIVALDI
Manager: Roberto Dazzo
Riva degli Schiavoni, 4150/52
Venice, (VE) 30122, Italy
Tel: (041) 27 70 477, Fax: (041) 27 70 489
24 Rooms, Double: €190–€525
3 Suites: €250–€770
Open: all year, Credit cards: all major
Vaporetto stop: San Zaccaria, also private dock
Region: Veneto, Michelin Map: 562

Many readers urged us to include the Londra Palace in our guide, and they were right—the Londra Palace is indeed a well-run privately-owned hotel. It enjoys a choice location, just a few minutes' walk from Saint Mark's Square, right on the busy waterfront, and boasts of 100 windows facing the lagoon. In addition, there is a small rooftop terrace, which captures an incredible panorama of magical Venice. The carpeted guestrooms are well-decorated, each with at least one authentic, 19th-century piece of Biedermeier furniture. In addition to antiques, each room has fine original paintings and sumptuous damask fabrics on walls and bedspreads, creating a classic Venetian ambiance of refinement. Five top floor bedrooms have mansard beamed ceilings and small terraces. The bathrooms too are special—all are tiled with pink Carrara marble. During the final phase of a multi-million dollar renovation, the hotel's lobby, restaurant, bar, public areas, and white marble façade were brilliantly transformed. When the weather is balmy, there is no more romantic spot to dine than the excellent Do Leoni terrace restaurant facing the lagoon, named after the Tchaikovsky piece of which several movements were actually composed here at the hotel. The indoor alternative is within the taupe and cream appointed dining room within with spotted marble floors and identical vistas.

❄ ☕ ✂ 💳 ☎ ⛑ @ W Y ⅋ 🖼 ⚗ ♿ ⚓ 🕴 ⚱

LONDRA PALACE
Manager: Mauro Zanotti
Riva degli Schiavoni, 4171
Venice, (VE) 30122, Italy
Tel: (041) 52 00 533, Fax: (041) 52 25 032
36 Rooms, Double: €330–€610
17 Suites: €490–€790
Open: all year, Credit cards: all major
Vaporetto stop: San Zaccaria
Region: Veneto, Michelin Map: 562

The owner of one of the finest small hotels in France recommended the Hotel Metropole as his favorite place to stay in Venice. After being a guest, I can understand his choice—the Metropole has great heart. On entering, I was immediately aware of an aura of hospitality that is usually encountered only in intimate, very small hotels—everyone seems to take personal responsibility that your stay will be a pleasant one. It appears that the owners, the Beggiato family, who personally manage the hotel, have imbued the staff with their own warmth of welcome. Many employees have been with them since the hotel first opened in 1971 and seem to care about the hotel as if it were their own. The Beggiatos are passionate about antiques and have over 2,000 pieces displayed in the hotel, including a fascinating collection of old corkscrews, fans, stunning bags, and crucifixes. The reception hall has an Oriental flare, reminiscent of Venice's rich past as a center of commerce with distant countries. All of the spacious bedrooms are individually decorated as in a private home and have fine antique furniture. An elegant tearoom serves fresh cakes and teas in precious porcelain. Another great bonus is the romantic garden restaurant, The Met, where Michelin star chef Corrado performs daily. Some of the bedrooms overlook this garden while others have a beautiful view of the lagoon, as the hotel enjoys a marvelous waterfront setting.

HOTEL METROPOLE
Owner: Beggiato family
Riva degli Schiavoni, 4149
Venice, (VE) 30122, Italy
Tel: (041) 52 05 044, Fax: (041) 52 23 679
67 Rooms, Double: €250–€600
6 Suites: €800–€1600
Open: all year, Credit cards: all major
Vaporetto stop: San Zaccaria, also private dock
Region: Veneto, Michelin Map: 562

For all of you who have been to Venice and fallen in love with both the Hotel Flora and its incredibly kind owners, the Romanelli family, we are delighted to let you know that they purchased a second building just a few minutes' walk from the Flora and have renovated it into another intimate accommodation, called Novecento. The hotel occupies two very old residences—one side of the building is rosy peach, the other soft ochre. Green shutters enhancing stone windows and a wrought-iron fixture overhanging the street add to the appeal of the ancient building. The interiors differ greatly from the Flora in that they incorporate the once-popular decorating style of Fortuny, who included motifs from exotic places such as the Orient, Africa, Egypt, and Morocco in his designs, therefore deep earth tones of browns, deep reds, mustards, and grays reign. Each of the nine rooms has its own personality appointed with antiques beds and a refined ethnic fabrics and art pieces. Although it doesn't have a central courtyard like the Flora, the Novecento has a nice garden in the back where guests can relax. The same Romanelli father-son team, who so expertly and with such heart manage the Hotel Flora, personally oversee Novecento. Son, Gioele, organizes art exhibits and welcomes artists. The Hotel Flora has been in our guide since its first edition and it remains one of our very favorites and that of many travelers.

NOVECENTO
Owner: Romanelli family
Calle del Dose 2683/84
Venice, (VE) 30124, Italy
Tel: (041) 24 13 765, Fax: (041) 52 12 145
9 Rooms, Double: €160–€280
Open: all year, Credit cards: all major
History Traveller
Vaporetto stop: Santa Maria del Giglio
Region: Veneto, Michelin Map: 562

A stay at the intimate and exclusive Palazzo Sant'Angelo offers guests an idea of what it was like to live in a private palazzo of nobility directly on the Grand Canal, complete with private front dock. The Bocca family, owners of eight other luxury hotels in Italy, had the centuries-old palazzo completely refurbished for private and guest use in 2004. Just fourteen bedrooms on the three upper floors are available (mostly junior suites and suites), either with front or side canal or garden views, and boast sparkling gray-and-white or green Carrara marble bathrooms with hydro jet tubs. Striped royal red and gold is the predominant color scheme throughout the classic hotel decor in carpeting, brocade draperies, silk wall fabrics and bedspreads. The spacious front lobby with Palladian designed marble floors, leads to a side bar with lead-paned windows looking out to the passing gondolas. A living room with antiques, sofa, and a gray-stone fireplace sits directly opposite the bar while the breakfast room looking out to a side canal is to the back of the palazzo. A full buffet breakfast is served here. The friendly and attentive staff can make personal suggestions for restaurants, cultural events, private guides, and concerts. *Directions:* The Palazzo with its own private dock, is halfway between San Marco and the Rialto bridge (both at an easy walking distance-10 min).

PALAZZO SANT'ANGELO SUL CANAL GRANDE
Manager: Paolo Morra
San Marco, 3878/b - 3488
Venice, (VE) 30124, Italy
Tel: (041) 24 11 452, Fax: (041) 24 11 557
14 Rooms, Double: €460–€630
Open: all year, Credit cards: all major
Vaporetto stop: Sant'Angelo
Region: Veneto, Michelin Map: 562

After two years of loving restoration, the Palazzo Stern reopened in the spring of 2008 as a stunning small boutique hotel; one of Venice's latest jewels. Because it is a sister-hotel of one of our favorites in Venice, the Locanda Vivaldi, we knew it would be just wonderful. And, it is. This 15th-century palace was built by the prestigious Malpaga Family. Later the Stern Family bought the mansion as their private home, totally rebuilt it, and enriched the interior with fine architectural details, gorgeous mosaics, magnificent chandeliers, frescoes, stained glass, and sculptures. The Palazzo Stern faces the Grand Canal, conveniently located next to the Ca' Rezzonico Vaporetto stop. The peach-colored building with arched Moorish-style windows is very handsome and is further enhanced by a spacious, waterfront terrace. As you enter the reception area, you find a marble staircase lined by columns. The wooden staircase to the next level is a copy of the one at Ca' D'Oro Museum. All of the guestrooms are lovely. Some face the Grand Canal, while others overlook a private garden, the tiled rooftops of Venice, or a side-canal called the Rio Mapaga. Throughout, the decor is splendid, reflecting a traditional Venetian flair with precious wall fabrics, sumptuous drapes, oriental carpets, frescoes, ornate furnishings, and Murano glass. On the top floor there is a roof-top terrace featuring a Jacuzzi tub. The hotel is planning to open a restaurant. Until then light meals can be ordered at the bar.

❄ 🍽 🥂 💳 ☎ 🐕 ♨ @ W ⅋ 🚭 🖼 ⚑ ⛷ ⚓

HOTEL PALAZZO STERN   **New**
Manager: Roberto Dazzo
Dorsoduro, 2792/ A
Venice, (VE) 30123, Italy
Tel: (041) 27 70 869, Fax: (041) 24 12 456
18 Rooms, Double: €200–€525
6 Suites: €300–€770
Open: all year, Credit cards: all major
Vaporetto stop: Ca' Rezzonico, also private dock
Region: Veneto, Michelin Map: 562

The Pensione Accademia, a Karen Brown favorite, is an enchanting Venetian villa with charming gardens and a quiet setting on a small piece of land that is nestled between two canals. You pass through a gate into a garden enclosed by walls, canal side (private dock), with tables and umbrellas for outdoor breakfast seating. Entering the wisteria-covered palazzo, you come into the spacious reception area with Oriental rugs and armchairs, with Internet point which opens at the other end onto another spacious garden with a fountain. A staircase leads to some of the guestrooms that are located in the original villa, while the remaining bedrooms are within an adjacent building connected by a second floor hallway. All have new individually designed bathrooms. Some of the villa bedrooms have partial canal views and vary greatly in size, although the décor is standard with cream-colored walls, rust colored bedspreads and individual heirloom antiques. Just above the lobby area is the typical high-ceilinged living room stretching from front to back. The back garden has two lovely family rooms and one double with independent access. The kind and attentive staff is like the ambiance, charming and accommodating. The only hitch to this charming picture is that your chances are slim of snaring a room in this romantic hideaway—the hotel is so special that loyal guests reserve their own favorite room for the following year as they leave.

PENSIONE ACCADEMIA
Owner: Giovanna Salmaso
Dorsoduro, 1058
Venice, (VE) 30123, Italy
Tel: (041) 52 10 188, Fax: (041) 52 39 152
27 Rooms, Double: €140–€300
2 Suites: €210–€330
Open: all year, Credit cards: all major
Vaporetto stop: Accademia, also private dock
Region: Veneto, Michelin Map: 562

The Hotel Violino d'Oro faces a small canal on one side and the Barozzi and San Moisé squares on the other. This hotel offers an excellent choice of accommodation for those looking for a small-hotel atmosphere with friendly service in a great location near San Marco. Two sisters, Federica and Cristina, using their family hotel experience, bought the once private home that had most recently been used as an office building, totally renovated it, decorated the rooms in the style of the 18th century, and opened in 2000. The 26 rooms on the upper three floors are accessed by an elevator or the main open staircase, which gives the place the sense of space and light, not very common in the city. Each bedroom accessed from each floor's large foyer with sitting area is very similar, with brocade fabric on the wall behind the bed and color-coordinated draperies and bedspreads either in royal blue or red. Murano glass chandeliers continue the mood of Venice's romantic heritage. There is a typical hotel setup in each room with desk and chair, luggage stand, satellite TV, mini-bar, and some with small balconies. The travertine marble bathrooms mostly have showers, although some bathtubs are available. The breakfast room is very appealing with walls painted sunny yellow. Another plus is a rooftop terrace where guests may relax and enjoy a partial view of the Grand Canal. Friendly and casual, the hotel is superbly located at a reasonable rate.

HOTEL VIOLINO D'ORO
Manager: Cristina Boscolo Chio
San Marco 2091
Venice, (VE) 30124, Italy
Tel: (041) 27 70 841, Fax: (041) 27 71 001
26 Rooms, Double: €80–€400
Open: all year, Credit cards: all major
Vaporetto stop: Vallaresso, also private dock
Region: Veneto, Michelin Map: 562

During the 16th and 17th centuries it was fashionable for wealthy Venetian nobles to build palatial retreats along the cool banks of the River Brenta, and so the waterway became lined with sensational villas all the way from Venice to Padua. Today villages and commerce have built up in the area, but many of the mansions still survive. Some mansions are now open as museums, but for those who really want to experience living the noble life, there is the lovely 16th-century Villa Margherita, an elegant small hotel. It is situated across the highway from the canal, just a short stroll from one of the villa museums and a short drive from the other highlights of Veneto. Many converted villas in Italy are beautiful but faded, reflecting genteel neglect: not so with the Villa Margherita where all is beautifully maintained and no detail overlooked. From the front veranda and sitting rooms with their elegant antiques and period paintings to the guestrooms with rich, color-coordinated fabrics, each detail shows the care and involvement of the owners, Remigio and Valeria Dal Corso who actually grew up here. Remigio is a renown chef and demonstrates his skills at his own popular restaurant in a villa across the street. Far from the hubbub of Venice, yet only a 20-minute drive (or bus ride) away, the Villa Margherita is an excellent hotel choice for those who prefer to come home to a good regional meal, kind hospitality, and a quiet and refined ambiance.

ROMANTIK HOTEL VILLA MARGHERITA
Manager: Mr. Dario Dal Corso
Via Nazionale, 416
Venice–Mira, (VE) 30030, Italy
Tel: (041) 42 65 800, Fax: (041) 42 65 838
19 Rooms, Double: €165–€320
Restaurant closed Wednesdays
Open: all year, Credit cards: all major
Romantik Hotels
On canal 2 km W of Mira, 16 km W of Venice
Region: Veneto, Michelin Map: 562

The sister hotel to the Villa Margherita, the Villa Franceschi, just a short distance down the road, is a classic venetian villa facing out to the Brenta canal. As with many of the 16th-century summer retreats of the Venetians, the pristine villa has a double façade to the front and to the back gardens dotted with statues. Elegant rooms are divided between the historic villa holding eight sumptuous corner suites and the adjacent "Barchessa", a building originally used for the servants' quarters and land maintenance. Located here are the main beamed reception area, ground floor rooms with direct garden access, plus remaining rooms on the two upper floors. "La Veranda" dining room is within this building, a sun-drenched airy room with large windows on two sides looking out to the back gardens where an ample buffet breakfast is also served. The more rustic Barchesssa guestrooms, mostly suites and junior suites with many amenities, tend to be spacious with a classic and more simple décor than the villa, and color combinations varying from blue and gold to yellow and burgundy. The cordial and highly professional Dal Corso family invites guests to dine in their separate restaurant just down the road. From this comfortable base, the Brenta and Palladian villas can be easily reached, among many other highlights. *Directions:* Exit the A4 at Dolo-Mirano and follow to Dolo, turn left at the canal for Venice. Follow canal for 4 km to Mira Porte. The hotel is marked.

❄ 🛏 🛎 ☕ 💳 ☎ 🐕 🚻 @ W Y P 🍴 🚭 🖼 🔔 ⛷ ☂ 🎿 🍇

HOTEL VILLA FRANCESCHI
Manager: Alessandro Dal Corso
Via Don Minzoni , 28
Venice–Mira, (VE) 30030, Italy
Tel: (041) 42 66 531, Fax: (041) 56 08 996
25 Rooms, Double: €185–€340
6 Suites: €340–€450
Open: all year, Credit cards: all major
16 km W of Venice
Region: Veneto, Michelin Map: 562

The Hotel Gabbia d'Oro, ideally located in the heart of Verona, is truly a gem that captures the romance of this fascinating city. From the moment you step inside you are surrounded by a relaxed, understated elegance. Although this is a deluxe hotel, there is no hint of stiff formality—the welcome is genuinely warm and friendly in this superbly managed small hotel. Just off the spacious reception area is a cozy lounge with massive beamed ceilings, ancient stone walls, fine antiques, and handsome old prints in gold frames. Beyond the lobby is an intimate bar where wood paneling—richly mellowed with the patina of age—sets off to perfection chairs upholstered in cherry-red fabric. There is also a charming, sun-filled inner courtyard, called L'Orangerie, where you can savor a cup of tea or sip a glass of champagne while relaxing after a day of sightseeing or while enjoying a well-chosen assortment of reading material such as books on travel, fashion, interiors, and flowers. The guestrooms continue the ambiance of loving care. All are individually decorated, reflecting exquisite taste: antiques abound and handsome color-coordinating fabrics are used throughout. Nothing has been spared to make each room beautiful. The standard bedrooms are very pretty, but if you want to splurge, opt for a junior suite. It is such a pleasure to see a hotel that reflects so beautifully the authentic rich heritage of the original building.

HOTEL GABBIA D'ORO
Manager: Camilla Balzarro
Corso Porta Borsari, 4/A
Verona, (VR) 37121, Italy
Tel: (045) 80 03 060, Fax: (045) 59 02 93
27 Rooms, Double: €354–€620*
*Breakfast not included: €23
Open: all year, Credit cards: all major
In the heart of Verona
Region: Veneto, Michelin Map: 562

The charming Hotel Torcolo is a real find and has one of the best locations in Verona—just a two-minute walk to the huge plaza in front of the Roman Arena, the highlight of Verona. Although officially categorized as a two-star hotel, it far outshines many hotels twice the price. If you appreciate simple, sweet hotels with lots of warmth and character, you will love the Torcolo. The building, which dates back over 200 years, was purchased and renovated by your hostess, Silvia, in the mid 1950s. After a few years, her grade school chum, Diana, joined her. Both women, and the entire staff, are exceptionally accommodating and are wonderful in assisting with sightseeing plans and restaurant suggestions. Together the two women run the hotel with great efficiency and outstanding warmth. You walk into a cozy little reception area. An elevator takes you up to the guestrooms, none of which are opulent, but each is very nicely decorated with style and good taste. Most of the furnishings are antiques which are accented by pretty fabrics such as white linen curtains. Although some of the rooms are larger, I fell in love with room 31, romantically tucked up under the eves with exposed beamed ceiling and two cute corner windows overlooking the narrow colorful street. *Directions:* Although very close to the Roman Arena, the hotel is difficult to drive to due to pedestrian areas and one-way streets. Ask for driving details.

HOTEL TORCOLO
Owners: Silvia & Diana
Vicolo Listone, 3
Verona, (VR) 37121, Italy
Tel: (045) 80 07 512, Fax: (045) 80 04 058
19 Rooms, Double: €75–€125*
*Breakfast not included: €7–€14
Closed: end Jan to mid-Feb, Credit cards: all major
In the heart of Verona
Region: Veneto, Michelin Map: 562

The entrance to the Hotel Victoria is starkly modern—almost with a museum-like quality. The white walls, white ceiling, white floors, and an enormous skylight are softened by green plants. At first glance I was disappointed since I had heard so many glowing reports of the merits of this small hotel. However, the mood begins to change as you enter the reception area with its Oriental carpets and by the time you arrive in the lounge area, there is a definite move toward an antique ambiance. Here you find original heavy ancient wooden beams and one of the original stone walls exposed, leather chairs, and some lovely antique tables. The bedrooms are extremely modern and beautifully functional with good reading lights, comfortable chairs, Internet connections, and excellent bathrooms. The Victoria actually dates back centuries and the new hotel is built within the shell of an ancient building. The architect incorporated some of the archaeologically interesting finds of the site into a museum in the basement level. When the hotel is not full and all of the tables are not needed, special "windows" open up on the floor of the bar and coffee lounge and the museum below is lit so that you can study the artifacts as you enjoy an aperitif or your breakfast.

HOTEL VICTORIA
Manager: Giusy Loro
Via Adua, 8
Verona, (VR) 37121, Italy
Tel & Fax: (045) 59 01 55
66 Rooms, Double: €210–€440
Open: all year, Credit cards: all major
In the heart of Verona
Region: Veneto, Michelin Map: 562

With great finesse and determination, Lucia and Paolo, an editor and art collector, managed to purchase Villa Campestri, a magnificent Renaissance villa—no easy feat, considering the 400-acre property had been in one family for 700 years. The cream-colored villa with handsome lawns and surrounding cypress woods commands a spectacular view over the immense valley and Mugello mountain range in an area north of Florence known for its concentration of Medici villas. The guestrooms in the villa have been restored to their original splendor, with high Florentine woodworked ceilings, carefully selected antiques, and delightful blue-and-white-tiled bathrooms. The honeymoon suite features a grand, gold-crowned, red canopy bed. Equally characteristic rooms are located in the side wing and small independent house. A sitting room adorned with rich paintings leads to the elegant, stencil-painted dining rooms where original combinations of fresh local produce are served with great attention to detail, accompanied by an excellent selection of wines. They have created Italy's first "Oleoteca" devoted to the culture of olive oil, offering courses in its history, science, and cuisine. Villa Campestri offers refined, romantic accommodations with professionalism and hospitality given by daughter, Viola. *Directions:* Exit A1 at Barberino di Mugello and follow signs for Borgo San Lorenzo, then to Vicchio, then Campestri.

VILLA CAMPESTRI
Owners: Lucia & Paolo Pasquali
Localita: Campestri 19/22
Vicchio di Mugello, (FI) 50039, Italy
Tel: (055) 84 90 107, Fax: (055) 84 90 108
21 Rooms, Double: €144–€210
4 Suites: €200–€310
Open: Mar to Nov, Credit cards: all major
Abitare La Storia
35 km NE of Florence
Region: Tuscany, Michelin Map: 563

Hotel Villa Malpensa is less than a five-minute drive from the Milan Malpensa airport. This stately, four-story formal mansion was once the home of the counts of Caproni (one of the wealthiest families of northern Italy). This is more of a commercial hotel than a charming small inn and lacks the personal touch of an owner-managed property, but if you are nervous about catching an early morning flight, its location can't be beat. You enter into a formal hallway painted a soft-cream color, with a soaring ceiling, walls enhanced by ornate plaster sculpturing, marble floors, and Oriental carpets. Throughout the original core of the hotel, the past magnificence of this 1931 villa lives on through ornate architectural features. However, throughout the rest of the hotel there is no great flair to the décor. The furnishings are contemporary, but you cannot fault the amenities. All of the guestrooms have built-in headboards with proper reading lights, comfortable mattresses, satellite televisions, mini-bars, direct-dial telephones, hairdryers, and air conditioning. The standard rooms are not large, but the superior rooms are more spacious and some have balconies where you can watch the planes taking off and landing. *Directions:* From Milan, follow signs to the Malpensa airport. Exit at Terminal One, turn right immediately, then go straight. The hotel is on your right, about a two-minute drive.

HOTEL VILLA MALPENSA
Manager: Giuseppe Gemmo
Via Don Andrea Sacconago, 1
Vizzola Ticino–Milan, (VA) 21010, Italy
Tel: (0331) 23 09 44, Fax: (0331) 23 09 50
65 Rooms, Double: €170–€290
Open: all year, Credit cards: all major
1 km SW of Malpensa Airport
Region: Lombardy, Michelin Map: 561

Volterra, a walled medieval hilltown, is not as well known as its ever-popular neighbor, San Gimignano, but it too exudes great authentic medieval character. Although not quite as colorful, it benefits from fewer tourists and offers a wealth of museums and many boutiques selling items made of alabaster, for which the town is renowned. Conveniently located within the walled city, very near the gate called Porta Florentina, the Hotel La Locanda is intimate and very attractive. The exterior is a pretty pinkish-beige color with arched doorway, flower boxes at the windows, green shutters, and a wrought-iron light sconce. You enter into a small foyer with gorgeous parquet floors and fresh flowers accenting the antique reception desk. Just beyond are a small lounge and then the cheerful room for breakfast, the only meal served (the restaurant for the hotel, under the same ownership, is the Etruria, just a short walk up the street). Throughout the hotel you find original art, with the work of local artists on display in all of the rooms. An elevator leads up to three floors of guestrooms, all as fresh and pretty as can be. Each level has its own color scheme—green, red, or blue—established by the carpeting and the richly hued, handsome coordinating fabrics used for draperies and bedspreads. The marble bathrooms are excellent and the suites even have Jacuzzi tubs. *Directions:* Inside the city walls, on the street leading to, and close to, Porta Florentina.

HOTEL LA LOCANDA
Owner: Assenza Andrea
Via Guarnacci, 24
Volterra, (PI) 56048, Italy
Tel: (0588) 81 547, Fax: (0588) 81 541
19 Rooms, Double: €129–€250
Open: all year, Credit cards: all major
76 km S of Florence, 50 km NW of Siena
Region: Tuscany, Michelin Map: 563

Places to Stay by Region

Abruzzo
L'Aquila, Sole, Hotel

Aosta Valley
Breuil Cervinia, Hermitage, Hotel
Champoluc, Villa Anna Maria
Cogne, Bellevue, Hotel
Courmayeur, Romantik Hotel Villa Novecento
Courmayeur, Maison Lo Campagnar

Apulia
Alberobello, dei Trulli, Hotel
Casalabate, Tenuta Monacelli
Martina Franca, Relais Villa San Martino
Matera, Sassi Hotel
Monopoli, Melograno, Il
Monopoli, Monopoli La Peschiera Hotel
Otranto, Palazzo Papaleo, Hotel
Otranto, Masseria Montelauro
Savelletri di Fasano, Masseria Torre Coccaro
Savelletri di Fasano, Masseria San Domenico

Basilicata
Maratea, Locanda delle Donne Monache, La
Maratea, Romantik Hotel Villa Cheta Elite
Maratea, Santavenere Hotel

Calabria
Tropea, Panta Rei, Hotel
Tropea, Porto Pirgos

Campania
Amalfi, Marina Riviera, Hotel
Amalfi, Santa Caterina, Hotel
Capri, Luna, Hotel
Capri, Villa Brunella
Capri, Villa Le Scale
Capri, Caesar Augustus, Hotel
Naples, Chiaja Hotel de Charme
Naples, Costantinopoli 104
Naples, Grand Hotel Santa Lucia
Positano, Buca di Bacco
Positano, Palazzo Murat, Hotel
Positano, Villa Franca, Hotel
Positano, Sirenuse Hotel, Le
Positano, Punta Regina
Positano, San Pietro di Positano, Il
Positano, Marincanto, Hotel
Ravello, Palumbo, Hotel
Ravello, Caruso, Hotel
Ravello, Villa Cimbrone
San Agata, Oasi Olimpia Relais
Santa Maria di Castellabate, Villa Sirio, Hotel

Santa Maria di Castellabate, Palazzo Belmonte
Sorrento, Grand Hotel Excelsior Vittoria

Emilia-Romagna
Bologna, Corona d'Oro, Hotel
Castel Guelfo, Locanda Solarola
Ferrara, Duchessa Isabella, Hotel
Ferrara, Principessa Leonora, Hotel
Ferrara, Locanda della Duchessina
Montegridolfo, Albergo Palazzo Viviani
Ravenna, Albergo Cappello
Reggio Emilia, Posta, Hotel
Soragna, Locanda del Lupo

Friuli-Venezia Giulia
Rivarotta–Pasiano, Villa Luppis
San Floriano del Collio, Golf Hotel
Valbruna, Valbruna Inn

Lazio
Anguillara Sabazia, Country Relais I Due Laghi
Bagni di Stigliano, Grand Hotel Terme di Stigliano
Bracciano, Villa Clementina, Hotel
Civita Castellana, Relais Falisco
Frascati, Flora, Hotel
Grottaferrata, Park Hotel Villa Grazioli
Ladispoli, Posta Vecchia, La
Poggio Catino, Borgo Paraelios
Ponza, Gennarino a Mare
Ponza, Grand Hotel Santa Domitilla

Rome, Barocco, Hotel
Rome, Bernini Bristol, Hotel
Rome, Hassler, Hotel
Rome, Lord Byron, Hotel
Rome, Piranesi, Hotel
Rome, Splendide Royal, Hotel
Rome, Inn at the Roman Forum
Rome, Residenza Paolo VI
Rome, Duke Hotel, The
Rome, Inn at the Spanish Steps, The
Rome, View at the Spanish Steps, The
Sabaudia, San Francesco, Il

Liguria
Camogli, Cenobio dei Dogi, Hotel
Chiavari a Leivi, Ca'Peo
Finale Ligure, Punta Est, Hotel
Garlenda, Meridiana, Hotel La
Genova–Nervi, Romantik Hotel Villa Pagoda
Levanto, Stella Maris, Hotel
Monterosso al Mare, Porto Roca, Hotel
Monterosso al Mare, Villa Steno, Hotel
Portofino, Splendido Mare
Portofino, Splendido, Hotel
Portofino, San Giorgio, Hotel
Savignone, Palazzo Fieschi
Sestri Levante, Helvetia, Hotel

Lombardy
Argegno, Albergo Villa Belvedere

Azzate, Locanda dei Mai Intees, Hotel
Bellagio, Florence, Hotel
Bellagio, Grand Hotel Villa Serbelloni
Bellagio-Pescallo, Pergola, La
Cernobbio, Villa d'Este
Clusane, Romantik Hotel Relais Mirabella
Erbusco, L'Albereta
Gargnano, Grand Hotel a Villa Feltrinelli
Gargnano, Lac, Hotel du
Gargnano, Villa Giulia, Hotel
Luino, Camin Hotel Luino
Milan, Four Seasons Hotel Milano
Milan, Grand Hotel et de Milan
Milan, la Ville, Hotel de
Milan, Regency, Hotel
Milan, Town House Galleria
Santa Caterina Valfurva, Romantik Hotel Baita Fiorita
Sirmione, Villa Cortine Palace Hotel
Valsolda San Mamete, Stella d'Italia
Vizzola Ticino–Milan, Villa Malpensa, Hotel

Marches
Acquasanta Terme, Castel di Luco
Ascoli Piceno, Palazzo Guiderocchi

Piedmont
Belgirate, Villa Dal Pozzo d'Annone
Cannero Riviera, Cannero Lakeside Hotel
Cioccaro di Penango, Locanda del Sant'Uffizio
Gavi, L'Ostelliere

Monforte d'Alba, Villa Beccaris
Orta San Giulio, Contrada dei Monti, La
Orta San Giulio, Villa Crespi
Pescatori, Isola dei, Verbano, Hotel
Romano Canavese, Relais Villa Matilde
San Stefano Belbo, Relais San Maurizio
Sauze d'Oulx, Capricorno, Il

Sardinia
Oliena, Su Gologone, Hotel
Porto Cervo, Pitrizza, Hotel
Porto Conte, El Faro, Hotel

Sicily
Agrigento, Foresteria Baglio della Luna
Agrigento, Domus Aurea, Hotel
Erice, Moderno, Hotel
Gangivecchio, Tenuta Gangivecchio
Marina di Ragusa, Eremo della Giubiliana
Modica, Palazzo Failla
Palermo, Centrale Palace Hotel
Palermo, Principe di Villafranca, Hotel
Ragusa Ibla, Romantik Hotel Locanda Don Serafino
San Vito Lo Capo, Capo San Vito, Hotel
Siracusa, Grand Hotel Ortigia Siracusa
Siracusa, Caol Ishka
Taormina, Grand Hotel Timeo
Taormina, Belvedere, Hotel
Taormina, Villa Carlotta
Taormina, Villa Ducale

Taormina, San Domenico Palace Hotel
Taormina, Villa Sant'Andrea
Valderice, Tonnara di Bonagia

Southern Tuscany
Sinalunga, Locanda dell'Amorosa

Trentino-Alto Adige
Bressanone, Elephant, Hotel
Castelrotto, Cavallino d'Oro, Hotel
Corvara, Perla, Hotel La
Fiè, Romantik Hotel Turm
Madonna di Campiglio, Biohotel Hermitage
Merano–Labers, Castle Fragsburg, Hotel
Merano–Marling, Romantik Hotel Oberwirt
Pergine, Castel Pergine
San Cassiano in Badia, Rosa Alpina
Sesto, Berghotel Tirol
Tires, Pensione Stefaner

Tuscany
Bagno a Ripoli, Villa Olmi
Castellina in Chianti, Locanda Le Piazze
Castellina in Chianti, Tenuta di Ricavo
Castelnuovo Berardenga, Fontanelle, Hotel le
Castelnuovo Berardenga, Relais Borgo San Felice
Castiglion Fiorentino, Relais San Pietro
Cetona, Frateria di Padre Eligio, La
Cortona, Falconiere Relais e Ristorante, Il
Cortona, Villa di Piazzano

Cortona, Villa Marsili
Florence, Antica Torre Di Via Tornabuoni
Florence, Albergotto, Hotel
Florence, Helvetia and Bristol, Hotel
Florence, Guelfo Bianco, Hotel Il
Florence, Lungarno, Hotel
Florence, Regency, Hotel
Florence, Marignolle Relais & Charme
Florence, Palazzo Magnani Feroni
Florence, Palazzo Niccolini al Duomo
Florence, Relais Uffizi
Florence, Torre di Bellosguardo
Florence, Montartino-Villa Le Piazzole
Florence, Villa La Vedetta
Florence–Fiesole, Villa Fiesole, Hotel
Florence–Fiesole, Villa San Michele
Florence–Fiesole, Pensione Bencista
Gaiole in Chianti, L'Ultimo Mulino
Gaiole in Chianti, Castello di Spaltenna
Lucca, Locanda L'Elisa
Lucca, Palazzo Alexander
Massa Marittima, Villa Il Tesoro
Monsummano Terme, Grotta Giusti Natural Spa
Montebenichi, Castelletto di Montebenichi
Montefiridolfi, Borghetto Country Inn, Il
Montefollonico, Chiusa, La
Montepulciano, Dionora, La
Montepulciano, Montorio
Montepulciano, Villa Poggiano
Monteriggioni, Monteriggioni, Hotel

Orbetello, San Biagio
Ottone, Villa Ottone, Hotel
Panzano in Chianti, Villa Le Barone
Pienza, Relais Il Chiostro di Pienza, Hotel
Pienza, L'Olmo
Pietrasanta, Albergo Pietrasanta
Pisa, Relais dell'Orologio, Hotel
Porto Ercole, Pellicano, Il
Porto Santo Stefano, Torre di Cala Piccola, Hotel
Radda in Chianti, Relais Vignale
Reggello–Vaggio, Villa Rigacci
San Casciano, Villa Il Poggiale
San Casciano, Villa Mangiacane
San Casciano dei Bagni, Fonteverde, Hotel
San Gimignano, Cisterna, La
San Gimignano, Antico Pozzo, Hotel L'
San Giustino Valdarno, Borro, Il
San Guiliano Terme, Bagni Di Pisa Natural
Spa Resort
San Gusmè, Relais Villa Arceno
San Leonino, Belvedere di San Leonino, Hotel
San Sano, Residence San Sano, Hotel
Scansano, Antico Casale di Scansano
Siena, Grand Hotel Continental Siena
Siena, Palazzo Ravizza
Sorano, della Fortezza, Hotel
Sovana, Taverna Etrusca, La
Sovicille, Borgo Pretale
Vicchio di Mugello, Villa Campestri
Volterra, Locanda, Hotel La

Umbria
Assisi, Umbra, Hotel

Assisi, Palazzo, Il
Assisi, Fortezza, La
Assisi, Residenza d'Epoca San Crispino
Assisio, Romantik Hotel Le Silve di Armenzano
Bevagna, L'Orto degli Angeli
Canalicchio di Collazzone, Relais Il Canalicchio
Citta della Pieve, Relais dei Magi
Colle San Paolo, Villa di Montesolare, Hotel
Cortona–Petrignano del Lago, Relais la Corte del
Deruta, Antico Forziere, L'
Gubbio, Relais Ducale
Montefalco, Villa Zuccari
Montone, Locanda del Capitano, La
Orvieto, Palazzo Piccolomini, Hotel
Orvieto, Villa Ciconia
Orvieto, Badia, La
Perugia, Brufani Palace, Hotel
Perugia, Locanda Solomeo
Ronti, Palazzo Terranova
Spoleto, Gattapone, Hotel
Spoleto, San Luca, Hotel
Spoleto, Logge di Silvignano, Le
Spoleto, Villa Milani
Spoleto, Eremo delle Grazie
Todi, Relais Todini
Torgiano, Tre Vaselle, Le

Veneto
Arcugnano, Villa Michelangelo
Asolo, Albergo al Sole

Asolo, Duse, Hotel
Asolo, Villa Cipriani
Bassano del Grappa, Villa Ca'Sette, Hotel
Cortina d'Ampezzo, Menardi, Hotel
Cortina d'Ampezzo, Poste, Hotel de la
Costermano, Locanda San Verolo
Follina, Villa Abbazia
Gargagnago, Foresteria Serego Alighieri, La
Montagnana, Ristorante Aldo Moro, Hotel
Pedemonte, Villa del Quar, Hotel
Peschiera Sul Garda, Ai Capitani, Hotel
Quarto d'Altino, Villa Odino, Hotel
San Pietro in Cariano, Villa Giona
San Vigilio, Locanda San Vigilio
Scorzè, Villa Soranzo Conestabile
Torri del Benaco, Gardesana, Hotel
Venice, Ca Maria Adele
Venice, Ca'Nigra Lagoon Resort
Venice, Antico Doge, Hotel
Venice, Cipriani, Hotel
Venice, Colombina, Hotel
Venice, Flora, Hotel
Venice, Gritti Palace, Hotel
Venice, Metropole, Hotel
Venice, Violino d'Oro, Hotel
Venice, Locanda Cipriani Torcello
Venice, Locanda Vivaldi
Venice, Londra Palace
Venice, Novecento
Venice, Palazzo Sant'Angelo sul Canal Grande

Venice, Pensione Accademia
Venice, Palazzo Stern, Hotel
Venice–Mira, Villa Franceschi, Hotel
Venice–Mira, Romantik Hotel Villa Margherita
Verona, Gabbia d'Oro, Hotel
Verona, Torcolo, Hotel
Verona, Victoria, Hotel

Index

M

Index

Volterra, 80
    Locanda, Hotel La. 454
    Sightseeing
        Museo Etrusco Guaracci, 80
        Piazza dei Priori, 80
        Porta all'Arco, 80

W

Weather, 28
Website, Karen Brown's, 29
Western Umbria, 98
What to Wear, 29
Wheelchair Accessibility, 13
Wineries, 80
    Cantina del Redi, 85
    Castello d'Albola, 82
    Castello di Brolio, 81
    Castello di Meleto, 83
    Castello di Volpaia, 83
    Dei, 85
    Fattoria dei Barbi, 88
    Poggio Antico, 88
Wines, 18

Index

Venice

KAREN BROWN wrote her first travel guide in 1976. Her personalized travel series has grown to 17 titles, which Karen and her small staff work diligently to keep updated. Karen, her husband, Rick, and their children, Alexandra and Richard, live in a small town on the coast south of San Francisco.

CLARE BROWN was a travel consultant for many years, specializing in planning itineraries using charming small hotels in the countryside. Her expertise is now available to a larger audience—the readers of her daughter Karen's travel guides. When not traveling, Clare and her husband, Bill, divide their time between northern California, Colorado, and Mexico.

JUNE EVELEIGH BROWN hails from Sheffield, England and lived in Zambia and Canada before moving to northern California where she lives in San Mateo with her husband, Tony, their German Shepherd, and a Siamese cat.

NICOLE FRANCHINI was born in Chicago and raised in a bilingual family (her father being Italian), but she has been residing in Italy for many years. Currently living in the countryside of Sabina near Rome with husband, Carlo, and daughters, Livia and Sabina, Nicole runs her own travel consulting business, Hidden Treasures of Italy, which organizes personalized group and individual itineraries. *www.htitaly.com.*

BARBARA MACLURCAN TAPP draws all of the delightful hotel sketches and illustrations in this guide. Barbara was raised in Sydney, Australia, where she studied interior design. Although she continues with architectural rendering and watercolor painting, she devotes much of her time to illustrating the Karen Brown guides. Barbara lives in Kensington, California, with her husband, Richard, and is Mum to Jono, Alex and Georgia. For more information about her work visit *www.barbaratapp.com.*

JANN POLLARD, the artist of all the beautiful cover paintings in the Karen Brown series, has studied art since childhood and is well known for her outstanding impressionistic-style watercolors. Jann has received numerous achievement awards and her works are in private and corporate collections internationally. She is also a popular workshop teacher in the United States, Mexico and Europe. *www.jannpollard.com.* Fine art giclée prints of her paintings are available at *www.karenbrown.com.*

Romantik Hotel Laurin, Salò

Romantik Hotels & Restaurants – Arrive, Relax, Enjoy!

At Romantik Hotels & Restaurants we invite you to arrive, relax and enjoy. Among our more than 200 Romantik Hotels you can find historic country inns, opulent estates and elegant city mansions in 11 European countries. We invite you to indulge in regional cuisines, discover award-winning restaurants or simply relax in one of our beautiful spas. We offer true Romantik hospitality, outstanding cuisine and a historic environment steeped in tradition. In Italy over 20 Romantik Hotels & Restaurants are awaiting you. For more information and availability go to www.romantikhotels.com.

Romantik Hotels & Restaurants are about personal service, attention to detail and true hospitality.

ROMANTIK
HOTELS & RESTAURANTS
INTERNATIONAL

We look forward to your visit.
Romantik Hotels & Restaurants GmbH & Co. KG
Hahnstraße 70, 60528 Frankfurt, Germany
Fon: +49 (0) 69/66 12 34-0
Fax: +49 (0) 69/66 12 34-56
info@romantikhotels.com

www.romantikhotels.com

A Customized Travel Service For Independent Travelers

HIDDEN TREASURES OF ITALY

*Personalized
Trip Planning*

*Charming
Accomodations*

Villa Rentals

Family Reunions

Private Guides/Tours

Cooking Classes

Museum Tickets

Trains

*Car Rentals/
Chauffeurs*

Boat Charters

HIDDEN TREASURES OF ITALY INC.
Chicago, Milan, Rome
US Toll Free: (888) 419-6700 • Fax: (773) 409-5044
International Toll Free: (011)(800) 280-4200-4
Email: info@htitaly.com • Website: www.htitaly.com

Ben Kong

Photography

Karen Brown's World of Travel

A FREE KAREN BROWN WEBSITE MEMBERSHIP
IS INCLUDED WITH THE PURCHASE OF THIS GUIDE

$20 Value – Equal to the cover price of this book!

In appreciation for purchasing our guide, we offer a free membership that includes:

- The ability to custom plan and build unlimited itineraries
- 15% discount on all purchases made in the Karen Brown website store
- One free downloadable Karen Brown Itinerary from over 100 choices
- Karen Brown's World of Travel Newsletter—includes special offers & updates
  Membership valid through December 31, 2009

To take advantage of this free offer go to the Karen Brown website shown below and create a login profile so we can recognize you as a Preferred Customer; then you can utilize the unrestricted trip planning and take advantage of the 15% store discount. Once you set up an account you will receive by email a coupon code to order the free itinerary.

Go to ***www.karenbrown.com/preferred.php*** to create your profile!

Karen Brown's
2009 Readers' Choice Awards

Most Romantic
Villa Carlotta
Taormina

Warmest Welcome
Villa Ducale
Taormina

Greatest Value
Villa Zuccari
Montefalco

Splendid Splurge
Villa di Piazzano
Cortona

Be sure to vote for next year's winners by visiting
www.karenbrown.com